Reviews for *Birds Gone Wild*

"Triumph, tragedy, and tomfoolery mingle with the history and science of raising ostriches. Molony provides the reader with a delightful romp among these flightless creatures!"

Jan Cleere, AZ Historian and Multi-Award-Winning Author of *Military Wives in Arizona Territory* (2021)

"A fun & offbeat look at Arizona's past."

Heidi Osselaer, Retired Professor of History (ASU) & Author of *Arizona's Deadliest Gunfight* (2018)

"Fascinating!"

D. C. "Rooster" Cogburn, Founder of the World-Renowned Rooster Cogburn Ostrich Ranch near Picacho Peak, Arizona

"Funny and entertaining; sometimes even tragic. I was quite intrigued at the enormous industry created in AZ by those who came this way in search of fortune and found it in ostriches!"

Carol Lynds, Descendant-Relative to the Pickrells

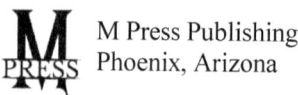 M Press Publishing
Phoenix, Arizona

Cover Design and Interior: J. Molony
Front Cover Images: Modified composite, licensed through CanvaPro.
Back Cover Images: Modified composite, licensed through CanvaPro, Tempe Museum & Chandler Museum.
Official Author Website: www.JanelleMolony.com

Paperback ISBN: 979-8-9905118-1-1
Hardback ISBN: 979-8-9905118-2-8
EBook ISBN: 979-8-9905118-3-5
Library of Congress: 2025922492
(0101b)

Non-Fiction Genres: Arizona History, Humor, Science
Keywords: Ostrich, Ranching, Pioneers, Cowboys, Southwest, Salt River Valley, Family History, Western

Trigger Warning: Violence, Politics & Satire.

Peek-A-Boo!

BIRDS GONE WILD
(AND OTHER STORIES OF ARIZONA OSTRICH RANCHING)

Janelle Molony

National Award-Winning Author & Historian

Other Books by the Author

On the Southern Side (Forthcoming)
Annotated and illustrated diary of Mrs. Sarah Rousseau Espy, seamstress from Northern Alabama. Widowed at the start of the Civil War, Mrs. Espy must keep the family business going with the help of her sons, until all four of them are called into the bloody battle.

The 1864 Diary of Sarah Jane Rousseau (2023)
The transcribed Overland-California trail experience of the Pella Company wagon train traveling from Pella, Iowa to San Bernardino, California. Their wagon master is Nicholas Earp, father of the Tombstone-famous Earp brothers Virgil, Wyatt and Warren.

Emigrant Tales of the Platte River Raids (2023)
Thrilling first-hand accounts and extensive research from the attacks of July 1864 in the "Black Hills of Idaho." Ft. families of John Brown, Daniel Boone, Wyatt Earp, Johnny Ringo & more!

Winner of the American Writing Awards (U.S. History) & WILLA Recipient from Women Writing the West (Scholarly Nonfiction).

Poems from the Asylum (2021)
The strange-but-true story of Martha Nasch: The Woman Who Never Ate, Drank or Slept! Features a biography, medical study, and the complete collection of her award-winning poetry as written while being observed during her prolonged fast inside the St. Peter State Hospital for the Insane.

Dedicated to

Mrs. Desdamona Rousseau

(Blank Page)

Table of Contents

Contents

Preface

To my knowledge, this is the second book ever written about Arizona's ostrich ranching industry. Writing it was both an honor and a blast. If you love history and science, this might be the best book on ostrich ranching you'll ever read. If you don't, this might be the best book on ostrich ranching you'll ever read.

After the deep dive this book project required of me, I now know a stupid amount of information on ostriches. Pretty soon, you will too. And I'm counting on you to tell all your friends. Though the book is thick, don't let it overwhelm you. More than half the pages contain an illustration, joke, fun fact, a deceased person's face, or a huge map.

Finally, the stories included are factual (even the unbelievable ones). Many occurred before the existence of the Royal Society for the Protection of Birds (1889), the National Audubon Society (1896), and the U.S. activist group People for the Ethical Treatment of Animals (PETA, 1980). The impact of advocacy group formation, activism, interventions and other legislative milestones are evident throughout the book.

- Janelle Molony, M.S.
Hottie Historian, Serious Books

(By the way, the first book was *Under the Desert Sky,* a romance novel about a sexy redhead, by Sara Luck. The author was inspired by her great-grandfather, who invested in an Arizona ostrich ranch at the wrong time and lost the entire family fortune.)

Birds Gone Wild *(And Other Stories of Arizona Ostrich Ranching)*

(Blank Page)

1. Arizona's Ostrich Craze

"The ostrich farm... has made Phoenix famous."
- The Arizona Republican (1901)[1]

Ostriches are among the most underestimated creatures in the world. They are, as some say, "regarded by most local historians as a laughable footnote."[2] I say, the history of ostriches in Arizona is one of the most engrossing topics you'll ever get into. You'll soon see, they are as iconic to the American Southwest as the stately saguaro cactus, picturesque sunsets, venomous scorpions and turquoise-laden silver. If this book's history nuggets do not satisfy, the scientific studies of these so-called "murder birds" will have you reconsidering every prejudice you've ever held against them as stupid or useless. For example, scientists currently regard the ostrich as a prospective ally in new medical breakthroughs, such as a cure for certain cancers.

Outside of their native habitat in Africa, Arizona's Salt River Valley is the perfect place to raise the long-legged, heat-loving, flightless birds of prehistoric lore. The megaducks' feathers were so popular that the state became Africa's top competitor in ostrich-related trade. Beyond feathers, ostriches were a tourism boon. At one point, Arizona was equally known for ostriches as the Grand Canyon. When motor vehicles became affordable, driving tours to ostrich ranches became popular, preceding the existence of the state's first zoo (or any other theme park, for that matter). Ticketed admissions granted views of risky egg collections and educational feather clipping sessions. The *Phoenix Gazette* reported in 1907: "To people that have never had the chance to see them, there is nothing more interesting to look at than a herd of live ostriches."[3]

In 1888, 13 ostriches arrived in Arizona Territory by train. The early birds were so prolific that by 1914, there were reportedly near 6,000 in Maricopa County alone.[4] That was 80% of the entire ostrich population in the United States! By the time statehood was granted, there were over thirty "feather farms" in the Salt River Valley and seemingly endless opportunities to expand. An early evaluation filed with the U.S. Commissioner of Agriculture read: "ostrich farming is a most lucrative business."[5] Early ranchers raked in the equivalent of a million dollars for feather clippings collected only once or twice in a year! The industry boom lasted longer than the silver mining activities that brought life to Tombstone, Bisbee and Globe. Yet, few people know enough to appreciate this subject as a serious part of territorial and state history.

What do you call a 300-pound, 8-foot-tall, spindly-legged fowl with an iffy attitude? An important part of Phoenix history![a]
- *Arizona Daily Star, 1997*

Ostrich ranching made a powerful impact on our early economy. In 1913, Arizona's first member of state legislature, Carl Hayden, got the President of the United States to agree that ostriches were one of the most important ventures Arizonans had ever taken part in.[6] "No one need have any fear for the future of the ostrich industry," Rep. Hayden said, "...all history indicates that the demand will remain as permanent and expansive as any other branch of trade."[7]

---

[a] "Ostriches are Part of Phoenix Past," *Arizona Daily Star*, May 25, 1997, 1.

Photogenic ostrich hen at the Rooster Cogburn Ostrich Ranch (Author collection, 2025).

With his support, the nation's first Ostrich Experimental Farm was built on Arizona soil.

Everyone wanted in on the deal. Notable breeders from back then were Dr. A.J. Chandler (founder of the city bearing his name), Louis Ellsworth (grandson of Brigham Young) and James Meadows (one-legged bull-wrangling brother of the famed Wild West trick shooter, "Arizona Charlie"). Though most individuals featured in this book are hardy and ambitious men, it was women who elevated the ostrich feather to such heights of desire and demand. The two-toed legend of the Sonoran Desert was made globally famous by the whims of empresses, queens, and first ladies. The elite adornment soon swayed in mesmerizing waves around anybody who was a somebody. And it was women who rallied for a cause that ended the luxury trend. This demolished the careers and livelihoods of virtual "nobodies"-turned-millionaires, who had barely warmed the seats of their proverbial thrones.

Beyond shoppers, there were also several entrepreneurial women in Arizona I wish to acknowledge. They advanced the early industry with their husbands. The list includes: Katie Pearson, a singer and stage actress and president of the largest commercial ostrich ranch in the country (unmatched to this day); Anna Adams, who became Katie's top competitor in the feathered goods retail industry; Georgiana Pickrell who helped launch the first feather processing facility in the state; Margaret Ann Toston, the first female owner and manager of an ostrich ranch in the state (possibly the whole country); and Helen Seargeant, a memoirist who shared the ins and outs from a local ostrich farm and preserved vibrant details of the Great Arizona Ostrich Drive.

There's also a special woman who died during that ostrich drive: Desdamona Rousseau, my distant cousin. Though she wasn't the first person to be killed by an ostrich in Arizona, as the first female to do so, I figure she should at least get a mention. (Even sad stories can be *great* stories.)

Let the Fascination Begin!

We're about to get into the backstory of fashion trends and how the first commercial ostrich ranch in the U.S. came to be. It's essential information, though it can be less than exhilarating for some readers. Don't worry though, soon after, you'll be reading about a naked ostrich who borrowed a man's pajamas, a deadly stampede through Phoenix, a four-legged ostrich, and even a *talking* ostrich! For the readers who just perked up, yes, you are about to read a borderline unhinged Western history book. For the serious readers, you can also feel confident that the book, though riddled with amusing and sordid details, has been well-researched, extensively cited, and vetted with local historians, descendants, subject experts, and onsite field trips. In consideration of different readers, I'll be mindful to balance the weird science and historical narrative as we go. But first, we'll start with a front-loading of the "best-of" facts on ostriches that you never knew you needed to know.

1. **Their excrement does not stink.**

   Though it isn't foul like most manures, it still has a light, earthy scent. Not only that, but they conduct their #1 and #2 in separate transactions, like mammals. Their scat resembles the dry, round pellets of a Mule Deer.

2. **Their eggshells are a wonder of physics.**

   Their eggshells are so hard to crack open that if hatched unassisted, chicks can emerge with broken or deformed legs. One time, the owner of the Rooster Cogburn Ostrich Ranch let Larry the Cable Guy stand on an egg to prove its maximal strength.

   Crows are the best ostrich eggshell breakers on the planet.

   They repeatedly drop stones on their target from a high point until they can access the gooey insides.

3. **They may dream more than any other bird.**

   Scientists at the Max Planck Institute for Biological Intelligence conducting a 2011 study confirmed that ostriches can sleep standing up, with eyes open and heads held still, as if awake. They also found that ostriches will slump their bodies and close their eyes when they reach rapid eye movement (REM) patterns associated with dreaming.[8] Other birds such as the owl also experience the drowsy droop, and can achieve a REM state, but cannot sustain it as long as the ostrich.

4. **They can go up to three years without water.**

Ostriches stay hydrated by absorbing water from what they eat. No one *really* knows how long they can go without drinking water, but one farmer at the Arizona Ostrich Company, R. J. Icke, claimed that when he worked in South Africa, his birds went three years without a single sip.[9] Farmed birds, however, have developed the habit of luxuriously lapping up a pint or so of water every day.

5. **Their "knees" are really their ankles.**

And that entire length of leg we *think* is a shinbone (tibia) is one very long foot (metatarsal). Ostriches walk on their two toes—a characteristic that landed them their scientific name *Struthio camelus*, or "Camel Bird."

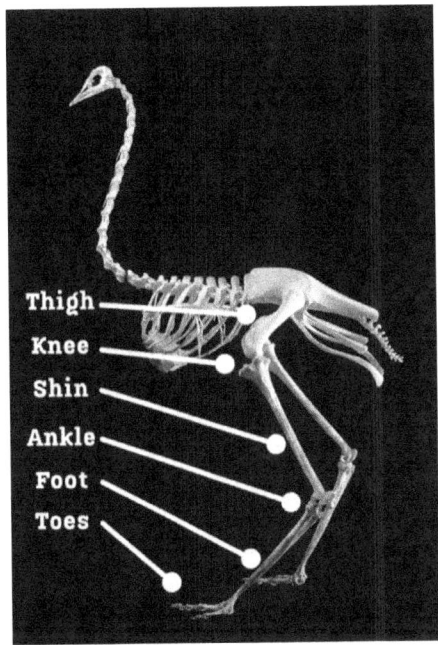

Thigh
Knee
Shin
Ankle
Foot
Toes

Ostrich skeleton from the Museum of Veterinary Anatomy FMVZ USP/CC BY-SA 4.0 (Wikimedia Commons, labeled by author).

6. **They eat rocks as a substitute for missing teeth.**

Swallowed rocks are stored in a section of the gastrointestinal system called the gizzard. Once tucked away in the gizzard, the rock gets a new scientific name: "gastrolith." When the gizzard muscles clamp, the rocks inside will grind down whatever food they have eaten. (This includes cans and other unnatural objects, but not all. Some foreign bodies cannot be broken down, and their continual presence harms the animal.)

Even with two rows of teeth, crocodiles *also* have a gizzard and eat rocks.

Seriously.

7. **Their teenagers have a plucking name.**

These birds are only considered "chicks" until about six months old. From then until a year, they are "young birds" ("children" to us humans). Between years one and four, they are developing into fine breeding and/or meat birds and are called "plucking birds" (*exactly as I told you*). They are not considered mature adults until about the three and one-half or four-year mark, with the hens maturing faster than the roosters.

8. **You can hear an ostrich chick chirping inside the egg before it hatches.**

I'm not 100% certain on this, but it might be saying, "let me out!" This phenomenon is possible because there is an air pocket in the egg located between the yolk sack membrane and the shell. When the chick breaks through the placenta-like membrane and accesses the air pocket, this is called the "internal pip" (internal breakage). At that point, the chick can practice using its lungs. When the chick punctures through the exterior shell, that is called the "external pip." Depending on the size of the pip (broken point), a viewer can see the bird moving around, trying to figure out what to do next. (I wish I could tell you this is where we got the term "peephole." It's not.)

9. They have a special morning dance.

Countless stories of dancing birds have been told from ranch owners, which will appear later in the book. The original flightless immigrants brought to the state were first seen dancing at New York's Central Park. A news report said the birds contained, "a rhythm that could be set to music."[10]

At the Pan-American Ostrich Company, cowboys observed male birds rising with the sun and having a stretch, then a quick walk-about that had a certain "dancey-pranciness" to it. An observer of this at the Arizona Ostrich Company described the performance starting off with a quick sprint that morphs into a cake walk, then into something like a Virginia Reel, but more grotesque.[11]

10. Mother hens will kidnap each other's babies.

These feathered families are known to brawl when caused to occupy the same space. The adults may fight or chase each other off until only one winner remains. Experts at the San Diego Zoo confirm that "the winning adult pair takes all the chicks with them.'"[12]

Now, readers, hang on to that spark of curiosity as we back up a bit to see how the incredible ostrich ended up in Arizona.

2. Feather Fashions & Fortunes

"A good ostrich feather, like a diamond,
never loses a certain intrinsic value."
- Cawston Ostrich Farm Souvenir Book (1909)[13]

The impetus for ostrich ranches in Arizona is unquestionably fashion related. A seismic shift occurred in the fashion industry of the "Gay Nineties," where feathers became the standard for elite expressions of couture and costume in European countries. A woman simply could not be considered stylish without the sacrifice of an exotic bird pinned to her hat, swinging limply around her neck, and fluttering in her handheld fan. For the next two decades, feathers were *la chose à avoir,* the must-have for every woman. And American women were not exempt.

At that time, ostrich feathers were only available from South Africa—either through illegal poaching, or through the ostrich "farms" that undermined that dangerous practice and were intended to repopulate the previously over-hunted bird. Demands for these plumes, sometimes as long as 30 inches, skyrocketed until, by 1912, the U.S. was internationally considered "one of the greatest feather-buying markets in the world."[14]

Women Wore Them Everywhere

These feathers were everywhere you would expect, such as trimming hats and fluffy gown pins. They were worn as thin

Featured hat styles from *The Millinery Trade Review*, January 1889 (highlighted by author).

French actress Jane Hading in a J. Lichtenstein & Sons hat and veil Advertisement in *The Millinery Trade Review*, March 1889 (cropped by author).

boas and full shoulder wrap stoles and seen as trimming on luxurious nighties. There were even feather garments for "Little Baby Bunting."[15] Women were enamored by feathered fineries of all sorts and the obsession spilled over into interior décor. Around the house, they'd appear in what we might now call "tacky" ornamental vase arrangements.

The *Millinery Trade Review*, a catalog of all-things hats,

> "As long as the ladies want their fashionable hats, there can be no end to the amount of money I can make."
> -*Mr. A.Y. Prinson, Under the Desert Sky (2016)*

announced in 1889 that, "As predicted by us, the coming-in of the large hats with lower crowns and wider brims has revived interest in ostrich feathers for trimming, the stiffer arrangements of fancy feathers, wings and quills, being unsuitable for the graceful shadowy effects aimed at."[16] The new styles the New York publication displayed caught the eye of some major influencers, such as the French actress Jane Hading, who modeled the latest trend during her American theatre tour that winter.

One major American icon of the 1890s was Lillian Russell, an American stage actress and singer who showed an affinity for the soft, flowing material. Before films, Lillian Russell was famed for comedy operettas such as Gilbert and Sullivan musicals, burlesque shows and vaudevillian productions. She was also active in advancing the Woman Suffrage Movement in her later years, which may have stifled her feather addiction for a moment. (More on that trend in another chapter.) My own great-grandmother, Martha Nasch, chose the ostrich feather to be the *pièce de résistance* in her wedding outfit.

Left to right: Lillian Russell ca. 1897 (J. Schloss, from the George Grantham Bain Collection/Library of Congress), Bust portrait by W. M. Morrison, ca. 1898 (Library of Congress), With a monocle, ca. 1898 (J. Schloss, Library of Congress).

1913 wedding portrait of Louis and Martha Nasch, St. Paul, Minnesota (Author's personal collection).

America's First Major Hat Competition

Soon, hat makers were competing more aggressively than ever before. In 1901, the International Association of Milliners held its first ever convention during the World's Fair in Buffalo, New York. The main event was an exhibit filling a hotel parlor with outrageously trimmed hats competing for cash prizes. A reporter for the *Buffalo Courier*, described the contents of the collection as having both "freakish" and "beautiful creations."[17] First prize went to a hat of black velvet and chiffon: a modification of an English Gainsborough and Scottish "tam-o-shanter" shape. It featured a buckle with turquoise and rhinestones. Tucked in the band, "an immense black ostrich plume is caught at the left, carried around the edge of the brim to the extreme right back and droops to the shoulder."[18] The winning designer received a check for $25, or nearly $1,000 in today's terms.

The reporter acknowledged everything adorned with an ostrich plume was a fan favorite but added that trying to sell those award-winning designs was "limited to those with ample purses."[19] Seen in the images that follow are ostrich feathers on Gainsborough hats adorning women in the 18th and 19th centuries.

Advertisement in *The Arizona Republican*, October 30, 1910.

Left: Élisabeth Vigée Le Brun, "Marie Antoinette with a Rose," 1783. Oil on canvas (on view at The Metropolitan Museum of Art. Right:. F. Holland Day, "The Gainsborough Hat," featuring model Ethel Reed, ca. 1895-1898 (Louise I. Guiney Collection, Library of Congress.)

These Were Pricy Plumes!

Arizona historian Roscoe G. Willson recorded the lengths women went to for their feather fix. "Around the turn of the century the price of feathers mounted to unusual heights, some of the fanciest ... selling for as much as $140 a pound on the London markct."[20] London's pricing and feather classification system was what the U.S. originally based their own on.[21] For context, it takes about 90 of the longest and cleanest, "white primes" to add up to a pound, so one fancy feather would come to U.S. distributors for about $1.55 raw, plus the difference in shipping costs, plus a 15% increase to retailers.[22] By the time the feather hit store shelves, it could be priced in the $15-$30 range.

Today, at the Rooster Cogburn Ostrich Ranch near Picacho Peak, visitors can purchase a long, luxurious white feather for about $4. At the end of the day, that's a 99.75% depreciation in value since the early 1900s.

Americans Couldn't Get Enough

As early as 1899, the United States imported nearly $2 million worth of feathers from South Africa to meet women's demands.[23] That was *with* the presence of five ostrich ranches in the U.S. already: two in California, one in Texas, one in Florida, and one in Arizona. But these five ostrich entrepreneurs could not keep up with the production demand, so sellers continued to ship over boatloads of the fluff with seemingly no end in sight.

In 1905, Watson Pickrell, one of the early Arizona ostrich ranchers, wrote in a report for the U.S. Department of Agriculture that, "The United States is one of the largest consumers of ostrich feathers in the world. During the fiscal year 1903-4 there was imported into this country $2,292,515 worth of 'raw' or 'manufactured' feathers."[24] The numbers continued to climb astronomically. Four years later, the U.S. imported $3 million worth of feathers.[25] In 1911, "Africa shipped $5,013,778.50 worth of raw feathers to this country."[26] That's about $170 million in today's terms!

At the peak of the boom, U.S. shoppers were purchasing 64% of all ostrich feathers harvested from across the globe.[27] Ironically, South Africans didn't even make up a drop in the ocean of sales. There, ostrich feathers were so commonplace that even members of the lower classes wore them. This caused upper class ladies to snub feather wearing even more.[28]

With the promise of fortune-making profits, ranchers, investors, military men, theatre managers, photographers, and miners—practically anyone with a whim and a dollar—considered how to get themselves an ostrich. If an American ostrich ranch could beat the prices of the global competition by avoiding tariffs, shipping, and other costs, then the lucky owner of the birds could find themselves as rich as royalty.

Shopgirls outside of the Ostrich Feather Emporium in Holburn, London, ca. 1900s (Miss Scarlet - "Real History," PBS.org, Masterpiece Studio).

Men Wore Ostrich Feathers, Too

Even before the American Revolution, soldiers were wearing feathers or "cockades" in their hats to denote distinction. During the American Civil War, qualifying Union soldiers could wear an ostrich feather in their dress uniform hat. Shown in the following images are examples of soldiers in their dress uniform. Towards the end of the Civil War, one of the highest and most touching feather distinctions was given post-mortem. During President Abraham Lincoln's funeral procession, his hearse was adorned with eight enormous bundles of black ostrich feathers (representing mourning) and his six-horse team all wore plumed bridles to match.

In "Yankee Doodle," a song about the American Revolutionary War, there is a lyric that says: "stuck a feather in his cap and called it macaroni!"
...Maybe it was an ostrich feather?

Left: Unidentified soldier in uniform and beehive hat. Right: Unidentified soldier in uniform and Hardee hat. Both images are dated between 1861-1865 (LOC).

President Lincoln's burial service in Springfield, IL showing a feather-adorned hearse. Illustration in *Harper's Weekly*, May 27, 1865 (cropped).

3. Ostrich Ranch Beginnings in Africa

*"There is not the remotest possibility of America ever
competing with Africa in raising the ostrich..."*
- The Millinery Trade Review (1904)[29]

Though ostrich products have been in human use for a
few millennia, farming them for their products is a relatively
new concept. Ostriches are native to all of Africa and parts of
the Middle East, believed to have originated from the
Mesopotamian region.[30] They are not migratory birds, so for
the longest time, they remained foreign to the rest of the
world unless trafficked by humans.

Agricultural historians agree that "the ostrich [feather]
industry began in Cape Colony in 1865 with 85 birds."[31] These
birds were caught from the wild as chicks then raised in
pseudo-captivity. The merchants working with the farmers to
sell those feathers were almost entirely Yiddish-speaking
immigrants who leveraged their connections to primarily
Jewish-owned manufacturers and resellers in both London
and New York.[32] Sarah Stein writes in *Plumes: Ostrich
Feathers, Jews, and a Lost World of Global Commerce*, "So
hugely overrepresented were Jews" as feather dealers, people
accused them of running a monopoly.[33]

Birds Gone Wild *(And Other Stories of Arizona Ostrich Ranching)*

Above: "Troop of Ostriches, and Cart with Prickly-Pear Leaves for Food."
Below: "Ostriches in a Hot Wind," on a South African farm. Illustrations from
Home Life on an Ostrich Farm by Annie Martin (1890).

Feather merchants in
Omdurman, ca. 1905-1910
(Sudan Times).

A Brief History of South African Politics

The native Zulu and Xhosa people had been at war with colonizers for years prior but were dominated in the mid-1600s by Netherlanders. The Netherlanders then established the Dutch East India Company on the west coast of the southern tip of the African continent. From Cape Colony, as they called it, the Dutch asserted power over most of South Africa, enslaving indigenous people in the process. This era of reign ended with the British Army's invasion and progressive takeover, starting in 1795.

In the 1860s, Cape Colony was fully under the dominion of the British crown. So were Natal and Zululand on the eastern coast. Under Dutch influence, those were collectively known as the Boer Republic of Natalia. The British renamed the Republic the Colony of Natal. It is important to distinguish these two British colonies (western and eastern) because of what happens later in the book. After being conquered, Dutch *Boers* ("Farmers") relocated east of the Orange River and formed the Orange Free State and Transvaal (later the South African Republic). Unsatisfied with the result, the British bribed the Basotho people to align with them in conquering the Boers again. This engagement (lasting from 1880-1881) was later called the First Boer War.[34]

All that to say... ostrich farming was established in the British-ruled Cape Colony during a time of economic depression. In many ways, it was as weird and out-of-place as an occupation back then as it is now. Within ten years, those first 85 ostriches reproduced into over 22,000. South Africans colonizers were almost as happy getting rich off feathers as they were with the diamonds they discovered in 1867.

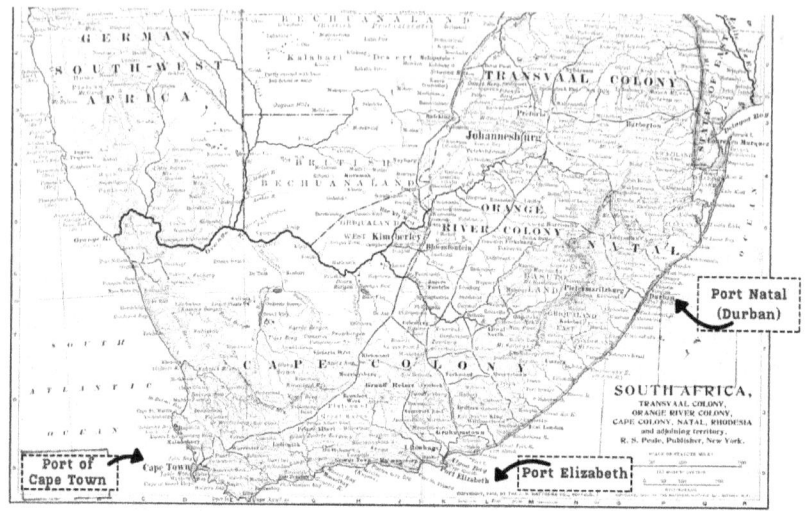

"Map of South Africa, Showing the Seat of War between Great Britain and the Dutch Republics," Chicago Record Newspaper, 1902 (LOC).

Watson Pickrell, an Arizona ostrich rancher, found that the earliest initiatives were in response to a noted decline in the ostrich population because of overhunting. He provided for the 1922 *Cyclopedia of Farm Animals* that the South African colonies had passed laws restricting slaughter practices and prohibiting poaching, which coincided with the establishment of the first ranches.[35] Raising these birds to support the feather industry was no different than keeping Merino sheep for their wool. It was humane and rational, plus it undermined the dangerous and wasteful poaching activities. Before this, Pickrell wrote, "nearly all the ostrich feathers of commerce were taken from dead birds."[36]

(By the way, the earliest breeders called themselves farmers, but "farms" are usually distinguished by growing crops, while "ranches" are distinguished by raising livestock. Because of this, I will give preference to the term "ostrich ranch," throughout the book. If, however, feathers are the salable output that happen to be grown on an ostrich's body, then perhaps an acceptable alternative is "feather farm," which no one seems to have used. That's a bit of a loss because it has a nice ring to it, doesn't it?)

Which Birds to Farm?

Those who formed the first feather farms were essentially making things up as they went along. They captured wild birds, branded them and learned the trade by trial and error. Because the animals' health and production now held global trade value, it benefitted breeders to begin distinguishing the characteristics and subtleties between native species before they bet their bottom dollar on an investment. Here's an overview of what we now know.

Ostriches are members of the ratite family. These include three other flightless birds: the rhea, cassowary, emu and kiwi. While the similarly built species are virtually useless to the planet, the ostrich has emerged as Mother Nature's most contradictory showpiece. She is the epitome of a dinosaur with special needs, yet she could be the scientific savior of this world. (More on that at the end of the book.)

A "ratite" is a bird without a keel bone. That bone supports large breast muscles necessary for flight.
Guess it's drumsticks for dinner, then?

There are basically three types of ostriches: red/pink, blue and black. They have fancier names than that, but they are all just subspecies of the *Struthio camelus*. Their nicknames refer to the shade of skin prominently displayed in the near-nakedness of their necks and their matching-colored legs.

- **Red necks** are the heaviest and most aggressive. The Common, Massai and North African are subspecies with this coloration. The North African bird is currently considered "critically endangered" and is almost entirely found in American zoos.[37]

- **Blue necks** are the tallest. The Somali Ostrich (in archaic literature, the Nubian) received its scientific name *Struthio molybdophanes* for its spot-on color match to iron ore. These are familiarly called the South African ostrich, considering the population in that region.[38] It quickly became the most common species found on American ostrich farms.

- **South African Blacks** are generally smaller than both of the above and are supposed to have black necks and legs. It's much more of a Cadet Gray, if you ask me. Sometimes these are referred to as "domesticated blacks." They were bred specifically for their feather production and are known to produce 20% more feathers on their body than the other species.[39] [b]

> "It has been successfully domesticated in America and elsewhere for its feathers."
>
> - *Watson Pickrell (1922)*

There Are No True Domesticated Ostriches... Yet.

According to an article in *Scientific American,* by 1885, South Africans had bred over 100,000 of the "tame" subspecies.[40] Despite the soft term applied to the headcount, there has been no official acknowledgement of South African Blacks (or any other subspecies) being formally domesticated.

---

[b] Watson Pickrell, "Ostrich," in *Cyclopedia of Farm Animals*, ed. L. H. Bailey (New York: MacMillan, 1922), 511.

Early farmers who learned how to manage captive birds only *claimed* that designation. Today's ostriches are still very much wild animals and will resort to their primitive habits when triggered. At best, they can be raised as livestock (not poultry), but no one should think of them as "tame" or gentle enough to be a family pet.

The scientific community generally accepts that domestication requires twelve or more generations to be raised outside of their native context. One example of removal from context would be like a pack wolf being brought from the woods and caused to sleep at the foot of a human's bed. Selective breeding would prioritize only the gentlest and fluffiest cuddlers to continue living in the house. This process would continue for the next twelve generations until the perfect companion pet was designed.

Early breeders in South Africa did not remove ostriches from their native context. They corralled a wild desert creature inside wire fencing, still located in the ostriches' natural habitat. Successful ostrich ranches in the U.S. also imitate native context. That being the case, little has been done over the course of 160 years to have earned the "domestic" qualifier. (By the way, breeders who tried to raise ostriches in snowy places like Pennsylvania not only failed to domesticate their birds, but they also discovered that ostriches don't adapt by growing more feathers to keep warm. Instead, they die.)

Another measure for domestication is evidence of evolution found in an animal's DNA (i.e. physically cuter, smaller, fluffier). The South African Blacks are one step along in that process. Finally, domestication can be achieved by a marked change in their behavior. While so-called "domesticated" ostriches present some adaptive behaviors towards human handlers, at present, none are being

Blue neck chicks being raised on a South African farm, ca. 1881-1890. Illustration from *Home Life on an Ostrich Farm* by Annie Martin.

selectively bred to reinforce those behavioral changes. Ostriches are presently bred for feather outputs or meat, without regard for the instinctual danger their behaviors may pose to their handlers. If a breeder chose to pursue true domestication, they might have to forgo a paycheck due to any physical changes that might result. For example, a tame bird might produce fewer feathers or eggs.

4. Introducing Ostriches to America

"Turkey has its mosques; Russia has its Cossacks;
Germany has its U-boats; and Mexico has its fleas; but the
United States has the queerest farms in the world."
- Henry Miles, "Strange Farms" (1916)[41]

Commercial ostrich ranching began in the U.S. in 1882. At this time, there were already over 300,000 birds bred in captivity in South Africa, turning its wishful conservationists into gazillionaires.[42] At that point, other countries not only wanted a piece of the profit pie, but they were practically drooling, begging, and driven to stealing for it.

Dr. John Protheroe is the man who should get all the credit for bringing ostriches to the U.S. to stay. He was an Englishman who'd invested in an ostrich ranch outside of Cape Town for several years. He'd become interested in this line of business after traveling through South Africa in his prior career as a physician. After discovering ostrich ranching to be more profitable, he duplicated his efforts with an experimental ranch site in Buenos Aires, Argentina. Then, after studying the topography and climate conditions of the American Southwest, he figured it being his next place of establishment.[43] By selling ostrich feathers locally to the largest importer in the world, he could increase his income exponentially and avoid the 25 percent export duty cutting into it back home.[44]

In 1881, Dr. Protheroe partnered with a naturalist, Dr. Charles Jarom Sketchley, who was formerly in the British

Army. As one agriculturalist of 1889 put it, Dr. Sketchley was "one of the largest ostrich farmers in Africa,"[45] having raised birds in the Dutch-ruled Transvaal Colony. Essentially, Dr. Protheroe was the money behind this venture; Dr. Sketchley was the muscle. Or, as my Arizona ostrich ranching friend D.C. Cogburn has put it, "some people in this industry buy jeans with fancy holes in them, while others earn theirs."[46] Dr. Sketchley earned his. (By the way, Cogburn has been a legendary wrangler of these birds longer than I've been alive, so he's earned the ability to drop gems like that throughout the book.)

Later records mysteriously omit Dr. Protheroe from the historical narrative. For example, in 1899, E. H. Rydall wrote for *American Farmer,* "About the year 1881, it occurred to Dr. Charles J. Sketchley, who was, before the Boer wars, one of the largest ostrich farmers in Africa, that if ostriches could be successfully exported and naturalized in America, the profit would be immense."[47] The story proceeds as I'm about to tell you, but instead of having any cooperation with Dr. Protheroe, it was Dr. Sketchley who hand-picked the birds, shipped them off alone, formed a syndicate and managed the first ostrich farm in the U.S.[48] I don't know if these two doctors had a falling out, but after the farm was set up, Dr. Protheroe faded from literary accounts.

From South Africa to the U.S.

Together, the doctors filled a ship's hold with two hundred mature birds from Cape Town and set sail for America.[49] They may have come from Sketchley's personal flock, or a combination from both of their collections, though there is no information to support either case. The *Arizona Republican* once drew a picture for its readers about this, printing: "Imagine two hundred of these gigantic creatures weighing from two hundred to four hundred pounds each, reared in the freedom of an almost boundless desert, cooped up in the stuffy hold..."[50]

The steamship made a stop in Buenos Aires, where the entire outfit could take a breather for several months at Dr. Protheroe's place. It's likely that the partners learned a great deal about shipping the gangly wobblers from that first leg of the trip. They claimed several birds got seasick along the way, and that only 28 made it to shore. Though ostriches have a hardy immune system, this illness might have been the result of limited ventilation and a constant flow of cold, moist air. Breeders later learned this was nearly a guaranteed recipe for respiratory illness and death.

It's also suspected that a rough wave could have sent a few birds knocking into each other or up against the enclosure, causing a broken bone or worse. Henry Miles, editor for a Canadian pharmaceutical journal agreed. He penned an article about some of the strangest farms in the world. He believed "the pitching and tossing of the steamer also was responsible for the death of many of the birds."[51]

The Second Sea Leg

In November 1882, Dr. Protheroe shipped 22 birds up to New York City. After passing their initial inspection and quarantine for imported animals, they were displayed in Central Park.[52] This was an important stop for the partners to get some attention on the birds, make a few bucks on admissions, and to draw in wealthy investors who might help fund their settlement in the States (i.e. reimburse them for significant expenses and losses).

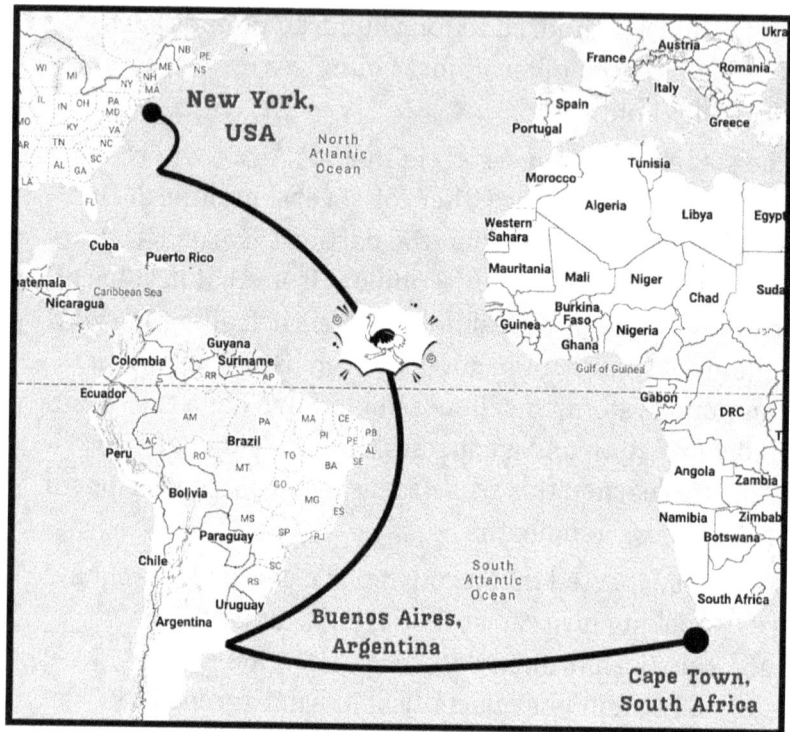

1881-1882 Ostrich journey to America (part 1) (Google Maps, marked by author).

A North Carolinian paper celebrated the entrance of the "African Colonist" who turned heads. The *New Bern Weekly Journal* printed on November 16: "Everybody who went to Central Park yesterday wanted to see the herd of twenty-two ostriches that just arrived. They are full-grown birds, and are the only lot ever imported for breeding purposes."[53] Dr. Protheroe told the paperman, though he had profitable businesses in two other countries, "I thought I could make more money elsewhere."[54]

Not everyone was excited to have these strange birds making a pit stop at Central Park, though. The park superintendent Mr. Conklin, for one, reported the birds being rather troublesome. "They are worse than a gang of pickpockets," he told the *New Bern*. "They won't leave a button on your coats if you don't watch them."[55]

The Statue of Liberty was not able
to greet the incoming birds.
(She didn't arrive until 1884.)

Winter in Central Park

The *New Bern* reported: "It was a cold day for the ostriches ... they were not at home except a few favored callers. They are confined to the deer hut, which is nice and warm."[56] Tourists loved the opportunity to gawk, but the climate of New York was too extreme for the birds to remain long. When asked about the birds' tolerance to the weather, Dr. Protheroe compared the chill to some nights back in South Africa when temperatures could drop into the 30's at night and an inch of ice could form on the surface of the desert. But back in South Africa, those conditions were long gone at sunrise.

The average temperatures at the Park in November ranged from low-40's to mid-50's; a significant departure from the high-70's the birds enjoyed during their June "winters" in Transvaal. In New York, the birds would have no relief from the chill, nor humidity. Keeping the birds inside a structure like the deer hut *sounded nice* but could lead to another ship hull disaster all over again. This show would have to get on the road, and quick.

Birds Gone Wild *(And Other Stories of Arizona Ostrich Ranching)*

"The Ostriches at the Central Park Menagerie, New York," Illustration from *Scientific American* 65, No. 23 (Dec. 5, 1891). Related text reads: "…handsome specimens of this bird now in confinement at the menagerie in Central Park."

THE OSTRICHES AT THE CENTRAL PARK MENAGERIE, NEW YORK.

Male ostrich preparing to make his call (Rib Ticklers, "Ostrich Sounds – Noises" on YouTube, Oct. 6, 2021).

Besides Dr. Sketchley, Dr. Protheroe brought out a herder from Cape Town known only as Mr. Johnson. A reporter from the *New York Sun* observed that when the herder opened the deer hut, "he was greeted by a series of sounds suggestive of the noise made by a fog horn[*sic*]. 'That's what the Dutch natives of Cape Town call *bromming*,' said Mr. Protheroe. 'It expresses the same feeling with an ostrich that cooing does with a dove.'"[57] That sound, also compared to a deep bellow or even to a lion's roar, can be heard from over a mile away.

Annie Martin, wife of an early South African ostrich rancher wrote about the birdcall in her 1890 memoir *Home Life on an Ostrich Farm*. To make this sound, the bird inflates its neck like a Scottish bagpiper (or croaking frog) and "gives utterance to three deep roars; the two first short and staccato, the third very prolonged."[58] In effect, the listener would hear, "*Vwoom-vwoom-vwoooooooom!*"

The birdcall was given its Dutch name by early South African breeders. In English, it means "humming." The onomatopoeic equivalent since adopted in the German-English language is "booming."

The sounds of an ostrich:
Ostriches can also chirp like a quail, trill like a turkey, screech like a seagull and hiss like a snake.

Once inside the deer hut, the *Sun* reporter was kindly accosted. First his shirt collar was nipped then tugged, then an ostrich plucked his walking cane right out of his hand. After a failed attempt to gulp down the stiff object, the greedy bird gave up and, allegedly, apologized.

The Third Leg of the Journey

On December 2, Dr. Protheroe announced his intent to sell the entire lot of birds to investors.[59] Folks from California responded immediately, as did some in Texas and Florida. Based on the favorable climate, Dr. Protheroe went into business out west. He, Dr. Sketchley and Mr. Johnson soon began the next leg of their journey to the opposite coast, where year-round sunshine would keep the bird's toes warm.

The journey was completed first by wagonload, then by railcar. A January 3rd announcement in a Wyoming newspaper explained that to get the birds into the vehicle, first Dr. Protheroe blindfolded the birds, then Dr. Sketchley "laid hold of each wing," while a third helper, possibly Mr. Johnson, prodded the bird from behind.[60] Coincidentally, the act of Dr. Sketchley handling the birds would become future propaganda image for the Arizona Ostrich Company in Phoenix.

Together, the team got all 22 birds loaded up into a large, covered wagon reminiscent of the old Oregon Trail days. I know what you're thinking: "I'd like to see that." I thought it, too. But I could not find an archival image from the 1882 cross-country mission. Undeterred, I asked an artificial image generator to assist with a composite illustration. It did not disappoint, and due to the absurd accuracy achieved here, there will be a few more of these co-piloted creations later in the book.

Disclaimer: The image shown is not real.

Protheroe & Sketchley's Overland Journey

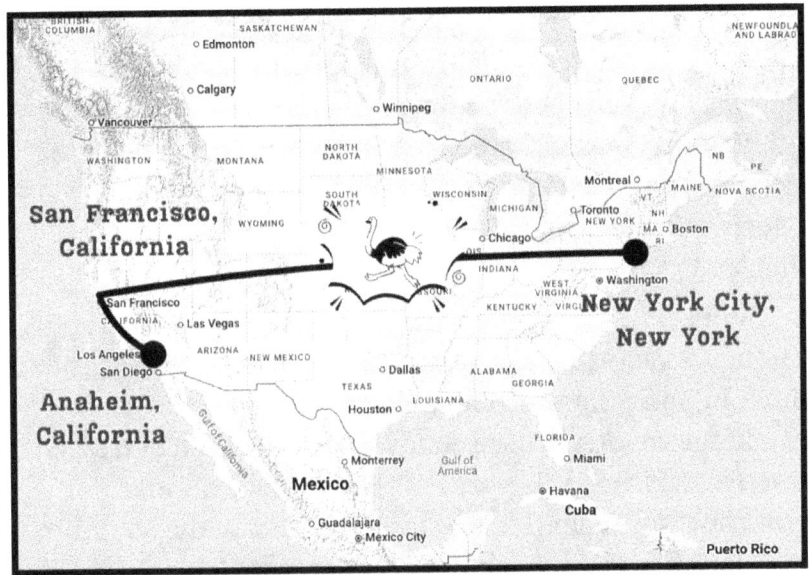

1882-1883 ostrich journey to America (part 2) (Google Maps, marked by author).

From the wagon, the birds were loaded into a railcar and transported through Chicago and Omaha to the Pacific Coast.[61] All 22 birds survived the trip to San Francisco, arriving in mid-January 1883. Some records say that the birds were again exhibited for the public. This time, in San Francisco. Then, they were moved to a temporary home on 800 acres in Borden.[62] The total journey took them 23,000 miles away from their homeland.

The California Ostrich Co.

In March 1883, the California Ostrich Company was formed (also seen as the Southern California Ostrich Farm Company or the California Ostrich Farming Company). Dr. Protheroe and Dr. Sketchley were vested members of the Company[63] that, through syndication with prominent locals, held a capital stock valued at $80,000 (or $2.5 million, presently).[64] Other investors were railroad barons, land developers, and ranchers. Burton Green, the founder of Beverly Hills, even got in on the deal. The syndicate paid $21,000 for the birds, or about $950 apiece.[65] The rest of the money was funneled into the development of a suitable property and the hiring of a full-time superintendent: Dr. Sketchley.

Robinson Trust (Stearns Ranchos Co.) leased out a portion of its acreage near Anaheim and opened its fences to visitors in April, thus becoming the first commercial ostrich ranch in the country. The grounds were warm, flat and sandy – exactly what the birds needed. The location was ideal for customers, too—being set up close to a stop on the Southern Pacific Railroad. Excitement for the new installment was shared among all the movers and shakers of the day. An article in the *Chautauquan,* a magazine for the promotion of culture, literature and science touted: "Every tourist to Southern California made the pilgrimage to Anaheim and the ostrich farm was well repaid..."[66]

Once in Los Angeles, the *Herald* interviewed Dr. Protheroe. He attested to his extensive knowledge of ostrich raising.[67] He described the perfect setup for a farm property, including the climate conditions, fencing requirements, and the labor demands. His prejudices slipped out when he told the reporter how glad he would be to employ white men in the U.S., considering them far more attentive and responsible than the migrant workers typically employed for farm labor.[68]

Though only 11% of the original cargo, the surviving birds flourished in their new home. "The first chick was hatched July 28, 1883," just three months after tours began.[69]

OSTRICH FARM

Capital Addition

NOW OPEN.

Fifty Gigantic Ostriches, beautiful display of Ostrich boas, plumes, fans, etc., at Producers' prices.

West end of Washington street car line.

Arizona Ostrich Company advertisement in the *Arizona Republican*, Jan. 7, 1904.

By the end of the first year in operation, those surviving 22 birds produced 270 eggs to grow the business.[70] His and Dr. Sketchley's accomplishment caused Dr. Protheroe to be hailed as "the first to pass the Rubicon," or the point of no return in the endeavor. [71] Their success bolstered others to soon follow in their footsteps. And *that*, kids, was how the U.S. got its first commercial ostrich ranch.

5. Blushing Grooms & Other Mating Stuff

"Much thought on the matter [of mating]
colors his shins and beak a bright red."
- The Arizona Graphic (1899)[72]

A warm summer in Southern California may have been exactly what Dr. Sketchley ordered for the restoration of the flock. While other livestock like cattle "go into heat" based on hormonal cycles, ostriches are some of the only animals to take that phrase literally. Warm weather invites ostrich breeding, with the egg-laying season in the American Southwest ranging from about February to August. Ostrich roosters blush deeply when mating season is upon them. This blush is not the human equivalent of the flirty feeling girls get sometimes. Rather, it's more like the heated rage and determination that a male feels during those same times.

"Beaks" are sharp and pointed.
"Bills" are flat and fleshy.
Now go (annoyingly) correct your friends.

Social & Breeding Systems

People mistakenly use the terms "flock, covey, gaggle, and flight" for groups of ostriches. Or, as we are discussing flightless landlubbers, sometimes they are called a "herd." In some parts of the world, they are a "Wobble," which seems most fitting, but the correct term for a group of ostriches is a "troop."[73] This may have been picked up from early literature such as Leo Africanus' *A Geographical Historie of Africa*

(1600). He describes their migration activities as such: "The ostriches wander up and down the deserts in orderly troops so that a far-off man would take them to be so many horsemen, which illusion hath often dismayed whole caravans."[74]

Ostrich troops don't operate as an organized unit with cohesive or predictable movements, such as seen in migratory bird groups like ducks. Ostriches essentially create limited alliances within a greater platonic community. In nature, the ostriches will create family groups of ten to twelve birds with a dominant breeding pair, plus additional hens claimed by the rooster.[75] Per the experts at the San Diego Zoo: "A dominant female is called the 'main hen.'"[76] Logically, that makes anyone else the rooster mates with a 'side chick.'

Within the family group, there is a hierarchy or "pecking order," like with chickens—and also, a bit like a pride of lions. There can be multiple family groups within a larger troop, but as one observer has put it: each dominant male "has its own domain, separated by some imaginary boundary line of his own, visible only to himself."[77] The observer, Helen Seargeant, lived on a Phoenix property that neighbored one of the largest ostrich ranches in Arizona's territorial days. From her home, she could see across the ostrich pens and noted: "There, in company with one or perhaps two hens, [the rooster] dwells monarch of all he surveys; any other ostrich daring to invade his territory is at once attacked."[78]

Matchmaking

An 1895 issue of *Poultry Monthly* provided that, in nature, "[t]he ostrich is gregarious and polygamous, the male, if left to his own inclination, often appropriating five or six females."[79] Breeders, however, manipulate the details of lusty encounters. On ranches, ostriches are generally paired off in duos, trios, or left to mingle promiscuously in a community pen.

If a breeder is looking for a specific output, such as feather quality, meaty muscles, or maximum fertility for egg laying, a bit of manipulation is required. If pairing off, the matchmaker must invest in extra fencing to contain each couple (or trio of one rooster and two hens) in their own separate corral. [80] Because of the instinct for hens within a family group to nest together, a trio can be a more natural setting for them than a duo.

According to Dr. Thomas Duncan's 1888 report to the U.S. Commissioner of Agriculture, when ostriches are, matched but have not

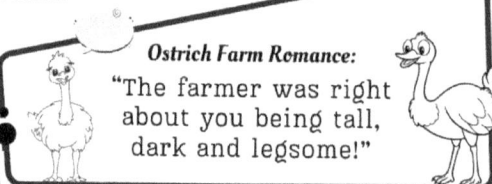

Ostrich Farm Romance:
"The farmer was right about you being tall, dark and legsome!"

yet bred, these birds are called "camped-off birds."[81] I prefer the term "flirty-birdies," but no one asked me. "After they have bred[,] they become 'guaranteed breeders,'" Dr. Duncan added.[82] The guarantee is supposedly backed by the birds' bond to each other.

Failed Matches and Lost Lovers

Not all man-made matches are successful, as ostriches can be rather picky when it comes to their partners. As seen in *Poultry Monthly*: "It is often the case that the male and female thus selected fail to agree and the male attempts to discipline his mate and occasionally kicks her over the fence."[83] Nonfiction author F. J. Haskin, once studied the birds' behaveiors at a Los Angeles ranch and found, "Some birds remain determined bachelors all their lives," refusing any and all of the partners offered.[84] Once captivated, however, a rooster becomes a "devoted slave" to his hen.[85] Challenging these claims is world-renowned ostrich raiser, D.C. Cogburn, who has offered: "the males will mate anything that looks mateable."[86]

On this note, once the birds have bonded to each other, they become protective and have been noted to show a preference for life, though not necessarily monogamy. Some literature supports the idea that when a rooster loses his preferred hen, he mourns the loss with a depressed mood, loss of appetite, and in some cases, a refusal to take a new partner. If in a larger family group, a bachelor bird could fight the depressed rooster for dominance. If there is no immediate replacement for the rooster, the ladies will stretch out their long legs and find themselves a new harem master. Or their breeder will assign them one.

Postcard featuring the Cawston Ostrich Farm in South Pasadena, ca. early 1900s (Los Angeles Public Library Digital Collection).

6. Sketchley Takes Over

"He left South Africa with 200 & landed in California with 22."
- Watson Pickrell, Cyclopedia of Farm Animals (1922)[87]

In 1884, Dr. Charles Sketchley planned a return trip to South Africa to secure additional adult birds that could amp up the breeding activities and increase the availability of filthy-rich feathers on U.S. soil. That year, 55 more ostriches were imported.[88] Besides shopper demands, pressure to increase the troop size may have arisen out of competition. In December 1883, the *Phoenix Weekly Herald* announced an Australian freighter, just recently arrived from Cape Town, carrying 23 ostriches in her belly, all of which would be rehomed near San Diego.[89] The new entrants to the industry were C.F.A. Johnson and his son Ed from Maine. The father-son team formed the American Ostrich Company.

In the four years following the 1883 Anaheim ranch opening, "three other parties ventured in the field of Ostrich-farming," wrote William Dutcher for *Bird-Lore* magazine.[90] Dutcher was once the president of the National Association of Audubon Societies. Besides the Johnsons', two other ranchers opened in Pasadena and Whittier. Mr. Johnson wrote about getting settled in: "a great deal of excitement here and you would split your sides with laughter to hear the absurd questions that are hurled at us from all sides."[91]

Considering all the new neighbors, Tom Pulley of the Orange County Historical Society claimed, "In the fall of 1885,

Los Angeles Ostrich Farm
——— AND ———
Zoological Garden

Will be open for the benefit of the G. A. R. and their friends for one week from to-day at half the usual rates.

au14 1w   **C. J. SKETCHLEY & CO., Proprietors.**

Ad for Sketchley's Ostrich Farm in California, *Los Angeles Herald*, August 14, 1886.

Sketchl[e]y wanted to return to South Africa to purchase additional birds for the farm. But his tightfisted board of directors refused his plan."[92] In response, Dr. Sketchley quit his position as superintendent, found himself new investors and formed C.J. Sketchley & Co.[93] In November of that year, he left to get himself another batch of birds to supply a new operation in Los Angeles.

Back to South Africa

What Dr. Sketchley might not have realized at the time of his departure was that the South African government didn't like what was happening with one of their most lucrative exports. After a few more retrievals from eager American farmers-to-be, South African ostrich farmers "became alarmed" at what it could mean for their future businesses.[94] In the early 1880s, South Africans had around $40 million of capital invested in this industry, and $4.5 million was shipped from Cape Town annually.[95] Dr. Duncan has explained, "if they allowed large troops of birds to be freely sent to the very land that took every year one-half or more of their feathers, this immense industry would be crippled."[96] It makes sense that South African ostrich raisers felt upset. Their livelihoods were being threatened!

In response, the African government increased the duty tax on exported birds of any age from 25% to $500 per, and $125 on every egg. [97] Railing farmers adjusted by increasing the price of birds to a prohibitive $1,500 each ($49,000 in 2025). Efforts to keep the fortunes in-house were too late, though. In addition to the American endeavors, there were early shipments that went out to India and Australia. The *Arizona Sentinel* later captured the way South African ranchers must have felt when there was a dip in profits: "...It is with chagrin bordering on despair that the Cape farmers find the retail trade gleaning the profits."[98]

After trekking through Cape Colony, Dr. Sketchley returned to his former hometown of Transvaal, on the eastern side of the continent. From there, he could avoid heavy export taxes by shipping his animals from Port Natal (Durban, KwaZulu-Natal). Since the Colony of Natal operated under different laws than Cape Colony, this became a temporary workaround.

A Stop in Galveston

Because there was no direct steamship access to California at this time (other than taking the long way around North America by crossing over the Isthmus of Panama), all imports of live animals had to stop over in South America, then to a quarantine station in New York, New Orleans or some other gulf port like Galveston, Texas.[99] Details of this journey were being tracked by interested Arizonans. The *Daily Tombstone* reported on an early April arrival at Galveston: "The Norwegian schooner [']Praecis St. Avenge['] arrived at the wharf ... after a two months' voyage from Africa. She brought a strange cargo to the new world, consisting of ostriches, parrots, monkeys, tropical birds, and last but not least, among her curiosities are five natives of the Madras [Chennai], India…"[100]

Again, some of the shipment became seasick, but historian Andrea Ringer claimed their accommodations may have been better planned than before. "On the Atlantic," she wrote, "they lived in single padded stalls near the middle of the hold, with paddocks between the stalls to offer some exercise and perhaps some interaction among the birds."[101] Ringer's research centered around the treatment of captive ostriches in zoos and circuses.

At the seaport, the ostriches were rested, inspected then exhibited at Galveston Park. According to an article in the *Daily Tombstone*, 36 ostriches debarked alive.[102] Dr. Sketchley's new birds, he told the media, were "the finest lot ever taken from Africa," moreso than the ones his predecessor could ever have found.[103] To compete with his former syndicate, he went as far as to claim that his birds were pedigreed like a racehorse, so he could prove their superiority on paper.

One ostrich threatened to embarrass the doctor when they were unloading from the cargo hold. When the bird was being led out, it became frightened and when "a couple of sailors approached to move him from the box, he gave one of them a gentle kick."[104] Despite courteous restraint, that kick sent the sailor flying into the side of the vessel where the man then checked himself to see how many bones he'd broken. The Malaysian animal handlers apparently told the sailor he was lucky to still be alive.

For the zoo-worthy collection, Dr. Sketchley reserved a specially prepared railcar on a California-bound train. Curious onlookers thronged the wharf to get a peek of the bewildering and diverse cargo before it boarded. While rail bound, expectant Arizonans looked forward to their chance to see the pro-

Dr. Sketchley's second Ostrich Farm in Rancho Loz Feliz in Los Angeles County, 1886 (California Historical Society Collection).

cession come through their state. The outfit passed through Tucson around April 16.[105] I don't know if Dr. Sketchley made time to showcase his animals while in town, or just take a breather, but one of them appears to have made a solo performance when it escaped into the Yuma Desert. (There's more on that in the Murder Birds chapter.)

The following year, the doctor made one more trip to South Africa. On that journey, he brought 30 ostriches to California and sold all of them to a circus.[106]

7. Cawston: the California Copycat

"The money-making possibilities of ostrich raising are simply wonderful almost beyond belief."
- American Ostrich Co. (1907)[107]

Two Californian gentlemen became the primary conduits to Arizona's ostrich industry. When competition appeared on the scene, there was one man who quickly dethroned Dr. Sketchley as the king of all ostrich ranchers. Hands down, claims Audubon's Dutcher, "the most successful of these persons being Mr. Edwin Cawston, who went to South Africa and returned [in 1886] with forty-four selected birds."[108] Cawston divided those ostriches between his ranch in Los Angeles and someone else's in Whittier.

Edwin E. Cawston was a young Englishman who could afford spending his inheritance funds on a new industry without thinking twice. It is believed that Cawston became fascinated with the idea of owning ostriches when he saw them on display at the 1876 Centennial International Exposition.[109] He spontaneously purchased the two ostriches being exhibited and took them back to Nice, France. (By the way, there are additional nuances to Cawston's story that might interest Californians, but I have left them out in favor of the big picture.)

Between 1884 and 1886, Cawston journeyed from Surrey, England to California to investigate the farming opportunity that was being spoken so highly of. It was an

Edwin E. Cawston, n.d. (South Pasadena Public Library/Public Domain).

Edwin Cawston drives a trap through his Norwalk ostrich ranch, ca. 1890 (Nicholas Beyelia Collection/Los Angeles Public Library).

Cawston Ostrich Farm Souvenir Book, 1909 (Smithsonian Institute/Public Domain). Image caption reads: "We have over 1,000 ostriches."

At the Ostrich Farm," ca. 1911. Postcard from the Dept. of Archives and Special Collections of the Hannon Library (Loyla Marymount University).

Cawston Ostrich Farm Souvenir Book, 1909 (Smithsonian Institute/ Public Domain).

instant sale for him. In 1886, he traveled to South Africa with E.P. Hoyle (the superintendent of the California Ostrich Co., who had replaced Dr. Sketchley). From there, the partners chartered a return ship to bring in what he believed were the "best obtainable ostriches in the world."[110] Certainly, Dr. Sketchley might have rolled an eye or two at this claim, as he would when Cawston put up a sign over the entrance declaring *his* ranch the "Pioneer Ostrich Farm of America."

Cawston made it back to the U.S. in January 1887. Of the original 52 birds shipped, just over 40 survived. He sold a few ostriches to others before setting up separate locations for his new business endeavors: a tourist attraction in Norwalk and a quiet breeding area in Pasadena. Cawston intended to be a "serious breeder" in Orange County and reserved 18 ostriches for that line of business.[111]

Cawston's Rise and Fall

In 1891, the California Ostrich Co. went belly up and 170 birds were sold to the superintendent R. J. Northam.[112] Northam then passed 40 over to Cawston.[113] Four years later, Northam's property could no longer sustain the birds, plus their second generation. Northam sent Cawston another large batch of chicks. Cawston's ostrich operation grew exponentially, and he became the number one supplier of ostriches and feathers in the country.

Ten years later, Cawston's obsession sparked anew. At the 1901 Pan-American Exposition in Buffalo, New York, Cawston saw blue necked "Nubian" ostriches on exhibit. He simply had to get his hands on them and, again, purchased some from the exhibitor, Aylma Young Pearson. Cawston hoped by crossbreeding the red and blue species he could experiment with increasing an ostrich's feather output.[114] The new additions stimulated a fresh wave of tourists to California and in 1905 the press reported that Cawston's Ostrich Ranch was "the finest show farm in the United States."[115] After 29 years in the business, in 1911, Cawston sold off his Pasadena land and ostriches, then retired to England.[116]

8. Arizona's First Birds

"...This will be the pioneer institution of this kind in Arizona."
- Arizona Sentinel (1888)[117]

There has been some debate over which Arizona entrepreneur brought the first family of ostriches into the state: Was it Moses E. Clanton or Josiah Harbert? The answer is both. Like Drs. Protheroe and Sketchley, they should share the glory, at least initially.

Moses Clanton was a stock-raiser in Phoenix in the early 1880s before he moved to Los Angeles around 1887. For a time, he lived in Santa Fe Springs, neighboring Norwalk. He may have been introduced to the ostrich ranching business through a visit to Edwin Cawston's show farm, but there is also a strong possibility that the livestock man was employed at Norwalk and learned everything he needed to know about ostriches through that experience. In this chapter is an image collage showing Cawston holding an ostrich (on the right) while an unidentified man harvests wing feathers (on the left). The groomer looks convincingly like Moses Clanton might have appeared in his mid-40s. (By the way, for Wild West fans—Moses is not related to Ike Clanton of the Cowboys who were caught up in the gunfight behind the O.K. Corral. There is, however, an associate of Wyatt Earp who appears later in the book.)

While in California, Clanton met Josiah Harbert. Harbert used to live in the town of Alhambra, just 19 miles north of Norwalk, and had recently moved to Arizona, located on

"'Plucking' of the Bird, Cawston Ranch," undated postcard from the South Pasadena Public Library Collection. Inset: Moses Edward Clanton (1840-1910), n.d., provided by Rose Ann Jensen on FindAGrave.com [memorial 10613941].

a large tract just three miles west of Phoenix. Before the Civil War, Harbert had spent seven years farming in Missouri, then ventured west in an ox train to Colorado, then Montana. He might have been seeking a fortune in mining. In 1876, Harbert continued to California, where he'd have seen three early feather farms become the new strike-it-rich opportunity.

Harbert had apparently done some thinking on the "disadvantages of the plume-growing business," as was observed in California. [118] He considered whether those issues might be overcome in the Arizona climate. In 1888, he formed a partnership with Clanton and they called it Clanton & Co. (Harbert being the "Co."). They planned to use Clanton's ranch lands outside of Buckeye, Arizona to host a new troop of birds purchased from Cawston. "While not claiming any experience in that kind of business," Harbert told the *Arizona Daily Star,* he felt confident that the valley would benefit from participating in the feather industry.[119]

Ostrich purchase reports from Arizona newspapers are a bit sketchy, but the majority agree that at the start of June, Clanton & Co. obtained at least one pair of guaranteed breeders and five pairs of chicks. All would surley propel their new owners into an immediate profit. The *Weekly Journal-Miner* in Prescott claimed the adult birds set Clanton and Harbert back $2,500.[120] Tucson's *Arizona Weekly Star* said the lot totaled $4,200, or about $350 per bird.[121] The *Arizona Sentinel* reported it was one-fourth of that price.[122] Chances are, the chicks were closer to $170, while the older birds demanded a much steeper price, having been directly from those Cawston recently imported from South Africa. At the end of the month, the *Arizona Weekly Enterprise* of Florence announced: "Mr. M. E. Clanton arrived last night from Los Angeles to prepare the way for a [rail]car load of ostriches which will arrive to-day, the nucleus of an ostrich ranch which he will start near Phoenix."[123]

Charles Colley wrote for *Arizona Highways,* as soon as the birds arrived at the Southern Pacific train station, there were "crowds of sweating townspeople braving the summer sun just to get a closer look at the strange birds..."[124] The attention lent itself to an immediate sideshow attraction. Clanton and Harbert capitalized on the opportunity by putting their ostriches on display in downtown Phoenix. After two weeks in the scorching heat, it was time to get the ostriches settled into more comfortable conditions. Such was Clanton's alfalfa field on the Gila River, out past Buckeye.

Clanton & Co.

Clanton's 160 acres on the Gila River west of Buckeye, Arizona, ca. 1900. 1914 township map section (1S 5W) from the collection of the History and Archives Division, Arizona State Library, Archives and Public Records, labeled by author (Fair Use).

Harbert hired someone with a high-sided wagon to deliver the birds to their new home. He emphasized how valuable the cargo was and how extra care must be taken in transport. Blanche Murray, also for *Arizona Highways*, wrote, "The men in charge were going to take no chances about their escaping, so the head of each bird was sheathed in a stocking and a tight canvas cover fastened over the wagon box."[125] Colley alleges that it was Harbert himself, "a greenhorn in the ostrich-trade" who secured the birds with a double measure of fabric.[126]

The ostriches were carted approximately 47 miles to the Gila River respite. After removing the top tarp, only the adults and one chick were standing. The rest had succumbed to the heat or been jostled too roughly. Clanton & Co.'s fortune had tanked just as soon as it arrived. Without the ability to claim seasickness as an excuse, Harbert may have felt an immense guilt. On July 12, he is reported to have bought the ostriches from Clanton, though it was more likely Harbert paid Clanton out for his portion of losses.[127]

Once business was settled, Harbert needed to make up for his mistake. He left immediately with the three surviving birds to showcase them at the Cincinnati Centennial Exposition, commonly called the "World's Fair" of 1888 (July 4-Nov. 8). Ostriches were not listed in the official event guide, perhaps owing to the late entry. Harbert's show business stint ended just in time to exhibit the birds for another week at the Arizona Territorial Fair (Oct. 15-20).[128] After the fair, Harbert kept the birds on his property in the Alhambra neighborhood.

More Ostriches Die in Transit

The next time an ostrich would stir up excitement in Arizona was that same October. John Robinson's Circus rolled through Yuma and Tucson on the Southern Pacific. While in route, there was an accident in the town of Cactus City, California. Newspapers reported that on October 16, "three cars were ditched, two of them badly wrecked, killing a full grown[*sic*] ostrich. The hyenas, tigers, ostriches and California lions were thus liberated."[129] All the animals were recouped (or re-cooped, if you will), except for the mountain lion and dead ostrich. This story repeats itself near verbatim several times in the same year, just in advance of scheduled shows. Without photographic evidence of the crash, I suspect the entire story was a ploy for ticket sales and there never was an ostrich to begin with.

John Robinson Circus poster showing interior view of various animals in cages, Courier Litho. Co., 1898 (LOC).

9. The Father of Arizona Ostrich Farming

"North of town, a flourishing ostrich farm is to be found.
There are about 160 birds ... descendants of a single pair."
- Phoenix City Directory (1899-1900)[130]

In office from 1892 to 1893, Arizona Territorial Governor Nathan Oakes Murphy provided a report to the Secretary of the Interior that Josiah Harbert should be recognized as the "father of the ostrich business."[131] He received the honorary title for bringing the original pair of ostriches to Phoenix. Obviously, that report was missing more than a few details. As for Harbert being credited as the person who made ostrich ranching popular, that much was absolutely true.

After a whirlwind investment, Harbert washed out of the competitive feathering ranks but continued to care for the three remaining birds, hoping that the rooster and hen might provide another brood come the summer of 1889. If he could successfully raise another troop, he might be able to restore his financial standing. Fortune seemed to smile on the Harberts when the two breeders showed a renewed interest in each other. Before the first nest could be scratched out, however, the hen suffered an accident. "The lady ostrich, apparently mistaking a piece of barbed wire for an exotic Arizona insect, was the next to succumb," Colley provided.[132] It was another devastating blow to the rancher who'd bet everything on what should have been providing him "stupid money" already.

Josiah T. Harbert (1828-1906), ca. 1890, provided by Ashley Evensen on FindAGrave.com [memorial 41651846].

Harbert's Ranch (1903)

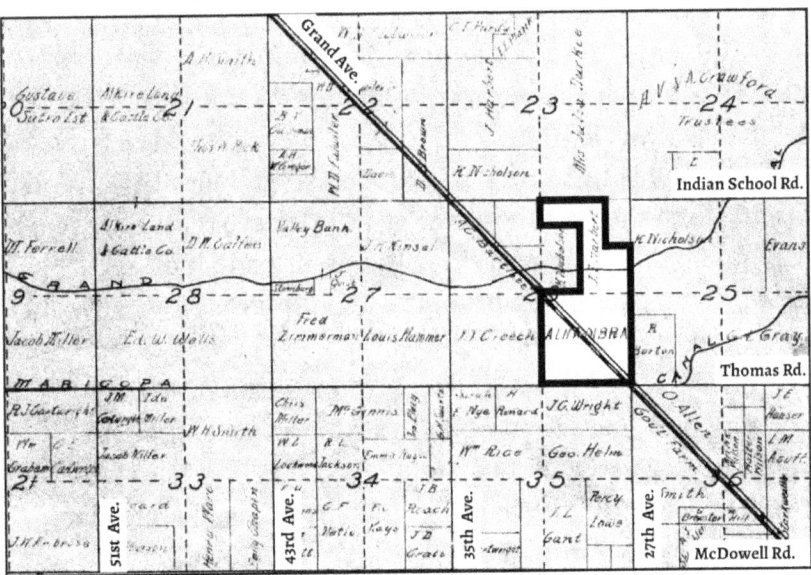

Township map (2N 2E), 1911, labeled by author (History and Archives Division/Arizona State Library/Fair Use).

The only birds left were the adult rooster and the young female believed to be its offspring. The *Coconino Sun* reported, "it was not thought wise to invest the amount of money necessary to replace the dead birds till it was better known what would result from the effort to raise them."[133] Harbert decided to keep the two birds as pets, learning whatever he could about them. And, as an experiment, he wanted to see if the two might still breed once the hen matured. According to the *Arizona Daily Star,* he put the ostriches out in the alfalfa pasture on the southern section of his land "where they can be seen by the curious public."[134] This section bordered the uniquely diagonal roadway Grand Avenue, near 31st Avenue. The ostriches had 40 acres to roam,[135] and they thrived on the nutritious greens at their constant disposal.[136]

In the meantime, Harbert moved on to other ventures, such as platting out the town of Alhambra and planting the first orange trees in Phoenix. The trees were imported from his former home in Southern California and planted at Arizona Falls (close to the Arizona Country Club). Harbert set his attention on canal projects, irrigation work and land development, eventually becoming the director of the Arizona Improvement Company.

After three years, Harbert's patience paid off. In 1891, the young bird had matured and was found acceptable to its pen mate. (Let's pretend we don't know their relationship for this next part.) Colley wrote that the birds "made up for lost time."[137] Murray wrote, "Mr. Ostrich scooped up a rude nest in the earth with his funny long toes, where his young mate laid a few precious eggs."[138] By 1895, the guaranteed breeders had produced 104 chicks,[139] and the following year, they added 19 more to the troop.[140] The *Oasis* announced, "the [ostrich] industry has long since passed the experimental stage."[141] With the exponential increase, Harbert purchased an incubator to assist with hatching greater numbers of eggs.[142] In the process, he noticed roadside audiences become more interested in seeing his strange pets grow up from wonky winged nursery tots to gorgeous goliaths.

Col. J.T. Simms, a railroad man-turned-canal developer visited Harbert's birds in 1894 and remarked, "I have seen ostriches in many parts[,] and from all parts of the world, but these are the largest and finest looking birds I have ever seen."[143] He said the Arizona birds put California's in the shade and the ranch manager Mr. Wright agreed, adding that their birds are worth three times as much, too.

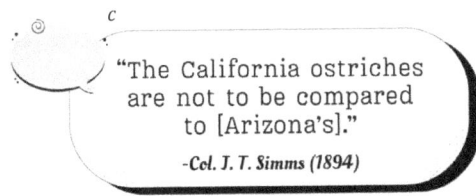

"The California ostriches are not to be compared to [Arizona's]."
-Col. J. T. Simms (1894)

The pen mates were successful breeders for nine years. "More than half the ostriches later raised in the United States were descendants of that pair," Murray wrote.[144] To address weakening the species via continued inbreeding, mature ostriches were crossbred with those in zoo collections and through arrangements with traveling exhibitions (like the circus or World's Fair).[145]

The father rooster became a bit of a progenitive legend, like Abraham of the Bible. He was reportedly named *Oom Paul* (Afrikaans for "Uncle Paul") after Stephanus Johannes Paulus Kruger, a celebrated politician and military figure from South Africa's Cape Colony.[146] In 1899, *Oom Paul* was removed to a quiet parcel and spent his senior years in the comfort and cantankery frequently enjoyed by old farts around the nation. "He has been honorably retired," read an article for *The Arizona Graphic*, "and with the dignity befitting his patriarchal

---

c "Omnivorous Birds," *Arizona Republican*, September 4, 1894, 1.

Left: Ostriches at Harbert's. Text reads: "Ostrich Farm, Phoenix, Ariz." Right: Girl with ostrich eggs at Harbert's (Jos. H. Hamill/Poultry Monthly, May 1895).

position[,] he knocks the stuffing out of everything that comes within his reach."[147]

Harbert Retires Next

After Josiah Harbert's wife passed away, his own health began to decline. He made a succession plan and sold off what he could, with 97 birds going to the Arizona Ostrich Co. between 1896 and 1897.[148] Harbert is listed as a "capitalist" in the next U.S. Census; perhaps enjoying the "lucrative" fruits of his labor.[149] In 1904, he retired to Oregon with his son but the legend of his failure-turned-success inspired many ostrich ranchers to come.

10. Nesting Habits

Downy fluff peeks out,
Wobbly legs take tiny steps,
New life on the run
- Haiku by C. Hicks (2025)

How can anyone learn anything correct about an ostrich's nesting habits when no author in history has ever taken this matter seriously? Not one, I tell you! The *Arizona Graphic* tells us the following:

"When [a rooster] finally determines that a family should be reared[,] he digs a nest in the ground. He then drives his mate up to the nest and calls her attention to his by giving her a kick. If she is dull of comprehension, and she usually is, he continues to kick her and scold her... He is often compelled to go to the extreme of kicking her over the eight-foot fence forming the corral. She finally, however, sees her duty and begins to lay eggs..."[150]

See what I mean?

Building the Least Nestlike Nests

Ostrich nests require no sticks, no grass, and no feathers. No shrubbery conceals where the hen drops her oversized clutch. No water source need be near, nor shade be overhead, "For she leaves her eggs on the ground and warms them in the dust," so the Bible says.[151] An ostrich's nest is not more than a simple hole in the ground—an indentation, more or less. The

Ostrich nest in the sand at the Rooster Cogburn Ostrich Ranch in Arizona. (Author collection, 2025).

rooster may scratch at the ground with a couple of toes before squatting to make a few shapely scoops with his calloused breastbone. The entire production leaves a rudimentary mark not more than one foot deep and three to six feet in diameter.[152] With one strong summer haboob, all might vanish from view on the Sonoran Desert floor.

Arizona ostrich rancher Watson Pickrell wrote about ostrich nesting behaviors in a report for the U.S. Department of Agriculture: "At first the female may not take to the nest, but may lay her first eggs on the ground, whereupon the male will roll them into the nest. Generally, after the male has put 3 or 4 eggs into the nest, the female will lay there. In about 30 days she will lay 12 to 16 eggs and will be ready to commence incubation."[153]

An observer at Harbert's Ranch wrote for the *Oasis*, saying that the hen is not particular about the final locality of the nest, "but she is very stubborn about giving it up once she has chosen it. One of the ostriches on the farm recently selected the middle of the road that runs through the paddock for her nest and promptly began filling it with eggs. Harbert dug another nest for her in a more protected quarter of the pasture, but instead of feeling grateful for his attention, Madam Ostrich quietly rolled the eggs, one by one, back to their original place of deposit."[154]

The Story of the First Three Eggs

In the Middle Ages, Zakarīyā Ibn Muḥammad al-Qazwīnī, an Arabic natural historian (more commonly a "naturalist") and self-proclaimed cosmographer (someone who studies all things in the universe), wrote his observations of ostrich nesting habits in his work titled, *The Wonders of Creation*. This circa 1280 text was an encyclopedia-like book that falls into the category of a "bestiary" or book of beasts. These books became popular literature in the Middle Ages (AKA the Medieval period). They were treasured not only for their clever ideas on each animal but also for the fantastical gold-inlay illustrations within.

Artists freely interpreted an author's descriptions about animals they'd never laid eyes on. The warped, dispro-portionate and discomforting creatures that result are only fit for Alice's Wonderland or a Dr. Seuss book. Or, in the case of the griffin and unicorn, a wizarding book at Hogwarts. One of the more bizarre inclusions is a creature called a Bonnacon. It seems to be a bull-sized, long-tailed ram with an unusual firepower system.

Bonnacon in Bestiary of Ann Walsh, ca. 1400-1425. From the Kongelige Bibliotek manuscript collection in Copenhagen, Denmark [GKS 1633 4° Folio 10r] (Public Domain).

Ostrich depiction in Wonders of Creation (Turkish manuscript W.659, 1280), in the Henry Walters Collection at the Walters Art Museum Collection [CPS_W.659.137b_Fp_DD].

According to al-Qazwīnī's book, when going into her egg-laying season, Madam Ostrich has thought of nearly everything for her nursery. Her first two or three eggs are infertile. The hen purposefully lays them outside of the nest because they will not need incubation, though they are an important provision for her chicks later. As soon as the chicks are freed from their eggshells, they need a meal that won't require them to travel to a watering hole where they'd easily be picked off by predators. As a meal and water substitute, the hen breaks open the first of the eggs in reserve. (Just to be clear here, the babies would not be practicing cannibalism—hypothetically, there would only be juicy goo inside those first few eggs.)

The nutritional reserves are considered an essential provision from the mother that is comparable to how mammals breastfeed their young. The chicks eat everything up, including the shell. The pseudo-scientist also explained a second stage of feeding: "When the chicks have grown strong, [the mother] breaks the last [egg,] on which vermin will collect, and this serves as food for the young until they are able to graze."[155]

Though interesting, that story is quite wrong. Infertile eggs can be easily identified by a hen based on their temperature and powerful scent. They are not stored for later. Instead, they are rolled away and destroyed or otherwise abandoned to vultures, creepy crawlies and decomposers. Newly hatched chicks can begin foraging on native resources almost immediately. If food is sparse, chicks can survive on very little to nothing for up to two weeks because they have (essentially) been super-charged with nutrients from within their egg.

Extending the Season

If left to nature's design, the dozen or so eggs will be the hen's complete brood for the season. A keen breeder, though, can trick the hen into extending her laying season for as long as the sand is warm. (In Arizona, ostriches can lay eggs from as early as March through August). Early breeders learned that "...Like its diminutive relation the chicken, the hen ostrich would keep laying if the eggs were systematically removed from the nest."[156] Once the pile of eggs had shrunk, the ostrich, seeing that her job was not done, would refill the pile until she reached her desired number. Unfortunately, for every new one or two she added, a sneaky somebody would pull one or two off the pile again. Being a bit of a perfectionist, the ostrich would keep laying an egg every other day, until she reached an ideal number. If done well, the final harvest can be as large as 40 to 100 eggs per hen.

Collecting those eggs, however, is one of the riskiest jobs on the ranch. In South Africa, native farmers were observed army crawling through the enclosures, while holding a long stick or shepherd's crook. "...He will skillfully draw out the eggs with a long stick until two or three are left," reported an Arizonan who personally observed the feat in 1882.[157] To avoid alarming the birds by letting them see the thief's bounty, the man employed for the task tucked each football-sized lump inside his waistband until he'd gathered two pant legs full of eggs. At that point, he'd have no choice but to slither back outside the enclosure.

Collected eggs were carried to the barn and incubated. After about 14 days, they could be candled (checked with a light to see if they were fertile or not). If fertile, the rancher would need to mimic Mother Nature by continuing to incubate

Ostrich chicks being hatched from an incubator at the Pan-American Ostrich Ranch in Phoenix, ca 1904-1907 (L.H. Chalmers/*The Earth*, Aug. 1909).

the batch for the next 40 to 45 days. In the earliest days of South African ranches, this would be done by a motherly maid whose full-time job was to keep eggs in her bed, tucked in around her body, and covered with a pile of blankets. As ostrich breeding became more common, appropriately sized incubator boxes replaced the bed maid.

Egg-Sitting Responsibilities

"The division of labor between Mr. and Mrs. Ostrich is more nearly fair than among most birds. It is an understood thing that if she takes the trouble to lay the eggs[,] he will attend to the hatching, which is very kind of him, considering the fact that he is bigger, stronger, prettier and worth more than she."[158] This inclusion in *The Oasis* is only partially correct. Though his feathers might be more striking, they provide infinitely less to the feather farmer over a lifetime than the multiplicative magic of one hen's summertime labor.

It is also only half-true that the rooster sits on the eggs to incubate. In nature, the dominant rooster takes to this sch-

Hens collectively tending to a nest at the Rooster Cogburn Ostrich Ranch (Author collection, 2025).

eduled chore only at nightfall, where he can sit on the nest out in the open, completely obscuring the moon-white pearls with his pitch-black down. Modern observations suggest that the rooster's contribution is the animal's way of maximizing their biological camouflage. "The male, being black, is not so easily seen at night, and the female, being drab or nearly the color of sand, can not be so readily seen in daylight," reported Pickrell.[159] "Once in a while," a hen might spare the rooster a respite, "to give him a chance to eat and stretch himself, but these kindnesses were by no means frequent," *The Oasis* writer concluded.[160]

In archaic literature, hens get a bad rap for not sitting on their eggs all day. This is also a misunderstanding. During the daytime, hens in a family group tend to a nest together; each checking on, turning over, sitting on and shading the pile of eggs they have all contributed to. For a long while, those studying the animal could not identify this communal behaveior and believed that hens were irresponsible mothers. A

Biblical account purported: "She's negligent with her young, as if they weren't even hers."[161]

From observations made of ostriches in captivity, the assumption of neglect was negated. When camped off in a trio, two hens can be witnessed splitting the egg-sitting duties from sunup to sundown. By isolating the birds from their larger community, it could be determined that ostrich hens were just as devoted as any other bird, even practicing "affectionate solicitude," towards their clutch.[162]

Her Morbid Responsibility

If an ostrich hen perceives something defective with an egg or the youngling inside, she dispatches of it quickly, rolling it away from the nest and, under strained circumstances, she may even eat it as a snack. The same nutritional boost that infants receive from eating shell pieces applies to the adults. The calcium from an eggshell helps hens create strong eggshells in the future. Ranchers can also support this need (and limit the cradle cravings) by offering their birds a bone meal mix. Sometimes, if other hens see that an egg has been cracked, they'll join in on the feast, taking care not to leave a single crumb behind. (And... just to be clear here, in this case, the hens *might* be practicing infanticide, or "filial cannibalism." This is a survival strategy employed by many bird species such as eagles, chickens, and even little quails. Lions do it, too.)

WANTED—10,000 pounds of old dry bone. Will pay one dollar per hundred pounds for good dry bones delivered at our ranch ten miles west of Phoenix, Yuma road. Phoenix-American Ostrich Co.

Want ad in *Arizona Republican*, May 10, 1905.

Inside the Eggs

An ostrich clutch does not, as archaic writers believed, get hatched out under the sun. In an Arizona summer, to leave the eggs unattended could mean certain death. The perfect temperature for incubation is about 97-degrees Fahrenheit. To warm the eggs up, nesters will sit fully atop of them. To keep eggs cool in the afternoon, nesters will squat over them, offering shade. And if inclined, a hen may even flap a wing or two for a slight breeze. Eggs within an incubator would need dual heat and cooling controls to do the same.

Newly hatched chicks are quite fragile. Arizona ostrich rancher Watson Pickrell shared for the 1922 book, *Cyclopedia of Farm Animals*, they need to be kept at about 90-degrees for at least the first 24 hours of their emergence. Then, chicks must be kept away from any chills in the air for the next 2-3 months.[163] Despite the available literature, ostrich chicks are unaware of the cautions they must keep and only about half survive to see their first birthday.

At one month old, ostrich chicks
can run up to 35 MPH!

Hyenas consider them a quick snack.

Initially, one chick is indiscernible from the next, and gender is a near mystery to their breeder unless they, for a lack of better phrasing, poke around a bit. James Geissinger described the appearance of chicks at an Arizona ranch in 1909. He wrote, "The ostrich chick is covered with a speckled brown feather coat somewhat like that of a partridge, which he wears for the first year.'[164] After a year, the bright black and white plumes will emerge, distinguishing young males from their counterparts.

Top: "Three-Day-Old;" Bottom: "Brood of Chicks," Cawston Ostrich Farm Souvenir Book, 1909 (Smithsonian Institute/Public Domain).

Chicks grow rapidly, at a rate of about one foot each month. They can reach their full height in eight or nine months. By the end of one year, the baby birds can be over six feet tall and near 200 pounds. Even before the year mark, chicks are surprisingly meaty. In 1914, a 6-month-old bird from the Belgo-American Ostrich Company in South Phoenix was served for a Christmas banquet. It provided a whoppin' 55-pounds of meat for that feast.[165]

11. Arizona's Early Ostrich Ranches

"Here is ... the best farming country in the world.
Here are thousands of ostriches."
- Arizona State Business Directory (1915-1916)[166]

Though Josiah Harbert had cashed out at the turn of the century, the ostrich industry in Arizona was about to boom. Harbert's robust troops provided evidence that the Salt River Valley could produce the best birds the U.S. would ever see. In 1905, Watson Pickrell agreed that Arizona's climate was particularly "favorable to the health of the birds, yield and quality of feathers."[167] And in 1910, T. W. Kemp, a so-called expert in the industry, agreed that there was no other place in the world where "climatic conditions, combined with an assured supply of water for the growing of crops, is so propitious for the industry."[168]

New entrants to ostrich ranching followed Harbert's example of keeping ostriches on an alfalfa diet. The feed crop could be offered year-round when irrigated by one of the canal systems fed by the Salt River. By 1915, the state's business directory boasted having everything needed to support thousands of ostriches across the valley. That number was no exaggeration, as you'll soon see.

Arizona Ostrich Company

With the 97 ostriches received from Harbert, William Smith Pickrell, a former stock raiser from Nebraska, established the Arizona Ostrich Company.[169] Pickrell had moved to Phoenix around 1894 and became a superintendent for the Phoenix Light and Power Company (one of the previous names for what is presently Arizona Public Service, or APS). His family lived out on Center (now Central) and Washington Streets, just down the way from the State Capital Building. Breeding the ostriches may have been a secondary income earner for him.

William formed the Arizona Ostrich Co. in 1897 with business partner Vernon L. Clark, a firefighter by trade and a well-known betting man. Clark was listed in the 1899 Phoenix City Directory as the Secretary of the Company, while Pickrell was the President. On the new line of business, the directory dedicated a section that read: "While this is not an industry that is calculated to invite extensive increase or investment of capital, it has nevertheless been a lucrative venture to the originators of the scheme."[170] Pickrell and Clark hoped to be the next to cash in on either feather crops or propagation.

Vernon L. Clark (1861-1950) in Phoenix Fire Dept. uniform, ca. 1907, provided by Tim Kovacs on FindAGrave.com [memorial 146320519].

Pickrell and Clark put those 97 ostriches on a plot of land three miles north of Phoenix's city center. It shared an address with the United States Industrial Indian School, though the specific portion of that government land that was leased out and dedicated to ostriches has not been identified. Arizona historian, Roscoe Wilson provided a description of the establishment from local "old-timers" as a basic plot of alfalfa (which pretty much describes 90% of the ostrich operations in the area).[171] Though raising ostriches is nothing like raising cattle, Pickrell appears to have gotten into the swing of things rather quickly. In just a few years, he tripled the population in his care.

Following William to Arizona was his younger brother George Watson Pickrell, who settled in Tempe. Watson, as he went by, is assumed to have helped his brother with the ostrich ranch, though he was a butcher by profession. From studying his subjects, Watson produced many writings on industry best practices. Several of his observations have already been shared in this book, but his ranching-specific story will appear in a later chapter.

Pearson Ostrich Company

Readers might recognize the name Aylma Young Pearson from an earlier chapter. Around 1899, Pearson established the Salt River Valley's third successful commercial ostrich ranching operation in the town of Cashion. Per the *Coconino Sun,* to launch his endeavor, Pearson purchased the entire troop of ostriches from Pickrell and Vernon's company. Though not specified, he paid "a figure which indicates that ostrich raising has passed beyond the stage of novelty."[172]

Of all the people who had absolutely no business being in the ostrich ranching industry, perhaps number one on the list should be Aylma Pearson. Pearson had zero experience with farming in general. He was a stage actor and theatre manager from New York. His career in show business was quite profitable with tours through the Midwest. He and his wife, a singer and dancer, had enjoyed sharing the spotlight until Pearson's health began to deteriorate. He spent three years at the Winyaw Sanitarium in Asheville, North Carolina, under the care of Dr. Karl van Ruck. There, he received an experimental climate treatment for tuberculosis and entered remission.

At some point during those restorative treatments, Pearson formed a connection with M. J. Taylor, an "extensive feather manufacturer and dealer, of New York City."[173] They came up with the idea for a combination ostrich and alligator farm in Jacksonville, Florida. It was an unusual business prospect, but why wouldn't they do just as well in Florida as the ostrich ranchers on the Pacific Coast? The weather was warm with sunshine aplenty, just like California. Pearson formed a syndicate with Taylor and in 1898, with the help of investors, they ordered a troop of 30 red neck ostriches from Edwin Cawston. Those ostriches were shipped by rail to Jacksonville.[174]

While Taylor saw to acquiring alligators for their new attraction, Pearson made a cross-country trip to earn more money for the startup. He took the ostriches to that year's World's Fair and put his show business skills to good use. Properly titled, the Trans-Mississippi and International Exposition ran from June to November, in Omaha, Nebraska.[175] The Exposition program listed Pearson's ostriches on the west midway, along with a giant seesaw and Herr Carl Hagenbeck's Wild Animal Show. Elsewhere at the fair was Buffalo Bill and his famous Wild West show featuring Arizona's controversial Apache Chief, Geronimo.

Following this multi-month field trip, Pearson returned to Florida with pockets bulging from ticket sales. There may have been a debate over "yours," "mine" and "ours" before Pearson and Taylor's working relationship fizzled. They went their separate ways the following spring. Taylor retained the financial interests of the farm in Florida, which became "one of the finest exhibitions places in the country," according to William Dutcher of the Audubon Society.[176] Pearson kept a portion of the show birds.[177]

The Ostrich Farm at the 1898 World's Fair. Photo by F. A. Rinehart, 1898.

Admission ticket to the ostrich farm. Both images are courtesy of the Omaha Public Library and Univ. of Nebraska, Trans-Mississippi International Exposition Collection.

Pearson Starts Over

Pearson briefly moved to California, still craving the attention and profits ostriches brought him. While seething over his bitter experience, he took note of the Arizona Ostrich Company. When he bought them out in 1899, they were already a lead competitor in the breeding industry. Pearson determined to steal the spotlight by aggressively acquiring ostriches. In 1900, the *Arizona Silver Belt* announced that Pearson was "gathering up all the ostriches of the United States," and that he planned to make the Salt River Valley "the center of the ostrich industry of the western continent."[178]

Adding to his initial troop were the 97 birds from Arizona Ostrich Co., 93 additional ostriches purchased from

Edwin Cawston,[179] and 154 purchased from R. J. Northem's successor, Edward Atherton.[180] (For clarity, Atherton was raising the descendants from Protheroe and Sketchley's original ostrich bloodline.) With the increase in animals, Pearson needed more land than the leased space at the Indian School. In November 1900, he purchased 320-acres of grazing land just outside of Phoenix.[181] The initial purchase was located on a portion of Frank Criswell's cattle ranch at 83rd Avenue and Buckeye Road. He rapidly acquired several nearby properties until he had 1,600-acres at his disposal.

> "In a short time, [Pearson] had bought all the birds in the [U.S.], except a few..."
>
> *Arizona Republican (1903)*

If Pearson wished to communicate to Taylor that he was now lord of the naked-long-legs and that Taylor should cower … the message was already clear. But Pearson wasn't finished with his mission. To achieve near total domination, Pearson established exclusive rights contracts with proprietors at ostrich ranches in Fullerton and Pasadena, San Antonio, Texas and even with Taylor in Jacksonville. With those contracts, Pearson would be the sole buyer of every chick they produced, that lived to two months. Atherton's contract spanned two years. In that span, he sent 150 chicks to Pearson.[182]

By the end of 1900, Pearson had gathered 780 ostriches in all, costing him around $100,000, so the *Silver Belt* reported.[183] He not only claimed the title of "Ostrich King" in Arizona, but his enormous collection in the town of Cashion

---

d "Funeral of A. Y. Pearson," *Arizona Republican*, January 28, 1903, 4.

Pearson Ostrich Company (Phoenix-American/Pan-American)

Township map (1N 1E), 1911, labeled by author (History and Archives Division/Arizona State Library. Licensed Use.)

Panorama of the Pan-American Ostrich Farm in 1908 from California Panorama Co. (LOC).

(now annexed to Avondale) would make Arizona the ostrich capital of the nation.[184] "And now," the *Silver Belt* included, "[Pearson] owns all [of the ostriches] in the United States, except about 100. ... Thus[,] he is in absolute control of the ostrich industry..."[185]

Pearson: The New Ostrich King

1901 seems to have been the height of Pearson's reign. The *Coconino Sun* announced that it was his farm attraction that had made Phoenix famous and touted it as one of the most successful enterprises within the Salt River Valley.[186] That May, a story came out about him in the *Los Angeles Evening Express*. The writer declared Pearson as "one of the few men who has ever engaged extensively in the theatrical business and has retired from it with honor and profit, to engage in other walks of life."[187] That story also included a jab on Cawston, saying that Pearson's "colony of plume-bearing birds ... rivals the famous herd at South Pasadena."[188]

Though Pearson had become a national celebrity for his record-setting achievement, the aggressive business practices that elevated his career simultaneously destroyed him. Pearson's health suffered. In 1901, Dr. van Ruck, Pearson's former physician visited Arizona. According to the *Arizona Republican,* Dr. van Ruck was looking for investment opportunities.[189] While the doctor was in state, Pearson quietly transferred the ownership of the Pearson Ostrich Co., "birds, lands, and all," to the doctor for $100,000.[190] One theory for this radical sale is that Pearson recognized his time was running short.

Pearson continued to be involved in the day-to-day operations of the ostrich ranch, though his later obituary revealed, "he was so sick he was unable to work more than half the time."[191] Still, that June, he accepted an invitation to show newly imported blue neck ostriches at the World's Fair in New York. It would be one of his final acts.

12. Blue Necks at the World's Fair

*"Clearly, the role of 'naked-legged, google-eyed' birds
in the Valley's economy was more than a mere sideshow."*
- Sylvia Bender-Lamb (1978)[192]

William Dutcher wrote for *Bird-Lore* magazine: "During
the Pan-American Exposition at Buffalo (1901), the last lot of
ostriches were brought to the United States. These were 12
Nubians, the most gigantic and magnificent of all the species."[193] Admission cost $.15 per gawker. Pearson's talent for
putting on a great show ensured daily crowds coming to see
the birds up close. He could pitch their unusual beauty and
extraordinary size or laud their raptor speed and ballerina
grace. Behind the scenes, however, it was really Pearson being
kept on his toes. When calamity struck, he quickly turned each
setback into a shocking (but profitable) sideshow.

Autopsies, Surgeries and S#*! Shows

The World's Fair had barely been open two weeks when
the *Buffalo Courier Express* reported June 16 that an ostrich
had "cashed in its checks, to the sorrow of its keepers who are
now taking up [donations] in order to bury it."[194] Rumor had
it the cause of death was Sioux Chief Hard Heart's doing. (He is
shown in the image from the Indian Congress at the Exposition). Various accounts alleged the chief amused himself by
feeding an ostrich "spikes." They may have been tent spikes or
railroad spikes—we don't know. Either way, Chief Hard Heart

got the bird to take down three gullet protrusions before someone stopped him.

> "When you ask me what are the greatest drawbacks I have met with ... perhaps the visitors are the worst."
> -Dr. Charles Sketchley (1883)

Considering the financial value of the birds in Pearson's possession (and the interests of the owner and investors), Pearson had quite a lemon to squeeze. So, as much as it might turn a stomach or two, he secured the services of a surgeon to conduct an autopsy of the deceased before a public audience. The surgeon conducting the procedure considered himself, "somewhat of a naturalist," though his credentials only supported the treatment of human conditions.[195] With the surgeon's enthusiastic support, Pearson scheduled the event for June 17.[196]

Pearson now had his birds and audiences eating out of the palm of his hand. Extra money had to be made to compensate for the loss, so it is presumed he charged a special fee to observe the autopsy. Squeamish, genteel or emotional visitors would have been encouraged to donate towards the advertised burial fund. No one would tell the donors that their sentimental dimes would never buy a single carnation, nor scoop an inch of dirt for the gimmick.

Within days of this stunt, the *Courier* reported another tragedy: One of the baby ostriches broke its leg. "It is worth $150," the story read. Pearson could not accept another major loss.[197] (As we'll get into later in the book, a broken leg is almost a guaranteed death sentence for an ostrich.) The $150 value on the chick was the equivalent of $5,700 today. And the adult bird that recently died was worth three times as much.

---

[e] "Anaheim Ostrich Farm: Dr. Sketchley's Experiment in California," *New York Times*, October 28, 1883, 6.

At the Pan-American Exposition, A.Y. Pearson or another showman stands among the ostriches (far right), 1901 (Buffalo and Erie County Historical Society/Public Domain).

"A Glimpse at the Indian Congress," Charles D. Arnold, Official Views of Pan-American Exposition, 1901 (Public Domain). Left to right: Sioux Chief Lone Elk; Sioux Chief Red Cloud; Sioux Chief Hard Heart.

Considering the medical bill a better alternative, Pearson hired Dr. Allen, the Exposition's staff surgeon, to help. The *Courier* printed: "despairing of saving it in any other way, [the chick] was finally taken to the hospital."[198]

Dr. Allen was praised for setting the chick's fragile limb. An adorable baby bird wearing a cast or crutch of sorts was a scene stealer. And putting it on special display: yet another moneymaker. An update in the paper read: "The youngster is reported to be doing well. The bird accepts the attention it is receiving with excellent grace."[199] (By the way, readers should not feel guilty for doubting this story. I do. Based on what we know of Pearson's character and motivations, I wouldn't put it past him to have slapped a cast on a perfectly healthy chick.)

Chief Calico and the Shiny Medal

Pearson's problems weren't over just yet. That July, one of his ostriches got a bit too greedy with a guest and the ordeal brought the grim reaper back to his gate. The story, as patched together (and fictionalized) from real newspaper reports, went something like this:

Chief Calico of the Oglala Sioux Nation was taking part in the Indian Congress with other tribal nation exhibits. One day, he had come down the midway to see all the strange creatures on display. During his visit to the ostrich pen, a bird developed a taste for the silver medal he wore around his neck.

For many years, the Chief led a band called the *Ta-pi-sie-cha* and had been in many battles just like his famous cousin and Sioux leader, Crazy Horse. He remembered one of the battles that white men at the fair liked to quiz him on. They called it "Little Bighorn," but his people named it after the greasy grass site it occurred on. He admired the white leader,

Lt. Col. George Custer. Custer showed his men how to be brave, and how to die well.

After the dust had settled, Chief Calico received a gift from the 18th president of the United States, Ulysses S. Grant. It was a large medal with the engraved words "Let Us Have Peace." This statement marked a promise to him and his people. It was also inset with diamonds. Other tribal band leaders (Chief Hard Heart, for example) had these medals and were encouraged to wear them at the Exposition, but no one had the diamond type like Chief Calico did. The precious stones may have been a nonstandard modification.

When Calico looked up to see the curious birds, one curled its neck and blinked a deep, glossy black eye at him.

"He moved like lightning and took my medal with such a strong pull that the strand around my neck snapped. The beads came loose, falling like sand upon the ground." Chief Calico recounted the event to Mr. Cummins, the General Manager of the Indian Congress. The chief was incensed and sweat profusely while he explained his situation. Witnesses even claimed he pawed at the air and stamped his feet in a rage.

"I reached out for him. If I could catch his neck, I would give him a thump then reach inside to take my gift back," he shared. The chief had every intention of finding an immediate solution. He told Aylma Pearson that the bird's stomach must be cut open, just like the autopsy.

Chief Calico pled his case to the General Manager. "The ostrich man said we cannot kill the bird. He said peace is for animals, too. If so, what can be done?"

Mr. Cummins promised Chief Calico he would help. They went to the ostrich farm together. After serious discussion, Pearson came up with a non-lethal plan. They would put the ostrich under constant watch, awaiting the return of the important item. An ostrich handler would collect everything the bird expelled and sort through it daily until the medal appeared.[200]

Considering Pearson's expert ability to turn every mishap into a razzle-dazzle opportunity, it should not shock readers to consider him posting signs or announcing from his soapbox that visitors could view the day's dig for treasure, or to place bets on which day the diamonds would appear.

Fortunately for the chief, for Pearson, and the ostrich, the culprit relinquished the precious object after three days. Based on this event, news reporters determined that an ostrich's stomach acids, while able to make soup cans disappear, were not strong enough to dissolve metals that held political power and purpose.

Silver medal gifted to Chief Piah of the *Ne-Va-Va* Utes, ca. 1874 (American Numismatic Society [1915.93.1]). The author was unable to find an image of Calico's diamond encrusted medal.

On Eating Sparkly Things

Visitors to early ostrich ranches believed ostriches had a diet similar to a petting zoo's leather shoe-eating goats, or to the family pig that ate not only the dinner scraps but also the plate they were served on. Even with proper viewing protocols in place, and with guests being warned that sparkly objects mesmerized these creatures, there were a string of expensive claims.

After finishing a visit to a California ranch, one man once claimed he'd been pickpocketed by an ostrich. He alleged that he'd kept a loose diamond deep inside his pants pocket (for no rational reason, I might add). After the visit, the diamond was gone. The ostrich owner was expected to not only compensate that man, but to accept his word regarding the estimated value of the rock. (By the way, if I could have been in that courtroom, I would have liked to have seen the claimant illustrate for the jury just how far into his pants pocket a live ostrich could get without him noticing.)

Avoiding scams like this required expensive mitigation strategies such as installing taller or doubled fencing and increasing property supervision. Posted signs stating things like, "feed at your own risk," and "not responsible for injuries or losses" could also deter some litigation.

Annie Martin, memoirist and wife of an ostrich rancher in South Africa, recalled avoiding unnecessary losses in the late 1880s when a gentleman from England paid a visit. She said he had been "looking over a fence into a camp, when the sharp eye of an ostrich spied a beautiful diamond in his pin. ...[I]n an instant[,] the jewel was picked out and swallow-wed."[201] Of course, the Englishman was upset, as anyone would be. In this case, however, the Martins were not inclined to pay a cent on the claim, nor go looking for the stolen object inside his feather-producing livestock, or its waste.

Annie shared: "A kind of court-martial was held on the ostrich; the relative values of himself and of the diamond being accurately calculated, that his judges might decide whether he should live or die. Fortunately for [us,] it was just the time when ostriches were expensive; and his value was estimated at £100 [about $137], while the diamond was only worth £90 [$123]. Those £10 saved his life..."[202]

At the close of the World's Fair, six of the blue necks were sold to Edwin Cawston and the balance brought home with Pearson.[203] Pearson's ambitious and stressful summer may have been the death of him. Four months in the cool and humid climate of Buffalo, New York exacerbated his tuberculosis. When Pearson returned to Arizona, he moved into one of Tucson's treatment centers. This was either at Saint Mary's Sanatorium or in what was nicknamed "Tent City" (AKA "Tentville" or "Lunger Hill") just north of the University campus.

In his last few weeks alive, Pearson sold off more ostriches to alleviate any financial burden on his family. In January 1903, 21 pairs of breeding birds went to William Pickrell and Company for $16,000 (just over half a million in today's terms).[204] It is believed this lot included the blue necks he'd recently shown in New York. Aylma Pearson passed away on January 26, after which Dr. van Ruck forfeited the business to his creditor: Phoenix National Bank.

13. Feather Clipping & Pricing

"What woman in her right mind tried to resist the seductive advertisements in the 1902 Sears Roebuck catalog for real ostrich feather boas?"
- Westways Magazine (May 1975)[205]

In the 20th century, harvesting feathers from an ostrich was done by harmless and sustainable means. American-raised ostriches were never plucked for the feather industry. Industry practices worldwide had moved away from the actual plucking of feathers decades prior, but the term continued to be used in literature and conversation, even though it meant something new. In this book, I favor the terms "harvesting" and "clipping." (By the way, regardless of how humane feather collections had become, ostriches still plucked each other's feathers out when establishing their hierarchy—the "pecking order." The barer a bird got, the lower it was on the social ladder, and less likely to find a mate.)

Clipping an Ostrich

Young ostriches can have their gray-brown unisex feathers for the first time at about 6-months old. When they reach 2-years-old, clippings can be repeated as often as in 9-month intervals, for the next 25-years or more.[206] It is a procedure as rote as shearing a sheep or re-shoeing a horse. If done carelessly, however, both the handler and the ostrich risk an injury.

To get the birds to cooperate with this procedure, they must first be subdued with some form of head covering. This might be a pillow slip or something as makeshift as the cut off sleeve of a sweatshirt. The concept may sound similar to covering a pet bird's cage to help quiet it down and signal for it to sleep. Ostriches do bed down when the sky darkens, but the head covering causes them to respond more like a cautious, blindfolded hostage.

Watson Pickrell explained to the USDA, "The hooded bird is very easily handled."[207] They can be gently prodded from the side or from behind to encourage them to enter a small pen, usually with a gate at the front and one at the back. Pickrell described the plucking box being "about 4 feet high, 20 inches wide and 3 ½ feet long."[208] The groomer stands to the side or to the rear of the animal known to deliver a violent forward kick when threatened or annoyed. Pickrell added, "The plucker is perfectly safe if he stands in the rear."[209] When finished, their helper opens the gate in front of the ostrich and removes its hood. When free, the bird zooms ahead, not unlike an angry bull entering a rodeo arena.

Feathers are only harvested from wings and tails. The handler uses shears to clip the feather quill at a distance at least an inch away from the ostrich's skin. This distance ensures that the portion of the quill with blood flow is never disturbed. Answering on whether there is any pain involved, William Dutcher, president of the Audubon Society has assured readers: "There is no possibility of inflicting pain ... not a drop of blood is drawn, nor a nerve touched."[210]

After being clipped, quill stubs dry up and die, pretty much as they would during the bird's natural molting season. During the molt, the stubs either fall out with minimal disturbance, or the ostrich plucks them out to make way for

Illustration from "Ostriches,"
by Watson Pickrell in
Cyclopedia of Farm Animals,
1922.

Close up showing shears in the hand of the groomer, ca. 1882-1930s
(C. C. Pierce Photo Collection/ California Historical Society).

emerging feathers. This process is about as uncomfortable to the bird as a human having their fingernails clipped. (Unless the person clipping your nails was my grandfather. God bless him, but he'd take a bit o' flesh every time.)

Raw Feather Profits

During the height of the industry, an exceptionally blessed bird could bring its owner around $150 in profit from a single clipping session. This amounted to a 25-40% return on investment, which excited folks who wanted to get in on the business. Dr. Charles A. Meserve, State Chemist and owner of fifteen birds in Tucson, estimated that it only cost him $15 a year to feed and care for each bird that potentially returned ten times that amount in feather sales. Sadly, he bought in at the wrong time and would never see that payout.

One Arizona ostrich was especially blessed in the feather department. "Doctor Cook" lived on the Pan-American Ranch (originally Pearson Ostrich Co.). "He was worth his weight in gold," wrote Blanche Murray for *Arizona Highways.*[211] Robin Doughty, researching the subject for *Agricultural History,* found that "Doc" earned its owner $10,000 during its lifetime.[212] This claim is ridiculous. From 1905 to 1914 (when Pan-American was in operation), this rooster could only have been clipped 12 times. If each clipping brought in a full $150 profit, that would only amount to $1,800. What is interesting about this boast, however, is how desperate "Doc's" owner became to get rid of him when the industry waned. (More on that in the Murder Birds chapter.)

Feather Classifications

The bounty of any clipping session is extremely limited. This contributed to the pricing that can be assigned to each plume based on rarity in color or form. Dr. T. C. Duncan has clarified:

"Each [rooster] has 25 white plumes in each wing[,] with a row of blacks[,] and still another row of shorter feathers[,] which are black in the adult male and drab in the hen."[213] Besides nearly striking black and white feathers in their wings, roosters also have romantic ivories in their tails. Hens wear a full spectrum of muted colors in shades from bone white to steel grey and in hues of light caramel to rusty brown. A feather's original condition was used to sort and rank it, but ultimately, ostrich feathers could be bleached and dyed to any color imaginable. Women could even order them to be matched with their dresses.

Which side of an ostrich has the most feathers?

The outside!

Before those final dressings, raw values paid to the rancher took into consideration the product length, breadth, luster, weight and general appearance.[214] Pricing standards were set by London markets and copied in the U.S. The classifying jargon used by dealers and sorters, such as "hairy blacks," and "spadones" (Italian for "longsword") sound like they were made up by 5-year-olds on a playground. I'm half-surprised the terms "tufty tickler" and "rump rudder" did not make it on the list.

Thankfully, Watson Pickrell defined these terms for us in 1905:

- ❖ "White primes," "white firsts," and "blacks" are clipped from roosters.

- ❖ "Blood feathers" are new growths still encased in a keratin coating. They are more commonly known as pin feathers.

- ❖ "Boos" or "spads" are tail feathers.

- ❖ "Drabs" are the browns and greys clipped from hens, although sometimes a decent enough white can be taken from a hen's wing.

- ❖ "Byocks" are the rooster's version of a drab body feather. They are a blend of black and white.

- ❖ "Spadones" are from chicks, usually in their first clipping. They are more voluminous than an adult feather.

- ❖ "Flats" or "Floss" are from the chest or underneath section of a wing. These appear sleeker and smoother than the other options but are less valuable.[215]

Example of a multi-colored byock feather from the Schmuckfedern Shop in Germany (http://www.gollwitzer-schmuckfedern.de).

Ostrich feathers being sorted and bundled for the fashion industry, ca. 1900-1901 (Alamy [D88B5A], Licensed Use).

Beautiful "White Prime" ostrich feathers approximately 20-inches long, Port of London ca. 1910s (Alamy [2BW2JEC], Licensed Use).

More about blood feathers is provided by Thomas W. (T.W.) Kemp, who observed an ostrich covered in them at a Phoenix ranch. At that time, Kemp was the superintendent of the Chandler Ostrich Ranch. Kemp had learned about the underlying condition when he was in South Africa. He noted that blood feathers were more common in actively breeding birds and during drought conditions (when ostriches lacked proper nutrition). His 1910 observation was published in the *Arizona Republican* as such: "I was shown a bird which had most of the outer sheath remaining upon the nearly full-grown primary wing feathers. This is a condition ... generally found upon examination that the bird lacks 'tone."[216] By tone, he meant the bird's overall nourishment, strength and energy.

The outer sheath, Kemp explained, "consists of the same outer skin as the epidermal scales[,] and it is the removal of these that allows the feather to become free..."[217] Kemp also said that a loss of energy may contribute to a bird's poor hygiene and under preening (grooming). "It can be taken as a general rule," he shared, "[that] the non-removal of the outer sheath of the feather are sure indications of poor health and want of tone in the system."[218]

During the preening process, ostriches remove dead feathers, break open the casing on pin feathers and generally manage dirt, pests, and excess skin oils. "The outer skin or epidermis of the ostrich, like that of other animals (and human beings) is continually freeing itself of dead tissue, and when this is removed[,] the skin is clean and soft," Kemp said. Ostriches that are not maintaining their skin and feathers will present with "a dull, scaly appearance."[219]

Processing and Dressing

Before a feather could be sold to the public, it had to go through a processing center where it would be washed and dried. Then, a manufacturing facility could curl, dye and otherwise manipulate the feather into the most spectacular version of itself before it reached the milliner or retailer. Each step in the distribution chain took a bite out of profits, but processing was a specific annoyance for Arizona ranchers because of the added shipping costs. Until a processing facility was opened in the state, Arizona's feathers had to be sent to New York or California.

The Pan-American Ostrich Company sent their feathers exclusively to Feather Producers Co. in New York City. Dr. A.J. Chandler had his feathers processed at Edwin Cawston's facility in California. One of the earliest feather farms that could process their own products was the Rancho Los Feliz, in California. There, one writer found, "a lady can visit the ranch, select her feather on the bird, and later have it delivered, curled and ready for wear: the entire process being done on the ranch."[220]

In New York, most of the physical labor of washing and modifying feathers was completed by people in lower classes (typically immigrants). They worked long hours and under unsanitary conditions. Skin and respiratory problems were prevalent in the warehouses raw feathers were processed in. Incoming shipments could be accompanied by ants or lice, manure, dust and other skin particulates. With any amount of handling, those particulates became airborne.

When ready to be dressed, feathers were sent to manufacturers who further enhanced the product. To make a visual stunner, manufacturers could slice two or three plumes lengthwise then graft them together to achieve unreal lengths. If pure white "primes" were not readily available, bleach could assist with a similar look. They might also have taken this one step further and custom dyed feathers to match a woman's dress fabric. One historian found that much of the final pro-

Manual washing and drying ostrich feathers in Amsterdam. Photo by
Cornelius Johan "Kees" Hofker, 1919 (Wikimedia Commons).

duct preparation was done by women, often from the Jewish
community, as the manufacturing centers were concentrated
in the Lower East Side.[221]

In the last stage of production, milliners or seamstresses
pinned, tucked, splayed and slung the plumes into their final
creation. At the peak of the industry, if a woman wanted to
purchase a finished feather as a stand-alone item, one long
"prime" held a retail value of $30 (around $1,000 in 2025).
Today, that same feather might cost a reader between $5 and
$20. That pricing reflects over a 99% depreciation in value.

Feathers could be dried by a 'Magdeleine' wheel to give them a plump appearance (Alamy [2K63WMJ, Licensed Use).

The feather bleaching or dying process, ca. 19th century (Alamy [2K63WK3], Licensed Use).

"Women at Work," inside a millinery sweatshop, ca. 1907-1933 (Lewis W. Hine Collection/NYPL Digital Collection).

14. Beginning the Arizona Boom

"Ostrich raisers in the Phoenix area had one thing in common…
a get-rich proposition."
-Sylvia Bender-Lamb (1978)[222]

To get a sense of how insanely important ostriches were to Arizona territory, we'll do a thought exercise. Today, Arizonans (and visitors) can walk into almost any of the state's museum gift shops, state park visitor centers or kitschy home stores with rock candy and soy candles… and every gas station on any corner… and they are bound to find an image of the Saguaro cactus painted, patched and stickered on at least half of the merchandise. That big, green "no-touch" totem has become so iconic that without it being on the cover of this book, it might not be shelved at so many stores. Now, imagine every cactus motif in that store replaced with a goofy ostrich head or curled feather design. And, if U.S. states had chosen their state birds before the national movement in 1931, it wouldn't be a stretch to consider the ostrich representing Arizona. It's a funny thought, but about as close as we can get to understanding the obsession.

Raising ostriches in the state implied having local wealth, making agricultural advancements, being unique within the country, and being a proud and serious global competitor. The ostrich ranching industry's period of rapid growth and ext-reme prosperity (known as the "boom") lasted from 1888 to 1914, a duration of 26 years. For comparison, the silver mining boom in Tombstone, Bisbee and Globe lasted from about 1873 to 1893, when minerals were exhausted and the effort to mine cost more than the ore's value. That was only a 20-year period of territorial history prior to the "bust" (depression or abrupt end).

Aylma Pearson's exclusive sales contracts delayed Arizona's industry growth until about 1903. Between then and 1905, the state increased from one to seven ostrich ranches in operation. Those seven, plus a few around the country, could not provide a steady or sufficient supply of feathers to U.S. milliners. These American hat makers and costumers still demanded one-third of the world's supply to satisfy their customers. As such, they'd continue to pay what they felt were punitive duties on feather imports.

A rant published in a 1904 *Millinery Trade Review* argued the increased taxes on their raw material was unjustified. The writer reasoned "there are but eighteen hundred ostriches in America and there will be no more full-grown birds imported."[223] They believed "there is not the remotest possibility of America ever competing with Africa in raising the ostrich."[224] They also predicted the U.S. would likely never accumulate enough stock for South Africa's government to feel an impact. It would take another decade to do so, but eventually, Arizona would peak at 65 ostrich ranches and become the number one competitor of South Africa's original breeders.

Pearson's Empire Becomes the Phoenix-American

After Phoenix National Bank was "compelled to take over their holdings," the Pearson Ostrich Company was reincorporated as the Phoenix-American Ostrich Company in 1904.[225] Leading the takeover was Herbert J. McClung, the bank's Vice President and a neighborhood man from 75th Avenue and Van Buren. Managing this business was beyond his area of knowledge, so Pearson's wife was hired to lead the team. In management were Mrs. Katie Pearson (Corporation President), Herbert McClung (V.P.), Edwin Barbour (Sec.), Louis H. Chalmers (Treas.) and John J. Hutchison.

By 1905, the Avondale location reportedly housed over a thousand birds, "making it[,] by several hundreds, the largest ostrich ranch in America."[226] Unfortunately, the ranch, "operated at a loss for several years."[227] Their upside-down financial situation was likely caused by the fulfillment of guaranteed chick purchases. Those chicks would take years to mature before there would be a return on the investment. In the meantime, the cost to raise those dependents outweighed what the adult birds could produce in feather profits.

PHOENIX
American Ostrich Farm

Boas, Plumes, Pom-poms, Tips, etc., at Producers' Prices. Bronze Ash Trays, Fancy Napkin Rings, Paper Cutters, etc.
CAPITOL ADDITION,
At End of Washington St. Car Line.

Phoenix-American Ostrich Farm advertisement from the *Arizona Republican*, Feb. 27, 1905.

Besides guiding the new ranch management team, Aylma's business savvy wife, Katie, maintained a sister operation at her home residence. The 1903 city directory listed Katie and her children living three miles south of Josiah Harbert's old property, around the intersection of the I-17 Freeway and Adams Street. The directory referred to their home address as "The Ostrich Farm." There appears to have been an arrangement where the Phoenix-American Ostrich Company used the Pearson's home as a show farm. The division was like when Cawston separated his breeding business from the tourist attraction.

When the Washington streetcar line extended west from the state capitol into her neighborhood, visitor traffic increased. The Pearsons were ready. A 1904 advertisement in the *Arizona Silver Belt* announced the opening of new "exhibition pens of the far-famed Phoenix ostrich farms." The pens held 50 ostriches on display. Also opening that year was a new retail store built on Pearson's property that touted glass cases filled with the "finest assortment of ostrich feathers in the country."[228] With the addition, Katie became the first woman in Arizona to manage a retail outlet exclusively for ostrich products.

The Pickrell Brothers Dominate the Industry

Within a year of receiving the lot of extraordinary blue neck ostriches from Aylma Pearson, W. S. Pickrell & Co. became the parent organization of at least three ostrich ranches in the Salt River Valley. In the partnership were William Pickrell, his brother Watson, and Vernon Clark. Together, they provided ostriches for the re-establishment of the Arizona Ostrich Co., for the Tempe Ostrich Co. and for National Ostrich Co. For expanding opportunities rather than suppressing them (as Pearson had tried), William Pickrell was considered "one of the hardest fighters for the success of the ostrich industry in the valley."[229]

In 1903, Pickrell opened the Arizona Ostrich Company for a second time. Again, he leased 40 acres from the Indian School, now on the opposite end of the streetcar line from Katie Pearson. Over next few years, his breeding skills shone, and he needed room to expand. In 1907, Pickrell moved his ostriches south of the city, onto 480 acres near the Salt River.[230] He would ultimately top out at 550 birds on 880 acres.

In addition to a land expansion, Arizona Ostrich Co. opened a salesroom on the corner of 1st Avenue and Adams Street. Mrs. Anna Adams, wife of a newspaper print supervisor, managed the store until Mrs. Georgiana Pickrell took over in either 1908 or 1909. As seen in the advertisement from the *Arizona Republican,* the Pickrells carried upwards of $10,000 in products for both modest and luxury shoppers.[231]

Ostrich Goods

Our Ostrich Feather Goods add elegance to the most refined or elaborate costume. We sell them to the consumer at producers' prices, direct from the farm where we raise the ostriches and produce the feathers.

We carry the largest line of Plumes, Fans, Boas, Mufes and Tips in the Southwest, made from the finest feathers grown, or

Make Special Pieces to Order

Don't buy until you get our prices.

We have a few very fine soft, hand-made ostrich Feather Dusters on sale, the only thing for new furniture.

Goods delivered anywhere in the United States prepaid.

Arizona Ostrich Farm

PHOENIIX, ARIZONA.

Cor. Adams and 1st Sts.   Opp. New Noble Bldg.

Pickrell's brother Watson was another benefactor of the Pickrell & Co. investment. He received a few ostriches as seed capital for his own ranch. Watson's Tempe Ostrich Company was incorporated in 1904. It was located between Rural and McClintock Roads, on the south side of Baseline. Clark was a hands-off partner in this deal, mirroring the same type of relationship he had with William. Clark made occasional visits to the Tempe location, and in 1906 he observed, "The farm is growing more prosperous all the time and now has a hundred and sixty birds, all in good shape and doing well."[232]

For a while, members of Pickrell & Co. were in a fortunate sales position as one of only two U.S. providers of blue neck ostriches. They could ask any price and take in an astronomical profit. Some sources claim they sold a good pair for nearly $2,000.[233] Today, that'd be around $70,000. The low-supply, high-demand conditions made the Arizona-raised birds as expensive as those imported from the savanna. At the turn of the century, a South African ostrich was not only cost prohibitive but restricted to non-breeders. The *Arizona Silver Belt* reported, "[V]ery few are taken out of [South Africa] now

Arizona Ostrich Co.

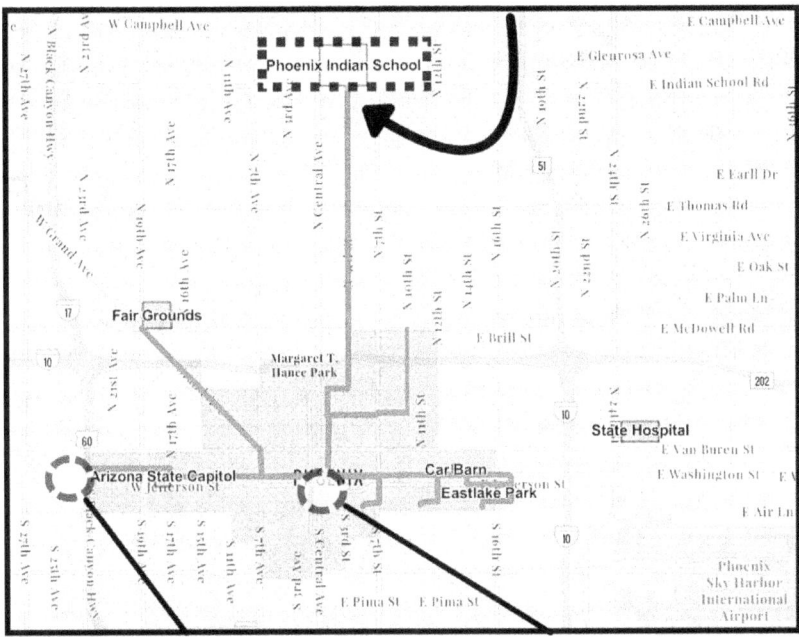

Pearson's Exhibition Pens   *William S. Pickrell*

1901 streetcar extensions (Jacob Conklin, "This History of Phoenix Streetcar and Light Rail," Valley Metro, 2024, marked by author).

Postcard from Arizona Ostrich Co., ca. 1900s (Phoenix Public Library, Susan Arreola Collection/Public Domain).

National Ostrich Company (1904-1910)

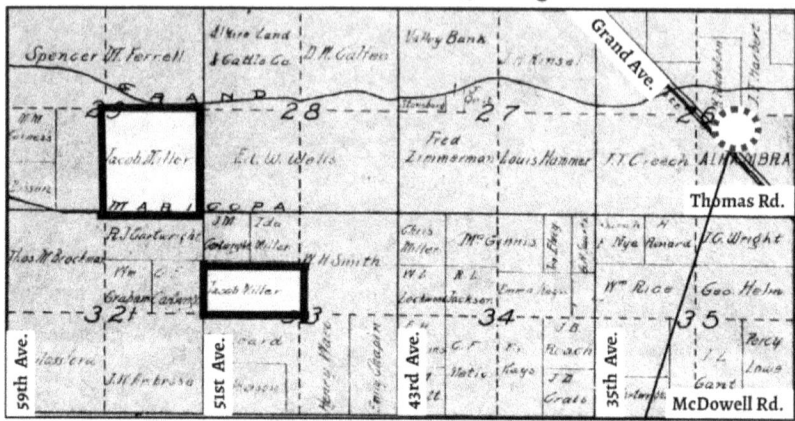

Josiah Harbert's Original Ostrich Farm

Township map (2N 2E), 1911, labeled by author (History and Archives Division/Arizona State Library/Fair Use).

and when they are exported there is only a pair at a time, and an understanding ... that they are intended for zoological gardens."[234]

Perhaps that $2,000 pair were sold to the third venture. In 1904, William Pickrell secured a deal with Joseph W. Zipperlein and William Hartranft from Pennsylvania and New Jersey. These men financed the launch of the National Ostrich Company.[235] City directories show this ranch being established five miles west of the state fairgrounds, on 240 acres of Jacob Miller's property.

The Industry Adds Two More

Others entering the ostrich ranching industry at this time were the McNeil-Wylie Company and the Big-Five Company, both in Phoenix. Dr. Winifred "Win" Wylie had a surgical office on the same street corner as Pickrell's new showroom. He may have purchased his ostriches from Pickrell & Co., though there is no record to support this. Dr. Wylie's business partner, Milo McNeil,[236] raised the birds as the ranch manager on Dr. Wylie's 40 acres at Center and Buckeye Road.

The Big-Five Co. was run by James Morgan Harmon. He was a local produce grower and cattleman, owning Harmon Ranch at 51st Avenue and Baseline Road. He'd also been the superintendent of Pearson Ostrich Company since 1901. Starting in either 1904 or 1905, he'd apply what he learned there to his own troop. He named his new line of after the five pairs of breeders he started it with.[237]

Considering the industry growth, in 1905, the *Arizona Republican* reported: "...Skeptics who first shook their heads at what they termed a 'hairbrained scheme' are beginning to see that before many years roll by[,] ostrich farming will be one of the largest industries of the warmer [S]outhwest."[238]

Dr. Winifred "Win" Wylie (1855-1939), undated, provided by Philip Barry (2021) on Ancestry.com (used with thanks).

15. Pressure to Compete

*"Within a few years there will be thousands of ostriches
in all the warmer parts ... where the land is cheap."*
- Daily Morning Times (1882)[239]

In 1906, the Phoenix-American Ostrich Company gained new investors and reincorporated as the Pan-American Ostrich Ranch. The new name could have been a play on the former World's Fair, or to signify the business's international standing. With the transition came a change in management. Phoenix National Bank still owned the Avondale ranch location, but Katie Pearson was no longer involved as the corporation president. Eliphalet Butler "E.B." Gage, the president of Phoenix National Bank, replaced her.

E.B. Gage was an undeniably busy capitalist. Before moving to Phoenix, Gage lived in Tombstone. There, he partnered with Frank Murphy and William Staunton to form the Tombstone Consolidated Mines Company, which earned him part of his fortune (until it busted in 1911). In Tombstone, Gage was a regular associate of Wyatt Earp and his brothers. Among the stories told, Gage helped pay Wyatt's bail bond after the famous 1881 gunfight behind the O.K. Corral.[240] Other accounts describe Gage bankrolling Wyatt's vendetta posse for horses and equipment.[241] Gage is also recognized for various activities in Northern Arizona. His resume there includes being a director for the Santa Fe, Phoenix & Prescott Railroad (SFP&P), the Fire Chief at the Prescott Fire Department, and the President of the Prescott National Bank.

Besides being the president of Phoenix National Bank for 14 years, Gage invested in and served as the President of the Phoenix Light and Fuel Company, specializing in hydroelectric power (as was fellow ostrich rancher Herbert McClung). Gage became so rich in his careers that he built mansions in both Tombstone and Prescott.[242] Because of h how impressive each was, both became historical landmarks.

E.B. Gage (1839-1913), ca. 1900-1904, from *Biographical Sketches of the Class of 1858, Dartmouth College* (S. Gerould, Telegraph Publishing Co., 1905), 53.

Until an E.B. Gage biographer convinces us otherwise, we might speculate that the most fascinating business Gage ever ran was the Pan-American Ostrich Company. He led it during its most profitable and expansive years of 1906 through 1912. Within a year of his leadership, the Pan-American's salable assets were valued at $600 thousand.[243] By 1908, an event locals called the "Big Hatch" occurred when 200 "lusty feather-makers popped out of the incubators."[244] Their adult bird population increased to over 1,200, enough birds to be considered the largest commercially owned troop of ostriches in the world (exceeding the troops held in South Africa). And those ostriches made the bank a staggering annual profit of $40,000, or $1.4 million today.[245]

In another departure from the Pearson family, Pan-American also opened a new retail shopping location at 1st Avenue and Jefferson Street, a mere block away from their chief competitor. A 1907 announcement for the store read: "Being the largest producers of feathers in the U. S. will enable us to make the most elaborate display ever made in Ostrich Feather Goods in this country, and that is why we can sell at the lowest possible prices."[246]

At that point, Pan-American was operating in high gear. One historian claims they had to keep six lawn mowers running constantly to harvest enough alfalfa.[247] Much of the success during that time can be attributed to the hiring of numerous "ostrich boys" and to the specific hiring of ranch manager Francis Peterson and superintendent William M. Cross. Blanche Murray wrote for *Arizona Highways*, "When Mr. Cross assumed control of that ranch his first objective was to build up strong, vigorous birds. He believed that only ostriches in the pink condition could yield the best plumage."[248] (By the way, the pink color reference could be about the red neck species at the Pan-American, or to the flush on a rooster's neck that is a good indicator of health regardless of the species.)

William McKee Cross (1865-1946), undated, as seen in his obituary Jan. 23, 1946 (*Arizona Republic*/Fair Use).

California newspapers praised William Cross for not only maintaining an extraordinarily profitable business, but also for being "the only raiser of ostriches in the world who successfully crossed the breed of the Nubian blue and Common red ostrich, thereby producing a feather stronger and superior in every way to anything that has ever existed."[249] What Cross did through hybridizing soon became a study of interest in both U.S. and South African governments.

Advertisement for feather sales from the Pan-American Ostrich Farm, *Arizona Republic,* Oct. 25, 1907.

Pan-American ostrich enclosures in 1909 (Walter Lubken's Photographs of the Salt River Valley/SRP).

Hile's Snowbirds

Other American ostrich raisers attempted to match the crossbreeding talent of William Cross, but many of those attempts went poorly. In one rather sad example, William Henry Hile attempted to compete with the ostrich business out West but failed on every account at his Pennsylvania-based ranch.

William Hile is believed to have discovered the exciting possibilities of ostrich raising while he was in Arizona doing some geological survey work.[250] One writer of 1916 suggested that while Hile was in Arizona, he caught something like Feather Fever.[251] In 1909, the Pennsylvanian formed the International Ostrich Farm and Feather Company with other Arizona speculators. This business was set to operate in Nogales, on the border of Mexico.[252] Strangely, their articles of incorporation, as posted in the *Border Vidette*, were primarily related to mining activities, his former interest.

In 1910, Hile traveled to Africa to acquire ostriches by any means he could manage (ethical or not). He collected two different species (red and blue) and brought 40 back to the U.S.[253] When Hile returned to the States, he was disappointed to find that he could not secure the Southern Arizona land he wanted. Undefeated, Hile kept the birds back in his hometown of Bloomsburg, Pennsylvania and renamed the business African Farm and Feather Company.

Hile had no animal husbandry skills whatsoever.[254] He probably expected his crossbred chicks to come out purple. But, as he soon learned, ostriches don't produce many eggs when they are cold. Actually, ostriches don't do much of *anything* in the cold. The entire operation quickly (and sadly) flopped. Towards the end, the American Society for the

Left: "Bringing in a Captive," image from Hile's book, *The Ostrich for the Defence* (Boston: Press of Geo. H. Ellis Co., 1913). Right: "The old birds in the snow at Bloomsburg Ostrich Farm," Postcard, ca. 1912 (Public Domain).

Prevention of Cruelty to Animals (ASPCA) had to intervene. In 1912, Hile published *The Ostrich for the Defence*, a fictionalized memoir about his career adventure. It was equally successful.

Europe Buys In

Though Hile appears to have struggled to find a home for his ostriches in Arizona, there was a group of Belgians who had a much smoother experience all around. In 1909, Louis Janssens Sr. and Pierre Danco of Belgium partnered to purchase the entire troop of 158 ostriches owned by Dr. Win Wylie and Milo McNeil.[255] The purchase price was about $24,400, to which the Janssens paid $19,000 in cash and signed a promissory note for the remaining balance.[256] The Belgian investors relocated the ostriches onto 270-acres of rented land, south of the Salt River.[257] Louis Janssens left his son, Louis Jr. (also seen as "John"), daughter Anna, and two Flemish servants in Arizona to manage the new ostrich farm while he returned to Belgium. One writer for the *Arizona Republican* predicted their residency being the "nucleus of a colony ... shortly to settle here."[258] They also remarked on the immigrants' inability to speak a single word of English.

The Janssens' new landlords were Adolphus Bartlett and his son-in-law Dwight B. Heard. At that time, the Bartlett-Heard Land and Cattle Company encompassed 7,500 acres at the base of South Mountain, making Dwight Heard one of the largest land barons in Maricopa County.[259] The Janssens reserved 195 acres of their slice for alfalfa; the remaining 75 was left as a desert landscape for the incoming ostrich troop. (By the way, in addition to land and real estate interests, Mr. Heard was the sole owner and publisher of the *Arizona Republican* from 1914 until 1929. He and his wife Maie also owned the collection of Southwest art and artifacts used to begin the Heard Museum.)

Once Phoenix real estate and insurance dealer Harry I. Latham saw what the Janssens had done, he felt compelled to act. Latham worked with the German Investment Co. in Central Phoenix. In 1909, Latham toured Europe and spread the word about the incredible profits being made in Arizona ostrich ranching. While he was fishing for business, a man named Leon Van Dorp of Belgium jumped at the opportunity. Van Dorp was an associate of Louis Janssens and wanted to experience the same success his friend had found. Instead of Van Dorp creating a competing ostrich ranch, however, he included Janssens and Danco in a plan to expand. Latham was about as American as they come, with Revolutionary War heroes up the line, but in the merger, Latham was identified as the official owner of the Belgo-American Ostrich Company, while Janssens Jr. remained the general manager.

Working together, the freshly funded corporation grew exponentially. The *Republican* announced, "Belgian Capital-

Bartlett-Heard Ranch (Belgo-American)

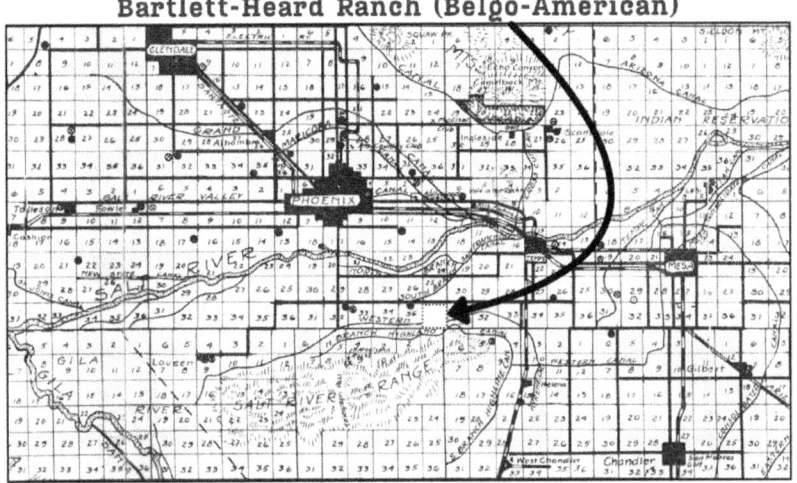

Map of Salt River Valley, Arizona, 1923 (Dwight B. Heard Investment Company, cropped and labeled by author).

ists Buy Five Hundred Birds!" This addition officially made them the second-largest ostrich ranch in the country, topping out with 658 birds. It also set them back about $100,000 (or $3.4 million, today).[260] The Belgians were beside themselves with anticipation for the wealth they would see in the days ahead. The *Republican* included, "They knew no more about the bird than the average European business man," but after investigating into the matter, they felt "they could not make a safer investment, or one more certain of a high interest return."[261]

The extra 500 ostriches they acquired came from William Hartranft's National Ostrich Co. Rather than selling out, like Wylie-McNeil did, Hartranft merged his interests with Latham. He also kept a small troop of ostriches on his personal property in Glendale.

Man with ostriches at the Bartlett-Heard Ranch in Phoenix, ca. 1910 (Tempe History Museum [1987.1.2727], licensed use).

Another Boom

From 1906 to 1913, the number of active ostrich ranches in Arizona leaped from 7 to 25—including the Belgians, excluding William Hile. In Mesa, Dr. Alexander John Chandler became the city's "pioneer ostrich owner" in 1906 with 100 birds purchased from one of the Pickrell brothers.[262] The second in Mesa was bank cashier John G. Spangler, who placed three pairs of birds somewhere on his property located off Guadalupe and Gilbert Roads in 1909.[263] Spangler eventually became the president of the Arizona Ostrich Breeders' Association after finding himself remarkably successful breeding his original birds into a troop of 51 in only ten months.[264]

The *Arizona Daily Star* also announced in 1911 that, "The Mesa country now has its third ostrich farm. W. J. Clemans, who had a large ranch south of Mesa, is the third

from the Belgo-Americans, "eight pairs of the magnificent birds, four old pairs and three young pairs."[265] (Or, perhaps, it was only seven pairs, but who's counting?) His ranch lands were located at Dobson and Elliott Roads.

Ernest Edmond Ellsworth (1869-1949), undated, provided by Michael Charles Malone (2022) on Ancestry.com (used with thanks).

That same year, Ernest Ellsworth established a ranch in East Mesa near Val Vista and McKellips Roads. He had been a cattleman for many years and worked with Dr. Chandler's birds before launching his own operation. About the change, Ellsworth shared with the *Arizona Republican* that he "has learned the business from the pin feathers up. He can handle the setting hens, regulate an ostrich incubator, pluck the ripe feathers at exactly the right time, and heal the sick birds."[266] He considered himself a bit of a "birdinary surgeon," which may have been an acquired skill from years of watching the former veterinarian tend to animals in need. His brother, Louis continued to work with Dr. Chandler's birds as the superintendent of the Mesa Ostrich Farm.

On the far west outskirts of Glendale, Addison Fox McCaleb and Charles Dee Young of the Arizona Alfalfa Mill Co. started the Desert Ostrich Company at 99th Avenue & Camelback Road. Another Glendale ranch was established through the partnership of a sheriff and a salesman. A bit of an "old bird" himself, former Sheriff of Maricopa County William "Billy" Cook was in his fifties when he got involved. Starting in 1907, he teamed up with his next-door neighbor Clarence Bruner Laird and formed the "Cook & Laird" livestock ranch, boasting cattle and horses. The sprawling 1,360 acres was located between the Agua Fria and New River, near 107th and Glendale Avenues. Laird was previously a school supply salesman. For a short time in 1909, he also worked on the Pan-American ranch as a foreman, possibly learning the ropes. That same year, Cook & Laird put a few birds out on their shared ranch and christened their side business the Salt River Valley Ostrich Company.

Tempe's second ranch was briefly managed by Thomas W. Kemp, L. N. (or L. H.) Hughes, and J. E. Sturges. They reportedly had 75 ostriches. The start date and name of this business is unknown to the author, but it appears the trio of investors packed up the operation in September of 1906. They transferred their Arizona birds to California and reopened the following April as the Los Angeles Ostrich Farm.[267]

In Downtown Phoenix, Pickrell & Co. invested in another ranch start up called the Maricopa Ostrich Farm. Continuing to push the industry forward, in 1908 William Pickrell and Vernon Clark engaged the services of C. H. Keep, a promoter and experienced feather manufacturer from London. Their plan was to establish the first feather manufacturing facility in the state. After a year of preparation, the Phoenix Ostrich Feather Manufacturing Company opened for business contracts in 1909. Keep became the president of the new facility. He trained employees on how to wash, fluff, color and stitch feathers into their final designer products. Pickrell's business savvy wife Georgiana played a major role as the Secretary-Treasurer of the company. They employed seven or eight hands, five of whom were women.[268]

PHOENIX OSTRICH FEATHER MANUFACTURING
CO, C H Keep pres. G M Pickrell sec-treas. 522-524
W Washington.

Listing in the Arizona State Business Directory 1909-1910.

WANTED—Girls to learn the ostrich
feather business. Apply at the Phoenix Ostrich Manufacturing Co., 522
W. Washington.

Advertisement in the *Arizona Republican*, April 19, 1909.

Wickey Ostrich Farm

R. WICKEY, Proprietor.

Buy Your Ostrich Feathers Direct From the Growers

We Have a Most Complete Stock of Willows, Plumes, Pom-Poms and Aigrettes and Anything in Ostrich Feathers at Prices Below Others. Bring Your Ostrich Feathers to Us for Repair Work We Guarantee Satisfaction.

Consolidated Phone Red 7042

Salesroom: 1016 GRAND AVENUE

PHOENIX   ARIZONA

Listing in the 1911-1912 Arizona State Business Directory, page 340.

In West Phoenix, Rudolph Wickey started the Salt River Valley Ostrich Farm in 1909 at Grand Avenue, between 7th Avenue and Van Buren Street.[269] By 1911, perhaps owing to confusion over a too similarly named business in the Valley (see Cook & Laird), Wickey renamed his operation the Wickey Ostrich Farm. Considering their location, Cook and Laird should probably have called themselves the Agua Fria or New River Ostrich Company instead.

16. No One Knew How to Farm Feathers

*"Everything there is to know about ostriches
has grown and died with the people that raised them."*
- Michael Lehman, President of the AOA (2024)[270]

For the longest time, no one in Arizona who kept an ostrich actually knew what they were doing. There were no instruction books. And the "experts" who'd seen ostrich raising firsthand in South Africa settled in Southern California. Most of those experts had already moved on to some other interest or left the area by the time ostriches were popular in Arizona. In 1906, Watson Pickrell plainly stated for the USDA: "The pioneer breeders in this country had to get most of their knowledge from their own experience."[271]

By 1908, though, there were enough locals in the greater Phoenix area learning by trial and error to gather for mutual support. An April announcement in the *Arizona Republican* stated, "A very important movement was set on foot yesterday at a meeting of the ostrich breeders of the Salt River Valley."[272] Ten men showed up and officially called themselves the Arizona Ostrich Breeders' Association. Herbert McClung from the Phoenix National Bank and Pan-American Ostrich Company served as the first chairman of the board.

Around this time, ostrich raising was performing financially at or above the cattle industry. With these numbers, and predictions for continued demand, the Association members believed themselves to be producing the most interesting and important livestock class, second to none.[273] As a team, they looked forward to having a bigger impact on city and state measures that might benefit the growth and economic stability of the industry. It seemed that anyone in the Salt River Valley who wanted to be taken seriously as a feather farmer joined the Association, with one exception.[274] That exception was with the Pima Indian Council at the Sacaton Agency. The Pimas started with 4 ostriches around 1915 and within a few years, they had 12.[275] Historian Lester "Budge" Ruffner has concluded that, based on patterns of untrustworthy behavior, the Pima people, "saw no advantage in membership in a white man's group."[276]

It was probably a good assessment for other reasons, as well. The Association was crippled by greed from the start. Promises to work as a united front were constantly undermined by selfish and personal ambitions. For example, one hope for their group was to consolidate sales processes to one representative who could coordinate all the collection, manufacturing, pricing, and distribution of feathers from around the area. The purpose would be to keep feather pricing fair for both big and small operations, but it would also create a monopoly. That dream was never realized, and locals continued to compete against each other.[277]

Eventually, ostrich raisers shared some of their best practices, but until then, Watson claimed that early ranchers and breeders "met with varying degrees of success."[278] In 1909, Louis Chalmers of the Pan-American attributed the emotional and financial frustration to "desultory" practices, meaning the ranchers continual lack of a plan or purpose.[279] Modern ostrich raisers argue the opposite, saying that giving ostriches leeway to follow their natural instincts has better results.

Ostrich raisers in South Africa shared the same frustrations on the lack of resources,

> "Ostrich are really not a domesticated species... you have to farm them as a wild species."
> *-Michael Lehman, Central Oregon Ostrich (2024)*

poor communication, and inconsistent results. Annie Martin wrote in her memoir that, for the locals she ranched near, getting anything right was a matter of luck, not skill. She gave as an example: "During a whole season, one farmer will lose nearly every chick; while brood after brood will be successfully reared by another[,] at no very great distance. Next year, perhaps, it is the turn of the latter to be the sufferer."[280]

Ostrich Farming Basics

Compared to cattle, ostriches are relatively easy livestock to raise. Many ostrich ranchers boast about the small ecological footprint involved in raising these birds. A 1908 news report claimed ostriches could survive on an average of 4 pounds of alfalfa per day, or about 7% of what a western steer consumed.[281] Current standards suggest ostriches receive closer to 14 pounds, or about 25% of what cattle would consume. What the livestock eat is similar—mostly alfalfa—but ostriches also enjoy seeds, grasses, legumes and berries, just like their four-legged friends. Even ostrich droppings are eco-friendly compared to cattle. Once mealtimes are over, their droppings emit 90% less greenhouse gases.

---

[f] Michael Lehman, "As exotic farms are on decline nationwide, Oregon ranchers are hopeful for the future," April 15, 2024. *Think Out Loud* podcast with Dave Miller, Oregon Public Broadcasting (OPB), MP3 audio, 14:08, https://www.opb.org/article/2024/04/05/oregon-ranchers-hopeful-future/.

Regardless of suggested minimums, ostriches can eat alfalfa to their hearts' content—and then some—and never grow fat. Fortunately for Arizona ranchers, alfalfa has long been a staple in our agricultural history. Pickrell reported, "Where good alfalfa pasture has been available, the birds bred in America have grown larger than those first imported."[282]

To make feeding time easier, feather farms usually adjoined an irrigated field of greens, with the ostriches kept on a smaller section of natural, dry landscape with wild forage or hardy grasses available.[283] At the Pan-American Ostrich Company, they maintained expansive acreage for grains and alfalfa to feed their 1,000-3,000 birds. Blanche Murray wrote for *Arizona Highways*, "Men, teams and wagons were kept busy preparing, chopping and hauling twenty tons of fresh alfalfa daily to stuff those demanding maws."[284]

Despite a prolonged myth that ostriches don't need to drink water, current standards for care include ostriches having access to a few pints daily—about 30% of the water required for cattle. Regarding the recommended minimum, D. C. Cogburn has shared that his birds at the Rooster Cogburn Ostrich Ranch can guzzle down however much water they want, every day.

Ostriches are omnivores. Besides plants, they're known to eat snakes, lizards, insects, mice & ground squirrels.

Chickens do, too!

Learning how to breed ostriches successfully started with a great deal of guesswork; Harbert's Ranch being a lucky exception. Most early ranchers felt their breeding pairs needed a quiet, stressless lifestyle. Part of that meant they should be spared from having their feathers clipped.[285] By avoiding these clippings, a rancher's profit would be delayed to the second generation. Modern studies agree with this practice, but not for the same reasons. Instead of supporting the idea of gentle handling during a sensitive season of life, scientific evidence pointed to biological cueing. An ostrich depends on having a full set of feathers to assist with natural attraction and mate selection.

Originally, ranchers prized ostriches direct from Africa for being purebreds. Some even kept documentation to prove their lineage. Though these details might matter to a zoo, ranchers cared less about purity and more about profitability. They began crossbreeding the birds and testing which offspring produced the desired result: a thicker feather, higher numbers of eggs, bigger muscles (more meat), and so on. As the superintendent of Pan-American, William Cross selectively bred red necks to achieve a higher quality feather. Perhaps he'd figured something out because by 1911, he was making a higher return on his investment. The hybrid species' feather output increased from 14 ounces per bird to over 2 pounds each.[286]

Once a rancher figured out the magic combination that could make a product they desired, they could sell breeding pairs or trios for an enormous price. Considering that ostriches are productive three times longer than cattle, the return on investment was expected to be high. Paige McNickle, a veteran keeper at the Phoenix Zoo, has shared that by now, "All the ostriches in North America are 'hybrids' of other breeds."[287]

As ostrich populations increased, Arizona ranchers learned they did not need to dedicate as much space as originally thought to sustain the large animals. Ranchers of the 1980s and 90s successfully kept as many as 100 ostriches on plots as small as one or two acres.[288] This spacing is not ideal for wild ostriches that travel for food and other resources, but captive ostriches could manage the tighter confines.

Agnes Estelle Craig Hackett at a Salt River Valley ostrich farm,
ca. 1907 (Tempe History Museum [1987.1.777], licensed use).

Even with a small plot, one of the largest expenses for
early ranchers was building a secure fencing system. In 1989,
Leon Vandiver, founder of the later formed National Ostrich
Breeders' Association, figured that it only took, "6 or 7
strands of strong, smooth wire," to contain an ostrich.[289] He
claimed the priority should be on preventing escapes over
anything getting in. The logic behind this was that adult
ostriches had a ready response to encroaching threats. They
could protect themselves from coyotes or mountain lions
with just a kick. Unfortunately, smooth, straight-wire fencing
designs posed a serious danger should ostriches stampede
within their pens to avoid a threat. When struck with the full
force of the bird's energy, decapitations and severed limbs
could result. A safer but more expensive option was woven-
wire fencing (as shown above).

One of the most serious considerations of raising ostriches is the lifetime commitment. These birds have a very
long natural lifespan of 40 to 45 years. That might be when
they become weak enough for a lion or hyena to catch up to

them. In captivity, they live into their 70s. Because of this, "feather farming" is a commitment not only for the ranchers who are first interested in it, but it can also demand the full involvement of the next generation (or two).

The Legend of the Barbary Feather

By 1911, the competition to breed ostriches for the best quality feathers got extra spicy when South Africans felt jealous of those sold in North Africa or along what was known as the Barbary Coast. European buyers considered these Barbary plumes a superior product and would selectively purchase them. The trouble with this, according to the *Atlas Obscura*, was that "by the time these feathers reached market, they had passed through so many hands that their European buyers didn't really know where they had come from."[290] It was only assumed that the location of the last sale was where the ostriches originated.

South African feather farmers were nervous that Americans were going to get themselves breeding pairs of the mythical Barbary species. If they did, the U.S. would dominate the industry. Because of this suspicion, South Africa sent Russell Thornton, a retired British military man, on a clandestine expedition to find these special birds. He was to secure a troop for Cape Colony. If he could do this, Europe would beat the ambitious Americans to the punch.

Thornton followed his leads into French Sudan and tried to purchase 150 birds but was denied. Unfettered, Thornton acquired a full troop elsewhere, allegedly through underground networking. After an incredible amount of effort and risk, he delivered the livestock; promising Parliament they were exactly what they wanted. The ostriches he brought might have been immature because when the feather market crashed a few years later, not one had yet been bred into the South African stock. His entire mission amounted to nothing.

Ostrich Ranchers Seek Help

Even with the overly simplified description of ostrich ranching, much of the day-to-day tasks of pen conditions, feed blends, veterinary care, incubation methods, retail contracts, distribution deals and such were out of the early rancher's comfort zones. Even with the formation of the Association, and its stated intentions of sharing best practices, by 1910, the same complaints remained. One story in the *Arizona Republican* revealed: "No concerted effort has ever been made to secure statistics and statements about ostrich growing by anyone in this country. Growers have mostly proceeded 'on their own book,' some with but slight knowledge of the methods employed in the home of the ostrich."[291]

Two years later, according to C. W. Wright, writing for *The Agricultural Southwest*, little progress was made. "No book of rules told the pioneer ostrich breeder how to care for his charges, the authorities on poultry culture refusing to commit themselves, where the fowl under consideration exceeded in size the goose or turkey. So[,] the ostrich breeder learned in the school of practical experience..."[292]

Watson Pickrell, the butcher brother of William, contributed more to the progression of industry knowledge than any other person of his time. In 1905, Pickrell laid out a basis for future farmers in a report to the United States Department of Agriculture.[293] Based on his observations of the ostrich, he identified the necessity of rotating incubated eggs from one to three times per day. He also found the ideal

Ostrich farm believed to be in Tempe, undated (Tempe History Museum [1992.4.3], licensed use).

incubation temperature to be 101° Fahrenheit—lower than the average summer temperatures experienced in the American Southwest. Some ranchers likely learned the hard way that an uncovered nest in Arizona's 120° thermal fury spelled the end of an entire brood. (By the way, this is one feature of the Salt River Valley that differs significantly from South Africa. The savannas max out in the high 80s.)

Pickrell recognized the ostrich hen's habit of destroying or abandoning infertile eggs. He also advised that newly hatched chicks have immediate access to sand and gravel, to prepare their gastrointestinal systems for digesting soft grains.[294] The *Arizona Republican* flagged his writeup as "the most reliable and authentic publication on the subject of ostrich farming in America, especially in Arizona..."[295]

Watson Pickrell's industry contributions ended abruptly while on a business trip to Omaha, Nebraska, in 1907. At 53, he contracted typhoid fever and died while hospitalized.[296] His four children, all under the age of 16, were taken in by uncle William and aunt Georgiana. William then merged the Tempe Ostrich Co. with the Arizona Ostrich Co.

In 1908, the *Arizona Silver Belt* announced that in the course of just a few years, the ostrich raising industry had, "grown to such proportions that almost four-fifths of the ostriches in the United States ... [were] being raised in the Salt River Valley, within a radius of 12 miles of Phoenix."[297] They added that, strangely, "aside from the interested tourist, few realize the growth of the business ... and none but the managers know how encouraging have been the returns ..."[298] Again, this suggests a lack of general education and broad promotions that would attract investors to contribute towards necessary industry advancements.

In 1910, Harry Welch, Secretary of the Phoenix Board of Trade, requested U.S. consuls in various parts of the world to observe what was happening in the ostrich industry. They were asked to report on what they'd learned that might support ongoing improvements and clearer standards. One such report was published after a visit to German Southwest Africa (*Deutsch-Südwestafrika*), a colony of the German Empire from 1884 to 1915, now known as the country of Namibia.

The consul reported on matters of pricing, availability and incubation: "A certain German animal dealer will supply Blue Nile ostriches at $475 each. If the biggest blood is not demanded, a pair of east or west African ostriches can be obtained for $715[,] or a pair from Somali for $430. The German dealer has 150 of the millinery producers. He hatches ostrich eggs in incubators. The buildings in which the birds are kept are not heated, even in winter."

The consul then shared an update from Cape Colony: "There are about 500,000 tame ostriches ... the extraordinary price of $5,000 has been paid for a single Cape Colony bird. Feathers are sold at auction. At the last, sale prices ranged $175 to $200 a pound."[299]

Also in 1910, a representative from South Africa conducted a similar assessment of the ostrich ranching situation in the United States. Mr. E. White was an Englishman engaged in ostrich raising in the Cape. He had heard stories about the amazing production of feathers from the Salt River Valley from New York feather dealer. This dealer referred him to William Pickrell and suggested a visit.[300] During that visit, White called himself an "ostrich investigator."

White found that his competition had a major financial advantage: Arizona land was 80% cheaper than could be had in South Africa. Plus, the U.S. did not charge prohibitive export duties on feathers. It made him consider that he and his colleagues might do far better if they invested out West. The birds he saw, though they resembled the wild red ostriches or the Nubian blues, they were markedly different. He called the Arizona ostriches he saw "magnificent specimens" and said they were "larger than those of South Africa."[301]

White delivered a strong criticism of Arizonan's careless inbreeding practices. He said the state's breeders would compare the feather products from a male and female, find two that were quality producers, then mate them indiscriminately, even if they were a parent and child or siblings. His concern was that each generation created this way would become more "delicate" than the next.[302] Pickrell gave this man the shock of his life when he explained to him how it all started with Harbert's two birds.

Another Expert Emerges

That same year, another Englishman, Thomas W. Kemp, chimed in. He offered his "Opinion of an Expert" to the *Arizona Republican*. He prefaced his letter on the subject with a note that he had spent 20 years raising the birds in South Africa and had toured every farm in California. He also (briefly) managed an ostrich ranch in Tempe before relocating it to California in 1906. Therefore, he knew, "by experience, observation and statistical information those things of which he writes."[303]

> [g] "Ostrich farmers of Arizona [have] conclusively proven that ostriches thrive and multiply in the Salt River Valley."
> -T. W. Kemp (1910)

Kemp continued his letter with a short criticism, sure to win over all who have invested in the industry. He said: "To me it appears strange to notice the lack of enthusiasm that exists in the Salt River Valley with reference to the ostrich farming industry and its great possibilities."[304] He confirmed that, "of all places in the world suitable for ostrich growing, no other offers the advantages to be found in this valley."[305] Kemp concluded that what Mr. White learned in New York was true: "the feathers grown [in Arizona] are of a good standard quality and find a ready sale in New York in competition with those imported from South Africa."[306] Kemp noted that demands for feathers were far greater than Arizona could supply. His impression that the industry lacked adequate support to expand, was spot on.

---

[g] T. W. Kemp, "Opinion of an Expert: The Ostriches in the Salt River Valley," *Arizona Republican*, October 30, 1910, 9.

17. The Biggest, Fastest and... Dumbest?

"The ostrich ... is one of the largest and stupidest living birds."
– Arizona Highways (1979)[307]

Even with Pickrell and Kemp's attempts to teach Arizonans about ostriches, until serious scientific observations were made and results published, people drew radical conclusions about the animal that have warranted repeated correction, extended clarification or specific emphasis. Some of the most misguided ideas humans held were more of a reflection on the human than the ostrich. Coming in at the top of the list for most frequently asked questions include whether ostriches are truly the biggest, fastest and dumbest creatures on Planet Earth. There are nuances to the answers and readers must take into consideration that the answers have also changed over time.

Are They the Largest?

Yes, indisputably. Ostriches currently are and have been the world's largest bird since the 17th Century. They claimed this superlative after the extinction of the 12-foot tall, 500-pound Moa (*Dinornithiformes*) in New Zealand and the nearly 10-foot-tall Elephant Bird (*Aepyornis maximus*) of Madagascar that ranged from 600 to over 2,000 pounds. Adult male ostriches can weigh in at around 400 pounds, with nearly half of that being pure muscle mass. Their wingspan reaches nearly 6 ½ feet, only a foot shorter than a glorious Bald Eagle's. Ostriches can tower over humans at heights of 7 to 9 feet. And, if they stand on their tiptoes, they can also come in at a staggering 7 to 9 feet.

Are They the Fastest?

Yes, but only compared to other flightless, two-legged animals. When in a sprint, an adult ostrich can maintain a speed of at least 40 miles per hour, sometimes even topping out at 45 for a sustained 30 to 40 minutes. Even an ostrich chick at three months old can burst into a 35-mile-per-hour run, if the mood strikes. Observations have also found that while the adults are in a run, a single leg stride can cover a distance between 10 and 16 feet.[308]

Ostriches are fast and efficient by design. The ostrich is a digitigrade, which means it walks entirely on its two toes. Humans, in comparison, are plantigrades, which means the whole foot usually contacts the ground when we walk. Both the ostrich's previous heavyweight contenders had three and four toes, an inefficiency that, in a theoretical foot race, would make them inferior to the ostrich. Actually, the ostrich is the only member of the *Palaeognathae* infraclass of birds with only two toes. This modification allowed them to become not only the fastest of the flightless, but to be recognized as the fastest two-legged creature in the entire animal kingdom.

Besides their fancy feet, modern studies conclude the entire ostrich body is built for speed. In 1939, one writer put it rather poetically for *Arizona Highways* magazine: "The ostrich, with its pointed beak, bare, snaky neck with its odd esophagus coiled around the vertebrae, bare muscular legs, the rounded elevation of the back, and the feather-producing area of wings and tail, is streamlined in every count; all of which is responsible for the tremendous speed it can maintain."[309]

Adjective-laden prose aside, there is a good deal of deep science behind this fact. One PhD researcher in Germany deep dived into the topic for the *Journal of Anatomy*. Nina Schaller of the Senckenberg Research Institute claimed it's specifically an ostrich's joint structure that "may enable energy conservation by providing joint stabilisation, optimised limb segment orientation and automated positioning of ground contact elements independently of direct muscle control."[310] She then went into matters of physics and geometry that exceed my comprehension.

> "They are the greatest of all other fowls and in manner of the nature of 4-footed beasts..."
> - *Pliny, The Historie of the World (1601)* [h]

Schaller has also broken the subject down in a complimentary resource for schoolteachers of sixth graders (for which I'm thankful). In that, she explained because of the way an ostrich's joints and muscle mass are arranged, they are physically optimized for high-velocity locomotion.[311] She ended with a recommendation for engineers to take note of the discoveries. An ostrich's structural design could benefit future applications in robotics, suspension systems, and prosthetics.

Are They the Dumbest?

Don't let the ostrich's goliath proportions and record-breaking speeds fool you, for though, "he looks wise, [he] has not a vestige of sense," wrote James Geissinger, a visitor to an Arizona ostrich ranch in 1909.[312] This dismissive attitude has perpetuated for hundreds of years, but the conclusive answer remains: it depends on whom you ask. The idea is being

---

[h] Pliny, *The Historie of the World. Commonly Called, The Naturall Historie of C. Plinius Secundus*, ts. Philemon Holland, amp. Claire Richie (London: Adam Islip, 1601), 270.

debated now more than ever, but sufficient test results have not been collected.

The first ever scientific attempt to measure an ostrich's intelligence was conducted recently in Bristol, England. The 2024 test aimed to see just how far back in a bird's evolutionary chain problem solving skills could be detected. One anticipated outcome was to gain insights on the relative intelligence of dinosaurs. The test pitted three species of the ancestral Palaeognathae clade of flightless birds against each other: the ostrich, emu, and rhea. During this test, treats were placed in front of a puzzle box that needed to be rotated so birds could access the food inside. Emus were able to solve the puzzle in 9 out of 10 tries. Rheas also solved the puzzle and even bypassed the trick by breaking the rotating mechanism. Ostriches, however, could not access the treat at all.

The researchers admitted there was a "substantial" ergonomic difference between test subjects that was not accommodated.[313] During the testing procedures, a simple accommodation could be placing the puzzle box at a taller height so the ostrich would not have to contort more than any other bird. Beak design was also not factored in. The results, printed in the *Scientific Reports* journal, warned that to conclude ostriches are unintelligent because they failed under notably flawed testing conditions is "highly speculative."[314] "Our study was an initial step into some unknown territory," the report summed, "however, there is still much work to be done."[315] A British *Times* reporter seized on this opportunity and announced that ostriches "have failed to shake off the dunce cap."[316]

Political messaging about ostriches is also problematic and often draws from the same empty barrel of scientific data. For example, in 2024, a troop of ostriches in Canada was ordered by the Canadian Food Inspection Agency (CFIA) to be destroyed after becoming infected with a commun-icable virus that affects humans. The Animal Justice League responded to this event with a public statement: "ostriches are intelligent, long-lived, and sensitive animals whose lives have individual value."[317] The only scientifically backed part of that statement is about a captive ostrich's lifespan. Everything else was an emotional appeal.

Historical premises for concluding ostriches are sim-plistic "bird brained" dummies were drawn from two things: their brain size and their behaviors. Scientists used to refer-ence the brain size-to-body size ratio as an estimation of a creature's intelligence quotient (IQ). It was an imperfect pre-diction system that has since been surpassed with new re-search methods. The modern evaluation of brain size consi-ders more complex nuances of neurological activity. Ostrich-es have not yet been subjected to this new study.

Ostrich brains are quite small (around the size of a walnut) and they weigh less than one ounce. "It can be placed on a teaspoon," one observer recorded.[318] When the ostrich brain was compared to its overall body size in 1904, it was "the smallest of any creature relative to its size."[319] That fact would have led to a most severe determination of stupidity. The ratio would rank ostriches in company with the titano-saur Ampelosaurus, with a walnut-and-a-half-sized brain.[320]

Speaking of brains on a teaspoon, during the reign of Roman Emperor Elagabalus (about 218 - 222 BCE), ostrich brains were considered a mealtime "luxury."[321] Historical literature maintains that at one single meal, the emperor and his guests consumed 600 of these delicacies.[322] Also at the table were camel heels and peacock tongues. Besides having been the queerest eater, as an eccentric, Elagabalus was known to be one of the worst leaders of that empire's existence.

Ampelosaurus vs. Ostrich - Size Comparison

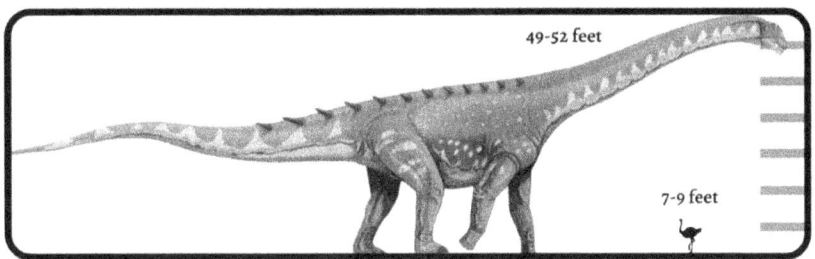

Illustration comparing the titanosaur sauropod to the common ostrich. Hypothetical lifelike reconstruction of the Ampelosaurus atacis (Wikimedia Commons, 2007/Public Domain).

Misunderstandings on ostriches found in historical literature are laughable. In *Physiologus*, a 2nd century Greek "bestiary" (book of beasts), it was taught that ostrich hens hatch their eggs by staring at them. With that absurdity, it would be fitting if this reference gave us the phrase "egg them on" (to encourage or provoke someone to action). It is not.

Biblical references dating back to the 6th and 4th century are only slightly improved. According to the author of the book of Job, God deprived the ostrich of wisdom by design. In exchange, she was endowed with incredible speed. The scriptural passage reads: "The ostrich flaps her wings futilely—all those beautiful feathers, but useless! ... She cares nothing about anything. She wasn't created very smart, that's for sure, wasn't given her share of good sense. But when she runs, oh, how she runs, laughing, leaving horse and rider in the dust."[323]

In 1890, Annie Martin, who raised ostriches with her husband in South Africa, questioned the ostrich's overall ability to exist without human intervention, considering its special condition. In her (most impressive) trash talk, she wrote: "Altogether, ostriches are queer-looking creatures;

they are so awkward, so out of proportion, and everything about them ... suggests the idea that they have only by some mistake survived the Deluge [the Great Biblical Flood] and that they would be more in their right place embedded in the fossiliferous strata of the earth..."[324]

Not everyone in ostrich ranching history agreed with such sweeping statements about an ostrich's intelligence

> "The ostrich is a series of contradictions..."
> -*James A. Geissinger (1909)*

or lack thereof. After visiting the Arizona ranches, C. W. Wright, writing for the *Agricultural Southwest*, concluded that the bird's curiosity was an indicator of at least some intelligence or situational awareness. As an example, Wright gave: "Let an unusual looking object appear in the vicinity of a flock of ostriches and they will line up with almost military precision and race across their feeding grounds to see what sort of thing the intruder is."[325] Anecdotal evidence to the contrary would suggest the next thing Wright should have seen was one of those ostriches swallowing the object whole, without regard for potential harm.

Paige McNickle, from the Phoenix Zoo, has publicly defended ostriches, saying they are both highly intelligent and emotional. In a 2017 interview, she said they even "choose what people they like and don't like."[326] (By the way, for those who have visited the Phoenix Zoo, you may have noticed that the ostriches are kept in the same enclosure as giraffes. That may be because the two animals have been found to make great companions. Some even believe the ostriches really look up to the giraffes.)

D.C. Cogburn of the Rooster Cogburn Ostrich Ranch in Red Rock, Arizona has since countered McNickle's assess-

---

[i] James A. Geissinger, "On an Arizona Ostrich Farm," *The Presbyterian Banner*, January 28, 1909, 9.

ment that ostriches might have preferences or special connections to any human handler. Rather, he's suggested that those higher-level concepts are being projected onto the livestock animal.[327]

Other than instinctual caretaking behaviors towards an egg, chick, or mate and predictive reactions to social cues, at best, ostriches have been observed showing submissiveness towards handlers. That reaction can be mis-construed as gentleness or emotional affection. The reaction is more likely a reflection on the handler's ability to maintain safe boundaries and effectively use calming strategies.

If one ostrich sees another yawn, it yawns, too... for no biological reason.

This social induction works on humans, too.

A ratite's personality or temperament can also be mistaken as a measurement of emotion and intelligence. As seen in popular online videos by Amanda of the Useless Farm in Ontario, Canada, her emu named Karen, though well cared for, is regularly violent with the handler. "I love the animals so much," Amanda told the *Whig Standard* in 2022. She argued that they have personalities.[328] Karen's personality is described on the farm's webpage as an "absolute b----."[329] Amanda (who has kept her surname out of public media on purpose) has gone on record to say the only thing her emu might feel towards her is "hatred."[330] If we married Karen's temperament with the fact that emus are the most intelligent ratite (according to their latest problem solving tests), then the next logical step would be to diagnose Karen as a sociopath. This line of thinking is ludicrous (though, Amanda might agree on the diagnosis).

Karen Weston Gonzales, a bird enthusiast, has explained for *Arizona Highways* that emotional intelligence may be quite a way down the evolutionary road. "Because they're only a few generations from being hatched in the wild," she wrote, "[ostriches] still act very wild."[331] In the late 1980s, Joe Hendrick, a professional race ostrich breeder and trainer (yes, that is a thing), told the *Arizona Republic* that ostrich jockeys must always keep in mind, that (unlike a well-trained horse) an ostrich does not intuit what is supposed to happen when they are being raced. "You have to do a lot of thinking for him," he explained.[332] More on ostrich racing is in the chapter on the Chandler Ostrich Festival.

It appears that the debate is still underway, but the expressions such as "bird brained" and "feather brained," continue to prevail, as do a few long-debunked illustrative phrases. At the top of the list for illogical, incorrect, and overused phrases is the one about ostriches burying their heads in the sand.

Ostriches Do Not Bury Their Heads

The sayings that a person has their "head in the sand," or that they are "acting like an ostrich," are supposed to mean that a person is purposefully ignoring or refusing to acknowledge the situation they are in (usually a threat); hoping that the situation will go away, change or pass by. All of these behaviors can be bluntly labeled as "conflict avoidance," "delusional thinking," or "defiance."

You wouldn't believe the volume of myth busting in literature over the last 137 years of ostrich raising in America, yet this misconceived expression persists. Because of this, there are people who wholly believe that it is something ostriches do. D.C. Cogburn provided a prime example in a 2005 interview for *Arizona Highways*. He shared that two different marketing companies came to his ranch specifically to photograph the birds displaying said behavior.[333]

"Lustercomic" postcard illustration from 1958, attributed to Tichnor Bros. Inc. from Boston, MA (Fair Use).

Ostrich hens lay either in a dust bath or over a nest (J. Vodickova/ Shutterstock, 2016 [369986525], licensed use). Notice the physical similarity to the bush in the upper right corner.

I'd like to suggest readers imagine how an ostrich would dig a hole with chopsticks for shovels, Then, once they have put their head down inside that hole, try to imagine that same ostrich rearranging the sands to close in the hole, without seeing what they are doing, all while (essentially) upside down.

A few of the cheesier attempts to straighten people out are found in the news features by Walt Mason and Mary Graham Bonner. They are dated nearly a decade apart but plead the same case. In "Rippling Rhymes," a short prose series in the *Arizona Republican* by Mason, the poet began his 1915 limerick with: "'The ostrich hides, in sand or shale, its head, when men pursue it.' There's just one trouble with this tale – the ostrich doesn't do it."[334]

In Bonner's story for the "Daddy's Evening Fairy Tale" series in the *Arizona State Miner*,[335] she also tries to clear up the facts, but the result was as long as an ostrich's gullet, so I'm going to paraphrase a bit. The story that appeared in 1926 went something like this:

Poor Mrs. Ostrich

One day Mrs. Ostrich was in tears and Mr. Ostrich asked what was troubling her.

"Oh, it's that story," she answered. "The one that has been told over and over."

Mr. Ostrich empathized with her, explaining that humans will say just about anything without ever thinking beforehand.

That being the case, Mrs. Ostrich complained, "People will keep on believing, never even bothering to find out if it is true." Mrs. Ostrich reiterated that no one in her (ratite) family buries their head in the sand. She tried to explain that the rumor started because of what she does when she senses danger. She described how she lies down and either stretches out or tucks her head. It looks like when she is sleeping.

POOR MRS. OSTRICH

"Just because people cannot clearly see my head above ground, does not mean it is not there," she concluded. "I just wish people wouldn't say such things about a matter they know nothing about."

The birds agreed on that point. The story ends with a version of, "And they call *us* stupid!"

Though it might seem counterintuitive, the crouched down position Mrs. Ostrich described was a wise and reasonable line of defense for the prey animal. When the ostrich reduces itself so, it is conserving energy, listening intently, and watching keenly to pinpoint the direction and movements of the threat. Many predators will lose interest simply because the bird appears to be already dead, or its shape may be confused with some other lump of stuff commonly found in the grasslands.

If a predator is bold enough to continue encroaching on the bird, the ostrich can pounce to its feet and sprint away faster than the lion, hyena and even the African hunting dogs. A chasing lion can run up to 50 miles per hour, jackals 40, and African hunting dogs fall somewhere in-between, but none can sustain those speeds beyond a short burst of energy. These pride and pack animals' best chance for a tyrannosaurus turkey dinner is to team up to ambush the bird from all directions, or to continue a low- to mid-speed pursuit for upwards of an hour. Acting alone, there's a slim chance of success. But the cheetah, the *sprintiest* sprinter of them all, can get a step ahead of the bird within 30 seconds-- reaching speeds around 100 miles per hour. If Mrs. Ostrich took on a cheetah, who typically hunted alone, her life would depend first on endurance, then, if necessary, her kick.

Another Tired Ostrich Expression

Since we're at it, I'd like to suggest another expression to reconsider: "eating like an ostrich." It falls along the same lines as "eating like a pig," though the pig reference is more about the quantity of food one eats, while the ostrich reference is more about an unusual diversity of food selections.

The expression, as defined in an 1895 issue of *Poultry Monthly* magazine, is "speaking derisively of a person who has an abnormal appetite..."[336] The author scoffed at such an application then reflected on the ability of an ostrich to digest rather unusual objects that are non-food items, garbage and otherwise not ever part of their natural diet. "[T]ruly, an ostrich has a wonderful power of trituration and ... utter disregard of what it swallows," the author wrote. They continued: "Almost anything thrown to one of these ungainly birds disappears down its capacious gullet..."[337]

What is "Trituration"?

Trit·u·ra·tion is the process of reducing the size of a substance by grinding or mixing, often with a diluting agent (such as water or, in this case, stomach acid).

An exemplary story appeared in Tucson's *Arizona Daily Star* about a boy in Italy that allegedly ate like an ostrich. This kid boasted about eating nails, stones, and even kitchen crockery.[338] The reporter relaying the story issued the boy wonder an international challenge: to come and eat one of the codfish balls being served at a local Tucson boarding house. Then, and only then, will his gustatory powers be considered worth mentioning.

The misconception in the offending expression disregards the responsibility of a zookeeper or breeder (or the boy's parents) to properly manage their dependent's diet. And it may be that the expression, when applied to humans, should be understood less as "they'll eat anything," and more as "they'll eat anything *handed to them* regardless of sense or safety." The implication of this new definition would be less about food variety and more about the eater's gullibility.

One 1883 Alabama newspaper described ostriches at mealtime like watching "voracious chickens." *(Which could also be an awesome band name!)*

Arizona ostrich ranchers were very keen on the benefits of alfalfa and other local clovers and legumes, but the ideas this expression gave ranch visitors was dangerous, considering that some desired to test it out. To address this risk, a special edition of *The Oasis* in 1895 included the following:

"[N]otwithstanding the popular impression that the ostrich thrives on nails, bobble stones and tomato cans, the fact is that his taste is pretty much the same as that of a pig. He is particularly contented when turned loose in an alfalfa patch. Indeed, almost anything vegetable does [well] for him, from grasses to cactus leaves."[339]

In the early 1900s, if an ostrich in Arizona happened to accidentally swallow an item of hardware or kitchen crockery, there would have been no one who knew how to save their life better than Dr. Alexander Chandler, Territorial Veterinary Surgeon.

---

[j] William G. Le Duc, "Domestic Ostrich Farming," *The Courier*, Dec.13, 1883, 3.

18. Dr. A.J. Chandler Gets Involved

*"Raising ostriches in the Mesa country has been proven
to be a very profitable industry..."*
-Arizona Daily Star (1911)[340]

Dr. Alexander John Chandler was one of the late-start ostrich ranchers, joining in 1906 and expanding in 1914, when the *Chandler Arizonan* would claim, "ostriches are all the rage."[341] Dr. Chandler was a Canadian veterinarian who eventually became the founder of Chandler, Arizona. He moved to Arizona Territory in 1887 from Detroit, Michigan, after being commissioned as the first Veterinary Surgeon.[342]

One of his first challenges was to support the state's farming community, whose livestock numbers had been diminishing from a recent drought.[343] The daunting task was paired with the deadly flooding of Fall deluges familiar to most locals as "monsoon season." After observing how vegetation rapidly sprang up after these heavy rainstorms, Dr. Chandler decidedly fixed on solving livestock owner's complaints through irrigation.

Not having the capacity to push the irrigation idea yet, Dr. Chandler set himself up on eighty acres in Mesa, fulfilling his commission as best as he could. Within his first year, he tackled

Portrait of Dr. Alexander John Chandler,
c. 1888 Detroit, MI (Chandler Museum Collection
[2011.7.1a], Chandler, AZ, licensed use).

Several horses have died in and around Phœnix of a mysterious disease. Dr. Chandler, Territorial veterinarian is examining into the nature and cause of the disease.

Editorial in the *Arizona Silver Belt*, Aug. 4, 1888.

The Live Stock Sanitary Commission of Arizona.

C. M. Bruce, Chairman   Benson, Cochise Co.
A. J. Chandler, Sec. and Vet. Surg   Phœnix.
Thomas Halleck   Signal, Mohave Co.
N. B. Bowers   Prescott, Yavapai Co.
Isaac N. Towne   Calabasas, Pima Co.
Will C. Barnes   St. Joseph, Apache Co.

Dr. A.J. Chandler shown as Secretary and Veterinary Surgeon (*Mohave County Miner*, Dec. 1, 1888).

an aggravated form of influenza that plagued area horses.[344] Then he addressed the highly politicized "Sonora quarantine" that prohibited cattle from entering the state for several months, based on allegations of diseased cattle found in Tucson.[345] Those allegations were proven false by the veterinarian almost immediately, though political conditions superseded his expertise.

After five years in Arizona, Dr. Chandler abandoned all veterinary duties in favor of full-time land development. He began the Mesa Canal Corporation and started expanding the canal systems originally dug out by the indigenous peoples of the Salt River Valley. His irrigation efforts were a huge success. Once the arid desert lands appeared evergreen and productive, the Corporation then sold the improved plots at a profit. By 1900, Dr. Chandler expanded on this work, buying up 18,000 acres south of Mesa to duplicate the process in what would eventually become his namesake city.

Chandler Buys Ostriches

Numerous writeups claim that Dr. Chandler became interested in ostrich ranching only after seeing Edwin Cawston's collection on display at the 1893 World's Fair in Chicago, Illinois. A stronger argument is that Dr. Chandler had seen multiple successful examples in Arizona from 1888 on. Pickrell & Co. brokered his first purchase: a troop of 100 ostriches from Cawston's Pasadena farm. For the expensive startup, Dr. Chandler partnered with an investor from New York who had already been throwing money at local roadwork and mining projects.

A story found in the 1906 *Copper Era and Morenci Leader* read: "Between $30,000 and $50,000 will change hands between A.J. Chandler and Pickrell brothers for the purchase of one hundred ostriches within the next few days ... Chandler is preparing to take care of the birds on his ranch near Mesa, where he has 20,000 acres, a large part of which will be devoted to the cultivation and care for the birds."[346] Rumors circulated that Dr. Chandler wanted to become the new ostrich king of Arizona. The *Leader* declared that the large purchase was only the forerunner to several more, "that will bring the ownership of all the ostriches in the Salt [R]iver [V]alley under one company..."[347]

Dr. Chandler received his order in installments. The birds were shipped in "ordinary cattle cars" on the railroad, likely arriving at the Mesa train depot, which had just opened in 1903.[348] An announcement about one of Dr. Chandler's ostrich deliveries read: "A shipment of 35 ostriches will arrive today and be taken to the Chandler ranch to join others of their kind. ... There will be 68 birds at the Chandler ranch when the newcomers are registered..."[349] The article describes loading the birds up much like cattle, by driving

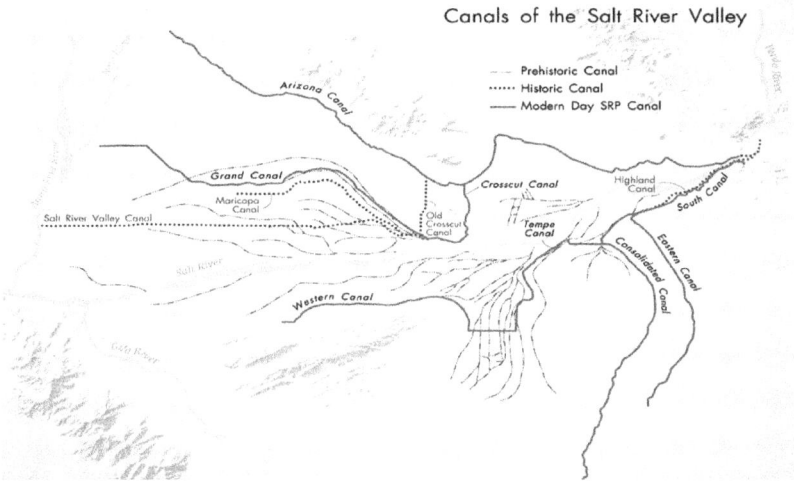

Map from Salt River Project, "A History of Canals in Arizona,"
SRPnet.com/about/history/canal-history (Fair Use).

Dr. Chandler at his Consolidated Canal Company home office, 1893
(Chandler Museum Collection [91-21-9], Chandler, AZ, licensed use).

Mesa Depot at 3rd Ave. and
McDonald in 1912 (Arizona
Museum of Natural History).

Tempe resident Agnes Estelle Craig "tends" to chicks at a local ostrich
ranch, ca. 1910 (Tempe History Museum [1987.1.2301], licensed use). If
determined to be at Dr. Chandler's ranch in Mesa, the mountain in the
background might be part of the McDowell range.

"Flock of Ostriches
Inspecting the New Canal,"
ca. 1908 (SRP, Walter J.
Lubken's collection/Public
Domain).

the ostriches through a chute. Upon arrival, the birds were transferred to a covered wagon before being taken to their final destination in Mesa. Chances are that news of the arrival elicited a crowd at the train station.

According to a description provided in the *Arizona Republican,* Dr. Chandler's newcomers were all under the age of eight months. The article read: "The birds are all young fellows and have not arrived at that period in their existence when they can walk around with expensive plumes in their [tails]."[350]

Introducing T.W. Kemp, "Ostricher" Extraordinaire

For several months in 1907, Dr. Chandler employed an experienced "ostrich man" named Thomas W. (T.W.) Kemp as superintendent over his new Mesa troop.[351] Kemp was said to be a long-time ostrich rancher in South America. Originally from Manchester, England, he'd traveled south, but when and for what reasons is unclear. He may have been part of the British Army, like Dr. Sketchley, but no records have been found to confirm his early career details.

While working on the South African ostrich ranch, he amassed a wealth of knowledge and skill. In time, he earned himself a reputation for knowing more about ostriches than they knew about themselves. Prior to working with Dr. Chandler, Kemp briefly raised a few ostriches in Tempe, in partnership with two other men.[352] The *Arizona Republican* reported: "He knows all about them. He talks about them all day and every day and dreams about them at night. When he falls out of bed[,] he dreams it was a forward kick of an ostrich..."[353]

Kemp left Dr. Chandler in 1906 and for the next year, he helped establish the Los Angeles Ostrich Farm as a profitable tourism spot with a "handsome salesroom."[354] The *Los*

Angeles Times reported that their establishment offered a "fine collection of ostrich feather goods and souvenirs," as well as "an extensive factory business."[355] At the new factory, employees would wash, sort, classify, price and package feathers for sale throughout the country. This move from pastoral care to production placed Kemp in direct competition with the feather factories in New York that most U.S. ostrich ranchers were reliant on. It also increased his knowledge base.

Dr. Chandler's Mesa Ranch

When Kemp left for California, Dr. Chandler replaced the senior bird handler with two brothers from an esteemed pioneer family in Mesa. Louis B. "Lou" Ellsworth and Ernest E. Ellsworth were locals familiar with cattle ranching, but willing to try something new. A third brother, Byron Ellsworth, also helped at the ranch on occasion. While the Ellsworth brothers handled the ostriches, Dr. Chandler continued to work on developing the East Valley into a green utopia.

With such young birds to raise, Dr. Chandler would have to wait for them to mature and breed to consider the investment secure. In 1910, Mesa's moderate troop of 100 birds had increased to 150.[356] That year, he arranged his first shipment of feather stock. Even though there was an established feather manufacturing business in Downtown Phoenix, the vet-turned-land baron sent his harvest to the Cawston Ostrich Feather Company in Los Angeles.[357]

In the meantime, Dr. Chandler resumed irrigation projects through his new business, the Chandler Improvement Company. Very quickly, with regular watering, the desert south of Mesa became fertile and green... and salable.

Top: "Drying Ostrich Feathers in the Warm California Sunshine." Bottom: "One of the Well Lighted and Perfectly Ventilated Workrooms." (Cawston Ostrich Farm Souvenir Book, 1909 (Smithsonian Institute/Public Domain).

During the summer land sales, "nearly $100,000 worth of Chandler Ranch lands were sold."[358] Not surprisingly, many of the new land buyers were from California, and several became ostrich owners shortly after arrival.

Kemp Reappears... Briefly

T.W. Kemp never stayed in one place very long, choosing instead to be an opportunist. Besides his proficiency in animal communication, he was notorious for moving "whither so ever he listeth."[359] In early 1911, Kemp toured ostrich ranches across the Southwest and offered his expert consulting services. Some records identify him as a promoter. While in town, a reporter from the *Arizona Rep-*

ublican interviewed him. He talked about various complaints most start-up ranches experience, the valuation methods of feathers and the dying and manufacturing processes. Kemp invited all those who were desired to start an ostrich ranch to come see him at the Adams Annex hotel for more specific advice (for a fee, I'm sure).

Kemp also revealed to the *Republican* his plan to form a syndicate and plant several new ostrich ranches in the Phoenix Valley (and beyond). He said, "[T]here is more money in ostriches than there is [in] anything else - except the hotel business."[360] During his last visit to Arizona, Kemp purchased ten pairs of breeding birds, though it is unclear from whom. He later said that the selection was made carefully and only the best feather producers were considered. Three investors teamed up with him to make the purchase. The final location selected for launching a new ostrich ranch was not in Arizona, as Kemp hoped, but in El Paso, Texas. The Southwestern Ostrich Farm, as it was called, was established on the U.S.-Mexican border, "one-half mile east of present-day Tigua," in Mission Valley.[361]

Kemp was hailed by the *El Paso Times* as the Texas ostrich pioneer who knew "more about [the ostriches] than they [knew] about themselves."[362] *El Paso Herald* spread excitement for the startup with an announcement that "A carload of live ostriches will arrive here next week…"[363] Twenty-five birds reportedly clambered out of the train car, having an estimated value of $10,000. A later historian noted for the El Paso Historical Society that, "The birds did very well in the fine El Paso climate, and things were going so well by 1913 that a big party was held… to celebrate the success…"[364] Shortly after, Southwestern Ostrich went out of business. Little was heard of Kemp again.

Dr. Chandler's Ostriches on Display

In November 1911, Dr. Chandler proudly sent off one pair of ostriches to be displayed at the National Land and Irrigation Congress in Chicago, Illinois. That year, the World's Fair was in Turin, Italy, so this was one of the largest stateside events he could take part in. The event was primarily for utilities-type companies to gather and address governmental issues regarding land use, agricultural developments, forestry protection measures and so on. (I imagine the birds were probably bored.)

The rooster he sent was reportedly the largest blue-necked Nubian in the entire Salt River Valley.[365] Accompanying the ostriches to Chicago was Lou Ellsworth, the Mesa ranch superintendent and foreman for the Improvement Company. The birds traveled to the wintertime scene in a specially designed steam-heated railcar with Lou remaining boxed up with them, rather than riding in a passenger car.

Other items sent from Arizona to exhibit the benefits of proper irrigation were oranges, grapefruit, baled alfalfa, barley, wheat and milo maize (sorghum). Only those that were "large, luscious and attractive to eye and taste," were included for display, according to the *Republican*.[366] After this first inclusion, Arizona utility companies tried to have ostriches regularly appear at the annual Congress, whether dead or alive. (More on that in the Ostrich Tourism chapter.)

19. Yuma Talks a Big Game

*"Yuma ... can raise ostriches more profitably
than in any other part of the world..."*
-Arizona Sentinel (1913)[367]

The Colorado River port town bordering Mexico and California, at the southwestern corner of Arizona, became the state's secondary hot spot for raising ostriches starting in 1909. Though the area started with twelve birds and peaked at about 150, the *Arizona Sentinel's* front page once rang out: "Yuma is [the] Best Field in the World for Ostrich Industry." Their reports claimed the dry atmosphere and steady temperatures were "equal or better than any other place on the globe" where ostriches could live.[368]

Tucson's *Arizona Daily Star* also printed a brag piece that suggested ostrich ranching, "undoubtedly[,] is destined to become a great Yuma industry and should command the attention of every one[*sic*]."[369] The reporter even said, as Yumans continued to excel in this line of business, the Salt River Valley ostrich raisers should start "looking after their laurels." [370] That inky boldness should be tempered by the fact that there were only two ostrich owners in the area and neither was pretentious enough to compete.

The first families of ostrich ranching in Yuma were the Meadows and Biechtelers... with one brief exception for a man named Miller. He once locked an ostrich in the blacksmith's shop. (More on that in the Murder Birds and Other Tragedies chapters). These neighbors lived in what was considered the Lower Valley of Yuma, near County 10th

Street and Somerton Avenue. In December 1909, James Harvey Meadows and his neighbors expected the arrival of 12 ostriches. When the train came in, four ostriches went to the Biechtelers and eight to Meadows.

Meadows can be credited with bringing the idea of ostrich ranching to Yuma, possibly after being influenced by Dr. A.J. Chandler. Meadows had previously worked as an engineer on Yuma's canal project to draw water from the Colorado River into the area for agricultural developments. Then, in 1909, he and his brother John Jr. worked with the Salt River Valley Water Users Association (now recognized as the Salt River Project, or "SRP").[371]

For years, the Association had been constructing the Roosevelt Dam on the Salt River, about 67 miles east of Mesa. Dr. Chandler was a key member of the vanguard who pushed the project to completion. When Meadows came home from that job, his mind was full of ideas. Meadows would replicate the way Dr. Chandler set up his ostriches on an irrigated alfalfa field, but on the banks of the Colorado River.

Yuma's First Ostrich Owners (Meadows & Biechteler Bros.)

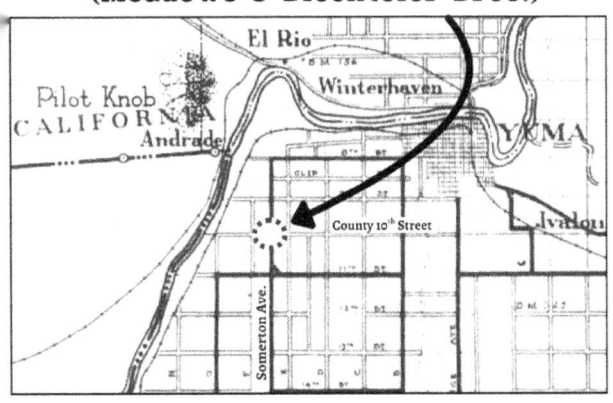

Portion of the "Official Map of Yuma County, State of Arizona," marked by author (Yuma Co. Hwy Dept., 1923).

Meadows Family Backstory

Before canal work and ostriches, James Meadows was best known as one of the little brothers of the world-famous, fancy shootin' celebrity, "Arizona Charlie" (born Abraham Henson Meadows). James was one of 12 children who'd moved to the Payson area from Visalia, California in 1877. They settled on the East Verde River on the Mogollon Rim in what was then called Diamond Valley. The Meadows family name became famous back in 1882 when the Meadows Ranch was targeted during an Apache raid. During that event, Cibecue band leader Natiotish led between 40 and 80 warriors through Pleasant Valley and above. They burned down cabins and indiscriminately murdered settlers in an agitated response to dangerous rumors. (To be fair, that story is far more complicated and sensitive. Also, here's where we begin a rabbit trail.)

Early in the morning of July 15, 1882, James' father John, a former sheriff in Tulare County, left the cabin to see why the dogs were barking. After walking some distance, he was ambushed by Apaches lying in wait. They killed him at close range. John's sons, John Jr. and Henry, went outside in response to the gunfire. Once in range, the Apaches also shot at them. In that encounter, John Jr. was hit in both arms. The bullets blasted through his left wrist and right elbow. A third bullet entered the left side of his chest, remarkably missing his heart by first striking the tobacco pipe in his vest pocket, then deflecting. Henry took a bullet in the abdomen. Then, he suffered severe impact when an Apache shot the cartridge holder strapped to his waist. The explosion left a gaping hole in his groin.

Both brothers kept brave faces on as they retreated to the cabin. While fleeing, Henry was shot again. This time, the bullet struck his foot, and he had to be dragged inside.[372] The

Meadows family hunkered down as if defending the Alamo. Help finally arrived in the form of a U.S. cavalry unit. U.S. Army Scout Tom Horn, wrote in his autobiography that on July 15, he was tracking down the "renegade" Cibecue band when they'd come to the Meadows Ranch.[373] "About 10 o'clock we came to the Meadows Ranch on the east fork of the Verde, and found old man Meadows killed, Hank shot all to pieces, and John also badly shot up."[374] Horn believed "[T]he renegades had most likely seen us coming," and Mrs. Meadows guessed they'd only gotten a half mile away by the time the cavalry arrived.[375] An Army doctor stayed behind to stabilize "Hank" (Henry) and John Jr.

Charlie, age 22, was away from home when the raid happened. He was also a U.S. Army scout, like Horn, and had been at a nearby fort. He arrived in the late afternoon of the 15th to find his father's body still in the yard and his mother and siblings on high alert. When Charlie recounted the event to a sister, he said the 12-year-old future ostrich farmer James was one of "three small boys" who had to be protected by their brave sister Maggie.[376] Charlie claimed that 13-year-old Margaret Ellen Meadows had grabbed a rifle and aimed through a port hole. Charlie assumed Henry toughed out his wounds and, incredulously, manned another.

In an alternate account from Jean Beach King, granddaughter of Maggie Meadows, she found that Maggie and James were the only able-bodied defense remaining. John Jr. could not hold a weapon and Henry, being disabled from his midsection down, acted primarily as a shot reloader and instructor to his younger brother and sister. King wrote that the brother-sister-duo "stood on tubs and flour sacks, tensely manning their smoking rifles and helping to repulse the whooping raiders like seasoned gunfighters."[377]

After two days of cat and mouse skirmishes, the U.S. Army finally caught up to the faction of Apaches on July 17. The event has since been called the Battle of Dry Wash. About a mile north of Diamond Valley, the Army and Apache renegades fired on each other for nearly six hours. The event ended abruptly when a summer monsoon blackened the skies, blew in sheets of torrential rain, and dropped violent hail on the Mogollon Rim. The weather was so intense, Tom Horn claimed he still felt wet and cold from it, years later. "We could neither see nor shoot," he wrote, and after 20 minutes, "the fight was over."[378] The storm provided the perfect cover for the Apaches to escape. As expected, the U.S. Army claimed they'd won that battle. More to that story can be found in a resource other than a book about ostrich ranching.

After this traumatizing event, John Jr. recovered from his gunshot wounds and went on to invest in mining claims and became a Justice of the Peace in Payson. Henry died two months later from complications. As the new head of household, Charlie sent his mother and younger siblings Maggie, James, Jacob and Mobley down the Salt River via boat. After landing in Tempe, the children attended school in Phoenix.

Showtime for the Meadows

In 1884, Charlie Meadows, with the help of John C. Chilson, organized a cowboy skills competition in Payson, which has continued annually ever since. Through rodeoing, Charlie established himself as a champion trick shooter, cattle roper, and bucking bronco master. The excitement from those tournaments lent the scout and cattleman a heap of celebrity. In an 1889 steer roping contest, Tom Horn bested his friend and host: setting a record of 58 seconds.

Starting in 1890, and continuing into the early 1900s, Charlie gallivanted around the globe, performing in popular Wild West shows. Charlie accepted an invitation to join Wirth's Wild West Show on a tour through Australia. At the last minute, John Jr. joined him for that tour and was billed as the "ruthless spirit of the Plains" in his role of "Captain Happy Jack."[379] The brothers were later picked up by Harmston's Wild West Show.[380] When that show toured around East Asia, John Jr. stayed back and opened a horse training and lassoing school in Brisbane. He also spent a few years mining for gold before returning to the U.S. in 1908 and working on the Roosevelt Dam.

Charlie later joined "Buffalo Bill" Cody's Wild West Show for a tour through Europe. Horn was invited to join, too, but was content to keep working as a field operative for the Pinkerton Detective Agency. After Charlie's overseas adventure, he formed his own performance company. He continued to be a traveling entertainer as a Buffalo Bill look-alike for nearly a decade.

Left: Charles Henson Meadows in costume, ca. 1890-1900 (Jean B. King's *Arizona Charlie*/Fair Use]. Right: "Buffalo Bill" (William F. Cody), ca. 1890-1900 (Nat'l Cowboy and Western Heritage Museum, Willard H. Porter Rodeo Collection Item 2001.049.003).

Occasionally, Arizona Charlie's Historical Wild West production featured one or more of his little brothers: James, who could be counted on to wrangle an angry bull for excited audiences; Jacob David ("Jake" or "JD Meadows"), renowned trick rider and overall stuntman; and Mobley Augustus Meadows ("Kid Meadows"), a bronco buster and the fastest Pony Express re-enactor. James never had a cool stage name, though he sometimes went by "Jim."

When the showbiz gig fizzled, Charlie ventured to Yuma and, like James, got involved in canal work and other civil engineering projects. He also made the acquaintance of Guillermo Andrade, Consul General of Mexico. Gen. Andrade offered him the deed to the Isle of Tiburon so they might engage in a cattle and mining partnerships there, but there was a catch: Charlie would have to rid the island of its inhabitants, the Siri Indians.

In 1902, Charlie, Jacob and James Meadows (and a few other men) took a yacht down the Gulf of California to the island to explore the possibility. The on-land expedition lasted two weeks. They collected mineral samples, found out how many Siri lived in the area and scoped out where their tactical advantages could be, should they be allowed to return with a small army to subdue and evict the indigenous people. Nothing appears to have come from that expedition other than wild yarns of cannibals and secret troves of gold.

When Charlie retired and James turned to ostrich raising, Jacob and Mobley became legendary peace officers in Yuma and Imperial County. Those two tracked outlaws across the searing sands of the Yuma Desert, took down a Mexican desperado on a murder streak, and unmasked a diamond thief in disguise. Mobley was honored with a statue in front of the Imperial County courthouse. (By the way, I could write an entire book about James Meadows' brothers

Left to Right: Jacob David "Jake" Meadows, constable in Yuma. Charles "Arizona Charlie" Henson Meadows, Western rodeo legend and cattle rancher in Yuma. James Harvey "Jim" Meadows, ostrich breeder in Yuma. Dated between 1891 and 1902 (Jean B. King's *Arizona Charlie*/Fair Use).

—and maybe I will—but none of them owned ostriches, so that's all you'll get in this book.)

Back to Ostrich Ranching

In 1909, onlookers were skeptical when James Meadows unrolled five miles of "funny-looking" mesh wire fencing for a section on his 160-acre alfalfa ranch in Yuma. He needed the installment to be perfect: the fence should start one foot off the ground and stretch four feet high to accommodate the birds' odd anatomy.[381] No sharp toenails could be allowed to get caught in the lower wires and no legs should be able to step over the upper rail.

After settling his eight birds in, Meadows immediately prepared for the forthcoming egg-laying season. The following March, three incubators arrived at the post office for him, each capable of handling 22 eggs.[382] Meadows looked forward to the summertime hatchings until he realized that the stories of hens laying an egg every other day was true. A May 26 story in the *Yuma Examiner* read: "Jim Meadows was in town yesterday from his big ostrich farm and states that the baby ostriches are arriving so fast now that he has ceased to be excited about it."[383] The first baby ostrich in the Yuma Valley hatched on April 7 as a motherless wonder. On learning how to care for the new arrivals, Meadows shared with the *Examiner* that "it takes about five days for these birds to decide to live or not to live ... after that[,] they are very hard to kill."[384]

That December, Meadows took his family to Los Angeles, where they stayed for a month so he could learn several new things about the developing industry and how to manage his unusual livestock.[385] It is possible that he interned with Edwin Cawston or another California ostrich farmer (like Moses Clanton did). He also sold his latest collection of feathers to a California manufacturer and received an enormous dollar figure.

In December 1910, James Meadows had to have a leg amputated, making him the world's first one-legged ostrich rancher! *Still... no cool nickname.*

When the following year's clippings returned from processing in Los Angeles, they were reported in the press as "the most beautiful ever seen in Yuma"[386] They were clean, treated and curled to perfection. Meadows could have raked in another pleasing profit but for no stated reason, he sold them off at wholesale prices.

A week later, the same newspaper announced that Meadows had also sold off most of his troop to people in Phoenix, reserving only the youngest to keep on with his interests as a breeder and reseller (instead of feather farming). This business angle kept his overhead expenses low, the demand for acreage in check and limited how much he would have to fuss over his birds. King claimed her grand-uncle's ostriches were reduced to a side business next to his alfalfa production, vegetable rows, fruit orchard and beehives.[387]

The Biechteler Brothers Give It Their All

The other first family of Yuma ostriches were bachelor brothers Ernest and Hans Biechteler from Kempten, Germany. They immigrated in 1904 and arrived in Yuma the same year the ostriches did. At 27 and 30, respectively, the brothers appear to have no clear connection to ostrich raising other than the potential to have discovered it as a lucrative opportunity when they lived somewhere in Los Angeles County.

Raising ostriches brought several woes to the Biechtelers. In 1911, a fire started at the farm and destroyed the incubator house they'd built, along with 15 chicks and the 57 developing eggs.[388] Hans also got a taste of an ostrich's bone breaking kick in 1913.[389] "Once they finally figured out how to keep the farm running and chicks alive, the Biechtelers quickly multiplied their four original birds into a troop of 100, making them the largest ostrich ranch in the county. Ernest told the *Tombstone Epitaph* in 1913 that "the ostrich business in Yuma Valley is growing by leaps and bounds."[390] He said that their post-fire generation of birds were "healthy and lively youngsters," and mentioned their plan to clear even more land so they could expand the operation.[391]

"Scene on Biechteler Ostrich Farm," *Arizona Sentinel and Yuma Weekly Examiner*, Nov. 19, 1914. The man on left is suspected to be Ernest Biechteler.

BEECHLER BROTHERS, OSTRICH FARM, YUMA, ARIZ.

A. O. Boeres Co. postcard collection, ca. 1910-1914 (Public Domain).

Of the two neighboring families in the business, the "Biechteler Bros." were the area showmen. Their critter corral appeared in newspapers and postcards for the enjoyment of Yuma promoters, who would use them as an example of how the desert was evolving into as green a scene as Mesa and Chandler. The Biechtelers also impressed Dr. R. H. Williams, a professor of animal husbandry at the University of Arizona who had visited to learn the tricks of the trade for an Experimental Farm on campus.[392] (More on that in the chapter on the U.S. Ostrich Experimental Station.)

More Families Follow Suit

In 1914, the *Tombstone Epitaph* reported there being an increase to four ostrich ranchers in Yuma County.[393] The third belonged to Henry Hansberger and his sons James "LeRoy" and Edwin, who stationed a troop of 20 in Gadsden, on the border of Mexico.[394] Edwin Hansberger recalled, "Ernest Bietchler in the lower Valley was growing ostriches in the early teens. And around 1913[,] Papa decided to try it out."[395] They designated five acres of their farmland to their ostriches. In addition, they tended an alfalfa field, date orchard, and pecan grove.

The fourth was established by Mr. Blount in Wenden, a former miner's supply point in the middle of nowhere.[396] Neither operation panned out. Edwin Hansberger recalled, "We kept the birds for a time but finally killed them off in order to make better use of the land."[397] They gifted eggs and meat to a restaurant on Main Street that served ostrich omelets and steaks until they ran out. Within the next five years, any memories of ostrich ranching in the county were practically forgotten by all.

Hansberger & Sons

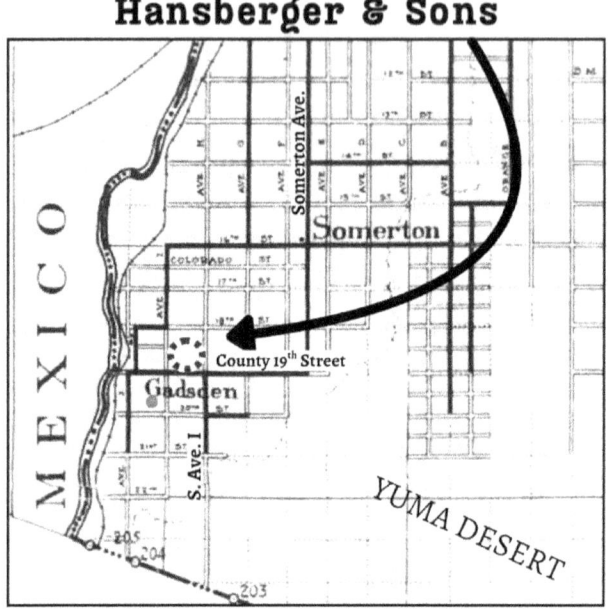

Blount Ostrich Farm

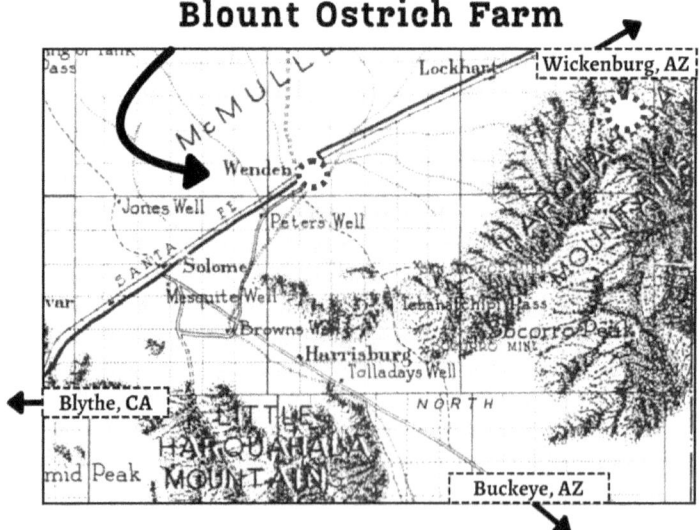

Top & Bottom: Selected portions of the "Official Map of Yuma County, State of Arizona," marked by author (Yuma Co. Hwy. Dept., 1923).

20. Extreme Growth

"Arizona, doubtless, will be as famed for its
ostriches as… for its Grand Canyon.
- James A. Geissinger (1909)[398]

Without question, the period from 1910 to 1914 saw the most extreme growth in the Arizona ostrich ranching industry. Ranches began popping up everywhere, feather costs continued to rise, and wealth from these once laughable endeavors oozed from the owner's pores. One rancher out of Phoenix reported that their sales in 1912 alone reached $350,000, or $11.6 million in today's terms.[399] Ostrich raising turned businessmen into googly-eyed dreamers bringing in 25% to 40% (or more) on their investment—an unheard-of reward for feeding a few big ducks.[400]

Arizona historian Roscoe G. Willson sums it up this way: the industry "boomed until almost everyone tried to get in it."[401] One investor, Louis Chalmers, predicted in 1909: "The day is not far distant when every farmer in the Valley will not be content without having on his farm a few fine pairs of these birds."[402] He was not far off in his estimation. New ostrich companies "sprang up all over the Valley," and feather dealers and distributors sidled up next to whomever they could get an exclusive contract with.[403] By 1910, the agricultural value of ostrich livestock was $1,696,140.[404] That value averages out to about $320 per bird, regardless of age or breeding status.

Breeders were more than happy to distribute their extra birds to those who wanted a piece of the profit pie. At this time, "ostriches were selling at prices higher than cattle, $100 for a chick and $800 for a 4-year-old…"[405] Within three years, those prices would jump to $150 and $1,000 and the *Arizona Republican* would declare: "As a moneymaker, the ostrich takes second place to none."[406]

To get an idea for how fast the industry grew, back in 1905, "more than half of the ostriches in the U.S. were in Arizona," and by 1910, the state housed 80% of the animal's population, all within the bounds of Maricopa County.[407] The 1910 census reported there being 5,316 ostriches in the Salt River Valley. Kemp said of the population increase: "The Salt River valley has already more ostriches than any other one spot in the world[,] with the exception of South Africa."[408] By 1914, Pan-American Ostrich Company boosted that statistic even more when their troop population increased to 3,500. Historians have estimated that at the peak of the boom, there were "at least 8,000 ostriches in the Valley."[409]

Production Demands for Arizona

With more than a decade of hands-on experience "domesticating" the African ostrich, Arizona breeders had finally proven themselves capable of competing with the best. Local exhibitions of Arizona feathers on the market (more or less competitions) displayed plumes that could make a husband's wallet wilt. Stunning white primes came in as long as 27 inches (without modification) and nearly 17 inches wide.[410] In the 1910s, there was an extraordinary plume that pulled in a lofty price of $50 for its owner. That's close to $1,700 in today's terms, for one feather.

"Ostriches in Field," believed to be from Pan-American, ca. 1914, in Walter Lubken's Photographs of the Salt River Valley (SRP).

The Sonoran Desert-raised birds attracted an enormous amount of attention from buyers and ranchers across the world. Watson Pickrell predicted that, as long as the industry had customers, land, and irrigation water, there was no reason for the American Southwest not to become the foremost provider of feathers in the country, if not, the world's.[411] And Arizonans tried.

Even though ranchers in the state devoted extensive acreage to raising ostriches, and held the largest population in the nation, the state, a writer for *Quad-City Times* argued that "the American supply of ostrich feathers is so small that it has little or no effect on the world's market."[412] It was true that Arizona only held a few thousand birds compared to South Africa's tens of thousands. That factor alone would continue to keep shoppers reliant on imported goods. But what Arizona could not offer quantity, it outdid itself in quality. And that, for sure, made Arizona South Africa's most annoying competitor.

Sale of feathers from the Pan-American Ostrich Farm, *Times Leader*, May 21, 1913.

Extreme Responses and Rival Taxations

As Arizona's ostrich industry expanded, both South African and U.S. governments took serious note of the increasing potential for Americans to become self-reliant ostrich feather producers. In response, South Africa passed exclusionary laws to end the sales of fertile eggs and breeding birds to all foreign buyers. This new system replaced prior tariff and tax structures. This motion was supposed to protect South Africa's precious assets from being comercialized to the point of putting their original feather farms out of business.

An article about the nuances came out in a 1911 issue of *Overland Monthly* titled, "The Ostrich Feather Industry in the West Vs. Africa." It read: "In German Africa, it is found, the export of ostriches and ostrich eggs is now prohibited by Imperial decrees of February 16, 1909."[413] The Imperial decrees went as far as restricting who could even collect wild ostrich eggs or capture birds for captivity. Breeders had to have special governmental permission to acquire new birds. The only permitted condition for getting a new ostrich was for breeding (primarily to prevent extensive inbreeding).

The article provided that the restriction did not apply to trade operations with neighboring states, "in which similar measures are in force, and in which exception is made as to the export to German Southwest Africa."[414] What South Africa did not expect was that *Deutsch-Südwestafrika* or DSA would become the regional exception for smuggling ostriches off the continent. Buyers would claim to export ostriches from South Africa to DSA, then export them from there to the U.S. To hamper greedy Americans who turned to the black market and evasive schemes, South Africa issued a steep fine and a two-year prison sentence for anyone involved in taking (or allowing) ostriches to be taken from the continent. This reduced the number of go-betweens in DSA, but not by much.

During World War I, South Africa militarily assumed control over DSA, which ultimately squelched prior German authority. That control lasted from 1915 to 1920, when South Africa was given full administrative power by the League of Nations. This shift enabled the launch of the Apartheid system. (By the way, the Anti-Apartheid movement was a significant factor in the second boom of the ostrich ranching industry. More on this in the Late 80's Comeback chapter.)

In 1990, Deutsch-Südwestafrika was liberated as the independent country of Namibia. One of the first things they did was legalize ostrich exports.

By 1910, Uncle Sam finally took ostriches under his own wing. Considering the cutoff of valuable trade items, the U.S. imposed a protective tariff on feathers coming in from South Africa, making imports outrageously expensive. This action drove the prices of feathered goods across the board. In addition to the duties and tariffs placed on the items by their own country, South African exporters were taxed by the U.S. an additional 20% on raw feathers and 60% on manu-factured items.[415] This likely infuriated the Cape Colony multi-billionaires, who expected U.S. fashionistas to finance a gilded wing on their Feather Palace. Feathers were already a luxury

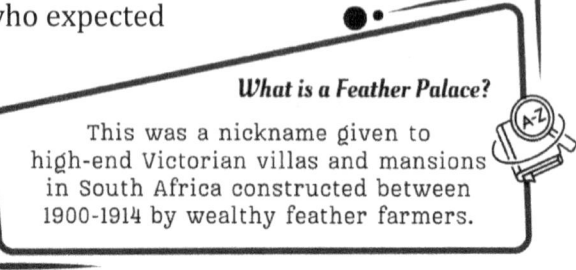

What is a Feather Palace?

This was a nickname given to high-end Victorian villas and mansions in South Africa constructed between 1900-1914 by wealthy feather farmers.

expense, so to keep shoppers happy, this motion placed the American Southwest under significant pressure to increase its (relatively affordable) output, and faster than ever.

Dr. Chandler's Secret Weapon: George Peabody

During this time, one rancher's marketing skills tipped the shopping scales in Dr. Chandler's favor. With the help of a promoter, Dr. A.J. Chandler's multiplying troops quickly became the state's new show ponies, and Pan-America's fiercest competition.

In late 1911 or early '12, Dr. Chandler employed a Californian named George T. Peabody to help publicize his land developments in the East Valley and attract buyers specifically from California. The veterinarian's initial urge to irrigate the land via canal system improvements had turned the City of Mesa into an agricultural oasis. On May 16, 1912, the newly recognized townsite of Chandler was also touted to be as lush and fertile as Southern California's Pasadena. Besides canals, cattle, citrus, and Egyptian cotton, Dr. Chandler's ostriches became an icon of the Salt River Valley's immense prosperity and fertility.

Peabody was not a marketer or "promoter" by profession. He was previously a field assistant for Gifford Pinchot at the Department of Agriculture, Division of Forestry (the U.S. Forestry Service) before he became an absolute dynamo for Arizona's agricultural community. Though he only lived in the state for about four years, in that time he became the founder of the Chandler Chamber of Commerce, the assistant manager to Dr. Chandler at the Chandler Improvement Company, he served as the Maricopa County Fair commissioner, was one of the founding members of the Egyptian Cotton Growers Association, and was the originator of a boy's "Cotton Club" (the predecessor of today's 4-H club).[416]

George T. Peabody (1879-1942), c.1910-1920, Courtesy of Roy Fetterman (Chandler Museum Collection [87-1-5], Chandler, AZ, licensed use).

The *Arizona Republican* called this man of many skills a "live wire," who had made satisfactory improvements to the East Valley within his first year of arrival.[417] When he accepted the position of Dr. Chandler's assistant manager for the Chandler Improvement Company, the board was pleased. The press announcement read: "...with his dynamic qualities and ability to push things, he makes an ideal man for the position."[418] And in 1915, Peabody accepted a full-time position as the business manager (secretary) of the Chandler Chamber of Commerce. It was a tremendous undertaking, so the *Arizona Republican* claimed. That said, the report continued: "if anyone can make it go, it is George Peabody. He has the technical knowledge, the address, and enthusiasm unbounded."[419]

It seemed George Peabody had the so-called "Midas touch." That was exactly what Dr. Chandler needed. According to Chandler Museum literature, Peabody "jumped into the business of promoting Chandler and all it had to offer,"[420]

View of the San Marcos Hotel in 1914 (SRP, Gary Lubken Collection).

and trumpeted the forthcoming sale of the greenbelt gem in a national advertising campaign. Early promotions for investors to consider Chandler were a bit liberal with exaggerations, such as one in 1906 that read: "There are no pests in the valley and diseases are practically unknown."[421] But once Peabody took the reins, Dr. Chandler's formerly hard and dry townsite was framed as "the very cream" of the Salt River Valley's agricultural crop.[422] Chandler townsite was pitched as one of "the prettiest, busiest, and wealthiest communities in Arizona."[423] Chandler acreage sold in record time, adding $50,000 to his coffers practically overnight.

As Dr. Chandler's right-hand man, Peabody also helped drive traffic to one of the new town's greatest tourist destinations: the San Marcos Hotel. As if Dr. Chandler didn't have enough going on already, he opened one of the most technologically advanced vacation spots in 1911 with hardly a word. A November 5 blurb in the Arizona Republican read: "Quietly and as ostentatiously as any well-appointed hostelry

George Lewis at San Marcos Golf Links, 1913, Courtesy of Janet Gross (Chandler Museum Collection [92-7-92], Chandler, AZ, licensed use).

should, the San Marcos hotel made its bow to the public Monday and threw wide its doors of hospitality to the tourists of the United States."[424] The hotel was a dream, five years into the making when Chandler Townsite was only a few buildings, "surrounded by thousands of acres of beautiful alfalfa."[425]

It was to be an "oasis in the desert;" a luxury resort for tourists that featured horseback rides through the wilderness, the first all-grass golf course in the state, tennis courts, polo fields, and 35 fully electrified rooms with both lightbulbs and telephones.[426] Dr. Chandler frequently offered his guests excursions out to his ostrich ranch in Mesa. The ranch visits included a shaded grove of palms and orange trees and respite at the ranch house. Sometimes formal meals were served on the lawn with entertainment to enhance the visit.

Perfect Mr. Peabody

George Peabody's talent for making the best of a situation extended to his own personal property as well. He lived on 20 acres, adjacent to Chandler, near Frye Road.[427] In March 1914, his home became a stellar example for how new residents could maximize the use and profitability of their own backyards, if they felt so ambitiously inclined. The *Arizona Republican* detailed: "If anyone wished to see a perfect exhibit of intensive farming on a small scale, he wants to visit George T. Peabody's back yard... The ground used is about 50x90 feet, and so far[,] Mr. Peabody has a fruit orchard, strawberry patch and vegetable garden. A chicken yard of Columbian Wyandotte, another of Bantam Cochins, and aviary of wood or Mandarine[*sic*] ducks – they are not labeled yet – and a pheasant run."[428]

The journalist went somewhat overboard with the rest of the story, adding in rumors Peabody would soon be digging a bear pit. After that, he might add a coon hollow and start a tree nursery to complete his vision.

21. Arizona Sets the New Standard

"Olives, Oranges and Ostriches.
These big O's [are] grown to perfection in the Salt River Valley."
- *Arizona Republican (1914)*[429]

Despite ongoing trade wars between countries, Arizonans were glad to have their ostriches in the global spotlight. In 1910, Phoenix's Board of Trade produced a promotional film to highlight some of the major attractions in the Salt River Valley. The hope was to entice new residents and encourage developers. The film debuted in October before an audience of political movers and shakers. "Over 6-feet of moving picture film was run through the Coliseum machine last night," the *Arizona Republican* shared.[430] The first scene opened on a vast alfalfa field, tall and ripe for harvest, followed by views of the new Roosevelt Dam, lush orchards, and agriculturalists hard at work. "Perhaps the best part of the film comes last," the *Republican's* journalist allowed, as the final sequence was and close look at an ostrich ranch. "[T]he pictures of the big birds are certainly fine ... a band of several hundred ostriches is seen coming toward the spectator, turning and wheeling like a company of well-trained soldiers."[431] (By the way, that analogy is sorely misguided. Troops of ostriches rarely behave in an orderly

> [k]
> "Fine horses, cattle, sheep, hogs, bees and ostriches are among the opportunities that are money makers."
> - *Phoenix City and Salt River Valley Directory (1912)*

---

[k] 1912 Phoenix City and Salt River Valley Directory.

181

manner. You'll see more on this in the Bird's Gone Wild chapter.)

With all the publicity Arizona ostrich ranchers were receiving, and with the obvious wealth to be gained from such an occupation (or side hustle), people from all around the world considered Arizona as having set the standard for selective breeding operations and farming conditions. Though there were still ostriches in California, Texas, Florida and Arkansas, Arizona's ostriches were the best feather producing specimens in the world. Because of this, visitors came from around the world to discover the secret for success.

In April 1913, a judge from Slater, Missouri, visited Phoenix and painted quite a picture of the Pan-American for his hometown news outlet. The *Slater News-Rustler*: "Here on the sandy place[,] these monster birds of speed and strength are retained ... the climate and soil are admirably suited to these birds that seem to be on stilts."[432]

A few months later, Oscar Evans from Cape Colony visited Phoenix, burning with envy. He was some kind of government representative from Melrose and claimed to be a scholar on "ostrich culture" (as if that was a thing).[433] Evans made appointments to speak with Herbert McClung about the Pan-American Ranch and with Dwight Heard about the Belgo-American Ostrich Co. Evans demanded to know how Arizonans were producing such healthy birds with high-quality feathers. "He seems anxious to gain all the knowledge possible about local conditions," the *Republican* reported.[434]

That same year, an Australian named Mr. Palmer visited Pan-American with the goal of reporting to the British Parliament about their need to support more ostrich farming activities in his home country. After the visit, Palmer argued before Parliament that ostrich farming "may become a considerable importance to the Commonwealth."[435] He cited the

Berryhill Company postcard of an ostrich ranch in Phoenix, ca. 1910s (Susan Arreola Collection/Phoenix Public Library).

value of feathers, the ability to avoid steep importation costs, and the successes of those who had taken a chance on the investment in the U.S. Palmer also angled for the Australian government to subsidize farmers and support the growing industry.

"While at Phoenix, Arizona, I took the opportunity to visit several of these farms," Palmer relayed at the 1913 Parliamentary session. Referring to Belgo-American, he said, "One of those I visited, conducted by some Dutch farmers, is in use mostly as a stud farm for breeding stock for sale; while another," the Pan-American, "is the largest farm in America, carrying over 5,000 birds in various stages, from chickenhood to maturity. This ranch is owned by a New York company and pays immense dividends on the capital invested."[436] He reported on the efficiencies of Arizona ranch management, citing, "The number of hands required to run [the ranch] is not much greater than the requirement for a small farm."[437]

Nothing but golden insights were provided to the Australians but naysayers argued they could raise three times as many sheep on the same amount of ground an ostrich farm would use. Examples were also given of prior attempts where feathers produced by Australian breeders "were characterized by four times as much quill, and very much less plume."[438] The response did not acknowledge how current ostrich farmers could improve their outputs with the benefit of further study (perhaps, abroad).

Ultimately, members of parliament wasted time quibbling over where to get the ostriches, how much duty to impose on exports, and whether their current birds had inbred too much to be of any further use. The biggest kicker, though, was a governmental grudge. If South Africa would not allow Australia to import any more ostriches, then Australia would consider prohibiting the exportation of sheep, specifically to South Africa. Animosity and circular talk continued at length until the debate was adjourned with no course of action decided.

Arizona's Biggest Year

With the entire world watching to see what Arizona ostrich ranchers would do next, the industry saw its biggest period of growth. From 1913 to 1914 alone, the industry practically doubled to at least 47 active ostrich ranches (not double-counting businesses that were renamed and not counting any that had closed). New owners popped up in Tucson, Yuma, Wenden and Thatcher. An explosion of ostrich purchases can be attributed to a massive offloading from Pan-American. They provided a tally of those purchases to the *Republican*.

That year, there were ostriches in so many places that an explanation had to be added to the Phoenix City Directory. It read: "Ostrich farms are among the many sights of the valley.

Here in the Salt River Valley are 80% of the ostriches in all of the United States. There is one farm that has over 3,500 birds. ... There are a number of rather large flocks or herds in the valley and the industry has come to stay."[439]

To be fair, not all sales from Pan-American were going to ostrich ranchers. The Phoenix Elks Lodge and the Harvey Eating House deployed their ostriches to the kitchen. A press release from the Harvey House explained that a total of 60 ostriches from Phoenix were "sacrificed on the altar of American gratitude," when served up as Thanksgiving dinner to riders on the Santa Fe railroad and guests of their affiliated hotels.[440]

Dr. A. J. Chandler	300
C. B. Laird	5
Geo. Alkire	40
L. Ellsworth	12
H. Claridge	3
O. M. McCulloch	2
F. Brown	2
Dr. Fisk	2
S. E. Sparks	3
H. C. Cleveland	2
J. M. Sanders	6
E. E. Ellisworth	2
A. G. Barnes	2
Lovell & Clobby	4
Elks Lodge	1
Harvey Eating House	40
Gen. M. H. Sherman	200
E. E. Morrison	50
L. H. Morrison	20
T. M. Toston	20
M. Lecky	10
W. H. Heffner	10
F. D. Lane	100
University of Arizona	24

Buyers of ostriches from Pan-American (*Arizona Republican*, December 1, 1914).[441] Note: "M. Lecky" should read "D. L. Lecky."

The *Chandler Arizonan* reported on the sudden influx of large birds in their vicinity: "Chandler will soon be dotted with little ostrich farms."[442] Among the Chandler buyers were Charles Peterson (purchased 20), Thomas and Margaret Ann Toston (40), D. L. Lecky (10), and brothers Ernest and Leroy Morrison (40). The Morrison Brothers were the first grocery store owners in Chandler Townsite. E.E. Morrison Grocery was the third original structure built in 1912, after the town-site office and dining hall. A historical plaque marks their store location at 40 S. San Marcos Place.

Even Dr. A.J. Chandler's assistant, George Peabody, made room in his backyard paradise to raise 10 ostriches for com-mercial gain. Rumor holds that Peabody housed the ostriches between his new polar bear ice slide and scorpion sand pond. The Peabody Ranch business appears to have lasted three years, when the owner withdrew from all his Arizona interests and moved back to California.

The State's First Female Ostrich Rancher

The Toston purchase is notable because through it, Margaret Ann "Maggie" Toston became the first female ostrich ranch owner in Arizona (and possibly in the nation). The Tostons were California transplants who lived in Chandler from 1912 to 1917. Though her husband Thomas is named in a news article as having purchased 20 ostriches from Pan-American, the township maps, city directories and county land records confirm that Maggie was the sole business owner and sole property owner between the two of them when these ostriches were acquired.[443] Her husband was consistently identified as either a farmer or dairyman.

Toston's relatives have called her a "dynamic woman," which is evidenced by her ambitious entrepreneurial ways.[444] At 22-years-old, Margaret Ann Todd (Toston) had

Margaret Ann "Maggie" Toston (1873-1950), undated, provided by Dorothy Combs (2013) on Ancestry.com (used with thanks).

not found a suitable match in her home state of Kentucky, so she ventured west with her sister to become a schoolteacher. She arrived in Montana as a "spinster," according to granddaughter Dorothy Combs, while Maggie's sister married a man she'd been writing love letters to for the last 10 years.[445] Maggie's new brother-in-law George Toston was a Norwegian American stock raiser and in 1895, he was considered the wealthiest bachelor in Park County.[446]

While the newlyweds settled in Livingston, Maggie secured a teaching position 30 miles north, in the town of Meyersburg (also seen as Meyersville). While there, Maggie constantly crossed paths with another Toston. Her brother-in-law's big brother, Thomas "Moz" Toston Jr., happened to be "one of the most prosperous of the young ranchmen of that vicinity," according to the *Livingston Enterprise*.[447] Maggie and Tom married in Bozeman at the late ages of 27 and 48. (By the way, I'm not convinced about the "young" label, considering Tom was 21-years her senior and already aged beyond the average life expectancy of a male in the 1890s.)

By 1907, Maggie and her husband lived in Tulare, California. There, they individually owned properties, showing precedence for how the couple conducted business. In the fall of 1911, the Tostons were exposed to George Peabody's propaganda advertising lush, irrigated Mesa lands and a booming Chandler Townsite. In January 1912, the *Los Angeles Times* announced the Tostons had purchased 160 acres in Mesa; 80 of which were owned by Maggie Toston exclusively. All were located a mile north of Chandler townsite. Besides the original land purchase, Maggie bought another 40 acres in her own name, which she later sold to Dwight L. Lecky.

In the summer of 1913, at the age of 61, Toston's husband was involved in a buggy accident resulting in a concussion and skull fracture. He was rendered unconscious for several hours. No one expected him to survive.[448] When he came-to, the Tostons may have re-evaluated their situation through a very practical lens. Between July and October 1914, all of Thomas' holdings were sold off and the only property remaining in the Toston name was 40 acres of Maggie's land, known to locals as Toston Ranch. Consolidating the estate would have protected the family interests and inheritances. The couple had a 10-year-old and 8-year-old to consider, plus, in September 1914, a third child arrived (a geriatric surprise). Two months after her youngest was born, 40 ostriches arrived at the Chandler Train Depot for the Toston Ranch.

Besides owning ostriches, in November 1914, Maggie Toston was among the first women to vote in a Presidential election.

SEEK ARIZONA LANDS.

Southern California Buyers In Evidence In Acreage Activity Under Roosevelt Dam Irrigation System.

Sales of Chandler ranch lands near Mesa, Ariz., are reported by the Los Angeles office of the Mesa Improvement Company as follows: Maggie Toston, eighty acres, $11,000; Thomas Toston, eighty acres, $12,000; G. H.

Toston land sales (*Los Angeles Times*, Jan. 14, 1912).

CLASSIFIED BUSINESS DIRECTORY	495

OSTRICH RAISERS

Chandler Improvement Co (Chandler)
Leckey D L (Chandler)
Peabody Ranch (Chandler)
Toston M A (Chandler)

1917 Phoenix, Arizona City Directory, p. 495.

Ostrich Ranches in or near Chandler (1914)

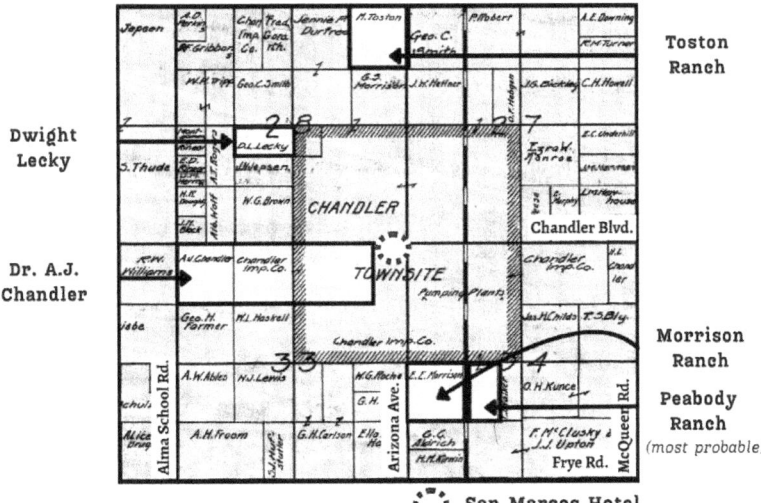

Township map (1S 5E), 1914, labeled by author (History and Archives Division/Arizona State Library/Fair Use).

189

Unfortunately, Maggie did not end up with all 40 ostriches at Toston Ranch. In a mid-delivery accident, one died. Chandler townsite and the surrounding area became infested with the others that were loosed in that event. (More on this is in the Murder Birds chapter.) After giving it a go for a few years, the Tostons left Arizona in either 1917 or 1918 and returned to Southern California. Maggie refurbished an apartment complex and supported the family as a landlady. When Tom passed away in 1920, Maggie retired to a farm on the San Vicente River near El Cajon and helped raise her grandchildren.

22. The U.S. Ostrich Experimental Station

"Diamonds and ostrich feathers...
neither are necessary to our actual welfare,
yet they satisfy one of the greatest human desires..."
- Rep. Carl T. Hayden (1913)[449]

The economic value of the ostrich industry to state initiatives and agricultural sciences had become so clear that Arizonans appealed for federal investments. Governmental funding would assist in taking the industry to the next level—whatever that meant. Between 1912 and 1913, members of the Arizona Ostrich Breeders' Association (AOBA) shared their convictions about the importance of an investment with Carl T. Hayden.

Hayden had been a Tempe pioneer and longtime Territorial Sheriff of Maricopa County. In 1912, Hayden traded in his Sheriff's badge for a seat in the state legislature. Five days after Arizona gained statehood, Hayden was sworn in as its first member of the U.S. House of Representatives.

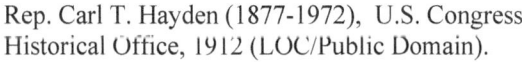

Hayden spent the rest of his career as a member of U.S. Congress and in 1969, he set the record as the longest continuously serving member at just shy of 57 years. (This record has since been broken. Twice.)

Rep. Carl T. Hayden (1877-1972), U.S. Congress Historical Office, 1912 (LOC/Public Domain).

191

Hayden was not a man who wasted words. In fact, he gained the nickname the "Silent Senator" because he rarely spoke in Chamber meetings.[450] By the time he presented a case, though, he had already exerted so much influence, extended favor and formed trusting relationships with other congressmen that, as one pundit put it, others would approve a request for a Navy in the landlocked state of Arizona, if it was Hayden who asked.[451]

Several Arizona ostrich ranchers had already benefitted from Hayden's connections and talent when he was a Tempe town councilman. In 1902, he visited Washington, D.C. and successfully lobbied for funding of the Salt River (Canal) Project. Surely, Hayden was already sold on the serious potential for feather farming after having seen the industry's progression (and profits) for himself. When members of the AOBA asked for his help, he was a ready ear.

After meeting with the AOBA, in 1912, Hayden introduced an amendment of bill H.R. 18960 to Congress, requesting an appropriation of $5,000 to support the founding of a research station specifically to study ostriches. The insights from this station would propel the industry to new heights. Issues to be addressed were pros and cons of modifying ostrich feed (such as should ranchers stick to alfalfa and bonemeal-only diets?), the comparative results of harvesting feathers at different rates of frequency (like are year-old feathers better than those clipped at 9-months?), and veterinary care standards. Since ostriches were still a relatively new livestock animal, veterinarians were mostly guessing when treating them. If experiments could be conducted, Arizona ranchers could protect their investments with vaccinations, medication blends, and feed blends that perfectly suited the ostrich at every stage of life. Hayden's proposal was turned down.

Undeterred, Hayden gathered additional proof of concept from his ostrich-raising friends and from Dr. Alonzo D. Melvon, Chief of the U.S. Department of Agriculture's Bureau of Animal Husbandry. Armed with information to extinguish every doubt, Hayden wrote one of his rare speeches.

On February 7, 1913, Hayden delivered a compelling 30-minute presentation to the House of Representatives, declaring ostriches to be one of the most important ventures the country had ever engaged in.[452] He cited the latest statistics; that the country had recently imported $5 million dollars of feather products from South Africa (almost one-half of their output) and he emphasized that one day, all that money could stay in the country's economy. (That is, should federal funds be applied towards research.)

> "Ostrich feathers have always been worn by those who love the beautiful, and always will be."
>
> - *Rep. Carl T. Hayden (1913)*

Hayden assured representatives that the investment was secure, saying: "No one need have any fear for the future of the ostrich industry. The feather is undoubtedly the most beautiful ornament of its kind, and as such[,] is independent of fashion." He continued, "[A]ll history indicates that the demand will remain as permanent and expansive as any other branch of trade."[453] His confidence in the U.S. being able to progress into global feather trading was a testament to the success of industry pioneers who had faithfully stewarded the original few ostriches and their descendants.

Hayden reminded the congressmen that he previously put forth a request for $5,000 in federal funding. But he was not there to echo himself. Hayden explained that for anyone to improve and protect the industry, an experimental station had to be developed eventually, but the terms could be flexible. He adjusted his request to half as much, with the understanding that it would fund an experimental station for one year (like a trial period, or perhaps, an *experimental* experimental research station). He believed, in time, the government would see the value in renewing the investment.

Hayden emphasized the pressure to move the bill forward. South Africa had already conducted similar experiments to improve its livestock and the U.S. needed to catch up.[454] And nowhere else on earth could this operation be envisioned other than in the U.S., since ostriches and eggs were prohibited from trade in most other countries. Hayden also argued that Arizona was best suited to the

"The breeders of Cape Colony recognize the American ostrich farmers to be their most dangerous rivals."
- *Rep. Carl T. Hayden (1913)*

establishment, local ranchers able to share everything they knew and willing to accommodate the project, however needed.

For a moment, it seemed Hayden's glowing tales of Arizona's success thus far backfired. Representative William E. Cox of Indiana questioned him. "It seems to me that the gentleman is making out a splendid case *against* the necessity for his appropriation, that his people have a pretty good knowledge of how to breed ostriches and that this appropriation will not add anything to the knowledge that they already have."[455]

Hayden was ready with a stalwart answer. He responded, "...The necessity for this appropriation is due to the fact that the industry in the United States has grown slowly on account of the excessive mortality among the ostrich chicks. ... When you consider that chicks six months old are valued at $100, you can readily understand why my people are interested in reducing this great mortality. ... There is no literature on the subject that is available to the beginner in the business, and the ordinary American ostrich breeder is not inclined to conduct experiments himself on account of the great value of the birds."[456]

(By the way, Hayden allowed that one instructive book had been published. In 1881, Arthur Douglass, an ostrich raiser from the early 1860s, penned *Ostrich Farming in South Africa.* Hayden credited the author as being "the man who put the 'riches' in 'ostriches.'"[457] Still, the book could be faulted as outdated, heavily tailored to the South African economy and culture, and experiential—not scientific.)

He continued his speech. "The study of the feeding, breeding, and diseases of ostriches is pioneer scientific work in the strictest sense and deserves the support of this Government."[458] In his final statement, Hayden appealed to politicians' vanity by reinforcing the idea that Americans do things better than everyone else, including how they dress. "Whoever wears an ostrich plume is adorned with an emblem of justice," he said.[459] He condemned those who support the cruel extermination of birds for fashion. Like a diamond, "the ostrich feather fulfills [a very] legitimate need in the way of adornment," but (unlike diamonds and other frivolities) this adornment would not shed innocent blood.

As will be seen in a future chapter that covers animal rights movements circulating the globe in the 1910s, it was a prudent (if not popular) choice to make a nationwide statement in favor of the ostrich. Hayden concluded, "If for no other reason than this, the industry deserves encouragement by the American Government."[460]

Hayden's charm and accompanying stats convinced Arizona State Senator Henry Ashurst, who, according to the *Slater News-Rustler*, supported the appropriation.[461] The amended bill H.R. 28283 was put to vote and passed by a

landslide of 25 "ayes" to 17 "noes."[462] President Woodrow
Wilson signed the bill into effect on March 4, 1913. $2,500 was
awarded to the USDA's Bureau of Animal Husbandry, who
would oversee the fulfillment of this project.[463] AOBA
members were thrilled about the news and believed that with
this support, "the breeders of this section should break all
existing ostrich records."[464]

Opening the Nation's First Ostrich Experiment Station

A search for the perfect place for a research station
began immediately. Tempe, Glendale, Phoenix, Chandler, Mesa
and Buckeye all vied for selection. At the February 1913
meeting, Hayden requested the Secretary of Agriculture start
by visiting the state to study its conditions and the birds being
raised, and to listen to the troubles of the ostrich ranchers.
Hayden told his AOBA colleagues he believed the USDA would,
in due time, "discover the cause of our troubles and find a
remedy for them."[465]

When asked how scientists would be accommodated,
Hayden assured Congress: "My people are most hospitable,
and I assure the gentleman that the Government experts will
live on the fat of the land."[466] AOBA members Pickrell,
Chandler, Ellsworth and Cook were important contributors
towards the first year of observations and towards the land
search. They secured the USDA's confidence and proved
Hayden's promises true. For the fiscal year ending June 1915,
the USDA was awarded $24,500 towards fulfillment of the
project (an increase of 880%). The amendment read:
"Provided further, that of the sum thus appropriated [to the
USDA], $24,500 may be used for experiments in poultry
feeding and breeding, including the feeding and breeding of

HUNTING SITE FOR EXPERIMENTAL FARM

Headline from the *Arizona Republican,* Aug. 6, 1913.

ostriches and investigation and experiments in the study of the ostrich industry."[467]

After evaluating all the options, the USDA awarded a contract for the original ostrich experiment station to the University of Arizona in September 1914. Tucson was likely shown favor on the bid because the school already had a cooperative arrangement with the USDA for hands-on educational extension opportunities involving plants and other livestock animals.[468] The University's Board of Regents set aside 27 acres of the northeastern portion of the campus for the experimental station. Five acres near 2nd Street and Cherry Avenue were reserved for ostriches.

The at-large director of the extension program was college dean Dr. Robert H. Forbes. Directly overseeing the ostriches was H. C. Cross (also seen as C. H. Cross), who was employed as the Executive Clerk of the Animal Husbandry Division.[469] Dr. Forbes said of the incoming animals, "We expect to have four pens of ostriches here, so that we can live with them and study them."[470] According to the University publication *Arizona Land and People,* the ostriches were "the center of interest" at the campus addition.[471]

Tucson Citizen, Sep. 12, 1914.

U.S. Ostrich Experimental Station
(Tucson, AZ 1914-1915)

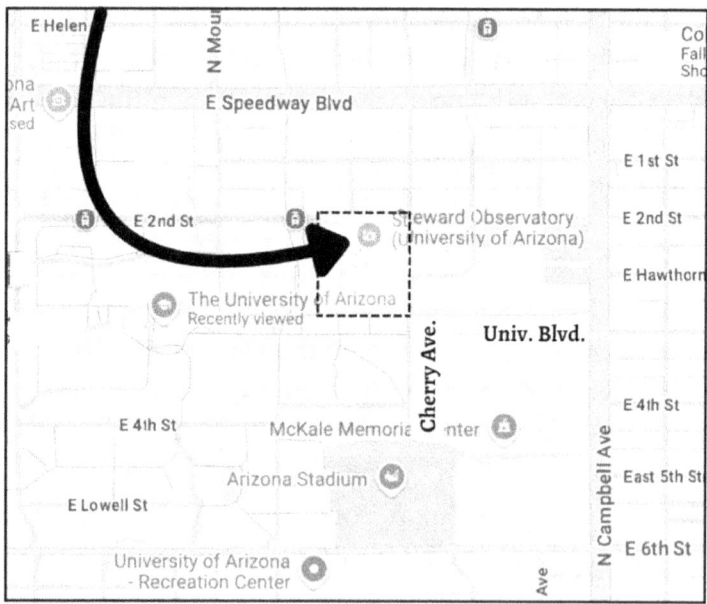

Site of first U.S. Ostrich Experimental Farm on the campus of the University of Arizona (Google Maps, 2025, labeled by author).

The *Snowflake Herald* announced that ostriches would come to the program from a local ranch.[472] Dr. Forbes' starter batch was a donation of 24 ostriches from Pan-American.[473] Those were loaded into a railcar and sent down to the University and arrived sometime between November 11 and 27 of 1914. The *Arizona Republican* reported on their arrival: "They will be used in studying the industry and in experimental breeding for fine feathers."[474] Forbes explained to the *Tucson Citizen* that besides preparing for ostriches, there would be ten pens for other poultry birds.

Researcher Robin Doughty found for *Agricultural History* that "The U.S. Bureau of Animal Industry purchased [both] northern and mixed stock from local enterprises."[475] Besides the red necks from Pan-American, in 1915, Cross purchased ten "Wickey birds" from Rudolph Wickey's lot of red South Africans, including two blue "Nubian" species.[476] The following year, Harry M. Lamon, Senior Poultryman for the Bureau, added in another pair of blue "Somali" ostriches (also called German East African) from a ranch in Yuma.[477] Those fresh additions never set foot (or, should I say toe) on the University campus.

That year, federal funding increased to $34,500 and the ostrich research program moved to Glendale. Likely by request of Arizona's poultrymen, an emphasis was placed on adding poultry breeding experiments to the list of activities. At this time, there was already an established poultry experiment farm in Beltsville, Maryland (the first U.S. Experimental Farm, ever). Poultry raisers across the American Southwest were delighted to have a nearby resource, as were the ostrich breeders who had wanted a more accessible location to start with. The *California Poultry Journal* announced: "This station is designed to do work for the entire Southwest, and experimental work carried on there will be directly for the Pacific Southwest in its scope and character."[478] By 1920, Glendale's experimental farm was the largest in the country.[479]

On the divorce from the University, Doughty wrote: "The Bureau stationed a man at Glendale, Arizona who began to collect information in cooperation with the Arizona Ostrich Breeder's Association."[480] The University of Arizona kept the Pan-American ostriches, and the Bureau purchased 12 of its own, intending to nurture a new bloodline.[481]

Over the next few years, Tucson's cooperative program saw little-to-no value in keeping ostriches around. University literature recorded that by 1917, only eight roamed the University Farm.[482] By that summer, the number of ostriches in all of Pima County dwindled down to three, "and evidently have had no increases in the family," reported the *Arizona Daily Star*.[483] Likely, the three remaining were purposefully not being bred as the experimentation wound down. The University of Arizona tried to diversify the station by adding deer,[484] but that was not enough to keep the station in operation. Besides, the spot where ostriches lived was better suited for the construction of the new Steward Observatory.

In January 1918, there was a university-sponsored feast highlighting several agricultural products. On the menu was "Hoover's Hottentot Ostrich à la Mode" from the University Ostrich Farm, with accompanying options of giblet gravy, peas, butter, mashed potatoes, corn bread, and Neufchatel cheese balls.[485] And then, there were only two ostriches left in the county.

Glendale's Experimental Station

Starting in December 1915, H. C. Cross lived with his twelve new ostriches in the far-west outskirts of Glendale,

Arizona. For a couple of years, the USDA had an informal land use agreement with William Cook and Clarence B. Laird. In 1917, they secured an official claim, a short distance away. Contained with the station logs held by the National Archives is a note from November 15, that read: "Made a preliminary survey of the land to be turned over to the Bureau by Messrs. Cook & Laird; it was agreed by Mr. Lamon that the Bureau would accept approximately 80 acres."[486]

The area set aside was located immediately on the west bank of New River, where access was limited by a single dirt road and concrete bridge structure that was frequently flooded. The USDA would have full use of the land on a 99-year lease, to be paid annually at the rate of $1 per year.[487] That was a small drop out of the $37,000 awarded by the government that year.[488] The deed was executed on March 11, 1918.[489]

When Cross moved to the new property, he brought 40 ostriches with him. Out of the 80-acres at their disposal, 20 housed ostriches and another 20 grew alfalfa. The final 40 were unaccounted for. To prevent erosion of the riverbank, riprap needed to be installed immediately. The banks were likely covered in heavy stones, then wire mesh was applied overtop to keep the rocky retainer held fast. Once the bank was secured, Cross erected fences. Breeding birds were corralled in six pens that backed up to the river. Besides three pairs of (near) purebreds used as controls, the other three pairs were crossbred combinations. Unmated and young birds were kept in a small corral to the west and mated freely.

Between the pens and corral was the station's "plucking box." Feathers collected were bundled by bird and then sent to Pasadena to be graded. Cross trusted Cawston's feather processors to "give us their opinion as to the quality of the feathers sent."[490] Once quality was assessed, Cawston's had

U

Ulrey Walter R rancher
Union High School C A McKee prin
United Produce Growers Assn of Ariz Wm Thompson sec and mgr
United States Ostrich Experimental Farm R F D 2

Glendale listings in the Phoenix Metropolitan Area City Directory, 1918.

U.S. Experimental Poultry Station
(Glendale, AZ 1921-on)

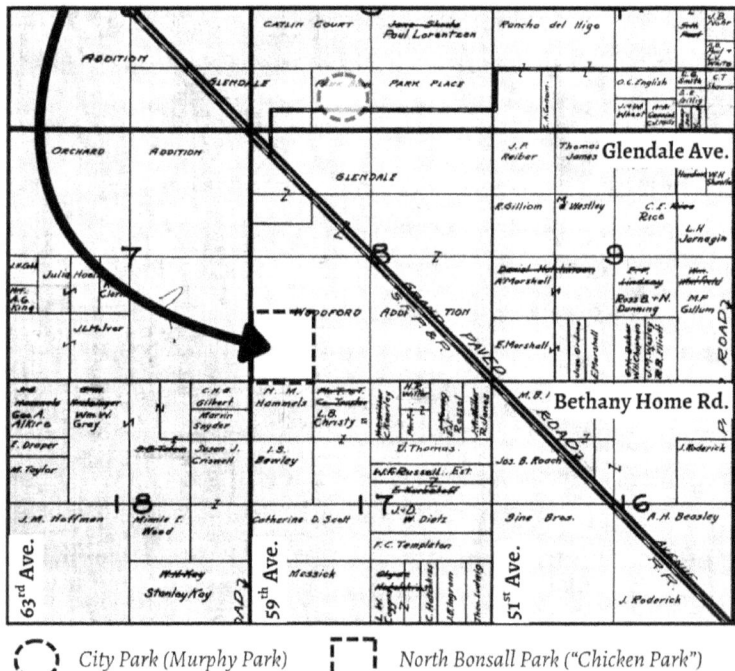

◯ City Park (Murphy Park)   ▢ North Bonsall Park ("Chicken Park")

Township map (2N 1E), 1917, labeled by author (History and Archives
Division/Arizona State Library/Fair Use).

the first rights to purchase the feathers.

Cross, who had never raised ostriches before this assignment, was supported by locals who had a wealth of information to share. Of particular help were William Pickrell and Lou Ellsworth. After consulting with the Arizona Ostrich Breeders' Association, one of Cross' first puzzles to solve was the low hatch rate of ostrich eggs. An example he recorded was that from a batch of 140 eggs collected and incubated, only 50 chicks hatched.[491] Fewer lived past the first 90-days. Another item to explore was nutrition modifications to produce bigger, healthier birds with larger, clearer, wider or brighter feathers. Cross experimented with the addition of oatmeal, corn, and various oil blends, but suffered losses and setbacks when the ostriches became constipated. Douglass' guide referred to the deadly condition as "stop sickness."[492]

Besides requests from the AOBA, Cross's station logs contained reported problems with flooding, fertility and filial cannibalism. July 1918 was a challenging month for ostrich chicks. Cross had not accounted for Glendale' higher summer temperatures and lower elevations. These amplify an incubator's warming effect. Cross burned almost all the eggs inside. He also struggled with his hens eating uncollected eggs and adults sitting on chicks and either crushing or smothering them to death.

In July 1920, when Nat E. Luce took over as the stationmaster, he watched a hen pick up and throw a chick into the air like a cat toying with its mouse before swallowing it whole.[493] (Don't worry; the ostrich didn't swallow the chick. Instead, she experimented with the idea that it might sway side-to-side, like a feather when floating to the ground. It didn't.) After observing those behaviors, Luce kept chicks separated from adults for their first 90-days.

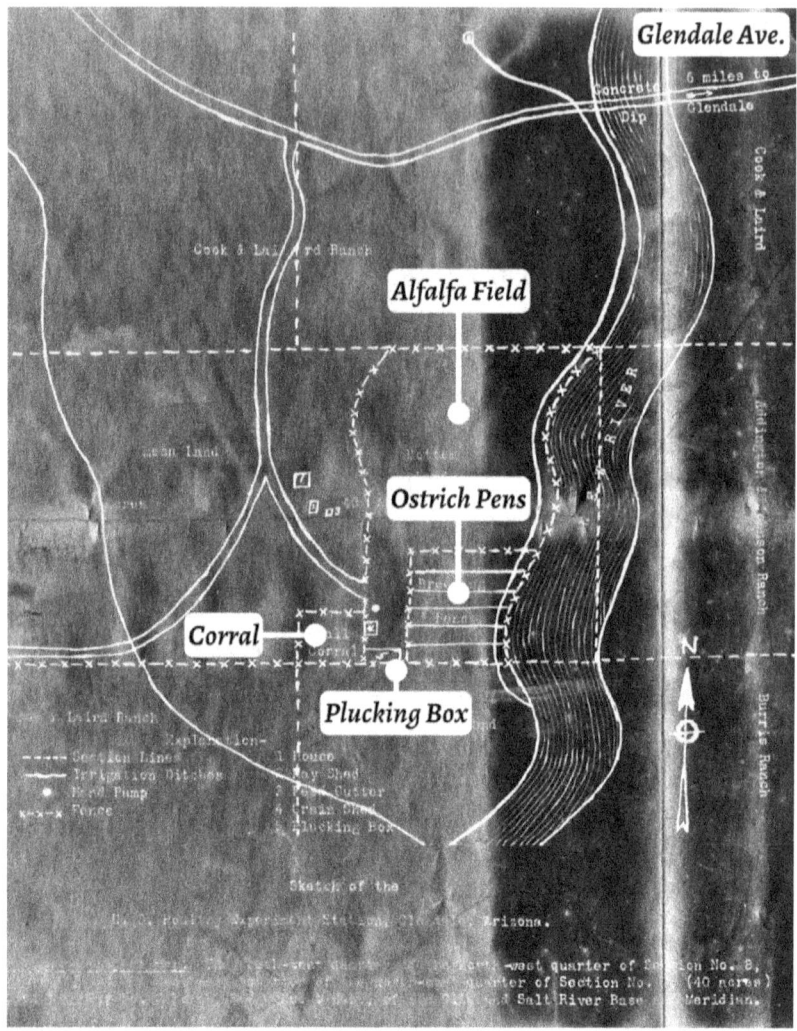

"U.S. Poultry Experimental Station," Drawing by H. C. Cross (May 1919), labeled by author.

Arizona's monsoons repeatedly devastated the research station's property and residents. Whenever New River's water level rose, the crossing (Glendale Ave.) would become too dangerous to use. This (and subsequent road repair time) prevented vendors, government officials, and locals from accessing the property. In August 1918, the river flooded and washed away a portion of the fencing behind the ostrich pens. Cross sent an account of damages to Harry Lamon:

> "Mr. Reynolds [a live-in site foreman] states that only his prompt action prevented the birds from getting away and running wild, he having gone out and by working hard and fast got the posts temporarily placed… The water was up to the top of the wooden feeding troughs, the engine under water, about a ton and a half of hay rendered useless and water two feet high in the plucking box."[494]

In November 1919, another flood occurred. The surge washed away a portion of the bank, along with one ostrich rooster and four newly built chicken coops (called colony houses). Two colony houses banked about a quarter-mile downriver. The other two floated even farther, being found six miles downriver at the Litchfield crossing of the Agua Fria River. Those were rescued from the river and used by locals as a shed and for spare lumber. Asst. U.S. Attorney John H. Langston issued those residents demand letters, citing Penal Code violations and instructions for returning stolen goods.[495] The rooster was never found and presumed drowned.

In 1919, Cross's ostriches struggled with infertility issues and some flat-out refused to breed. Bacterial infestations inside eggs suggested hygiene problems in the hens' nether regions. Rather than figuring out how to overcome that challenge, Cross (then assisted by Dan Green) held a public auction. He needed to get 19 birds off the farm that may have been carrying cooties and were otherwise useless for breeding. "No one came to the auction sale," he wrote in the station log, "so the birds were put back in the small corral and I came to Phoenix and interested Armour & Company in butchering them and selling the meat on the Pacific Coast."[496]

Armour & Co. could not find a meat buyer. They suggested Cross look for some place that might want the birds to be taxidermied for displays.[497]

Cross kept trying to pawn the birds off. Mr. Reynolds bought one for $1. Harry Hurley at the Phoenix Packing Plant wouldn't take any, not even to feed his hogs. R. P. Davie in Phoenix took one look at the ostriches before snubbing them, too. Finally, Fred Kendrick of Fairhope Farm in Glendale accepted balance of 18 ostriches for $20.[498] Kendrick fed the ostriches to his 5,000 chickens.

Morbid Farm Math

An average adult chicken eats 4oz. of feed daily (5,000 chickens: 20,000oz.). Eighteen adult ostriches might provide up to 28,800oz. of meat, offal & bone.

Enough Was Enough

As time went on, ranchers and poultry raisers complained that the station, though no longer in Tucson, was still too inconvenient. Visitors tried to come daily to get information to help them give their flocks the best care.[499] Every time someone needed to consult with the government agent, they had to travel outside of city limits and hope, with fingers crossed, that neither the bridge was flooded, nor road washed out.

Luce, a New Yorker who replaced Cross as stationmaster on July 21, 1920,[500] compiled a "History of the Poultry Experiment Station" the following year that explains the phasing out of ostriches. He wrote: "Conditions became such that it was not advisable to carry on the research and experimental work with ostriches further..."[501] In fact, the stats were so poor that federal appropriations dropped the word "ostrich" from the verbiage. To convince the USDA to remain invested, Arizonans needed to pivot to something more sustainable: chickens and turkey. Harry D. Bonsall Sr. of Southwest Flour & Feed is credited with pitching the idea to the government and convincing them of the value of pivoting towards a poultry-only operation. The *California Poultry Journal* elaborated on the shift to chicken and turkey: "the poultry industry in the Valley had reached large proportions,

and the ostrich business being practically lifeless..."[502] Harry Lamon was optimistic that the experimental farm could remain financially feasible with poultry and approved the change.[503]

Nat E. Luce (1864-1924) from the *California Poultry Journal*, 1920. His obituary in the San Bernardino Sun read: "Mr. Luce was an incurable poultry enthusiast..."[504]

On August 17, 1920, Luce logged: "Now making Glendale headquarters for the U.S. Poultry Experiment Farm."[505] He still had 14 ostriches and 15 chicks to take care of, though no further tests would be conducted. If any future issue arose with an ostrich, he teased about the veterinary care they might receive. Cross quoted him saying that the only treatment the USDA would provide, "could be found in one corner of the food house" (where a sharp axe sat).[506]

Because of the demand to be more metropolitan, Arizona residents began a search for a suitable property more central to their work. A petition for Glendale to remain the site of the operation circulated around town. It read: "Petaluma and Venice, California want this station. Phoenix and Mesa want it. Glendale *must* have it."[507] Phoenix Chamber of Commerce rallied for the government to choose Christy Park, diagonally

Chamber news from
Arizona Republican,
Oct. 7, 1920, 9.

Harry Welch. secretary of the chamber of commerce, asked that the commission donate or lease to the United
States government about 10 acres of
Christy Park, to be used for the purpose of establishing a permanent poultry experimental station in the valley.
The matter was taken under
advisement. .

across from the State Fairgrounds at 19ᵗʰ Avenue and
McDowell Road. When competition increased, M.E. Bemis, a
representative for Southwest Poultry and Swine Breeders and
the Assistant Secretary of the Chamber asked Mayor Willis H.
Plunkett to flat-out donate the land.[508] It was a big ask, and
one that Glendale District couldn't beat, if awarded.

To show their commitment to the bid, in December 1920,
Glendale residents pledged $2,757 towards the purchase of a
property within their city limits.[509] William Cook pledged the
highest amount, at $500. Bonsall Sr. pledged $200. The petition with individual pledges read:

> "We, the undersigned residents of the Glendale District
> hereby subscribe the amounts opposite our respective
> names for the purposes of purchasing ten acres of
> ground in the Glendale District to be deeded to the
> United States Department of Agriculture for the estab-
> lishment of a Poultry Experimental Station thereon. ... to
> serve the entire Southwest."[510]

State Representative O. D. Betts (also a member of Glendale's town council) petitioned the state for an additional
$1,500 contribution,[511] but the motion was repeatedly vetoed.
Governor Thomas Campbell reasoned that an existing location
had already been built (so, keep using it) and that the Univer-

sity of Arizona was already conducting chicken-related research.[512] The city would have to move forward on the generosity of its own people.

Rep. O.D. Betts' first name was "Ova," which is Latin for "Egg."
I'm not even yolking.

Poultry Journal reported: "The businessmen of Glendale, realizing the value of the station, determined to provide a tract on which the work could be carried on, and still make it pleasant for anyone desiring to visit the farm."[513] Bonsall and Cook offered more support. Cook promised to furnish teams and labor to move all the equipment to the new station.[514] Bonsall personally negotiated with landowners for reasonable pricing and acreage.

Luce recorded on May 18, 1921: "After a thorough inspection of different sites [,] it was unanimous that the site offered at the corner of Ave 18 (called Central in City limits) and Ave. L, situated on the northeast corner of the streets named was the choice."[515] More familiarly, the site chosen was on the northeast corner of 59th Avenue and Bethany Home Road. Ten acres were secured by Bonsall from the Woodford neighborhood addition, "about a mile south of the heart of the city," the *Arizona Republican* announced.[516] The central location, "will enable farmers to visit it without a waste of time."[517]

Even though it was designated exclusively for poultry, a "good-sized flock of ostriches" would remain part of the collection through 1922. Luce claimed the 29 ostriches that transferred to the new location "comprise the finest bunch of ostriches in America."[518] Bemis agreed Glendale held "the finest stock of South African and Nubian birds in America."[519]

U.S. Experimental Poultry Station
(Glendale, AZ 1921-on)

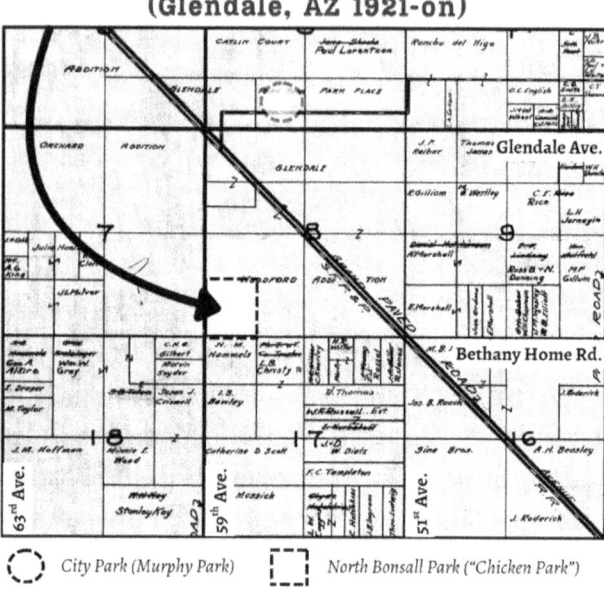

⭕ City Park (Murphy Park)　　⬜ North Bonsall Park ("Chicken Park")

Township map (2N 2E), 1923, labeled by author (History and Archives Division/Arizona State Library/Fair Use).

"While this is not the main work at the Station," Luce continued in his station record, "we are still working with the ostriches on breeding for better feather production and more sure methods of raising the young."[520]

Happy Chicken Day!

The new farmland was dedicated by Glendale residents on Friday, May 20, 1921, with a festival unlike any the city had ever seen. Newspapers invited everyone to come celebrate the breaking of ground and presentation of the deed from Secretary of State Ernest Hall to George M. Rommel, Chief of the Animal Husbandry Division. Residents planned for 5,000 attendees and saw closer to 6,000, which was (at that time),

MONSTER CELEBRATION MAY 20
Good Eats GLENDALE'S CHICKEN DAY Good Music

Headline from a full-page ad in the *Arizona Republican*, May 18, 1921, 3.

"the largest crowd in the history of Glendale."[521] A parade launched the day's festivities, followed by speeches and musical performances. At noon, 5,000 chicken sandwiches were served with either lemonade or water.

After the dedication, it took several months to construct appropriate fencing around the new acquisition and move all the equipment in. The chickens and ostriches arrived incrementally. Luce's first day working at the "New Station Grounds" was on October 10, 1921.[522]

Bye-Bye, Birdies!

Ranch records show there were only two pens for the Downtown Glendale ostriches. Luce reported, "all the ostriches young and old are in a good[,] healthy condition."[523] Considering they were no longer assets, Luce sold the remaining ostriches as quickly as he could. He shipped 12 to the National Zoological Park in Washington, D.C. as a donation. One pair was sold to the Sells-Floto Circus. Another pair went to W. A. Lane in Glendale. A third pair went to Judge L.L. Pearson in South Phoenix. The other 11 (mostly chicks) went unaccounted for. As of May 27, 1922, no ostriches remained.[524]

A year later, Luce suffered a "complete nervous breakdown,"[525] and he struggled to leave his house to complete any work. In 1924, he moved into the Loma Linda Sanatorium where he passed away in June at the age of 59 or 60. For the next three years, his under-foreman L. J. Pettigo managed the basic care of the flocks. The workload was too much for one person and testing went neglected. In 1927, Burt Heywang from Pennsylvania took charge and ran the station until his passing in 1964.

In 1931, as President of Glendale's Chamber of Commerce, Harry Bonsall helped extend the station's footprint by another 10-acres. Over the years, the site was renamed (or nicknamed) the Glendale Government Poultry Farm and the Southwest Poultry Experiment Station. After receiving several shipments of poultry from Beltsville, Glendale became host to the largest experimental poultry station in the world.[526] In 1868, the USDA conveyed the land back to the City of Glendale. The properties were honorarily renamed North and South Bonsall Park(s). For old timers, however, the area has been and always will be called "Chicken Park."

Harry Bonsall Sr. featured in the *Arizona Republican* March 16, 1925 (Fair Use).

23. "Ostrich Boys" & Their Cranky Charges

"[An ostrich] kicks like a mule,
but perhaps I would be nearer right to say like TWO mules!"
–James A. Geissinger (1909)[527]

Even though it may seem like anyone and their nephew was getting into ostrich raising in 1914, not everyone was cut out to handle the backyard behemoth. The ostrich had, as historian Budge Ruffner put it, "some personal habits which presented problems to the handlers."[528] For a sensible owner, employing a thick-skinned fellow with such confidence that toed the line between genius and stupidity may have been the way to go. If lucky, the job of an ostrich boy went to a mettle-tested farmhand or cattle wrangler. If desperate, the new guy might have signed on for a thrill. As long as the wrangler was willing to respect the wildness of their charges and learn on the go, they might stand a chance of surviving a one kick coma or the toenail of terror.

One Kick Killers

The force with which an ostrich can kick ranges from 500 to 2,000 pounds per square inch, or in other words, it'll knock you back and then some. That's enough blunt force impact that even if their razor-sharp claw fails to latch, human bones will break and lungs can explode. Though ostriches warn their harassers to back off with a hiss, tilted wing posture and a bit of fancy footwork, kicking is their primary form of attack and a wrangler better always keep an eye out for it.[529]An 1899 news article from the *Arizona Graphic* warned prospective ranchers from the start: "She does not flee from the human pursuer, but meets him half way, and if he is not as clever as [the boxer] Kid McCoy[,] she gives him a solar-plexus searcher straight from the shoulder."[530]

Up-close encounters with the hot tempers of Arizonan birds have been told from the very infancy of this industry. An 1895 issue of *Poultry Monthly* featured the original Abraham of Arizona's ostrich population back in Josiah Harbert's patch of green. "A man who was attacked by an enraged bird on Harbert's ranch, only saved his life by throwing himself prone on the ground."[531] While this maneuver may have saved the man's life that day, it did nothing to preserve his pride. Once down, "the ostrich got some satisfaction out of his victim by jumping on him."[532]

Four years later, William Pickrell got a taste of the *Oom Paul* special. The *Graphic* printed: "It was not long ago that [*Oom Paul*] engaged Mr. Pickrell, president of the Arizona Ostrich company, in an impromptu 'scrap,' and while Mr. Pickrell is a husky old bird himself and was armed with a wooden pitchfork, old '*Oom Paul*' hit him one welt and knocked him out for several days."[533]

An Ostrich Hunt Gone Awry

Long before Pickrell's near-death experience, a story was told of a couple of ambitious Arizonans who'd gone sport hunting in South Africa and learned a lesson for life when they thought they could outsmart what they judged would be "the most idiotic game in the world."[534] What they got was a pissed off Penemue, the mythological

Who's Penemue?

The Pe·ne·mue fallen angel (demon) posed as a teacher and scribe. He convinced people to put their thoughts on paper to obtain power. However, not all thoughts were wise to write. Penemue counted on mass communication sowing corruption.

creature considered by Ancient Greeks to be the Curer of Man's Stupidity.

An 1882 issue of the *Pinal Drill* shared the story of Captain James Fewsmith and Thomas Harrod, who had gone to South Africa for sport hunting.[535] The story first describes the bird as an exciting adversary to challenge even the most experienced hunter: "The ostrich's sight and hearing are wonderfully keen, and he can run at the rate of a mile in two minutes for a long time, but, with every advantage on his side, his own stupidity proves his destruction."[536]

Historic tactics that indigenous South African hunters used for this venture included dressing up in an ostrich costume, trying to get as close as possible, then using a bow and arrow to silently take the closest one out. A grim drawback of this strategy is that the costumed character unfortunately drew the attention of hungry lions to themselves. For many North African hunters, persistence was their preferred strategy. Fewsmith and Harrod reported: "In North Africa, the game is pursued on horseback, the chase being kept up for several days, until the bird is literally run down and incapable of going further or making resistance."[537]

The travelers explained that another method of capture was to cause the birds to run into a body of water. While modern research has proven that ostriches can swim, they are terrible at it. At best, they might attempt a dash through a shallow river or splash in a pond like the sparrow and dove do in a Victorian bird bath. While ostriches swam, their kickers were busy, thus eliminating one threat. Once bogged down, their hunters simply bonked the bird on the head. Other methods of old included chasing ostriches into a hidden pitfall or a readied snare trap.[538]

Well, the American boys opted to prize hunt their own way: mounted on horseback with rifles. After Fewsmith nailed an ostrich in a single shot from his saddle, he hopped down with a knife to finish the downed animal. Harrod aimed to copy his friend's instant success. He took his shot, but the intended target did not respond as politely as Fewsmith's prey. In fact, "the bird seemed to brighten up."[539]

Surely the animal would fall at any moment, Harrod believed, but it would not be so. The eager hunter joined his fellow on the ground and, bearing his own blade, he squared off with his goliath opponent. So the story goes, "Before the gentleman suspected his intention[,] the ostrich] delivered a terrible kick which tumbled the hunter over on his back as if struck by a falling tree."[540]

"Mr. Harrod fell so quickly that Captain Fewsmith ran forward in alarm. Assisting him to his feet, he was found to be a little injured, although, he declared, with a grim smile, that he [now] knew more about ostriches than he ever did before." [541] When that high-stepping bird vanished into the savanna at a prideful trot, both hunters were glad for it.

Surviving an Ostrich Attack

Those Arizona dudes specifically went looking to pick a fight with a totem of tragedy, and though they thought they were well-armed, suffered for it. But what should someone do if ever spontaneously entered in a danger duel with an ostrich? It helps to have some type of stick, broom or shepherd's crook to keep the bird at distance. If weaponless, or already in combat mode, a swift sidestep and do-si-do can help you evade the frontal assaults. If out front, one might raise their hand into the air to keep the bird's attention away from perfecting the aim of their strike.

Some success has been seen by survivors flattening themselves down on the ground with head and face covered

Ostriches fighting (Alamy Stock Image [G0FF4W], Licensed Use).

(in case the predator pounces a bit, like at Harbert's). Survivors might get stepped on or pecked at with a dumbo duckbill, but an ostrich's most devastating blows become harder to land at that angle. Once down, victims should stay down until the bird loses interest. Then, they can get up and make a run for it... straight through the pearly gates, because following *any* bird wrestling tips from a historical writer is bound to be a terrible mistake.

How Wranglers Managed the Violence

An ostriches' advantageous weight and height, "coupled with the ability to kick ... with the power of a battering ram," made death a known hazard for those working with them, summed *Arizona Highways* writer Blanche Murray.[542] Wranglers were wise to withhold trust during every bird encounter and to enter an enclosure only if armed with a long, crooked staff. Murray found, "If the bird started to attack, his long neck was caught in the crook and pulled low. In that position, he was helpless to strike," and could be subdued or redirected.[543]

One tale from Dr. Chandler's Mesa ostrich ranch made bird kicks sound predictable enough that avoidance was rather easy for those with a trained eye. "Whenever an ostrich gets to kicking," the reported claimed, "there is never anyone around close who assumes the awful responsibility of trying to stop it."[544]

Watson Pickrell advised ranchers to never go near an ostrich over a year old without some type of bayonet in hand.[545] It could be almost any variety, such as a rake or broom, a shepherd's crook, a club, or a tree branch with some leaves or thorns at the end. The goal, he said, was never to engage in a striking fight, because an injury to the bird meant an injury to one's bottom line. Instead, he suggested using the staff to firmly push the bird away as needed or frighten them enough to back down.

> Singer-Songwriter Johnny Cash once fought his pet ostrich. He ended up with five broken ribs and a song titled "(I Learned) The Hard Way."

When Ostrich Fights Break Out

The unbridled violence shown during a melee between two birds happened regularly and, though damages were expensive, wrangler interventions were flat out of the question. As explained in *Poultry Monthly,* "In their fights between themselves they are vicious[,] and often disable one another."[546]

Famous ostrich promoter T.W. Kemp described the sight for an audience in Texas, which ended up in the *El Paso Times*:

Fighting ostriches, Cawston Ostrich Farm, California (John and Jane Adams Postcard Collection, San Diego State University, # A-61519).

"To watch an ostrich fight, said Mr. Kemp, is one of the most exciting experiences in the world. The birds advance upon each other with erect heads and fluffed out plumage. Then they come within kicking distance of each other, powerful legs shoot out to the front and deliver sturdy whacks that can be heard for a distance of a quarter of a mile. The fights do not last long, however, and do not seem to settle anything. They end as suddenly as they begin, with one of the contestants taking to his heels..."[547]

When a news reporter visited Dr. Protheroe's Central Park collection, he also mentioned there being warning signs: distended mouths, flapping wings and glaring eyes. The fight might even progress to a testy "pecking match" before kicks are deployed.[548]

Legendary Lou

Some of the best ostrich ranching stories come from Louis B. Ellsworth of Mesa, Arizona who was the foreman at both the Mesa and Chandler locations for Dr. A.J. Chandler. In time, he became known as "one of the best known ranchers of the southside," and his 1935 obituary testified that "Lou Ellsworth, as everybody knew him, was one of the beloved men in all [of] Arizona."[549]

Before we get into that, I couldn't resist including Lovable Lou's backstory. His parents had originally moved to Salt Lake City, Utah from Nauvoo, Illinois in 1847 with his grandfather and then leader of the Church of Jesus Christ of Latter-Day Saints, Brigham Young. Since his father Edmund had made the journey before, he was considered a fitting leader for the original Mormon handcart company from Iowa in 1856. In fact, church historical records claim it was his idea to engineer the handcarts as an inexpensive form of transportation to make the journey easier on families.[550]

Edmund Ellsworth, a polygamist, moved his family (with two of his four wives) to the Show Low, Arizona area in late 1880. He was arrested in '84 for unlawful cohabitation and spent two months in the Yuma Territorial Prison for that.[551] By 1898, 33-year-old Louis (also "Lew" or "Lou") and a few of his brothers moved to the town of Lehi, later annexed by Mesa. William, his older brother, became the town marshal, while Ernest, his younger brother, was a cattleman and farmer. Like Lou, Ernest eventually dabbled in feather farming, but William stuck to upholding the law and tending one of Mesa's largest orange groves. In fact, for William's fiftieth birthday, following cake and ice cream was a trip to an ostrich ranch to see Lou "get chased by the ostriches," while Ernest cracked jokes.[552]

Like Kemp, Lou Ellsworth had a certain knack for working with ostriches... and people. For Lou, being an ostrich handler was one part cowboy, one part rodeo rider, and another part crowd pleaser. A 1912 write-up on Lou said, "the ostriches on the farm look upon Mr. Ellsworth as their father by adoption: they obey his orders and have as much affection for him as an ostrich is capable of expressing. He goes among

them fearlessly, plucks their plumes and herds them in the various pastures in which they feed. They recognize him as their master and seldom make any objection to anything he may do."[553]

Louis "Lou" Ellsworth (1865-1925), from Ancestry.com contributor louisemily. Original source is undetermined.

In 1907, Dr. Chandler invited the Chamber of Commerce to his Mesa ranch for a private benefit, complete with a picnic buffet, theatrical performances, and popular music blasting on an old Victor Talking Machine.[554] During the afternoon, Dr. Chandler escorted his guests to the ostrich enclosure to see the birds grazing on alfalfa. The *Republican* detailed, "Lew Ellsworth added to the interest of the occasion, by gathering the eggs from the nests."[555]

It's probable that Lou made a show of his army crawl through the bone-legged forest, holding onto a stick that he'd have to ever-so-carefully *tap, tap, tap* to roll a few eggs away from the hens without detection. Perhaps he rolled one egg in the opposite direction of his collection sack or basket. Then, when an ostrich saw the misplaced item and bent its head to push the egg back, Lou clowned it up with an exaggerated disappointment that he'd failed the task. And maybe, when he finally presented the bounty from this perilous endeavor, the crowds cheered and applauded. Or maybe not. I probably made most of that up.

Lou and the Boy Intruder

Of all the stories in the Ellsworth collection, there couldn't be any better than the one about him and the ranch intruder. The *Arizona Republican* titled the 1912 story, "Hunting for Trouble." It went a bit like this...

A young man once visited Chandler's Mesa ranch looking for trouble. As many boys of a certain age who crave a similar hunt, this kid anticipated regaling his pals with the exciting details of his quest: to "do battle with an ostrich."[556] Now, one would think that by this time, enough stories had circulated about the dangers of being near an angry bird that this young man should have known about the life-ending or *near*-life-ending options reserved for those who could not escape.

So, good ol' Ellsworth noticed that this boy standing up against a fence, gesturing and shouting out to incite a ratite reproach. That boy had no notion that he had chosen the most troublesome opponent, "one of the big fellows, whose temper is not the best at any time."[557]

"Kid, what do you think you are doing?" the foreman asked.

With an ever so plucky response, he shared, "Watch me. I'm gonna have a battle with a full-grown ostrich."

"Are you now?" Mr. Ellsworth looked the boy over to check if he might truly have made serious plans to kill the expensive bird. He had no weapons on him. Not even a slingshot and a stone. "And why's that?"

Ostrich Farm on Chandler Ranch, Courtesy of the Price-Propstra Family 2011 (Chandler Museum Collection [2011.7.2b], Chandler, AZ, licensed use).

"You see, Mister, I've never been afraid of nothin.' No man or beast, and certainly not any *farm* animal. But my friends said these were the scariest birds they've ever seen. And now, I want to conquer one."

It was a somewhat logical plan, Ellsworth admitted. Mothers always told their boys they'd need to face their fears one day. Still, he had a feeling that this kid's tough talk was only for show. "Well, you can't go in unarmed, like that. Wouldn't be a fair fight."

The boy cocked his head and looked at him sideways through slitted eyelids. "Hmm… I suppose that's right." With that, he skipped off, canvassed the area, then returned with a stick about three feet long.

The kid's audacity impressed Ellsworth. Thinking that it was still only a bluff, he opened the gate and let the boy into the pen with his intended. When the boy encroached, the ostrich responded by lifting its wings at an acute angle. With

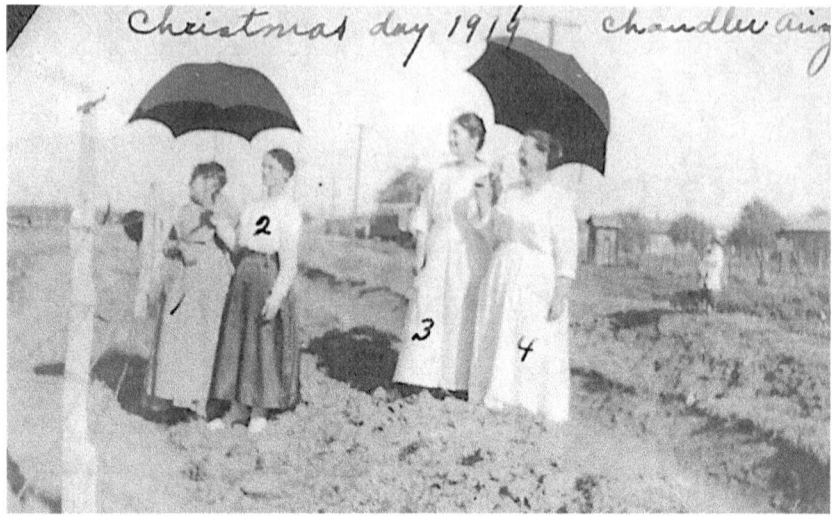

Women observing ostriches in Chandler, on Christmas Day, ca. 1919. Courtesy of James Sossaman (Chandler Museum Collection [08-1-227], Chandler, AZ, licensed use).

feathers twitching, the bird hissed and bobbed his head. Its eyes appeared to glow red.

That kid watched with intensity as the bird lifted its clawed toes in an alternating rhythm. This was, as Ellsworth knew, the mesmerizing ballet of impending doom. The boy must have been dull-headed because he didn't even flinch at the declaration of disaster about to strike him faster than a speeding train. Realizing there was no bluff to be called, Ellsworth ran in between the bird and its prey, grabbing the boy by the armpits and heaving him into a sprint back towards the gate.

"Hey! Let me go! I was gonna get 'em!" The scrawny boy flayed and twisted out of Ellsworth's hold once outside the pen.

Ostrich rancher at work, possibly from Thomas Behan's farm in Queensland, Australia (Public Domain). This farm was in operation from 1907 to at least 1913.

This kid didn't sense the bloody drubbing he was about to receive, Ellsworth thought. "Now that's enough of that," he told the boy. "Go back and tell your friends you were kicked out for trying. And don't you even think about coming back!"

That day Ellsworth learned not to second-guess any visitor's intentions. But what did the boy learn? The news reporter concluded:

"It seems almost too bad that Mr. Ellsworth did not allow the ostrich to give the youngster just one kick; the lesson might become useful to him in the after life."[558]

(By the way, there is another exciting account of Louis Ellsworth saving another ranch hand from peril in the chapter about Murder Birds.)

What's it Really Like Being an "Ostrich Boy?"

Arthur Chapman, an old cowboy poet, once wrote a few licks about the woes of a new hire on an Arizona ostrich farm. These lines are from his 1917 collection, *Out Where the West Begins (And Other Western Verses)*. I'd like to share that poem with you now... on one condition: that you read it out loud.

"The Ostrich-Punching of Arroyo Al"
Arthur Chapman (1873-1935)

I was broke in Arizony, and was gloomy as a tomb
When I got a chance at punchin' for an outfit called Star-Plume;
I did n't ask no wherefores, but jest lit out with my tarp,
As happy as an angel with the newest make o' harp.

When I struck out from the bunkhouse, for my first day on the range,
I thought the tracks we follered was peculiar like and strange,
And when I asked about it, the roundup foreman sez:
'You ain't a-punchin' cattle, but are herdin' ostriches.'

Well, we chased a bunch of critters on the hot and sandy plain,
Though 't was like a purp a-racin' with a U. S. A. mail train;
But at last we got 'em herded in a wire fence corral,
And the foreman sez, off-hand like: 'Jest go in and rope one, Al.'

Well, the first one that I tackled was an Eiffel Tower bird,
But that noose ain't pinched his thorax 'fore several things occurred:
He spread his millinery jest as if he meant to fly,
And then he reached a stilt out, careless, and smote me above the eye.

They pulled me out from under that millin' mass o' legs,
And they fed me on hot whiskey and the yolks of ostrich eggs;
And as soon as I was able, I pulled freight for Cattle Land,
And the ostrich-punchin' business never gits my O. K. brand.

Jonathan and Helen Seargeant, ca. 1910s, as shown in *House By The Buckeye Road* (1960). Ms. Seargeant was raised on a coffee plantation in Chiapas, Mexico for seventeen years (1888-1905) before returning to Arizona to become a stenographer.

While that's cute fiction, there are plenty of stories out there from folks who've been there, done that. A wealth of observations came from Helen Humphreys Seargeant, daughter of an Arizona Territory pioneer who, with her husband Jonathan, operated a cattle ranch near the Pan-American. The Seargeants' home was near the largest lot of ostriches on Buckeye Road (formerly Maricopa Road). From upstairs, Helen Seargeant could watch the going-on's. Seargeant wrote her memories of various farm activities in a 1960 memoir, *House by the Buckeye Road.* The time of her observations ranged from 1913 on.

Lisa Hegarty at the Litchfield Heritage Center wrote that "from the balcony of the ranch house [Helen] could overlook

Sergeant Ranch

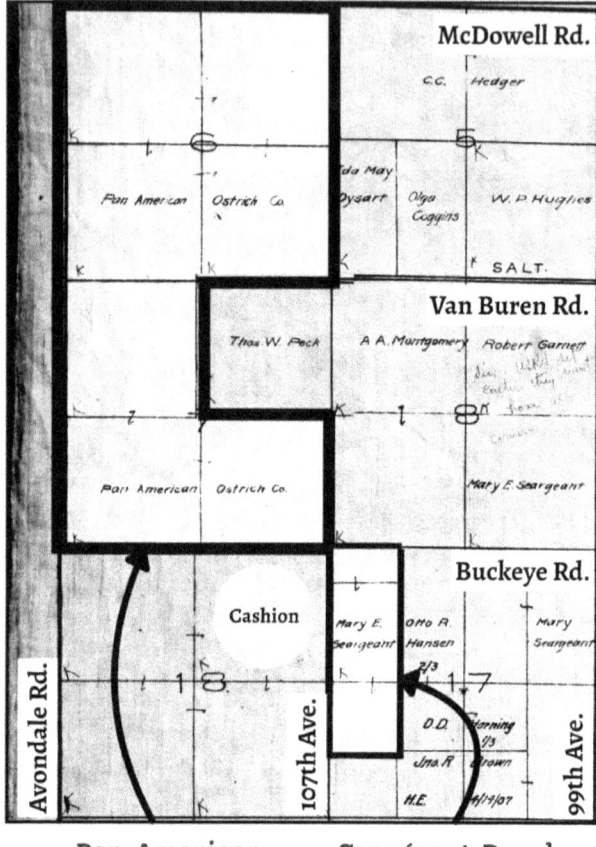

John and Helen Seargeant's property neighboring the Pan-American Ostrich Ranch. Township map (1N 1E), 1911, labeled by author (History and Archives Division/Arizona State Library. Licensed Use.)

the work and watch the cowboys (ostrich boys) on ponies[,] herding and moving ostriches from one field to another, and storing and separating some for different fields.'"[559] Watson Pickrell explained the logistics of herding as rather simple, but extremely thoughtful: "Ostriches are easily moved from one field to another by one person going ahead, calling them, and

"Herding the Ostriches" in the 1880s at the Pan-American Ranch (Arizona Historical Society Library, licensed use).

tolling [enticing] them on with grains, while another follows on a horse. The birds are very timid and do not like to be driven unless someone goes ahead of them."[560] As you'll learn in the Ostrich Drive chapter, this last detail was much more critical than folks realized and when ignored, invited calamity.

The day-to-day of an ostrich boy's job could be mundane enough to elicit trouble from within, such as hazing the new hires by placing bets on whether they could eat an entire ostrich egg or not, or by practicing the best mount and dismount strategies for riding one of the adult birds. "Doubtless," claimed Dr. Duncan about future endeavors, "we expect to hear that the cow-boys utilize ostriches in herding cattle."[561]

Some stories from ranchers are quite endearing. One such came from Karen Weston Gonzales, who worked on an ostrich farm in Arizona back in the 1990s. She told the *Tucson Weekly*: "To watch baby ostriches dance is beautiful. I will never forget, once, when I had the radio on loud and 100 or so chicks all started dancing to the music at once. They shifted their bodies from side to side, wobbled their necks to follow their body motion and started spinning around with their wings held in the air."[562] She concluded that they'd spun themselves until they were dizzy.

Ostrich ranchers are also privy to strange knowledge that only someone who handles a live ostrich or butchers it for meat would know. For example, did you know that ostriches have three sharp, hooked claws at the end of their wings? Real visuals are gross, but if you'd like to skip the internet search, just imagine their distant cousin, the velociraptor, hiding its slap scratchers in an oversized down mitten.

An ostrich's claws are remnants
from their theropod ancestors.

This clade included the Tyrannosaurs Rex.

One of the strangest, yet most memorable events Lou Ellsworth observed was the hatching of conjoined ostrich twins. The story, "A Freak Ostrich," appeared in the *Arizona Republican* on June 30, 1909. It read: "The incubator in which the ostrich eggs are hatched produced a bird with four legs, three wings, two necks and one head. When the chick first came out of the shell it seemed as active as any ... but in a short time it began showing signs of drowsiness..."[563] The twin birds' overtaxed body could not sustain life more than 30-minutes and Ellsworth disposed of the remains.

If the twins had been preserved, they surely would have traveled the world as a glass jar specimen in some kind of circus. Though Ellsworth described his discovery in quite clear terms, I figured I would hand them over to an image generator to see what it might imagine. The results were grotesque and absurd. Try not to look (on the next page).

The "Freak Ostrich"

Disclaimer: This bird is not real. This illustration was created with the assistance of generative programming and generous author manipulation.

24. The Great Arizona Ostrich Drive

This was "...the first time in the history of the valley that ostriches have been herded from one point to another..."
- Chandler Arizonan (1914)[564]

In 1914, the Pan-American Ostrich Company was getting out of the ostrich business. Contributing factors for this were overall feather sales entering a slump, new entrants willing to buy out their livestock, and the enticement of Egyptian Cotton projecting high profitability (which would replace the bird-filled acreage). The mega-ranch had also taken a few financial hits that made Phoenix National Bank's ongoing investment unfavorable.

One loss occurred back around 1909 when then president of the company, Katie Pearson, "transferred the birds and property to [her husband's] predecessors," which as *The Daily Arizona Silver Belt* detailed, ruffled more than a few feathers.[565] Both of her children sued the owners, claiming the transfer (not sale) was of an "irregular," sort, that the land and ostriches (and profits gained since Aylma Pearson's death) were community property and the family was entitled to some sort of payout.[566]

Aylma Jr. and his sister demanded a cut of $250,000 ($8.8 million in 2025). The bank settled this case out of court in 1910 for 20% of that request, to be paid in a combination of cash and ostriches.[567] With the settlement, Aylma Jr. paid for his Harvard law degree, and sister Kate became a nun. The strain of litigation was so difficult on the bank president, E. B.

Gage, that it was cited as one of the reasons he left Arizona behind (that, and his mining company failed, and he was suffering from stomach cancer).[568]

In 1912, another disruption was the installment of railroad tracks extending the Arizona Eastern Railway from Phoenix out to Buckeye and beyond. While the route skirted the largest and westernmost ranch property, it passed immediately through the eastern plot, possibly requiring an earlier sale (or abandonment) of that land. After Gage's death in 1913, Roger W. Warren, a New York investor, managed the estate. Because of these recent hits to the bottom line, the industry slump may have felt a bit more painful to the bank than to others. With Gage's passing in 1913, Warren began the dissolution of the Pan-American Ostrich Company.[569]

Blanche K. Murray found that their final raw feather sale netted $101,000, bringing in a profit of $64,000 (just over $2 million in today's terms).[570] As printed in the *Arizona Republican*, by the end of the year, they'd sold off 860 birds to new feather farmers in the Salt River Valley, and to the University of Arizona, at bargain basement rates. Warren contracted with residents in California and the Yuma Valley for large batch purchases. An ad he placed in the *Republican* on November 22 claimed, "The European war had made the feather market temporarily dull[,] but it will come back with a rush. ... You will regret it if you do not act quickly."[571]

One of Pan-American's most interested buyers was Dr. A.J. Chandler. In early November, he had made a purchase of two hundred "mighty fine specimens" from the Belgo-American Ostrich Company, which were, according to the *Chandler Arizonan*, "installed on a 140-acre tract just on the west edge of town."[572] This purchase coincided with the promotion of a new golf course that also extended out past the west end of the San Marcos Hotel. This decision may have

Ad for the closeout sale, *Arizona Republican*, October 30, 1914.

been part of George Peabody's vision. Rather than add more ostriches to the Mesa ranch, they were sent to Chandler to intensify traffic to the new emerald sea.

The November 12 press announcement in the *Arizonan* read: "Work on building the [pens] has been going on for several days, and it will require about 240 rods of fencing wire to keep the birds inside... The introduction of the birds to Chandler will prove a novelty to many and will be a splendid attraction for tourists."[573] Two pens containing the largest collection of ostriches in the East Valley were set up to the west of the hotel and were easily within sight of guests.[574] (See map in the Ostrich Hunting chapter.)

Dr. Chandler purchased 300 ostriches from Pan-American, to be delivered in two shipments: 200, then 100. The addition of these birds would bring the veterinarian's total both in Chandler and Mesa (which had multiplied rapidly) to around 800 birds.[575] Newspaper headlines read: "Chandler to Have Big Ostrich Farm" and "More Ostriches for Chandler."

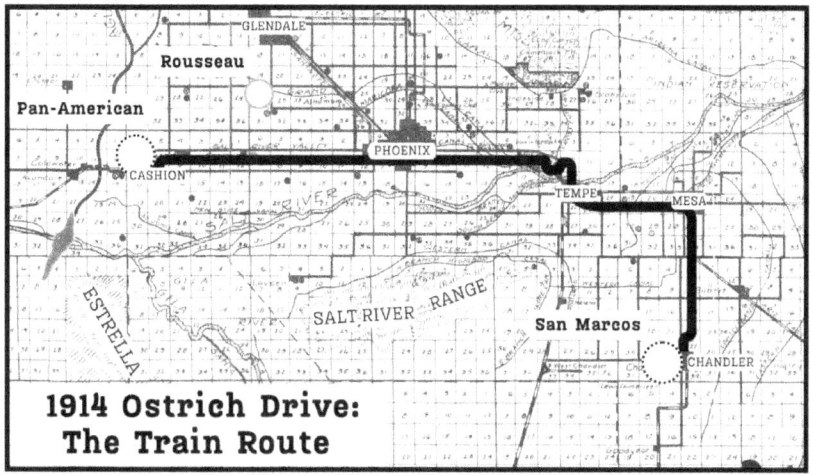

Map of Salt River Valley, Arizona, 1923 from the Dwight B. Heard Investment Company, labeled by author.

The Plan to Move 200 Birds

The standard method for transporting ostriches from Cashion (Avondale) to Chandler would have been to load them onto a railcar and send them east on the Arizona Eastern Railroad (A.E.R.R.) through Central Phoenix and Tempe, dropping down through Mesa, then heading due south, paralleling Center Street (which bends into Delaware Street). With this route, the birds could have made their grand arrival at the A.E.R.R. Depot at Commonwealth Street and Delaware then marched exactly half a mile west to the San Marcos Hotel. That trip would total 36 ½ miles on tracks, plus a half mile on toes.

In 1984, Lovell Thomas Rousseau recounted to the readers of the *Arizona Republic* what had been passed down to him about this event. His grandparents Lovell and Desdamona Rousseau were Territorial pioneers who lived about five miles away from Pan-American. He explained that instead of taking the train, "Some enterprising chap talked [Dr. Chandler] into driving them to Chandler like cattle."[576] Helen Seargeant told the same story in her memoir. She claimed Dr. Chandler "thought that if they had enough cowboys to handle them[,] they could drive his ostriches to Chandler, as they would drive a herd of cattle."[577]

There was logic but no common sense in this plan. It would delay the delivery, it would add more hourly wages and mouths to feed (including the birds), and the roadways were not at all suitable to herding livestock (especially through a major downtown area, and especially when there was the potential to interact with motor vehicles). Some literature suggests the featherheaded escorts had not even considered how they would feed the ostriches along the route. They assumed ostriches would graze on whatever greens they passed.

> To be "featherbrained" is to be foolish, or lacking
> in seriousness and maturity, as if one's head
> was stuffed with feathers.
> *"Noodlehead" is similar.*

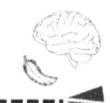

Based on the route the ostrich boys started out on, it appears their projected route would eventually follow the canal system byways, which would reduce the likelihood of encountering vehicular traffic. And it's in this detail, we might make an educated guess at who would think up the idea to march ostriches along the Grand, Maricopa, Mesa, Consolidated, and Chandler Canals. George Peabody comes to mind. As a reminder, his primary role in Dr. Chandler's company was as a promoter, and what better press could be had from a parade of this magnitude? In fact, the *Chandler Arizonan* declared it would be, "a novel sight and one worth seeing."[578]

Coming along for the journey was a professional photographer-turned-salesman. The photographer, Arthur

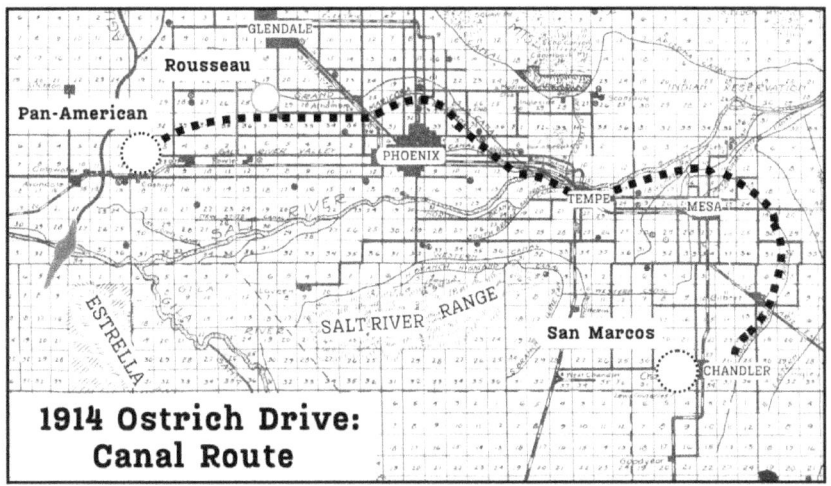

Map of Salt River Valley, Arizona, 1923 from the Dwight B. Heard Investment Company, labeled by author.

Amet, was briefly employed by the Pan-American as a ranch hand, as was his father-in-law Harry Thacker. Neither were well suited to the job (Thacker was formerly a city clerk).[579] Whether by Amet or not, both candid and staged photographs were taken during the historic transport. According to related news articles, the expected schedule for the arrival of 200 ostriches was as follows:

Thursday, November 12

Depart from Cashion. Follow major roadway for fastest and most direct access to the Maricopa Canal. Allow the birds to bed down when the sun goes down.

Friday, November 13

Continue following the canal roads around the outskirts of major cities. Arrive at the San Marcos by nightfall.

A "band of horsemen," believed to be twelve in all, was formed from Dr. Chandler's and the Pan-American's profess-ional network.[580] Among those identified were George Peabody, Louis Ellsworth (with the assistance of his brothers Ernest and Byron), Art Amet, Harry Thacker, J. C. McDonald (a hotel guest), and Webster Jay Lewis. Why Dr. Chandler allow-ed a hotel guest from Kansas City to help herd ostriches across a desert is a mystery, other than to continue having this event appear in the papers. McDonald was, according to the *Repub-lican,* "afforded an experience not often included in a ... hotel's list of 'Things to Do'."[581] In this case, I suppose the answer to the question was, *Why the heck not?*

Whatever business Webster Lewis had going along is also unclear. This 26-year-old geological engineer had moved to

> "Their arrival in Chandler... will be made the occasion for a big celebration."
> - *Bisbee Daily Review (1914)*[1]

Phoenix only a few months prior and had yet to find employ-ment. In the meantime, he'd volunteered as the Secretary of the Chandler Chamber of Commerce. He helped his father raise chickens and managed a modest citrus grove. (Lewis must have had some degree of patience for working with birds because he'd later be praised for showing off a few of his father's Wyandottes that year.)

News clipping from the *Chandler Arizonan*, Dec. 11, 1914.

W. J. LEWIS POULTRY KING OF ARIZONA

---

[1] "Roosevelt Dam is Making New Record," *Bisbee Daily Review*, November 19, 1914, 7.

Ostrich Drive, 1914, Courtesy of Janet Gross (Chandler Museum Collection [92-7-81], Chandler, AZ, licensed use).

Had This Ever Been Done Before?

Annie Martin remembered a time when her husband had tried to herd 90 ostriches across the Cape of South Africa. Citing that the birds were clumsy and delicate in a railcar (leading to losses every time), Mr. Martin opted to try herding a troop from near Cape Town to Port Elizabeth, a distance of 400 miles.[582] "[A]nd as for their behavior when travelling on foot, [my husband] has had some experience of the infinity of trouble they can give to those in charge of them," Martin wrote.[583] "One night there was a stampede; and when daylight broke over the vast plain[,] not one ostrich was in sight."[584] Over such a distance, losing track of a few birds seems within reason, but to lose all at once was a hard lesson learned.

Recovering lost or runaway birds was also a challenge for the couple. Martin recalled trying to round up one rambunctious ratite who was, ironically, considered a regular "flight risk." She wrote:

"One day [my husband] and I had the excitement of an ostrich-hunt on horseback. One of our birds ... had got away, and we had a long ride after him; [my husband] following him up by his *spoor*, or footprints... until at last we were rewarded by the sight of a small head and long snake-like neck above the distant bushes. Then came the very enjoyable but somewhat difficult work of driving our prisoner home. He would trot before us quietly enough for a while, with his curious[,] springy step, till he thought we were off our guard, when he would make an abrupt and unexpected run in the wrong direction..."

To contain that sideways sprinter, Annie and her husband employed all the skills of a "picador in a bull-fight" to prevent the ostrich from slipping away again. She remembered, "[t]he horses quite understood what they had to do, and seemed to enter into the spirit of it, and enjoy it [as much] as we did."[585] (Now imagine the "infinity of trouble" the Martins had with all 90 birds at once!)

The Fence Assist

Wanting to herd the Arizona ostriches was a very understandable effort, not only to save money, but to create all sorts of media fanfare. And the request was probably not too strange to ask the Pan-American wranglers, because they'd had the most time and practice moving birds back and forth from their detached properties with no issues. On those brief excursions, however, the ostrich boys could keep the birds somewhat cornered, following along property fence lines.

Ostrich Drive, 1914,
Courtesy of Janet
Gross (Chandler
Museum Collection
[92-7-82], Chandler,
AZ, licensed use).

Lisa Hegarty, executive director at the P.W. Litchfield
Heritage Center wrote that the ostrich ranch's neighbor, Helen
Seargeant, "had a front row seat to the action. She saw about
100 of the big birds - with cowboys to the right, cowboys to
the left, and cowboys behind them, being moved down
Buckeye Road."[586] Someone reported to the *Chandler Arizonan*
that, "The birds are willing to meander along the highways so
long as they are unmolested and are permitted to range as
they move along."[587] The plan for the overnight care of the
birds was to allow them to "roost where ever[*sic*] they may
be," with the herding team hunkering down for the night in
that very same spot, while taking turns looking out for their
charges. Without much more thought, the "cavalcade" left Pan-
American for Chandler that Thursday.[588]

Twelve proud wranglers marched their downy charges
along Buckeye Road. Following the Pan-American protocols,

Ostrich Drive, 1914, Courtesy of Janet Gross (Chandler Museum Collection [92-7-68], Chandler, AZ, licensed use).

ostriches were kept somewhat pinned to the fence line that ran for several miles along private properties. Everything seemed to work well, but it seemed no one thought this plan through past the fence line. Once cleared of the fence, wranglers would need to direct the birds towards the canal route without any assistance.

The thing about ostriches is that they can't really be steered without a physical barrier to block non-preferred paths. And, if running loose, they don't really have a reason to stop other than some sort of physical barrier, physical exhaustion or sundown. In a way, ostriches are tutors of Isaac Newton's first law of physics. "[W]hen the fences gave out," Seargeant wrote, "ostriches broke away and scattered everywhere. They couldn't get them bunched again."[589]

> "These flat-headed birds just DO NOT...
> follow the leader!"
> -Helen Seargeant, Witness to the Event (1960)

---

[m] *House by the Buckeye Road* (San Antonio: Naylor Co., 1960), 75.

At this point, records got messy. The *Bisbee Daily Review* reported that the ostrich owners acknowledged they "might be forced to face serious damage suits" regarding the event.[590] In this case, a reader might understand that any official reports from Dr. Chandler's associates were being cautiously minimized. Other news stories lean into the yellow journalism style, offering eye-caching headlines and sensational details that deliver a "wow" factor, usually at the cost of factual accuracy. Though we might never get the full story, we can certainly get down to brass tacks: the ostrich boys lost control of the ostriches, who then terrorized the state of Arizona.

25. Dr. Chandler's Birds Gone Wild

"He often runs so very fast, he leaves himself behind."
- Mary E. Wilkins Freeman, "The Ostrich" (1905)[591]

Desdamona Jones Rousseau died because of the Great (uncoordinated) Arizona Ostrich Drive. The context of her demise involves the unbelievable game of "playing chicken" with the ostriches on the loose. Before we get to that, however, allow me to better introduce you to Lovell and Desdamona Rousseau, two well-respected Arizona Territory pioneer ranchers and... my distant cousins.

Headline from the *Waukegan News-Sun*, Nov. 13, 1914, page 1.

SPECIAL

OSTRICHES IN A STAMPEDE; WOMAN MEETS HER DEATH

The Rousseaus arrived in the newly incorporated Maricopa County back in 1892, in a covered wagon. According to their grandson, they'd left Kentucky in 1884 with one toddler and one infant and crossed the Great Plains to Oregon. From there, they traveled south along the Pacific Coast to Fresno, California.[592] Taking a roundabout way to Arizona, the Rousseaus ended up in Roswell, New Mexico from 1891, staying only until August of 1892. They backtracked to Phoenix with two other families. In 1984, their grandson Lovell Thomas Rousseau shared the following anecdote with readers of the *Arizona Republic*: "My grandfather shot some quail out of a mesquite thicket at Seventh Street and Washington for their first meal in town."[593]

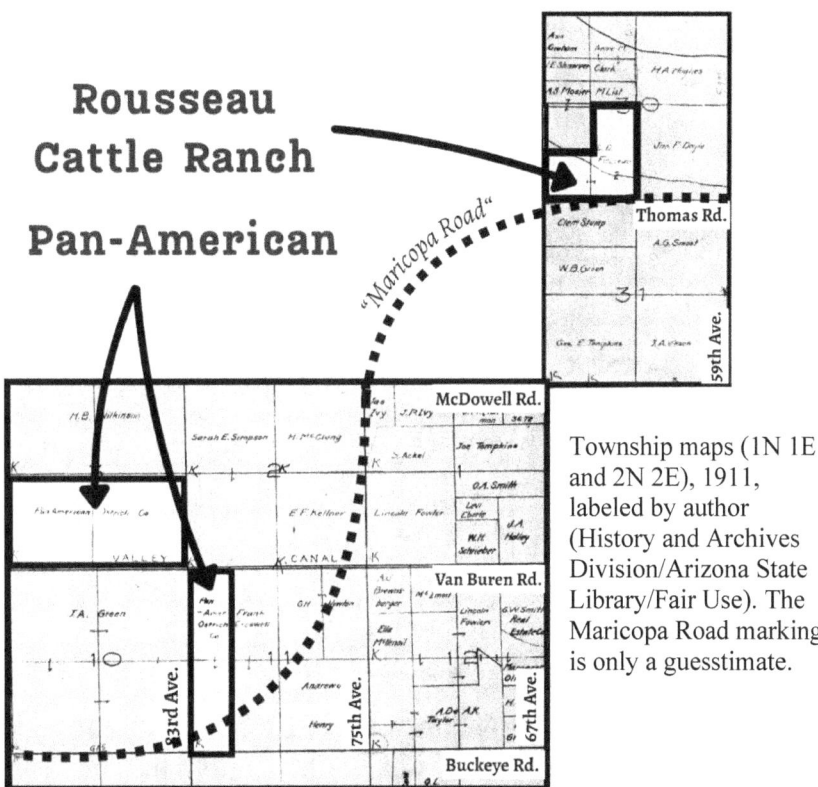

Rousseau Cattle Ranch

Pan-American

Township maps (1N 1E and 2N 2E), 1911, labeled by author (History and Archives Division/Arizona State Library/Fair Use). The Maricopa Road marking is only a guesstimate.

By 1899, the Rousseaus had built themselves a modern ranch home on 240 acres, at 67th Avenue and Thomas Road (formerly the Maricopa Road). Though not distinguished on modern maps, the "Maricopa" was a historical East-West trail that crossed the state. Instead of a gridline pattern like many roads today, the trail skirted the natural landscape of the Salt River and South Mountain, which explains why the Seargeants (on Buckeye) and Rousseaus (on Thomas) both claimed to have lived on this road. The Rousseau family became quite affluent raising cattle and were very active in community and church events in the historic Cartwright neighborhood.

After processing my initial shock over the "Murdered by Ostrich" headlines that spread across the nation, I realized that Desdamona's tragedy was more than just a sad family story: it was a *darned good story.* Now, the version I'm about to share is based on over a dozen variations that appeared in national news, as well as in the recollections of descendants and relatives. Records generally agree that it happened around 7:30p.m., approximately half-way between the Rousseau's home and the local Methodist church.

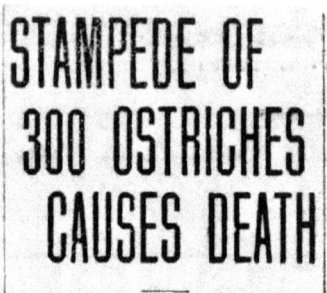

STAMPEDE OF 300 OSTRICHES CAUSES DEATH

Mrs. L. D. Rousseau, Wife of Well-Known Rancher, Instantly Killed in Runaway on Maricopa Road Last Night

Headline from the *Arizona Republican* Nov. 13, 1914, page 1.

Desdamona and the Ostrich Stampede

On the evening of November 12, 1914, Lovell Rousseau, a wealthy cattle rancher in Maricopa County, patted his son William on the shoulder and said, "Thank you for coming through for us in this pinch. We'll be home late, but don't wait up. We may be old, but we haven't lost our wits and ways yet."

His son laughed and wished Lovell and Mrs. Rousseau a good night before retiring back to the house.

A friend was getting married that Thursday night, and though Mr. and Mrs. Rousseau had planned on arriving early for the ceremony, their automobile refused to start. Fortunately, Will was available to hitch up a horse and buggy for them in short time.

"Come on, Desde. If we hurry, we'll still make it to the church before the vows." He assisted his wife Desdamona into their outmoded chariot for the evening. He watched her scrunch up her full-length dress a few inches into a gloved hand. Taking hold of her free hand, Lovell steadied her. She took the iron step up to the buggy's platform and settled herself on the far side of the padded bench.

His wife was especially dolled up for the occasion, and he very much enjoyed seeing her get ready by pinning on the new black velvet hat he'd recently gifted her. A solitary black ostrich feather swayed above her now, its finery secured with a thick satin band. It complimented her dark green dress and long strand of glossy white pearls that marked today as a special one.

"I hope Mr. Hawley will have time to come over first thing. He really understands an engine," Desdamona said. "Besides, I'd rather you drive me to the fairgrounds to collect my jar of *blue-ribbon* sweet pickles than to ask Miss Betty Mare, to keep pulling us around with her old knees." Desdamona shimmied her shoulders to emphasize how pleased she felt with her win at the 10th Annual State Fair.

"I'll ask him after his son's vows," Lovell responded. He grabbed onto the frame of the buggy and hoisted himself up to join her for the ride. The elderly couple rode east from their home. The ceremony was only a short distance down the old dirt road.

In their rush to change vehicles, Lovell had retrieved a kerosene lantern and set it on the floorboard but never paused to light it. That night, the half-full moon cast a bright glow ahead of them. They'd get to the wedding just fine, he figured. Besides, at this hour, not many people were on the road, and surely any passing vehicle would see them with their headlights.

Out in the distance, they could see the sparkle of the Ferris wheel that lifted its passengers over 260-feet into the sky for a view like no other. And fanning left and right across the horizon were two spotlights attracting everyone to come see the stunt shows, hot air balloons, musical talents, and galleries filled with the best artisan and agricultural products Arizona residents could offer. The splendid gala would continue through the weekend.

Off to their right, the dark outline of the Salt River Mountain range divided territorial settlers from the indigenous Gila River people, now living on the reservation south of the city. Running parallel to the mountain, the Salt River used to flow generously, year-round. Since the Roosevelt Dam was built and irrigation canals dug for the town of Chandler, the water levels were down, but still consistent enough to keep the local corn and cotton fields producing through regular irrigation.

"Do you remember when we first saw the Salt River?" He asked his wife.

"That was a long time ago, but of course I remember."

Lovell considered how much of the area had changed since that time. "Hardly a thing was around here back then. And now, we can zip into town in our automobile or even shop from a catalog. Just about anything from around the world can be brought in on the railroad."

"I know, Dear." Desdamona smiled at Lovell. "We've seen some things in our lifetime, haven't we? We made it through the Rebellion and now have the telephone, the electric lightbulb *and* the airplane! Can you imagine what will be next?"

They continued their casual recollections for half a mile when a cluster of tall, round figures appeared to bobble in the distance. Thin shadows streaked across the county road like dizzying zebra stripes. The shapes before them reminded Lovell of a fluffy dandelion head extending out above its neighboring grass line.

"Hold these for a minute." He passed the reins over to his wife and reached down for the lantern. Pinching the base of the lamp between his knees, he felt inside his coat pocket for the matchbook.

"What's going on over there?" Desdamona pointed towards the movement he'd already been watching.

"I don't know. Just give me a minute to get this thing lit up." In one quick strike, his match blazed. He touched it to the wick, set it alight, then tucked the folded matchbook back in his pocket. Holding the lantern's handle, Lovell raised it up above his head. The bright beam bounced off of a dozen or more pairs of large, glossy eyeballs that seem to have leapt into the eastern horizon.

"Oh my!" Desdamona's screech launched a commotion from the creatures that must have been bedded down along the side of the road. Gigantic birds rose up from their resting place, and the largest one flapped its wings with a heavy *WHOOSH*. It's bright white wing tips flashed in the moonlight.

The Rousseau's horse startled at the sudden display and reared back on its hind legs. Lovell and Desdamona grabbed hold of whatever they could on the buggy. When Miss Betty brought her front legs down, the birds advanced on them, hissing and flapping their wings.

"Turn us around!" Lovell shouted.

"Betty, yee. Yee!" Desdamona tugged on the left rein, but the horse yanked back against the line. Instead of turning the buggy around, Betty launched into a gallop, straight into the oncoming stampede of feathered monsters.

The buggy rattled violently. Lovell feared they would run off the road and crash.

"We have to jump," He said. "Desde, now!"

Desdamona got to her feet just as the buggy hit a bump in the road. Out she went, but he didn't see her land. Lovell readied himself for the hard knock awaiting him next. Then out he went.

Desdamona (Jones) Rousseau's headstone at the Greenwood Memory Lawn Cemetery in Phoenix, AZ. Provided by Gloria Simpson on FindAGrave.com [memorial 33683748].

As soon as he hit the ground, he heard a horrible cry from his horse and a terrific crash. Ostrich after ostrich smashed into the buggy, overturned it and crushed it into a pile of splinters. One bird pivoted and ran his way, so Lovell scrunched his body into a tight ball. He held his head in his hands and prayed the bird would change course. It must have seen his form because he felt a gust of wind pass over him before all was settled.

Lovell slowly uncovered his face and peeked down past his feet to see the heap of buggy parts with two of Miss Betty's legs sticking up from the pile in an unnatural way.

Lovell rolled over to push himself up and felt an excruciating pain in his shoulder. He felt himself over, noticing that his coat sleeve had torn down the same side that hurt. He must have broken something in the fall. That's to be expected, he supposed.

He looked around for the lantern, but that, too, had broken and the flame blown out.

"Desde." Lovell looked back down the road to where his wife had jumped out. At least, he thought she had jumped. "Desde! Are you okay?"

He got up and approached his wife, still down on the ground. Her pearls gleamed in the moonlight but the feather decorating her new hat had broken and now hung limp. Desdamona was dead.

"Oh, Desde…"

Ostrich Encounter

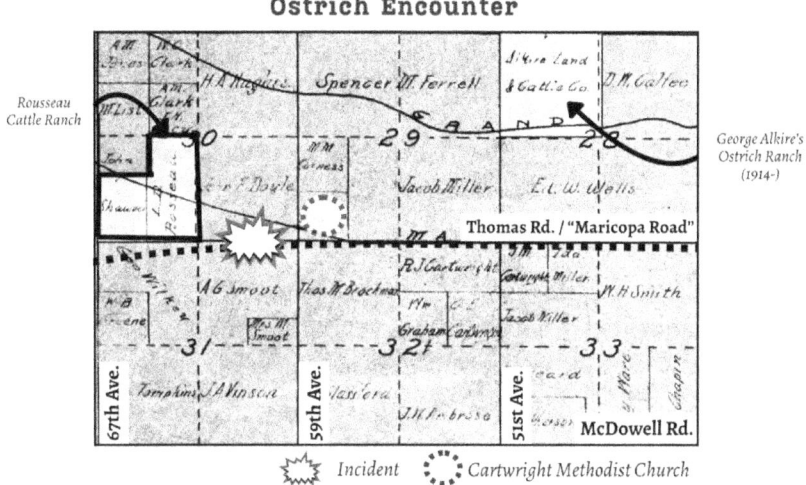

H. F. Robinson's *Plats of the Salt River Valley*, 1903 (2N 2E), labeled by author (History and Archives Division/Arizona State Library/Fair Use).

Description of a Frightened Ostrich

It might surprise readers that a horse, that can see over most human's heads and that weighs at least twice as much as (if not five times greater than) an ostrich, would spook over a few wing flaps. Any sort of strange flapping things in the distance, such as a flag or laundry line, could be grounds for the horse to become anxious unless that specific horse has been desensitized to the item. Even for those that were desensitized to ostriches, such as the horses being ridden by the Pan-American and Chandler Ranch wrangler, the sudden appearance of one or, in this case, popping out from nowhere, is still likely to cause a knee-jerk reaction.

To help readers visualize the scene Annie Martin's provided a description of a startled ostrich in her memoir. She wrote: "Only startle an ostrich; and very little is sufficient to do this, his nerves being of the feeblest ... What a jump he gives, and what a swerve to one side! Surely it must have dislocated some of his joints. But no; off he goes, flinging out his clumsy legs, and twisting himself about as he runs, till you almost expect to see him come to pieces, or, at any rate, fling off a leg, as a lobster casts a claw, or [how] a frightened lizard parts from its tail."[594]

The Nation Was Shocked

News of this tragedy went nationwide, including New York, New Mexico, Illinois, California, Missouri, Montana, and back in their hometown in Kentucky. It was a novel story, something of a "freak accident," that would make for an easy payday for journalists. Depending on the source of the information, details varied as did culpability. In what I'll refer to as "version one" of the reports, loose ostriches spooked the horse and Dr. A.J. Chandler is fully responsible for the damages and death.

Some sources say the wranglers managed a rather uneventful journey until they had called it a night near the Salt River bottom. The *Arizona Republican* reported, it was then that, "60 or more of the original 210 slipped away through the brush."[595] (By the way, if the evening's camp was more im-mediately along the river, then the prior theory about follow-ing the canal roads may be wrong. In that case, perhaps they intended to stick to the riverbank until they reached the crossing in Tempe. This would also mean that the ostriches had scattered several miles already, without being rounded up.)

Thomas Rousseau reported: "[A]ll of a sudden, an ostrich jumped up beside the road and spooked the [Rousseau's] horse," which then took off running, out of control.[596] A next-day announcement featured in the *Kentucky Advocate* read: "Frightened by a stampede of 300 ostriches ... a horse driven by L. D. Rousseau ran away ... overturning the buggy and instantly killing Mrs. Rousseau."[597] Helen Seargeant also remembered that the Rousseaus were "thrown from their buggy," but she also thought both parties died that night.[598] Family accounts contend both parties jumped or fell away from the wagon and in the process, Desdamona (age 58) died instantly with a broken neck and fractured skull. Lovell (age 61) survived with a broken collarbone and dislocated shoulder. We know from corroborating sources that not all 300 ostriches were involved in this incident, like most journalists declared.

> [n]
> "If red or blue necks got out like that, they'd go in 40 different directions and tear down every fence for miles."
> - D. C. "Rooster" Cogburn (2025)

Version two of this story was that the ostriches were still being driven down the country road (not already loose) when the incident occurred. A news report from the following week's *Republican* shies away from the liability that would fall squarely on George Peabody and Louis Ellsworth, who were managing the troops. In that version, it was only "presumed" that the ostriches the Rousseaus encountered were part of Dr. Chandler's purchase."[599] If that were the case, I'd question who else in the immediate neighborhood owned hundreds of ostriches at that time (no one) and, of those, who had recently lost control of them (hint: the answer is still no one).

Seargeant hypothesized that the birds became scattered once the fences along the road ran out, stating that the fences, kept the birds together, and once freed of those boundaries, the ostriches instinctively broke away. If this occurred earlier in the day, then Peabody and Ellsworth's immediate prerogative would be to contain the situation as fast as possible. While securing the troops that remained within reach, the rest

---

[n] D.C. Cogburn, phone communication to author, September 27, 2025.

of the birds took to the sand in any direction that fancied them. "Having no herd instinct," Lisa Hegarty wrote, "they could not be rounded up, and most of the birds scattered into the desert and river bottoms like phantoms."[600]

Blanche Murray's account for *Arizona Highways* concluded that "Some of [Dr. Chandler's] stampeded troop had settled down to spend the night in the road; when the horses approached[,] they rose with outspread wings and scurried away in the darkness, causing the calamity."[601]

Another variation of this event was that the horse and buggy spooked the ostriches, allegedly still in the control of their handlers. The Chandler Museum recorded, "[T]he effort to drive the herd the long way around South Mountain backfired [when] [l]ate one evening the birds were spooked and stampeded."[602] "The ostriches became unmanageable," the *Arizona Republican* declared the morning after the event.[603] One might say how dare the Rousseaus interfere with the neighbor's ostrich drive. If only they hadn't been on the road to mix everything up, the ostriches would have been easy to recollect, right?

Version four of the tale came from Alan Thurber, columnist for the *Arizona Republic,* who had researched the details and interviewed witnesses in the 1980s. After doing so, he surmised: "[T]he cowboys and horses and ostriches didn't get along, and the birds stampeded. Went all over the place."[604] If this is the case, then the initial loss of control may have occurred earlier in the day. Additional support for this shift in timing came from a man named James Carlton, who was working in a field just off the Maricopa Road when it happened. Carlton was 27 when the event occurred, but he recalled it to Thurber at the age of 97 with wonderful clarity.

* * *

Three hundred ostriches, outracing 14 mounted guards, overtook Mr. and Mrs. L. D. Rousseau, who were driving near Phoenix, Ariz. Ther buggy was overturned and Mrs. Rousreau was killed.

* * *

"From Around the Planet," *Semi-Weekly Leader* (Brookhaven MS), November 21, 1914, page 2.

He said, "We had three or four teams working the field when the herd stampeded ... One ostrich came right at us, with its wings spread out and a couple of dogs chasing it. The horses took off ... I had a five-horse team on the plow, and they were going in circles."[605] After stirring up a frenzy, the ostrich ran back out onto the road and disappeared.

A fifth version leans towards the ostriches becoming demon possessed. A Stockton, California paper reported that the birds were "maddened" and "bore down on [Mrs. Rousseau] at great speed. Her horses, terrified, bolted and overturned the trap they were pulling. The ostriches swept over the wreckage and the horses, which were entangled in the harness."[606] That reporter also claim Desdamona's and the horse's cause of death was by direct trampling (a horrifying thought). Montana's *Billings Tribune* followed suit and claimed the ostrich damage "reduc[ed] the carriage to a scrap heap."[607]

Who Was to Blame?

News of the debacle was telegraphed straight out to Waukegan, Illinois, where former city clerk Harry Thacker and his son-in-law Art Amet were from. The Waukegan story revealed the fact that this was the second stampede Pan-American had that year. Oddly, Arizona news outlets said nothing of the first event. The article leaned on the idea that stampedes were a "known hazard" of ostrich management and should have been accounted for.[608] Despite this, fingers still pointed in every direction.

The *Semi-Weekly Leader* in Mississippi reported that the herders had lost all control of their charges when the tragedy occurred.[609] A November 13 article in the *Republican* said the ostriches were still in the charge of the herders when they stampeded and that, "In spite of efforts to control them they swept down the road at terrific speed, meeting the conveyance containing Mr. and Mrs. Rousseau and causing the runaway."[610]

Some communications created doubt about where to draw the line for who was responsible for each separate reaction. The *Stockton Evening and Sunday Record* presented conflicting information, stating "Twenty mounted vaqueros had them in charge," then immediately reported that "None of the men knew what caused ... the great birds to bolt."[611] Perhaps the lack of a fence line simply set the captives free but the horse and buggy incited a stampede and made the herding task impossible.

Regardless of the narrative one believes, the Salt River Valley lost an incredible woman that day. Her funeral was held two days later, on Saturday morning. Her obituary reported that "An unusually large number of friends and acquaintances followed her remains to its last resting place," at Greenwood Cemetery.[612] The Sunday *Republican* also included "Resolutions of Respect and Condolences" for the Rousseau family. In an awkward coincidence, printed immediately next to the condolences was a story of hotel guest excitement over the arrival of ostriches at the San Marcos. The latter was written without a single acknowledgement of the incident.

26. The Long Way 'Round

"Country Below the City Overrun by Great Birds!"
- The Arizona Republican (1914)[613]

After the ostrich stampede, George Peabody and Lou Ellsworth had a mess on their hands. Loose birds caused chaos far and wide, and "a panic among ranchers and their families followed," claimed one newspaper, adding that locals were fleeing to the safety of their homes.[614] Someone, either a wrangler or a local resident, made a phone call to Dr. Chandler fand reported what had happened. In the meantime, the press continued, "the birds had scattered over miles of country."[615]

The herding team busied themselves trying to contain the birds in the immediate vicinity. For this, they were assisted by a Mr. Huerta, a Pima Indian, and Mr. Choo or "Chappo," a Maricopa Indian. One account described two men on horseback, each holding a post with barbed wire linked between them.[616] The two riders coordinated their moves to try scooping ostriches into a makeshift net before taking their prisoner to a temporary jail cell in the pasture of a nearby rancher. This ad-hoc strategy makes me wonder if they just yanked out a couple of fence posts from one of the local properties to get the job done. The *Stockton Evening* relayed: "An hour after the stampede, less than half of the birds had been captured."[617]

The next morning, the ostrich boys tried to capture more runaways. Many were found bedded down on the sandy shores of the Salt River.[618] They only recovered 40, leaving 70

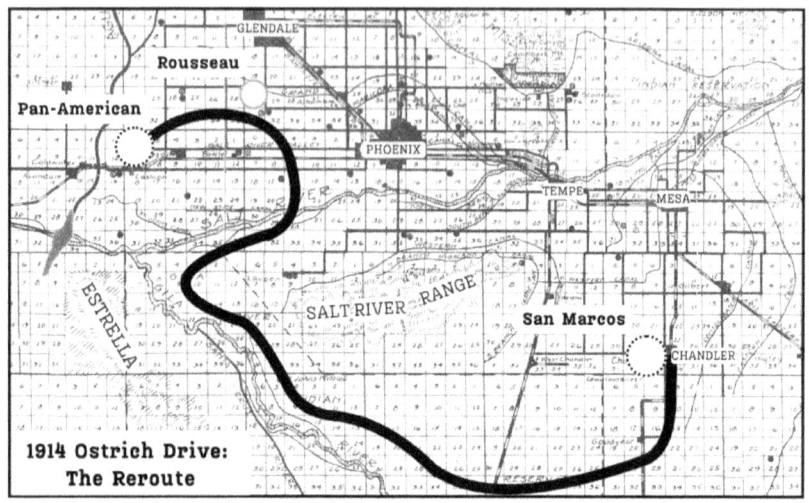

Map of Salt River Valley, Arizona, 1923 from the Dwight B. Heard Investment Company, labeled by author.

still at large. Birds that headed north ended up needing to be rescued out of the Grand Canal, reported a project manager, O. McDermith. He told the *Bisbee Daily Review*: "We found four that got away when they stampeded the other night."[619] Murray claimed as many as ten ostriches were, "immersed to their necks in water ... lassoed from the Grand Canal."[620]

After doing all they could in the short-term, Dr. Chandler's men needed to secure and finalize their delivery, however, continuing east along the Salt River or along the canals in any populated area was now out of the question. "It was necessary," the *Chandler Arizonan* reported, "to make this wide detour of some fifty miles in order to avoid humankind as much as possible."[621]

The alternative route took the team south to the Salt River, then backtracked to thread between the Estrella and Salt River (South) Mountain ranges towards the Gila River

Ostrich Drive, 1914, Courtesy of Janet Gross (Chandler Museum Collection [92-7-71 and 72], Chandler, AZ, licensed use).

Indian Reservation. After passing St. John's Indian School, they could follow the Gila River for a portion of the route before turning northeast, straight to downtown Chandler. The November 13 announcement of the detour claimed a the "leisurely" journey would only delay the ostriches' arrival by a day or so.[622] The announcement contained no mention of the Rousseau incident.

For two days, Dr. Chandler's team led Pan-American's ostriches along the Gila River, which afforded the photographer some stunning views of the Sierra Estrella Mountain (or *Komatke* to the Pima and Maricopa). On Friday night, the wranglers camped near the southern end of the foothills. The river and mountain pass would create natural boundaries to limit the amount of wandering off the ostriches could do.

(By the way, the Gila River used to be a major waterway that riverboats could travel by from Southwest New Mexico until it met the Colorado River in Yuma, Arizona. Its perennial flow sufficiently supported the tribal communities' various agricultural activities. When the Coolidge Dam was installed in the 1920s, the Gila River was reduced to a trickle, contributing to a major famine on the reservation. In 2020, New Mexico

State Senators Martin Heinrich and Tom Udall introduced the M.H. Dutch Salmon Greater Gila Wild and Scenic Rivers Act (H.R. 1611/ S. 1476) to the congressional legislature.[623] The act would protect 445-miles out of the 649 stretch to keep the water free flowing and restore fish and other wildlife habitats. Protections to the waterway would limit areas accessible for recreation and agriculture and designate portions to be kept wild. As of April 2025, the updated and proposed bill has yet to be passed by the House of Representatives or Senate.)

Camp Tales and Teamster Tricks

The birds did not appear to give Dr. Chandler's wranglers too much trouble on this leg of the journey, though, J. C. McDonald, the hotel guest, had one complaint to share. He said the ostriches "would come into camp early in the morning, drink all the hot coffee from the kettle over the camp fire[*sic*] and carry off the blazing sticks."[624] I found this story highly implausible. An ostrich doesn't bother with hot coffee because by the time it reaches the bottom of their throat, it turns cold.

Another splendid story attributed to this event was centered on a cookout that may or may not actually have happened, but legend says it did, so that basically settles it. Similar to how I have reimagined and paraphrased some stories in this book, there was an Arizona storyteller in the 1940s and 50s, named Roscoe G. Willson who did the same thing. This guy had worked in mining operations and for the forest service for decades, but in his retirement, he enjoyed sharing creative reiterations of the Sonoran Desert's days of old. Willson produced short story collections under the titles *No Place for Angels* and *Pioneer Cattlemen of Arizona*, as well

Rest period on the ostrich drive, 1914 (Chandler Museum Collection [92-7-73 and 74], Chandler, AZ, licensed use).

as contributing to a regular column in the *Arizona Republic.* Willson was a self-proclaimed "Stickler for Facts," but his reputation was based more on his ability to tell a tall tale set so close to the truth that everyone *wanted* to believe it.[625]

In one such story for the statewide news, Roscoe Willson regaled readers with an incident between the cowboys handling Dr. Chandler's ostriches. He said on that first day of the ostrich drive: "A hastily gathered crew of horsemen had spent an exciting day rounding up a bunch of the 8-foot-tall birds that had broken loose from the Pan-American Ostrich Farm. They camped on the Salt River that night with nothing in sight to eat."[626] To throw off any truth seeker from questioning the details, he added: "They had plenty of dishes but the food had not arrived."[627]

Willson then wove a yarn about some greenhorn whose stomach growled while the Arizona Eastern Railway's fine dining cart derailed from the tracks to carve its way slowly through alfalfa and honeydew fields to reach the tired and hungry hunters. The greenhorn, Pete, said things like "Golly," and "Would'ya believe it?" He probably had an accent, like someone from Kansas City, Missouri, who'd never seen an ostrich up close before. That tale went something like this:

"If I had some ham, and if I had some eggs, why then, I'd eat myself some ham and eggs," Pete concluded.

Someone on the ostrich drive who identified as the cook spoke up and assured the young man that there was a hunk of ham tucked inside the boss' spare boot and that if he'd just wait for the team to return from a wilderness Easter egg hunt, they'd all have an ostrich omelet to share.

"Gee willikers!" exclaimed Pete. "I've never had an ostrich omelet!"

The cook seemed to brighten up at the confession. "Haven't you?" He looked around camp and hollered out to the cowboys nearby. "Ya'll hear that? Petey boy has never tasted an ostrich omelet! Guys, come on in for this special treat."

"And Pete," the cook added, "have you ever *seen* an ostrich egg?"

"No, sir. Like you said, I'm looking forward to this treat."

That was just what ol' Cookie was hoping. "Well, in that case, how many eggs do you normally take in an omelet?"

"Oh, maybe two or three."

Cookie sucked some air through his teeth. His grin now resembled the Cheshire Cat. "Two. Or three. Nope. That don't work. Pete, I'm willing to bet you won't be able to eat even one."

"What a silly bet that is! I could eat half a dozen chicken eggs if I wanted to, but I figured the ostrich might be a bit larger. I stand by my claim."

"Okay, Pete. I'll put you to it and I'll even pay you fifty dollars if you can do it."

That made the greenhorn light up. "*OooWee!* Two weeks' pay for eatin' my breakfast!"

"Yeah." Cookie let that sink in before asking, "Since you're just visitin' and I'm sure you need your purse free, what do you say you throw in your saddle. You know, in case you can't eat all that egg."

"Yer on!" Pete's confidence soared.

The whole crew gathered around to watch the exchange. Cookie pulled out the largest cast-iron skillet he had, settled it over the fire and greased it up with a block of ham fat. Looking all around, Cookie saw the guys licking their lips as the sizzling scent reached their noses.

"Okay, who's got an egg?" he asked. Cowboy Carl produced the heavy orb from his shoulder sack and Cookie held it up for Pete's inspection.

Pete's eyes bugged out.

The cook proceeded to bust open the shell and pour the runny egg into the skillet. He gave it a few stirs with his knife, and the yellow mixture rose up like a cake in the oven until it spilled over the edge of the enormous pan.

Charles C. Colley imagined the end of this exchange in an article for *Arizona Highways* that reads:

"His voice caught in his throat as he turned away from the huge[,] glutenous[,] yellow-eyed mass filling the frying pan in front of him."[628] Finally, Pete told the cook that the saddle was all his.

Illustration from "Arizona Days with Roscoe G. Willson," *Arizona Republic*, August 22, 1954 (Fair Use).

The Grand Arrival

Finally, on the afternoon of Saturday March 14, the *Republican* announced: "A herd of 140 ostriches arrived in Chandler ... after a three days drive from Pan-American, in charge of George T. Peabody, assistant manager of the Chandler Improvement Company, and Lew Ellsworth, who is foreman of the Chandler Ostrich farm north of Mesa, and assisted by ten or so other drivers."[629] The ostriches were led to pasture out in the grassy pens.

About the remaining 100 to be collected from Pan-American, Helen Seargeant explained that "[Dr. Chandler] had them sent by rail... It was not so hard to get them into boxcars."[630]

27. "Ostrich Hunting: An Arizona Sport"

"Ostriches, ostriches, everywhere, but not one to eat..."
- Chandler Arizonan (1914)[631]

News headlines rang out the chapter title, adding that the country below Phoenix is "alive with ostriches" and that "Indians and white men on horse back[*sic*] are chasing them over the desert with little result."[632] Another story reported that "Scores of cowboys were requisitioned to round up the birds."[633] After 140 of the 210 scattered ostriches were secured, George Peabody and Lou Ellsworth made a quick turnaround to go after those roaming wild. Joining with them for the so-called hunt were Ellsworth's brothers, W. J. Lewis, Ellis Morris, Oris Holdron, Mr. Huerta and Mr. Choo.[634] The hotel guest, J. C. McDonald, also tagged along. He may have lost his saddle but hadn't had his fill of adventure yet. "Messers. Peabody and Ellsworth ... report many interesting and exciting experiences in recovering the birds which strayed," the *Arizona Republic* told readers.[635]

Many stories that came in from this roundup remained light, positive and entirely absent of liability. It was as if the entire ordeal had a public relations team behind it... (which may have been truer than folks realize). From 1912 to 1929 the *Arizona Republican* was owned and managed by Dwight B. Heard, the land baron and ostrich-ranching enthusiast with deep pockets, a powerful influence, and a partial beneficiary from Dr. Chandler's recent purchase of Belgo-American birds.

Ostrich Drive, 1914. Standing-right is George Peabody. Standing (left) is believed to be Lou Ellsworth (Chandler Museum Collection [87-8-7], Chandler, AZ Museum, Licensed Use.)

The *Chandler Arizonan's* managing editor, Samuel A. Meyer, also had to toe the line because he was under the immediate thumb of Dr. Chandler – the newspaper's owner, main stockholder, and the owner of the publisher (Chandler Improvement Company).[636]

Many of the wandering ostriches were attracted to the cultivated areas in Phoenix and invited themselves to eat fruits from private orchards and clover from neighborhood fields. "For the most part, [they] walked over or through such pasture as looked good to them, and stayed right of possession," the report read (as if the owners allowed ostriches special privileges).[637] I can imagine that some neighbors, such as James Carlton, were not at all pleased to have such company. Others appear to have made the best of the situation and claimed suitable compensation for the feeding and housing of strays. The *Republican* gave the following example: "One bird was picked up by a farmer who evidently liked ostrich feathers, for when Peabody came to get it, he found the bird plucked as clean of feathers as the palm of his hand. It was just right for baking, but in poor condition for the field. Just now the bird is wearing Peabody's pajamas and a Navajo blanket."[638]

I know what you're thinking: "I'd like to see that." Since this is a ridiculous look for a bird of such majestic proportions, I asked for help from an image generator to tell this story. It did not disappoint.

Peabody's Ostrich

Disclaimer: This bird is not real. This conceptual image was created with the assistance of generative programming and generous author manipulation.

Another story was told of a young boy from the Gila River Reservation standing out by the roadside with a handful of long, white plumes. He was offering them for sale at a ridiculously cheap price. "He got thirty cents for a particularly handsome one," the press explained.[639] What became of the ostrich those feathers were gathered from remains unknown.

One *Republican* journalist declared: "The horse is no match for the ostrich in speed," while describing Dr. Chandler's horsemen out trying to lasso the birds, one-by-one, like cattle.[640] The article continued: "Occasionally, one [bird] would be seen and the cowboy would put spurs to his horse and get his riata in readiness, but when he approached the bird, it would merely lengthen its stride in the sand. It would not appear to be running, only walking hurriedly, but it rapidly widened the distance between itself and the horse."[641] This November 15 report included the refreshingly blunt statement: "These ostriches are a part of a flock of 250 that escaped on Thursday night when they were being driven from

CHANDLER ARIZONAN

CHANDLER, ARIZ., FRIDAY, DECEMBER 4, 1914

OSTRICHES ARE ALL THE RAGE IN CHANDLER, AND DOT THE LANDSCAPE BY THE HUNDREDS

Front page, *Chandler Arizonan*, Dec. 4, 1914. Caption reads: "Ostriches are all the rage in Chandler, and dot the landscape by the hundreds."

the Pan-American ranch to Chandler where they had been sold to Dr. A.J. Chandler. It was the stampede of these birds that caused the runaway in which Mrs. L. D. Rousseau was killed."[642] Perhaps by then, enough of the truth had gotten out that there was no use denying it.

Despite how fast and far the birds traveled, the expeditionary force was still expected to have all the flat-billed bandits rounded up by Saturday the 28th. That was the date when a train car would arrive at the Chandler Depot with 100 more Pan-American ostriches to unload.[643]

Several days after the stampede, the news reports started to sound a bit cheekier. "They will be picking ostriches out of their hair," read the November 24 *Republican.* In that story, readers were entertained by how two Phoenix boys ended up in an ostrich chase that resulted in a scientific discovery. Paul and Ted Peterson, who lived downtown, captured one "frisky" bird who had escaped the prior week "with such tragic results."[644] These brothers went for a ride on the family

Dr. Chandler's Ostrich Pens (at San Marcos)

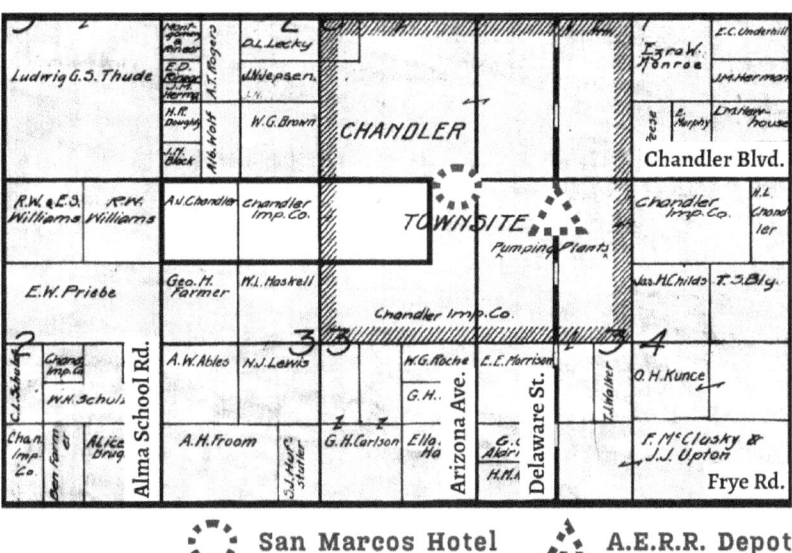

San Marcos Hotel ☀ A.E.R.R. Depot

Likely location of Dr. Chandler's ostriches, ca. 1914 to 1923. Township map (1N 5E), 1914, labeled by author (History and Archives Division/Arizona State Library/Fair Use).

motorcycle 11 miles southeast of the city, in the desert, which may have been above the Mesa Grande site (*Sce:dagĭ Mu:val Va'aki*), in present-day Scottsdale. They chased that bird on their rig and clocked its speed at 40-miles-per-hour. They kept at it until the ostrich tired out, which was anywhere between 30 to 40 minutes, at its top speed. Once tired, the ostrich gave up the game and was easily taken into custody.

I'm not sure how the Peterson boys held the ostrich down, or brought it back into town, but a funny example of what it may have looked like is found in Annie Martin's memoir. When Martin and her husband received a stray in South Africa, she said it was a rather joyful, but laughable sight. She wrote in her memoir, "As he was marched along between the two men, each with a tight grip on his shoulder, he looked just like a pickpocket in the hands of the police, going to prison."[645]

Scene at Behan's ostrich farm in Australia, ca. 1907 (University of Queensland, Henry William Mobsby Papers/Public Domain).

Another discovery came from a duck hunter who was out east along the Salt River. According to the news, "He was sitting on the river bank waiting for duck. He heard a splashing in the water far below him and thought it was a cow or a horseman. He moved back from the bank and waited. At last[,] he was surprised to see a huge ostrich pass, wading in water four feet deep. When he yelled at it, it turned and surveyed him for an instant and then passed on up the river."[646] From this encounter, natural historians learned that ostriches are not afraid of water, as was so long believed.

Helen Seargeant recalled, "There were a number of accidents caused," and sightings reported "in odd places," for multiple weeks.[647] One ostrich decided to head south and ended up causing a ruckus on the north side of Tucson. The *Arizona Daily Star* reported: "An ostrich wandering at large near the Rillito River four miles from the city caused two runaways yesterday. One woman[,] whose name could not be obtained[,] last evening, was thrown out and cut about the face. The ostrich is believed to have been one from a flock that escaped from Phoenix last week and … have been wandering on the desert. The strange birds have never been seen in Tucson until a flock was brought here the present week for the university and horses are afraid of them."[648]

That ostrich appears to be one of 20 that were lost for better or for worse. On Sunday, November 22, Peabody only brought back a catch of 50 ostriches.[649] As for the rest, the press concluded, "Probably not many of the birds will ever be taken alive. Some of them may now be on their way to join their four-legged cousins, the camels, of which reports have been received from time to time in the last 25 years."[650]

The last part of that statement was a reference to the U.S. Camel Corps once employed as beast of burden in California, Arizona, New Mexico and Texas for reconnaissance missions in the late-1850s. Back then, a large caravan of camels had headquartered at Fort Beale, outside of Kingman, Arizona. The military may have assumed that all deserts were the same, so they expected these beasts from Egypt to thrive in their new home. The military also believed the camels required less general care (i.e. less feed, water, rest, etc.) than horses and mules. For a short while during the American Civil War, camel drivers operated the Southwest's version of the Pony Express, creating a mail route between Fort Mohave (on the Arizona-Nevada border) and Drum Barracks (in San Pedro, California). Commanders at both forts apparently objected to the use of camels. In 1866, the experiment with camels was fully abandoned. Many camels were sold off at auctions while others released into the wild, to survive off the land.

In the 1870s, some camels were repurposed for packing ore from the Silver King Mine to Yuma.[651] Still, others were used to assist with the completion of the Southern Pacific Railroad.[652] Once those camels' usefulness had ended, they were released near Maricopa Wells, on the southern bank of the Gila River. Legend holds that, over the course of a decade, Arizona's camels were hunted to extinction by members of area tribal communities.

The Red Ghost

Additional lore tells of the humpbacked hobos being seen long into the early-1890s, with one special camel appearing to residents down on the Gila River, up north on the Verde River and into the San Francisco mining district near Oatman. This ghoulish sight was described as a red-haired demon beast carrying the bleached-white bones of a dead man on its back.[653] The apparition (which storytellers claimed was a real animal, carrying a real, grizzly burden) received the nickname, "Red Ghost." In 1893, a man named Mizoo Hastings claimed to have killed the Red Ghost and made boots out of its hide. These boots were for sale (of course) and priced according to their rarity. After sharing the incredulous details of various corpse-carrying camel encounters from the past and securing a buyer for the boots, Mr. Hastings allegedly climbed a beanstalk into the sky, and no one ever heard from him again.

Settling In

"After a number of exciting adventures", the *Republic* summed, "the birds were all captured, and they, with one hundred more half-grown birds from the Pan-American ranch are now on their way to the new ostrich ranch at Chandler."[654] Good or bad press aside, the menagerie became a popular tourist attraction. You might even say that people flocked to it. Because of one claim that Rough Neck was the ostrich who started the stampede leading to Rousseau's death, he became a celebrity (some sources say he's the one who did her in).[655] According to the *East Valley Tribune*, people came out to the San Marcos just to see the "killer ostrich."[656]

Woman at the Chandler Ostrich Farm, 1920 (Tempe History Museum [1987.1.1752], Licensed Use.)

⊁ **Inspect the Ostriches**

Large crowds all day Sunday strolled to the ostrich farm on the west edge of town Sunday and admired the kings and queens of the desert. The birds seemed contented and happy and in no evident mood to stampede.

Chandler Arizonan, November 20, 1914, 6.

It seems unfair that the woman's killer would become famous while the birds' owner appears to have made no official apology. With that in mind, I think there is a reasonable allowance for Rousseau's ghost to haunt the halls of the San Marcos Hotel (presently the Crowne Plaza). Alas, no sightings have been reported… yet.

28. Murder Birds & Other Tragedies

"The ostrich... is a most formidable & dangerous opponent."
- The Arizona Sentinel (1886)[657]

In 2017, the Encyclopedia Britannica listed the ostrich in the top six most dangerous birds in the world. Based on the statistics, ostriches take the title as the number one deadliest bird in the world.[658] They appear listed next to their relatives, the emu and cassowary, who have attacked but made very few confirmed kills on humans. Others on the list were the Lammergeier vulture with its 10-foot wingspan, the Great Horned Owl, and the Barred Owl, who had a track record for harassing and injuring humans, but murders were not on the scorecard.[659] As of 2024, the "most dangerous" list has been updated to add the Harpy Eagle (well deserved) and the Red-Tailed Hawk. Still, ostriches continue to be regarded as the grimmest of all reapers and were number two for most violent overall, after the nasty cassowary.[660]

Annie Martin described how intimidating an ostrich can be once enraged: "The creature, when preparing for an attack, draws itself up, stands on tiptoe, stretches its neck to the full extent, and really seems to gain several feet in height."[661] That shift can happen with practically no notice, and anyone and anything could become a target, especially during mating season.

Before he passed away, Watson Pickrell warned the ostrich ranching world that, "After ostriches are over one-year-old, no one should go among them without a brush or stick in hand, as at times[,] they will want to fight." This and further instructions from Pickrell on ostrich handling appeared in the 1922 *Cyclopedia of Farm Animals*.[662]

Pan-American's Sonoran Slayer

Arriving in 1914 with Dr. A.J. Chandler's Pan-American order for 300 ostriches was one of the state's most notorious roosters: Rough Neck. He earned his ruthless name because of all the scars that lined his throat: trophies of supreme dominance from winning various battles with other roosters.[663] According to one story in the *Bisbee Daily Review*, "[Rough Neck] was decidedly ferocious and boldly attacked the men as they entered the field."[664] Despite being an exceedingly "big, handsome, feathered biped," when he was made part of the sale, he already had at least two counts of murder on his criminal record.[665] And the ranch hands knew those facts well. If he was, as some proposed, involved in the Rousseau's buggy bust, that would have been his first count of manslaughter and third overall kill within a calendar year.[666]

Months before meeting Mrs. Rousseau, Rough Neck had been guilty of taking out a field attendant at the Pan-American "by one blow of his foot," so survivors told.[667] The man's chest completely caved in from the impact. Within a matter of days, he attacked another employee. Those injuries resulted in a slower, but still quite certain death.[668] The papers warned: "Woe betide the person that went unarmed..."[669] Regardless of his kill streak, Rough Neck was left to remain in the troops, possibly for being a successful breeder. The ranch hands at the San Marcos toughed out the various moods of the tuxedoed tormentor until March of 1915. That spring, the rooster held a wrestling match with a barbed wire fence and lost.[670]

Now, it sounds like the Pan-American was glad to be rid of a "bad egg," but Dr. Chandler's ranchers appear to have been familiar with how to manage these types of challenging personalities. There was also a blue-necked rooster on the hotel's campus named Scar Neck. This guy was considered in the papers as, "perhaps the most vicious ostrich in the valley, [that] has more than once put a horse to flight."[671] In December 1914, Scar Neck starred in a 10-minute tournament worthy of a gladiator's applause. According to the *Arizona Republican*, he "viciously attacked a team and[,] afterwards[,] two men on horseback."[672]

What made Scar Neck upset? Nothing. Well, sort of. An employee of the Chandler Improvement Company had driven into the pen in a wagon cart loaded with fence posts. The rooster allegedly made eye contact with a mule and the mule responded by snorting its disgust (or something like that). That was enough for Scar Neck to launch into rage mode. He darted toward the mule and kicked with savage intent. Fortunately, his spear-toe struck where the mule was wearing a protective neck pad.

The paper read: "George Peabody then [rode] up to the mule's assistance, when the bird turned on him, threatening to rip [his] horse open with his vicious kicks."[673] At this point, every available man was engaged against this highly determined divo. Peabody was unarmed. He didn't even have a length of rope to lasso a flying leg. While the mules pulled their delivery out of the way, Peabody kept dodging those killer kicks until he and his horse were backed into a corner. Just then, "Lew Ellsworth, armed with a riata, came to his rescue."[674] The news story concluded that between the two men, they were able to "subdue" Scar Neck. What wasn't written in the paper was that this was the last time the public would ever see or hear of Scar Neck ever again.

Other Attacks of Note

Time and again, these types of encounters ended with either a total win for the ostrich, or at least a few well-scored points for the next tallying up of the "world's most dangerous" list. At the Pan-American, there was another beaked beast written about in later years, named "Doctor Cook." He was, as Blanche Murray put for *Arizona Highways*, "a feather Ishmaelite with a cantankerous disposition."[675] "Doc" was both a known killer and a farm favorite. "He could run like the wind, dodge like a quarterback and fight like a demon[,] yet [he] was always the first to greet visitors," which may have granted this rooster a few extra days in the sun.[676] At one point, Carl Hagenbeck of Germany offered William Cross $5,000 for Doc to become part of his touring circus of exotic animal performances and the *Völkerschauen* (ethnological human zoo).[677] That amount is close to a staggering $180,000 in today's terms, but Cross refused the sale. Ultimately, with the closure of the Pan-American, Doc. Cook sold for a measly $5.[678]

Another account from the Avondale area came from Frank Hill, who lived further west of the Pan-American, where Buckeye Road becomes Yuma Road. He once told Helen Seargeant, "He and his mother were attacked by an ostrich one evening, when they were driving home in their automobile."[679] Seargeant did not record the date of this event but continued: "It was late enough for the car lights to be on and the ostrich began to kick at the lights. It kept fighting the car until it got the toes of one foot caught under a wheel." At that point, Mr. Hill wielded his pocketknife and made sure the ostrich would never kick again.

Back in South Africa's early industry days, Annie Martin reported on a newcomer to a local ranch who thought he was

"Doc Cook" at the Pan-American Ranch, undated. As seen in B. Murray's "Ostriches in Arizona," *Arizona Highways*, Nov. 1939 (Fair Use).

so tall and sturdy, he'd be immune to the ostrich's angry advances. Fortunately for the readers, he was wrong. Martin shared that he started right into a pen for an early morning walk. Beforehand, he was specifically cautioned against venturing where the camped off birds were stationed. Friends told him the birds were aggressive, but Mister Six-Foot-Whatever, "told *them* he was 'not afraid of a dicky-bird!'"[680] He used the phrase usually reserved for a bird of small size and harmless to children (such as a finch or parakeet). He even refused the "tackey" (defensive staff) and foolhardily marched in toward danger. Martin concluded: "He did not return home to dinner; a search was made for him; and eventually he was found, perched up on a high ironstone boulder; just out of reach of a large ostrich, which was doing sentry, walking up and down, and keeping a vicious eye on him."[681]

In 1901, there was another group participation situation with an Arkansas-bound bird that might have been purchased from Aylma Pearson's collection on display at the World's Fair in Buffalo, New York. This unnamed ostrich had a wounded neck requiring medical intervention. While trying to pin down the bird for that treatment, "feathers flew in rare style, and six men fancied for a time that they were wrestling with a 50-foot walking beam and several healthy mules."[682] The *Buffalo News* delivered the following play-by-play for their devoted readers:

"There was a struggle, much grunting, a few expletives not usually printed, then more struggle..."[683] The six-to-one match included hammerlocks, half-nelsons and even an attempted foot hold before the team finally succeeded staying the ostrich long enough to receive treatment.

Arizona's Nature Takes Its Toll

Sometimes the ostriches would be at a disadvantage in their Arizona abodes. Coyotes were not brave enough to take on a full-grown ostrich, but sometimes they'd be curious about the appetizer-sized options left unguarded. In 1907, "six young ostriches were killed and nine others were injured by coyotes at the large farm nine miles west of Phoenix."[684] The birds were around 6-months-old, but must have given the canines enough of a fight to cause them to only get a nibble of each hide. Of the 18 chicks mauled, only six were expected to live.

Arizona's summer monsoons were also a problem for ostriches as lightning rod simulators. In the fall of 1911, the *Arizona Republican* reported on two ostriches at Pan-American that were struck when "standing alone in the middle of a large field."[685] The story continued, "This is the first time in the history of the ostrich raising industry of the Salt River Valley that any of the big birds have been killed by lightning." Rather than consider ways to prevent this type of scenario from happening again, "The owners of the birds [the Phoenix National Bank] are more concerned about the loss of $1,000....," or about $34,000 in today's terms.[686] (By the way, this is not where the term "sticker shock" came from... but it should have been.)

Ostrich Stampedes (Not for the Sensitive Reader)

It might be that the greatest threat to a captive ostrich is not the diseased flea, rabid coyote, prowling mountain lion, or even the butcher. Statistically speaking, the worst possible thing for ostriches to do is stampede. It's an event that will slam them into fences and each other at velocity, claws catching into flesh, necks curling around and tangling, and bones breaking in a horrendous cacophony. "Some people might find that [reaction] very stupid," wrote Karen Weston Gonzales for *Arizona Highways*, however, "the instinct to run at the first sign of danger is very strong in them. That's what keeps them alive in the wild."[687]

Multiple stampedes have been recorded at the Pan-American, all with tragic outcomes. One instance happened during a lightning storm. "It started in a pasture where 300 birds were sleeping," wrote Murray. "Their panic set flock after flock into mad flight. The next morning, 650 mangled, bleeding bodies were removed from the broken wire."[688]

Another loss occurred early in 1914 when a dog ran through one of their fields and startled the ostriches into another violent rush. That time, 200 birds died while trying to flee the perceived predator.[689] If the ostriches were valued at the average 1910 price of $320, Pan-American may have taken a loss valued upwards to, or above, $96,000 (and exponentially much more for the lightning event).

Since nearly the beginning of ostrich ranching history, it has been known that "Ostriches are mortally afraid of dogs..." and as such, dogs were outlawed near the grazing giants.[690] The risk for losses was so high that back at Dr. Sketchley's Anaheim farm, a notice was posted to the public stating: "All dogs brought to the farm will be shot."[691] Dr. Sketchley's ranch hands were equipped with a loaded weapon in case they needed to carry out that threat.[692] In Murray's creative retelling of Desdamona Rousseau's sad ending, she claims that "a request was broadcast asking that all dog owners pen up their pets on a certain day."[693] Despite the command, Murray claims "an animated wisp of yellow hair and bark rushed noisily out; apparently from nowhere." It was at that point, she believed, the troops in the Great Arizona Ostrich Drive scattered. Alas, more theories.

Other Ostriches That Escaped Captivity

Though Dr. Chandler's troops claimed quite the spotlight in 1914, there were a few other times when loose ostriches roamed the Southwest. Down in Yuma, a wandering bird made one rancher famous overnight... twice. An 1886 issue of the *Arizona Sentinel* provided the story:

> "Among the many curiosities that are the attraction of Yuma, Mr. Walter Miller has probably got the greatest. It is known as Miller's ostrich, and was [caught] on the desert of California by some Mexican hunters on Thursday last. ... He is a vicious bird, and yesterday laid an egg that is ... about the size of a sledge hammer. This is very peculiar as this is undoubtedly a male bird. Those who desire to see this wonderful bird can do so by going up to the old Dotton blacksmith shop, wherein he has it confined."[694]

This biology-defying story is an illustration of the "black hen." In this genetic anomaly, a female ostrich presents exactly as a rooster except for its sexual organs. It is a rare occurrence. Black hens do not normally produce eggs in captive environments, considering the confusion of breeders who camp them off with other females. After a period of what appears to be infertility or incompatibility, the black hen—a fraudulent rooster—is liable to be discarded from the troop.

Within seven days, Miller's black hen slipped out of its Yuma enclosure. This was its second recorded escape since leaving Dr. Sketchley's animal entourage earlier in the month.[695] The hen scared the locals, who did not take kindly to her making appearances around town. The *Sentinel* likened the ostrich's end to a boxing match: "Walt Millar's ostrich is dead. He was lariated out when some boys took him for a horse thief..."[696]

In the big Pan-American clearance, a food scientist from Tucson ordered 15 of the ostriches to his property northeast of the city. Dr. Charles A. Meserve was the U.S. government-appointed scientist who oversaw the State Health Department's Pure Food and Drug Laboratory (at the University of Arizona).[697] Shortly after his shipment arrived, the ostriches got loose. All but three were recovered. One didn't fare well on the journey, another decided to scratch an itch with barbed wire, while the third simply vanished. The *Tucson Citizen* headline for this story read: "Meserve's Ostrich Still Roams the Mesa."[698]

A similar event occurred in the Toston family's delivery of ostriches to Chandler.[699] On November 30, 1914, the Toston's wagonload of 40 Pan-American purchases encountered a pair of kids making a ruckus on the road.[700] One boy was on horseback with tow ropes pulling the other boy in a boxcar-type toy called a "pushmobile." He pulled his friend by at a dangerous speed. The rattle and strange appearance likely caused the ostriches in the wagon to startle. When they did, they crowded to one side of the vehicle. This sudden shift in weight resulted in the entire vehicle tipping over. Those injured were Byron Ellsworth (driving), brothers Earnest and Lou Ellsworth (riding with the birds), and Lou's son. It remains unclear if Thomas Toston was involved, or if, owing to his prior traumatic brain injury, he was excused from the transportation task.

After the crash, all but one ostrich "scattered all over Chandler."[701] The one remaining was dead. While rounding up the escapees, one was found having fatally injured itself on barbed wire. Another was caught spying in the window of the *Chandler Arizonan* newspaper office.[702] It took about five days to find the remaining ostriches, with the last being spied at Dr. Chandler's hotel.

The original tale of capturing the lost rooster appeared in the *Arizona Republican* on December 3, and it went a little like this:

Toston's Tearful Goodbye

One chilly December eve, a Toston-owned ostrich wandered all through the Chandler townsite, knocking on doors and asking if anyone would let it come in for a cocoa to warm its long slide. From house to house that ostrich went until... it found the biggest house of all: the Hotel San Marcos. The hotel practically glittered like gold through the windows. The warm glow of incandescent bulbs looked just like a roasting fire, perfect for a shivering gent.

"Surely they will let me in," the ostrich said. "I'm well dressed in my black and white, my face is clean shaven, and I've heard they can now put their restaurant charges on my bill." The bird walked through the main entry gate but found himself perplexed. With all the soft feathers covering his stubby fingers, he simply couldn't open the heavy door to the lobby.

"I'll just knock on the window instead," he figured. So, he walked through the garden under the pergola and found a window where he could see the front desk inside.

Behind the desk stood Mr. Sloan, the clerk, looking through the daily mail.

TAP, TAP, TAP.

"What was that?" Mr. Sloan looked up at the door and thought twice. The noise he heard didn't sound right.

TAP, TAP, TAP.

Finally, Mrs. Robinson, the hotel's manager, walked to the window and startled. That was twice the ostrich had to knock before he could get someone's attention.

"Oh my! Who is that staring through our window with such a strange look?" Mrs. Robinson called the clerk over. "Mr. Sloan, you must come see this!"

The desk clerk joined her at the window and adjusted his spectacles. "Well, let's see… just give me a moment to think… Oh, yes, that looks to me like a millionaire I once knew in Vancouver."

Mrs. Robinson frowned. "That can't be. I rather think this might be the Phoenix pickle drummer that was here last week. I told him we had enough pickles and did not need any from him."

How interesting! The ostrich was mistaken as people they both knew, yet neither one would open the door for him. What kind of customer service was this?

"No, no, Mrs. Robinson. I really think this might be my old friend. Let me just wipe my glasses and get a better look."

Just then, the Korean bellhop appeared in the lobby, ready to receive another guest.

"Mr. Cho," the manager addressed, "could you please go see if this is a guest of ours, or a street peddler. We are undecided."

Cho went to the front doors with a merry gait and opened them. To get a good look, he stepped outside and peeked around the corner to see who the stranger was. After a brief

Hotel advertisement in the November *Arizona Magazine*, Vol. 5, no. 1, November 1914, 24.

assessment, Cho stood in the doorway and said, "He ain't no guest. He ain't got no bags. He an ostrich!"

"An ostrich!" Mrs. Robinson was surprised, but not too much, on account of the hotel's owner having a whole gaggle of them in the back pens. "Is it one of ours?"

"No, ma'am," Cho replied.

"In that case, tell him to go away."

Cho scrunched up his brows and thought about the request. "I don't think I can," he concluded.

"And why is that?" the manager quizzed.

"Because, ma'am, he an African ostrich and don't know English."

The hotel staff tried their best to communicate to the bird that he was unwelcome. They waved their arms and told him to "scat." But the ostrich would not *scat*. They shook a broom and called out "shoo!" But the ostrich did not *shoo*.

Finally, Dr. A.J. Chandler entered the lobby from the dining room. "What's all the commotion?" the doctor asked.

Once apprised of the situation, Dr. Chandler looked at the ostrich and confirmed, "Oh, he isn't mine."

As if on cue, the doctor's ranch superintendent, George Peabody, conveniently joined the crowd. "That's one of Maggie Toston's birds," he announced.

What a show, the bird thought. He took one more look at the hotel manager, now standing with her arms ferociously crossed in front of her chest. Feeling humiliated and scorned, he shed three large tears that splashed onto the patio furniture.

The dejected bird finally gave up and turned away. He left the Hotel San *Unwelcome* and began to mosey back to the Rancho del Toston.

Along the way, he met Thomas Toston on horseback.

"I've been looking for you," Toston told the bird.

The ostrich let out a sorrowful moan. The man with the broken head understood him.

"Oh, really?" Toston replied. "Well, I think your English is just fine. And how could they confuse you with a pickler? You look nothing like one!"

They made their way back home together.

Thomas "Moz" Toston, Jr. (1852-1920), undated, provided by Dorothy Combs (2012) on Ancestry.com (used with thanks).

Because I believe in truth in journalism, I decided to take only as many creative liberties in the retelling as the original author. I will admit, however, that I have no evidence for Mr. Sloan knowing a millionaire in Vancouver. That part might be entirely made up. Additional details of this event came out in the *Chandler Arizonan* the following day. Apparently, the ostrich threw a fit when he was refused hotel entry. It read: "'One audacious bird put his best foot through the window of the men's retiring room in the Hotel San Marcos, and created a furor of over-exaggerated joy among guests."[703]

Australia's War with Wild Emus

The ostrich's so-callled cousin has also had a litany of legends, but one that has recently stood out was when the Australian government rallied their military forces against their own emu population in 1932. Apparently, a mob of emus, numbering upwards of 20,000, had migrated from an area affected by drought, and the hungry birds ended up plaguing the irrigated farmlands down under. To address the field thieves, the 7th Heavy Battery of the Royal Australian Artillery was called into action... with machine guns. Their mission has since been called The Great Emu War.

As it turned out, emus were faster than the military's rapid-fire bullets. These birds, like ostriches, have no large flock mentality (such as ducks or pigeons who might be easy targets by way of keeping to concentrated groups). The emus broke up into small squadrons and, according to the new reports, they used guerrilla warfare tactics worthy of award. On day five of the battle, the *Kalgoorie Miner* reported that "Each mob has its leader," and even though the Seventh employed some of the best gunners, "...effective shooting was out of the question."[704] At one point, the commander conceded the military should consider employing emus instead of men, for their superior skill. He surrendered after eight days.

A 1953 issue of Sydney's *Sunday Herald* reflected on the events, calling their enemy a "tough, prolific, gangling marauder of the sand plains..." and commented on the military tactics as "farcical and humiliating defeats."[705] A modern writer has also summed, "...with thousands of rounds expended and only a few hundred emus confirmed killed, the operation was deemed a failure. ... The government had lost both ammo and dignity in what would become one of the most mocked military campaigns in history."[706]

The government followed up this initiative by putting a bounty on the bird's heads, setting traps, and building a 135-mile "emu-proof" fence through Western Australia. In 2020, Flightless Films released a comically-acclaimed short titled, "1932: The Great Emu War." The (should-be-R-rated) film perfectly blends elements of the "Jurassic Park" narrative, nearly every WWI trench war film of the past decade and any popular Zombie apocalypse movie set in the Wild West. It isn't for the faint of heart, but YouTube has made it available for all (see the Appendix for access).

29. Ostrich Tourism

"The baby ostrich is pleasing but not profitable;
the grown-up ostrich is profitable but not pleasing."
- The Outlook (1906)[707]

By 1914, ostriches were a well-established point of pride for the Sonoran Desert. Newspapers and magazines announced that even as ostrich populations increased in other parts of the country, Arizona remained the ostrich capital of the nation, with 6,000 of the recorded 10,000 on U.S. soil.[708] The January 1914 issue of *Arizona, The New State Magazine* devoted its feature piece to a Clinton S. Scott article about the industry, and the cover art featured a custom watercolor by Fay DeMund, a society woman and talented painter. That magazine cover showcased an Arizona mountain scene with desert features and two beautiful ostriches posing in the foreground.[709]

That same year, another promotional film featuring ostriches was produced. It was titled plainly: "Largest Ostrich Farm in the United States at Phoenix, Ariz." In Phoenix, it aired during The Mutual Weekly reel which was a series of scenes about the most important things happening around the world.[710] The downtown Lion Theater hosted the series on Sundays. That week, Pan-American's ranch dazzled viewers across the country, evoking summer road trip plans and eliciting even more civic pride from Arizonans.

Ostriches had become such a fascination that visitors were tromping on the grass and parking on the side of the street without the rancher's consent just to get a good look at

Selected pages from the Cawston Ostrich Farm fold-out brochure, created between 1896 and 1935 (South Pasadena Public Library/Public Domain).

(or inappropriately feed) the birds for their entertainment purposes. In response, Californian ostrich owners decidedly cashed in on the *lookie-loos.* Southern California ranches rapidly evolved into wildlife park attractions with ticketed entries, shops, refreshments, rides and feeding presentations to satisfy the curious. Robin Doughty wrote for *Agricultural History* that "The public looked upon ostrich farms in California (and Florida) chiefly as curiosities. They were well publicized as tourist attractions meriting a weekend outing..."[711]

Once the largest ostrich ranch in the nation, Arizona's Pan-American Ostrich Company received the bulk of tourist's attention. "It is half an hour by auto west of Phoenix

Advertisement from the *Arizona Republican*, October 8, 1906.

on the Yuma road, and worth traveling to see," wrote James Geissinger for the *Presbyterian Banner*.[712] Before the Chandler townsite could make such claims of being an oasis in the desert, it was the Pan-American that showcased, "in striking manner[,] the miracle of water."[713] The ranch was, as Geissinger put it, "Bitten out of this desert, snatched from the grip of relentless sand."[714]

Though Josiah Harbert's ostriches were generally visible from Grand Avenue, he charged a gate entry fee onto his Alhambra property to get a closer gander at his growing collection. The entry fees covered the expenses of livestock care while he continued to pay down his debts with the sales of eggs and feathers.[715] Also trying to increase income streams, William Pickrell once partnered with the Old Mission Museum on an early feather-themed museum exhibit. A 1906 advertisement for that exhibit read: "If the ladies of Arizona could realize that ... in our Free Museum they can see, without a cent of charge, thousands of beautiful ostrich feathers in their many finished forms and varied colorings, our Museum could scarcely hold the crowds."[716]

In Yuma, though not billed as an attraction of any sort, owing to the attention James Meadows was getting in the community, he allowed a high school class to tour his property. A summary of the visit appeared in the *Yuma Examiner* saying that Meadows showed the students the eggs inside the incubator, three baby ostriches that were only six weeks old and that he demonstrated how ostrich feathers were clipped once young birds matured.[717] The class left with one empty eggshell to take back to their school as a souvenir.

I'll Take a Dead Bird, Please

Speaking of museums... It's morbid, but not unreasonable for museums or other research facilities who might want to study the anatomy or other aspects of an animal to request one that has come to a natural or unfortunate end. But one 1910 request came from a member of the Board of Trade, now the Industrial Development Authority of the City of Phoenix, or simply "Phoenix IDA." Why would they need a dead bird? The *Arizona Republican* reported: "[The Board] feels that it must have an ostrich of some kind for its very own."[718] Secretary Harry Welch saw how well the birds were received when put on display at the 1909 Land and Irrigation Exposition in Chicago. After that, "The board thought it might secure one or two to send along for the same show this year."[719]

The Board representative rationalized that, "everyone who lives in this valley ought to want to own an ostrich whether he has any use for it or not."[720] Requests for dead ostriches for non-biological-study purposes were not entirely unhinged for the times. At the Cawston farm in Pasadena, "dead chicks could be stuffed and offered as mementos."[721] Since the expense was beyond the Board's ostrich-buying budget, "the next best thing [was] to get a dead ostrich and stuff him."[722] So, the IDA made a formal request of Pan-American for a dead ostrich.[723] Welch admitted this would be a penny saver because they wouldn't have to feed the large animal, nor would they need a large pen. Plus, it would always be ready for an audience. Soon, Welch learned that to get a corpse was just as expensive and difficult as buying a live bird! Hence, he extended the request to others in the state.

Display animals have historically been high-dollar expenses. As seen in an 1889 report from Dr. T. C. Duncan, he includes: "Even the skeleton on an ostrich commands a good price for public museums."[724] One example Duncan listed was from a professor in Rochester, New York. The professor (or his institute) put up an offer of $125 for a pole-mounted ostrich skeleton. That price comes to nearly $4,400 in today's terms, and that was *without* feathers. A corpse with its plumes attached commanded a much higher price.

Arizona ranchers refused to extinguish a member of their troop to meet the Board's request. So, the story continued, "There is nothing to do but wait for one to get sick and die."[725] Welch theorized that if a bird were to become available, he would offer acceptable terms to the owner. However, if they did not agree, Welch could wait for one day to go by, then ask the farmer again, albeit, with a lower offer. This bargaining tactic, he believed, would work especially well in the summer months.[726]

In 1995, a similar request was made of the Rooster Cogburn Ostrich Ranch at Picacho Peak. Relatives and descendants of the brothers William and Watson Pickrell wanted to help put on a museum exhibit on ostrich ranching at the Phoenix Museum of History. Watson's great-granddaughter, Connie Pickrell Siever, told the *Fort Worth Star-Telegram*, "We wanted a stuffed ostrich for the exhibit...."[727] The Phoenix Museum director agreed with the plan. "...To show a photo of an ostrich is one thing," the director shared, "but to actually see the size, shape and coloration is very exciting."[728] Certainly, a life-size cardboard cutout could never show those exact same qualities.

"We didn't want to kill one," the descendant clarified, adding, "We wanted to find one that somehow just died."[729]

The Pickrells had to wait for their wish to come true, but sure enough, an ostrich met an untimely death in the desert; it was a prized specimen

> "History doesn't repeat itself but it does rhyme."
>
> *- Quote attributed to Mark Twain*

that the Cogburns were sad to lose. It took a Phoenix taxidermist over one hundred hours to prepare the bird for its museum debut. In a strange act of kindness, the taxidermist also threw in a gift with purchase: four pre-stuffed ostrich chicks he happened to have already had on hand. For the record, the taxidermist wished to remain unidentified.

Siever mused on getting the creation to the museum: "'If you could have just seen that ostrich riding in the back of the truck with its feathers flapping away and that arrogant look on its face...'"[730]

A Few of the People Pleasers

During the height of the craze, an old-timer Willetta Riggs shared with the *East Valley Tribune*, "people could watch farmers clip ostrich feathers or buy decorated ostrich eggs and feathers in curio shops."[731] Inviting audiences to see the birds being clipped was so popular that announcements for upcoming clipping sessions appeared in the papers to draw in crowds. In 1905, Watson Pickrell made a public spectacle of the first plucking of his Tempe birds and de-quilling of those plucked a few months prior. For Pickrell, "[b]oth operations were gone through for the benefit of the spectators," he said, to educate those who thought the process was painful or otherwise damaging to the bird's health.[732]

Lou Ellsworth's clipping shows were among those best received. The *Border Vidette* reported on a busy day at the Mesa Ranch in 1910 when Louis Ellsworth, ranch foreman performed these duties for a crowd on New Year's Eve.[733] "This is an interesting sight to those who are not familiar with the operation, and is fascinating always to persons who have been in this part of the country long enough to know something about the ostrich," the report read.[734] Ellsworth was complimented on his plume selection and on the bird's healthy yield.

Another smart marketing scheme was to give sightseers an opportunity to see newly hatched chicks (which were usually kept contained in a barn or other enclosure to limit exposure to outdoor temperature variations and other threats). In March 1914, however, the Belgo-American Ostrich Co. set a few chicks out in a store window, perhaps to boost pre-Easter sales. The *Republican* included with their write-up: "Not all Phoenicians ... may have seen baby ostriches, just hatched from the shell. And but few of the Salt River Valley inhabitants ... have been privileged to see Motherless incubator ostrich chicks. For the next few days, however, everyone will have an opportunity to see them."[735]

The three-day-old chicks were set in the window display of the Sturges Hay and Grain Company, "and they will be kept in the windows where they may be seen at any time until they have become sufficiently old enough to no longer excite the

Ad from the *Arizona Republican*, March 18, 1914.

HATCHING OSTRICHES IN CITY STORE WINDOW

Little Fellows Beat Eddie Foy's Camel in Going Without Water

curiosity of the Phoenix sightseer."[736] The timeline for cuteness could be as long as six months, but certainly not in a shop window under the summer's intense glare. The day after the announcement, the paper reported that people were down at the Grain Co. "all day long" to see the babies.[737] Sturges' store owner likely benefitted from the crowd coming in to do a bit of shopping as well.

More People, More Problems

When Arizona Ostrich Company was located at the end of the Washington streetcar line, it became "quite an attraction for the citizens and visitors to Phoenix," similar to how the Phoenix Zoo has become.[738] (By the way, the state's first zoo was opened in 1923, and it was in Apache Junction.)

Though Pickrell's downtown location was popular for guests, not every guest was welcome. In 1910, Dick Aldrich was charged with stealing "a lot of ostrich feathers" from Pickrell.[739] Aldrich denied those claims, citing that the new laws passed in the prior year regarding feather property were not applicable to him. In March 1909, Governor Joseph Kibbey approved a bill that made plucking feathers from an ostrich without the bird owner's consent a misdemeanor crime.[740] Aldrich argued that he did not pluck any bird. Rather, he had taken his bunch from a barrel containing loose feathers. He also claimed he exchanged $5 cash, paid to a man who could not be identified nor located. Evidence against him included his attempt to conceal the giant feathers under his shirt and the fact that the feather quills were intact instead of cut.

A few months later, a desperate and greedy encounter of Secretary Harry Welch added to the uneasiness of ostrich raisers regarding site security and crowd control. After Welch posted his advertisement for a dead ostrich, he was approached by a stranger who got him alone in a corner of the office and offered to get him a corpse for only five dollars. "How?" was the question asked, but the answer was that this stranger planned to visit an area ostrich ranch and deliver cyanide to a bird during a feeding.[741]

At Dr. Sketchley's Anaheim location, he also faced some serious problems when visitors damaged the crops being raised to feed his animals. Some pulled down and otherwise breached the fencing, and many harassed his ostriches in ways that might harm their health. Dr. Sketchley had these offenders arrested and sought prosecution for every case.[742] Certainly, the early ostrich ranchers did not feel that they'd "signed up for" this type of added stress, which may have been a deterrent from more locations allowing public access. Dr. Sketchley found that what helped to keep the majority of miscreants away was to completely close off any public access to his property except by way of a formal, guarded entrance with a ticket fee of $.50 per person.[743] Edwin Cawston followed suit.

Another problem with having visitors is their ability to review their experience. Though not in Arizona, an amusing critique of Cawston's farm came from an unnamed visitor in 1906. This person, writing for *The Outlook*, a popular New York magazine, described the birds who crowded up to a fence as one-third "a pair of bare and revolting legs," another

Orange feeding time at Cawston's farm, undated postcard (David Boule Collection at Claremont Colleges Library, Fair Use).

third "equally bare and revolting necks" and the middle third being a dirty mass of fluff.[744] "To crown it all," he or she continued, the birds had "an indescribably fatuous [stupid] and yet malicious expression."[745] The critic said visitors were warned to keep at least two feet away from the fencing because ostriches will grab at and try to eat just about anything they could reach. "It will eat, so the ostrich farmers say, stones, leather, whole oranges, gimlets [a stiff gin and lime drink], and lighted pipes."[746] If spectators did not follow the rules, the ostriches were known to gobble down their hats, newspapers, and glasses right off their heads, hands and faces. This not only irritated the visitor but endangered the owner's

> o
>
> "They'll peck the pearl buttons off your Western shirt & pull stuff out of your pockets faster than a thief on the Rome metro."
>
> *-Sam Negri, Arizona Highways (2005)*

° Sam Negri, "No Dummies These Big Ostriches," *Arizona Highways* 81, no. 1 (January 2005), 31.

moneymaking. In one case of a hat-jacking, a woman was wearing a bonnet with a dyed-green veil. Two days after consumption, that ostrich was found dead of arsenic poisoning from the green dye.[747]

Finally, the critic declared Cawston's ranch "the dustiest place on earth," and figured that "[t]he ostriches have eaten up everything except the dust, which is where they draw the line."[748] Apparently that last comment was spot-on because other reviews called the place a "dust bowl."[749]

Dr. A.J. Chandler: Arizona's New Ostrich King

Leading in Arizona's most entertaining ostrich ranch competition was Dr. A.J. Chandler, who by volume of ostriches alone (approx. 800) became the new ostrich king. His show pens at the San Marcos Hotel and the bulk of his birds at the feather farm in Mesa quickly outshone both Pan-American and Arizona Ostrich Co. as the state's premier destination for ostrich ogling.

Dr. A.J. Chandler, 1915, Courtesy of Chandler Historical Society (Chandler Museum Collection [86-142-1], Chandler, AZ Museum, Licensed Use.)

Part of the draw to Dr. Chandler's ranches can be attributed to his many political alliances and social influences. For example, his superintendent George T. Peabody was a member of a local motorists' club, so the ostrich pens became a designated stop on their popular "auto tours." In prior years, Captain Frank Alkire had been leading similar club drive-bys to the National Ostrich Co. at 51st Ave. and Thomas Rd.[750]

In early December, after the San Marcos Hotel's pens were filled with the Pan-American purchases, Dr. Chandler hosted an auto tour group with special privileges. The *Arizona Republican* reported that "the entire party was taken to the roof of the San Marcos and shown one of the most attractive stretches of irrigated valley in the world. ...off to the west was a huge corral in which more than 200 ostriches were feeding."[751] The praise continued, assuring future motorists that this stop was "one of the most interesting of the valley auto tour" and made especially exciting because of such sights.[752]

As a whole, the ostrich ranching industry would decline after 1915 but because of the tourism aspect, the Chandler site would be one of the last ranches standing through the 1920s. And, if looking at the cumulative duration of Dr. Chandler's ostrich raising activities between the Mesa and Chandler location, he was the rancher to remain in business the longest, spending at least 18 years caring for the South African-turned-Arizona wonders. (That is, until D.C. Cogburn came to town and smashed the record.)

Unlike his competitors, Dr. Chandler never charged admission to see his birds at either location. At the Mesa Ranch, the birds were enclosed with double fences made of woven wires. This allowed the birds to be seen from the road, "so that visitors in the city have a good view of them at all times."[753] The up close and personal experience with feeding, petting, taking photos with and possibly riding on the ostriches from the San Marcos may have warranted a ticket, but it is reasonable to conclude that room reservations, golf events, corporate retreats and other merchandise sales earned enough to keep the ostriches accessible for "free."

Dethroned by Days' End

As the Pan-American ranch continued its closeout sales, a few more opportunists appear to have swooped in on an easy opportunity to turn a profit. After 23 major ostrich orders were listed on December 1, Pan-American still had 1,800 birds to rehome. Roger Warren made agreements with locals for bulk pricing of ostriches as low as $3 to help him offload the final few.[754] For Phoenicians with a bit of cash on hand, a situation like this was almost predatory. The *Imperial Valley Press* reported that Salt River Valley owners were willing to sell their precious birds for $50 per head with a $10 downpayment.[755]

Samuel H. Mitchell, manager of the Phoenix Railway Co. streetcar, was one such owner willing to sell his cheaply acquired 600 birds. He quickly turned his $1,800 investment into $30,000 (minus the cost of stamps and ink to coordinate a sale). His ostriches were sold to the Calipatria Ostrich Farm in California's around December 10.[756] Another surreptitious deal was arranged with a businessmen's association that planned to open a farm at Bidwell Park in Chico, California. They hoped the contribution would become "the nucleus of a zoo."[757] It is unknown who they purchased their starter birds from.

At the end of December, Arizona headlines announced another major sale, this time to Franklin D. Lane, a realtor who would eventually become the 35th Mayor of Phoenix. The December 27 story of Lane's coronation reads: "Franklin D. Lane is now the ostrich king of the valley, having purchased

"Frank Lane is Now Ostrich King," *Arizona Republican*, Dec. 27, 1914.

FRANK LANE IS NOW ARIZONA OSTRICH KING

the Pan-American ostrich farm and 1,000 birds that are still on the farm. Mr. Lane proposes to embark into the ostrich industry for all there is in it."[758]

Because land sales accompanied the livestock offloading, by the time Lane got involved, there was only 1,120 acres left for him out of 1,600 that passed into the hands of the Phoenix National Bank in 1906. "It is Mr. Lane's idea to raise eggs and feathers from his birds and not allow any of them to be eaten."[759] To be clear, the birds were not to be eaten, nor were their feathers, but Lane planned to market the ostrich eggs to bakeries and pastry cooks as "hen fruit."

It's likely that Lane may have jumped on this deal a bit too hastily and by April 1915, he sold his entire inventory to the British-American Mercantile Company in El Centro, California. They scooped up not only the remaining birds, but also the ranch manager, William M. Cross. The *Imperial Valley Press* headline read: "Have Big Plans for Bird Farm." In that deal, the mercantile announced it would be starting up with 1,200 birds.[760] Rumor has it, with that being the final sale, Lane surrendered the royal crown back to Dr. Chandler after giving it a quick spit polish.

30. What About Ostrich Meat?

*"The nation... will be informed of this fabulous
'new' red meat—Ostrich!"*
-*Dub Oliver, Ostrich Ranching in America (1993)*[761]

In 1914, ostrich meat made its national tabletop debut. A decade prior, Watson Pickrell told the U.S. Department of Agriculture that a young, domestic ostrich is "much relished by those who have eaten it,"[762] and that it is a viable meat product. Despite the praise, the fixation on feathers kept breeders busy chasing their fortunes in that avenue, exclusively. Competing on the meat market was partly prompted by the liquidation of Pan-American and the subsequent saturation of the industry, which lowered bird values. This caused breeders to rapidly shift towards a more economically stable product: meat. The caveat was that there had never been a market for this product. No one knew how to eat it, how to cook it, or on what occasion to serve it, so ostrich ranchers had to lead by example with fingers crossed that customers would follow suit.

Leading up to the 1914 Thanksgiving holiday, ostrich ranchers tried to promote their birds as the new centerpiece to dazzle one's guests. Early in the month, George Alkire sent two chicks to the Cohen & Co. grocer in Chicago, Illinois. The *Arizona Republican* touted: "These birds are destined to take the place of the long-gamed Thanksgiving turkey at a large banquet."[763] Mr. I. Choen let the live birds wobble around a display to draw in attention and told the press, "You can cook ostriches just like turkeys if your oven is big enough."[764] The

Headline in the *Bisbee Daily Review*, Nov. 25, 1914.

BABY OSTRICHES FOR C. Q. HOTEL DINNER

Headline in the *Arizona Republican*, Nov. 27, 1914, 2.

SIXTY OSTRICHES GO TO FEED GUESTS OF FRED HARVEY HOUSES

Chi-Town grocer marketed the birds as "squab ostriches" (i.e.. babies), which dressed them up as a delicacy for area hob-nobbers.

In Bisbee, Arizona, the historic Copper Queen Hotel added two 50-pound chicks to their holiday dining experience, citing they would be "the pièce de résistance," for connoisseurs of fine foods.[765] The hotel manager promoted the meat as having "the finest flavor."

One of Alkire's birds may have been purchased by the Chicago Athletic Association. They paid $35 for a 70-pound bird approximately five months old. "Members of the club decided to have something novel for dinner," the *Chicago Tribune* printed.[766] The chef for this banquet said that after being prepared, there were 17 pounds of meat for the meal (they were also surprised to find three pounds of gravel inside the bird's gut). The Chicago chef estimated it would take six hours to roast the ostrich and that it would sufficiently serve 100 guests at the affair.

To get an idea of how quickly an ostrich can provide such a large amount of meat, we'll look at turkeys and chickens. The heaviest turkey recorded in the Guinness World Record book was 86 pounds with a final dressed weight (the typically eaten portion) of 20 pounds. That's only possible in a turkey after 12-24 months of growth. Large roasting chickens mature faster and are processed at around three months. Even the largest can only provide 5-7 pounds of dressed meat. Comparatively, ostrich chicks have an extraordinary output for their short, five-month investment (plus 40-day incubation and hatcher care).

The Fred Harvey Company served up the trending fare that year. They ordered ostriches in bulk from Pan-American and distributed them along the Santa Fe Railway to be sliced and gravied for Harvey House diners and guests who were traveling over the holiday. The *Arizona Republican* suggested those birds were "Sacrificed on the altar of American gratitude."[767] The allusion to ostrich eating being a of patriotic gesture came on the heels of President Woodrow Wilson's proclamation for the day of prayer and thanksgiving to be held as usual, even as the events of World War I unfolded and North Americans feared for their European allies.[768]

Some concerns had also circulated that there might be a shortage of turkeys and a price hike, but turkeys remained available and affordable at $.30-$.35 per pound. (By the way, at Pan-American's extreme sale price, if each bird averaged a modest 20 pounds of dressed meat—depending on age—that would have come out to $.25 per pound. ...Just wait until you see what ostrich meat costs now!)

p In 1918, Phoenix rancher J. E. Cogdell was asked to provide 800 ostriches to local markets so the U.S. could send 25,000lbs. of pork and beef to soldiers in the trenches.
By June 1918, U.S. forces had been in combat for a year.

p "800 Ostrich[e]s to be killed for food," *Weekly Journal-Miner*, June 26, 1918, 3.

Also taking advantage of the fact that the price of ostrich had dropped to "about the same as the gobbling friend of our youth, and the meat is said to be fully as tender," the Phoenix Elks Lodge served a few heaping hocks at their monthly group meeting. The *Arizona Sentinel* announced to anyone hoping to claim the rights to the annual wishbone breaking ritual that the ostrich's large lucky charm had already been spoken for.[769]

An editorial in the *Arizona Republican* provided the follow-up to the year's feasts: "We have not heard from the guests of the Harvey Houses and Arizona hotels and restaurants where young ostriches were served last Thursday, but no doubt the verdict, when it is rendered, will be favorable..."[770] The write-up ended with a distasteful comment about people probably trying to eat the neck, which was thought to be rubber-like. (By the way, the neck is not in the traditional list of edible items. Back in the 1900s, however, ostrich neck tendons were harvested for use as surgical thread.)[771]

Ostriches continued to hold their reputation as a fancy feast maker through the end of the year, appearing on Christmas tables instead of ham or duck. In December, the *Republican* ran ads for young ostriches from Belgo-American to grace more family tables. Again, setting the example for others, the owners put their mouth where their money was. (You read that right.) "In celebration of the advent of the ostrich as a table bird, a number of the officers," the *Republican* included, "gathered at the American Kitchen last evening to partake of an ostrich dinner."[772] Guests included the Verwilghens, Janssens, Dr. and Mrs. Wylie, the Hartranfts, and the Heards. They chose a 55-pounder, prepared in a "most approved style" and they assured readers of the state newspaper that the meal "was pronounced delicious..."[773]

Eating roasted ostrich thighs, ca. early 1920s. (University of Southern California Libraries and California Historical Society/Public Domain).

Trying to break an ostrich wishbone at a feast in San Diego's Lincoln Park, ca. 1910-20s (University of Southern California Libraries and California Historical Society/Public Domain).

Why Don't More People Eat Ostrich Today?

Early ostrich ranchers were ineffective at convincing the nation to accept the meat as a regular food item. The over-the-top holiday promotion resembled a parent trying to feed spinach-loaded baby food to a skeptical infant (*"Mmmm..."*). The idea of eating a mean, gangly cartoon character, coupled with the perception of them as exotic, protected or an endangered species has continually deterred the masses from enjoying their luxuriously soft flesh for the last hundred years. The problem appears to be a matter of perception, which can be addressed with a bit of education and a heap of smart marketing.

First, we must acknowledge that ostriches have always been safe for eating and so are their eggs. Since the beginning of the industry in the U.S., ostriches were classified as a livestock animal and food product (just like cattle, pigs, goats, sheep, etc.). For Old Testament followers, ostrich is not considered kosher because of a Levitical decree designating it a "detestable" creature, along with the vulture and seagull.[774] That very clarification tells us that at least some people were eating ostrich back in Bible times. Besides religious or dietary restrictions, there is little reason for foodies today to miss out on the experience.

Right now, ostrich meat is one of the healthiest meats available on the market (plus there is the benefit of reduced greenhouse emissions and a smaller eco footprint mentioned in a previous chapter). Because demand is low, an ostrich steak or burger can be hard to find locally unless you live near an ostrich raiser or specialty meat market. It also commands a high price like lobster or venison. Depending on the cut, the meat can be between 95-98% lean. It is very high in iron and zinc and, compared to beef, it contains about the same calories but is lower in cholesterol. Unlike beef, though, ostrich does not shrink when cooked, so buyers get more bang for their buck.

D.C. Cogburn, currently the only ostrich rancher in the state, has shared on this: "A primary issue was that no one knew that it was safe to eat the birds and that they tasted good. The strangeness of the idea put off many cultures."[775] As an example, an 1899 article about the industry in California advised people against the practice of eating ostriches, claiming "Ostriches are not fit to eat, because they are so tough as to be uneatable."[776] The author confessed the source for this belief was an ancient writer who described the ostrich flesh like that of a zebra. Actually, the ancient writer was not far off. Zebra meat is very red in color, low in fat, dense in fiber, and slightly sweet. These are all applicable to ostrich as well.

Attributing toughness could also be the result of a hunter's selection of an older ostrich, beyond its prime, or due to the chef's attempt to cook the ostrich until it resembled the brown shade of beef steak. Due to the high presence of myoglobin, even when well done, ostrich meat still appears red like a rare steak, so cooking it requires careful monitoring of internal temperatures to avoid turning the velvety smooth fibers into something like chewy trailer tie-downs.

What Makes Meat Red?

The myoglobin protein is highly pigmented and largely responsible for creating the red color seen in muscle tissue (ie. meat).

How to Cook Ostrich

Though the USDA defines ostrich (the animal) as livestock, it categorizes its meat as poultry. But as much as these Thanksgiving stories may convince you to cook the bird as poultry, it should be prepared and paired like red meat. Ostrich can be ground, filleted and steaked just like beef, dried into a jerky, and even marbled into a salami-style cold cut. In the 1990s, blind taste tests revealed that people could not tell the difference between a common steak and a cut of ostrich. (By the way, there is a simple cooking guide in the Appendix.)

The portions of the bird eaten are in the legs, shoulder and along the rump, almost exclusively. Unlike traditional poultry products, ostriches do not produce breast meat, nor could anyone enjoy buffalo sauce on their bony wings. Annie

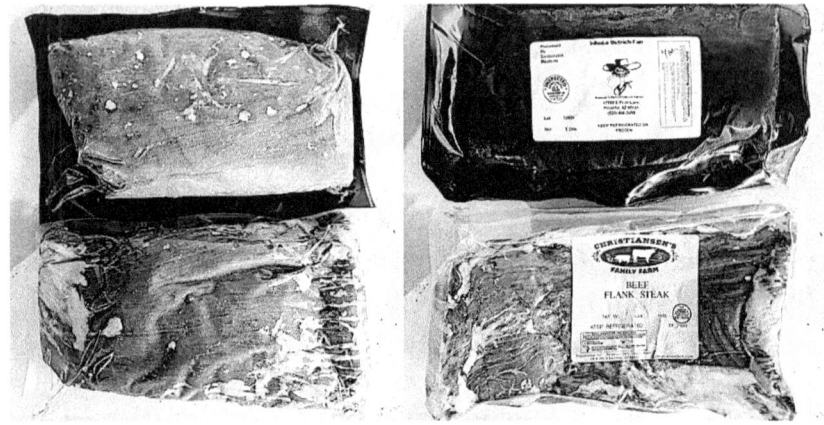

Comparison of fat marbling in similar (top) ostrich and (bottom) beef products. (Author's collection, 2025.)

Martin reflected on her first experience trying to prepare an ostrich to the cliché cuisine of the French. She wrote: "We ate the legs only; there being no meat whatever on any other part of the creature's body."[777]

For most feather farmers, the idea of eating their livestock was not even an option because it would eliminate ten to twenty years of potential profits from that bird's feathers. That being said, approaching this from an all-or-nothing stance left early raisers missing out on the opportunity to diversify the products they could put on the market.

There is a sweet spot for maximizing the gains from an ostrich sent for processing. In the range of 10-16 months, the bird will have grown mature plumes that can be harvested for fashionistas. Besides feathers, they will have become large enough to retrieve a sizable sheet of leather for luxury boots, belts, purses and more. Finally, at this age, they will provide enough meat to feed a family of four for a month. Dub Oliver, an ostrich rancher in the 1990s, learned while processing a

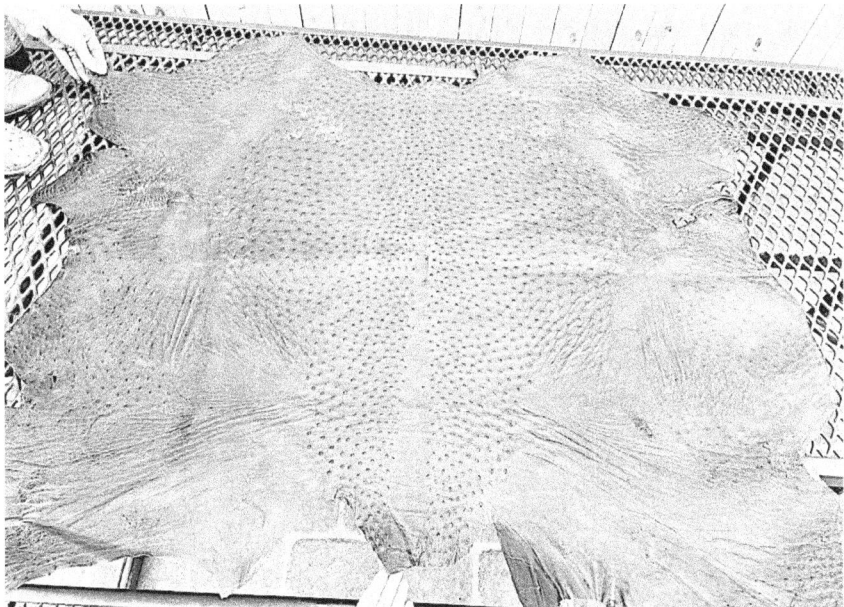

One ostrich leather from the Rooster Cogburn Ostrich Ranch can sell between $400-$600 (Author collection, 2025).

15-month-old bird, "after deboning, the actual meat ... came to a surprising 80 pounds, or 73% of the carcass weight."[778]

If an ostrich is processed before that sweet spot, its meat will be higher quality, but the feathers may not be ready and the leather supply shorted and undecorated. Beyond that sweet spot, its meat loses tenderness, and the bird will be exposed to more risk factors that can damage the quality of its leather (such as mating and fighting). Each breeder must decide for themselves which product they want to prioritize, then operate as efficiently as possible towards that end goal.

At whatever age processed, the ostrich gives more back to society than you might think. Ostrich skin is a highly desirable commodity to bougie Western shoppers. For those with a discerning eye, they can estimate the value of an ostrich leather boot by the quantity of its quill marks. More quills mean more decorative marks, which means more expensive products. Ostrich leg leather features distinct shin wrinkles that mimic a snakeskin pattern. Besides boots and purses, there are ostrich leather gloves and saddles that can reportedly outlast the lifespan of the rider who uses them.

The bird's bright yellow layer of buttery soft fat is another rich resource. Annie Martin claimed, "There is no fat equal to it for guns, saddles, harness, boots, etc."[779] The refined oil is also well-reputed for its Omega-rich anti-inflammatory properties made popular as a topical rub for sore muscles. Lesser known is how ostrich eyes can be used as a scaffolding structure for reconstructing damaged human corneas. Even ostrich bones go to good use as snacks for the carnivores at the zoo or as ground bone meal in pet food.

Menu	
Top Sirloin (12 oz.)	$26
Stingray Brisket	$35
Ostrich Steak (12 oz.)	$42
Cold Water Lobster Tail	$59
Wagyu Beef	$82
Zebra Tenderloin	$230

Can Ostrich Meat Improve Your Mental Health?

That was a legitimate question asked by professors at the University of Arizona, in 1918.[780] Dean R. H. Forbes and Professor Thornber of the College of Agriculture decided to test their theory using only the most scientifically sound way they knew: a foot race. That wacky story went something like this:

In 1903, before folks in the United States considered ostrich meat to be an available protein source, Dr. Forbes and Prof. Thornber engaged in a race that resulted in a disputed tie. Neither would concede the win to the other or allow for even a hint of embarrassment over the possibility that they may have been a millisecond short. So, the colleagues became enemies, spitting in each other's general direction if they were on campus on the same teaching day.

"How's it feel to be a loser, Thorny?" Dr. Forbes shouted across the main drag one day.

Prof. Thornber, the staff horticulturist, straightened his shoulders and tipped his signature newsboy cap. Calling back with absolutely no regard for the student body giving alarmed looks, he quipped, "It's hard for me to say, friend. For that, I'd turn to someone more experienced, like you."

Dr. Forbes received an audience of curious listeners hauling their bookbags across the greenway. He twitched his lip and looked down at his reflection in the mug of black coffee he was previously enjoying. He didn't have a quick response this time. The dean tossed his coffee out into a nearby bush with a huff and turned back to reenter the university's administration building.

The professor kept heading to the Ag. building, but with an added pep in his step.

Fifteen years passed by, and this grudge had become the only thing the Dean needed to think about in the morning to give him the zip to start his day. Then, in January 1918, as the agriculture department and friends of the university enjoyed their ostrich feast to close out the University Farm, Dr. Francis Lockwood from the department of psychology advised the Dean to settle the matter, once and for all.

"You know, this is the end of an era for you two. And Thornber's retiring. No need to stay spiteful," the psychologist offered.

Dr. Forbes glanced at, then past the instructor, eyeing his subject. "We may be older now, and certainly Thornber is significantly older than I, but there is only one way to settle this. Sir, we must have a rematch before the platter of ostrich turns dry."

That night it was decided that the Ag. Department would witness a rematch.

"But I've just eaten a plate of fine ostrich meat and I'm practically stuffed," Prof. Thornber complained.

"How exciting!" The psychology teacher suggested that the competitors incorporate that fact in the data collection as to whether the consumption of ostrich meat would benefit a runners' physical power and mental stamina. That was one of the last research experiments conducted on ostriches at the University Farm. Because the results of the rematch were not published in the *Arizona Daily Star,* we'll all just have to retest the theory for ourselves.

Ostrich Eggs on the Menu

Though folks in the early 1900s felt conflicted over ostrich meat, eating their eggs seemed to be an easier item to incorporate into a meal plan. Annie Martin shared that ostrich eggs, "were always most acceptable; and I have never had lighter cakes, nicer omelettes, custards, etc., than those made from them."[781] Some brides of this time even boasted that their entire wedding cake was made with only one egg—an ostrich's. Not only would that have been a nod to how large the cake was, but also an indication of wealth or connections. These "hen fruits," as Frank D. Lane called them, were priced well above the equivalent amount of chicken eggs.

When T.W. Kemp opened his El Paso farm in 1911, he celebrated his first Texas-laid egg with a political feast. He gave a luncheon for the mayor, the Secretary of the Board of Trade and ten other leading citizens, according to the *Arizona Republican.* Details of the celebration included the following:

Left: Author with an 8 oz. ostrich steak dinner. Right: Holding an ostrich egg at the Rooster Cogburn Ostrich Ranch in Arizona. (Author collection, 2025).

"Ostrich eggs fried, hard boiled and scrambled, with other good things ... centerpieces on the table consisted of a bouquet of long ostrich plumes, surrounded by other lesser feathers. Finger bowls of half ostrich-egg shells, mounted in silver were brought into use. Each guest was presented with a boutonniere of ostrich feathers ... [and] All spoke in highest praise of the ostrich eggs as an article of diet."[782]

"Eating eggs" have always been difficult to sell to the mainstream customer. One egg could contain as much to eat as the contents of 24 to 36 chicken eggs. After scoring one end of the shell with a drill and cracking through with a hammer, the customer needs to be prepared to supply an entire church banquet with quiche. Otherwise, the novelty of the meal might wear off when a small family is eating leftovers for the tenth time in a week.

 Hard boiling an ostrich egg can take from 1 ½ - 2 hours.

Currently, an eating egg costs between $40 and $50. Even when the 2024 bird flu caused chicken egg prices to

315

skyrocket, the average cost for three dozen chicken eggs was still only 1/3 the price of one ostrich egg. Today's buyer purchases them more for entertainment or "for the experience" than anything else.

31. The End of the Craze

"One day, every woman wore feathers.
The next day, you couldn't give them away for dusters."
- The Phoenix Gazette (1976)[783]

From 1914 to about 1918, the ostrich feather industry declined towards nonexistence. Past literature has jumped to conclude that World War I caused the ostrich feather industry collapse because these events coincide, but by then, feather farming was already doomed. Before the War began, women in Europe used ostrich feathers to make a powerful statement. And, historically speaking, when women organize for a cause, they can make an impact that is felt across the world.

I would argue that the initial domino that disrupted feather sales was an exaggerated response to the wearing of feathers by avian protection clubs. As early as 1904, advocates against bird poaching and the overt destruction of beautiful and exotic animals for fashion had gained traction in Europe. From club efforts, new legislation limited or altogether ceased wild bird plumage collection and resale. Anti-plumage-wearing supporters called for a total ban on feather importations ...except, from the very start of such movements, farmed ostrich feathers. The National Association of Audubon Society was in full support of the ostrich exception.

When the first Plumage Prohibition Bill was introduced to Europe in 1904, the *Millinery Trade Review* assured industry workers in New York, "The tender-hearted maiden may [continue to] wear [ostrich feathers] in happy consciousness that her pretty hat has cost the life of no hapless fowl, and," they asserted, "the dealer may handle [them] without fear of coming into collision with the Audubon society or the bird laws."[784]

In 1905, William Dutcher, the president of the Audubon, stated the society's formal position on wild bird poaching and cruelty for fashion, including a clear distinction and specific allowance for ostrich feathers. His write-up appeared in *Bird-Lore*, the official magazine publication of the Audubon. It read: "The Audubon Societies are not opposed to the use of feather ornaments which can be obtained without cruelty or the sacrifice of the lives of birds. ... Ostrich feathers are legitimate as well as beautiful decorations and are approved by the Audubon Societies. Their use does not entail the sacrifice of life, nor does it cause the slightest suffering to the Ostrich; taking plumes from an Ostrich is no more painful to the bird than shearing is to a sheep."[785]

To those considering a boycott against all feather types regardless of the organizational approval, Dutcher added: "Furthermore, the use of ostrich plumes encourages an important industry which gives people employment, in this country, to an annually increasing number of people."[786]

The Royal Society for the Protection of Birds & National Audubon Society were led by dedicated women who helped formulate & promote the Importation of Plumage Prohibition Bill(s).

Two years later, one woman threw a wrench in the hotly debated topic. Alexandra Edward, Queen consort of the United Kingdom and Empress consort of India impressed to her followers that she was opposed to *all* ornamental feather wearing, regardless of the source. It seemed an odd choice, considering Queen Alexandra frequently adorned herself with

Left to right: Queen Alexandrina of Denmark, 1898. Beagles' Postcard #306.F
(J. Russell & Sons); H. M. Queen Alexandra, Buckingham Palace, 1908 (W. D.
Downey Collection); H. M. Queen Alexandra, 1921, Beagles' Postcard #855.R
(Vandyk Ltd.).

feathers from head to toe, including lush fans with airy ostrich
plumes. Her loyal subjects and fan-followers mirrored her
attitude, and, for a while, ostrich feathers lost their popularity.

The impact Queen Alexandra had on European style was
so strong that by 1909, both the British and German settle-
ments in Africa ceased all feather exportations to the continent, regardless of the exception available.[787] As seen in the
images provided, one decade after the Queen took her anti-
plume stance, she must have changed her mind. In 1921,
ostrich plumes fluttered from her hat and trailed down her
entire collar. *How very fickle!*

In 1914, grassroot campaigns against feather wearing
resurged. This time, women's banding together coincided with
the Woman Suffrage Movement. New efforts to ban feathers in
Europe included heaps of negative publicity against comer-
cial operations that bought, manufactured or sold feathered
goods. Some advocates spread the narrative that feather-
wearing women were cruel women. Popular media became so

saturated by negative messaging that big-name ornithologists, literary men and politicians started to believe that "plume hunters were decimating scores of wild-bird species for the fashion markets of London, New York, and Paris."[788] Heroic politicians felt an obligation to intervene, or at least re-visit the prior law.

> "Clothes aren't going to change the world, the women who wear them will."
> -Anne Klein, American Fashion Designer (n.d.)

Adding to the problem in Europe was the start of World War I, when white feathers (the only legal type being ostrich) became a symbol of cowardice. A group of suffragettes used these feathers to publicly humiliate men who would not volunteer for military service. The intent was to emphasize the gender power gap by applying pressure on men to fulfill their role as voting-eligible, male British citizens, in the fullest sense of the meaning.

Women involved were called members of "The White Feather Society." When a society woman had an opportunity to present a symbolic feather to a non-serving man, she would do so, before a public audience, with boldness and little discretion. Staging the event maximized the ridicule her victim might receive. An example is shown in a comic from *Collier's Weekly*. The caption reads: "Suddenly, producing a large, white feather, she jabbed it into his waistcoat. And in another tone, fierce and scornful, she added: ... 'You coward! Why don't you enlist?'"

Suddenly producing a large white feather, she jabbed it into his waistcoat. And in another tone, fierce and scornful, she added: "You coward! Why don't you enlist?"

"The White Feather: A Sketch of English Recruiting," by Arnold Bennett in *Collier's Weekly*, 1914.

An unexpected reaction to one of these flagrant displays has circulated in historical literature about a man (possibly Private Ernest Atkins) who was on leave from the Western Front (some accounts say Passchendaele). While on leave, he was not in uniform and when the suffragette targeted him for this stunt in a crowded location, he shocked the audience. The soldier slapped the woman and declared something about wanting to take that feather back to the front line to show his comrades and ask what they might have to say.[789]

Feather farmers across the world saw these aggressive campaigns as an immediate threat to their livelihoods. Those immediately involved in the ostrich feather industry (and those financially invested) responded by heaping education and long-standing approval on retailers, shoppers and law-makers; reminding them that clipping feathers from domes-ticated ostriches was neither cruel, nor deadly.

In the February 28, 1914 issue of the United Kingdom's *Spectator*, one letter to the editor read: "We, the undersigned, have considered the Importation of Plumage Prohibition Bill. We are most heartily in accord with this measure, as we believe that it is the duty of this country to put an end to the traffic in the skins and plumes of wild birds. ... A great part of the work done in connextion[*sic*] with this fancy plumage is performed on... ostrich feathers, whose entry will be per-mitted, and even stimulated, by the provision of this Bill."[790] Sir Arthur Conan Doyle, a British physician and author of the world-famous *Sherlock Holmes* series was a signer on that letter.

A follow up issue of March 7 contained another letter which read: "The Plumage Bill now before [British] Parlia-ment prohibits the importation into this country of the plumage and skins of wild birds, with the exception of the plumage of (a) birds for the time being included in the schedule to the Act (ostriches and eider ducks). ... The Plumage Bill will increase the demand for ostrich feathers, trade in which is a perfectly legitimate business, involving no cruelty to birds and no risk of extinction to species."[791] (By the way, the eider duck was excepted because it's down feathers could be collected without cruelty or impact on population.)

European feather manufacturers were infuriated with the reputational damages caused by such events. Some felt it would be a fruitless effort to promote ostrich-only products to women who had taken an absolutist stance, especially when (somehow) their right to vote may have depended on it. Despite the clear legal allowance for ostrich feathers, "merchants of London ... argue that the use of ostrich feathers and of other fancy feathers rises and falls together," and they succumbed to the pressure.[792]

One year after U.S. President Woodrow Wilson funded the progression of safe and sustainable feather farming, the Plumage Bill promised a disruption to the American industry. Details of the debates and the July 1914 proclamation were printed in the *Arizona Republican.* In response, the journalist confidently reminded readers: "Owing to the representations that were made by this government ... ostrich feathers were excluded from the scope of the bill."[793] Arizona ostrich ranchers would not accept that a woman's parading and demonstrating for votes could derail an entire empire, especially when the state had given women the right to vote back in 1912.

The second domino in the industry's fall sequence might have been from major feather importers' sudden loss of business in Europe. Because of the political upheaval, South

African feather farmers redirected their products to North American manufacturers. In doing so, they flooded the market. Iowa's *Quad-City Times* reported: "South Africa ostrich men turned at once to New York seeking an outlet for their

> [q] "South Africans didn't use all the parts of the animal to stay in business."
> -D.C. "Rooster" Cogburn (2025)

plumes and in a short time that market was gutted. Prices then took a tumble, such as they never before had known."[794] Even the most stunning white primes lost their value by over 90%.[795] The surplus problem compounded when Pan-American sold off its troops. By the end of 1914, both the ostrich and its feathers were considered cheap and common.

One writer for the *Republican* posed that, because of feminine fickleness, "this slump cannot be of long duration."[796] They predicted "the business will boom again and a man who has a few birds will find himself in a way to make some money easy."[797] The *Bisbee Daily Review* also stayed encouraging, saying, "In another year ostrich feathers may come back in style and the value of the birds restored."[798] Dr. Charles Meserve, state chemist and owner of 15 birds, also expressed his hope for a comeback. He told the *Tucson Citizen*, "While the feathers are not worth much now, and may not be for several years, they will be valuable eventually."[799] Despite his optimism, the chemist kept his day job.

1915 was promoted as the year to invest in inexpensive ostriches, priced like an ordinary shoe, in readiness for a rebound.[800] At this point, George T. Peabody became an ostrich owner in Chandler, as did Dr. Frederick P. Perkins, Judge L.L. Pearson and Frances Shaw in Phoenix. The City of Mesa picked up a few ostriches for display purposes, and the Pima Indian Council at the Sacaton Agency also invested in

---

[q] Damon C. Cogburn, phone communication to author, April 29, 2025.

either two or six pairs of birds, depending on the source one reads.[801]

Wartime Fashions

As World War I escalated in Europe, and their women simplified their fashion tastes. Some needed practical outfits to better suit their entering the workforce, which led to a small surge of women wearing trousers. Most women wanted their clothing to express solidarity with the deployed. A 1915 news story from Iowa reported on how English women had "abandoned luxuries," and diverted funds to field hospitals and other relief organizations.[802] This type of positive attention on the demure or working woman further contributed to the collapse of the feather-buying market overseas. North America had not entered combat yet, so any sentimental dressing down would be delayed. It wasn't until the summer of 1917 when U.S. women saw their loved ones off to combat. By then, they could easily adopt Europe's sensible fashions and "keep up" with the movement.

A more immediate influence on U.S. fashion was related to the increase of automotive travel. Though enclosed vehicles were being developed at this time, most had no roofs, no windows, and only a minimal windshield. Helen Seargeant's thoughts were that "fine plumes are not suited to the windy air currents of open cars."[803] Even a short ride in an open-air vehicle could tatter a delicate feather down to its shaft. For a short time, women attempted to protect their investments in fine hats and accessories by overwrapping headpieces with chiffon or another light material to limit how much flutter the frills endured. That attempt wasn't very effective. Seargeant indicated that the additional tie-downs were an annoyance that could be avoided by choosing a different hat altogether.[804] Once vehicles were fully enclosed, internal head

Auto tour to an ostrich farm, 1912. Arizona State Archives at Arizona State Library (Licensed use).

space did not allow for big hats of any kind and women's hat selections had to change again.

The U.S. Hemorrhaged Ostriches

Though a few ranchers were determined to see the industry through the slump, Arizonans generally ridded themselves of ostriches anyway they could. Carloads of ostriches were shipped out to the Santa Fe Railroad to feed hired hands.[805] In an earlier chapter, we also saw that the U.S. Ostrich Experimental Station gave their birds away to zoos and circuses. In 1916, several Chandler breeders offloaded ostriches to the British and American Mercantile Company in Brawley, California.[806] Roscoe G. Willson found that the merch-ants acquired 2,500 birds at "$7 a head."[807]

Willson also claimed that if an ostrich could not be sold or given away, it was destroyed and used as fertilizer, though I have never seen empirical evidence to support this idea.[808] What I have seen, however, was that at the end of 1916, over 100 of Dr. A.J. Chandler's ostriches were fed to hogs.[809] 250 ostriches remained in Chandler and Lou Ellsworth complained that they were draining the bank when the land beneath them could be repurposed for cotton. In 1919, L.L. Pearson also pared down his troop by sending 700 ostriches to the same sad end. The 100 spared were those who produced the best feathers, according to a report from H.C. Cross.[810]

These numbers and mass destruction activities were a mere drop in the morbid bucket compared to what German-South African ranchers had to do with the 750,000 ostriches they reportedly held before the industry crashed.[811] "They were eating their heads off," one news story explained.[812] "They weren't worth their keep, and the owners began looking around for a way out… so they began to turn the ostriches loose on the plains and desert."[813] Within three years, 75% of their holdings were gone (sold, eaten, released or destroyed) in favor of high-demand produce and livestock that would support their fighting compatriots.[814]

(By the way, if a bird was turned loose in Arizona and its owner could be identified, lawsuits for damages could follow. Still, historical accounts prove several were released. Lowell Parker, writing for the *Arizona Republic* in 1974 claimed they roamed the desert for a while and "frightened the wits" out of motorists when spotted.[815] To avoid liability, whatever might have identified their owner was likely removed or defaced.)

There was no recovery in sight, but false hopes continued to be preached, and a few folks held out. Of those few was Dr. A.J. Chandler. Between 1919 and 1921, his San Marcos troops diminished from a virus and their numbers never recovered.[816] The remaining ostriches were moved back to his former ranch in Mesa, where they remained until the early 1930s.[817] Willetta Riggs, of Chandler, Arizona, recalled that when growing up, she could jump out of the family car and go right up to the fence holding the curious birds back.[818] By that point, however, ostriches had lost their overall attractiveness. In fact, Robin Doughty, writing for *Agricultural History*, found that "Most of the farms and show places [for ostriches] were dissolved by the 1930s."[819] Around the globe, D.C. Cogburn found that the total ostrich population dropped from about 30 million birds to 35 thousand "almost overnight."[820]

32. The Occasional Glimmer

"Every ostrich in Africa lost its plumage,
judging from the number of women wearing feathers."
- Anne Rittenhouse for the Buffalo Courier (1919)[821]

Through 1916 and 1917, Parisian opera houses continued to give their singers an extra puff of haughtiness with feathers in gaudy necklines, fancy headdresses, sleeve linings, and robe draping. The persistent appearance of feathers as a staple for artists and other creatives spilled over once again into modern fashion in 1918. French designers reincorporated feathers into dress trimmings, corsages, and skirt clips as a tasty *hors d'oeuvre* before the release of more outrageous designs in 1919.

One such item of artistry was the design by Arnold of Paris (image included) that beguiled and confused at least two continents.[822] "If clothes become more scanty and feathers more plentiful on the modern woman, she will run a neck and neck race with the ostrich [itself]," wrote Anne Rittenhouse, fashion editor for the *New York Times*.[823] The majority length of the skirt was draped with rows of ostrich feathers, which did not exactly cover the portion of a woman she usually kept to herself. The bodice was made from unlined tulle that dipped into a girdle at the

waistline. "Paris is," Rittenhouse observed, "sending over frocks that are little *but* ostrich feathers."

New Yorkers were not impressed. Nor were they interested in paying the prices that feathered frocks commanded. Because the feather production system had essentially broken down worldwide, the few raw feathers that could be obtained from breeders were once again pricey. Due to the surplus and cheapening of feathers in years prior, however, the average U.S. woman would not pay the asking price for such a common item that could be found in the back of any closet.

One surprising effort to encourage Arizona women to get back into the feather craze was found in a 1920 issue of the *Buckeye Valley News.* The article, "New Use for Ostrich Tips," said everything it in the subtitle: "Dainty plumes are placed on underwear as trimming..."[824] Though no photographs or user testimonies support this claim, the advertisers assure readers that trend was absolutely considered fashionable, and readers should just trust them to know. Parisian styles also incorporated feather bits and pieces into flapper accessories and at one point, the popular Kewpie dolls for young girls sported an ostrich feather dress.[825] The *Arizona Republican* declared that "the ostrich feather has been restored to favor," but American women didn't take the bait.[826] Even the microbursts of interest preceded by stage, burlesque and carnival celebrations could not hold a candle to the sleek, minimal and streamlined silhouettes women fancied.

The bump in sales did, however, strain one of Arizona's only suppliers. In 1924, a criminal broke into the ostrich pens at the San Marcos Hotel and "plucked two of the giant birds of all their feathers."[827] Only one survived from the trauma. The thief's cruelty went beyond stealing feathers that night. They also killed two other ostriches in a way that is so disturbing that the thief was considered evil and the details purposefully excluded from the book. At the end of the news story, the reporter for the *Arizona Republican* suggested the criminal be punished by being forced to "run a daily race with the fleetest of the remaining birds, with a penalty of subsisting on a sole diet of ostrich eggs until he wins."[828] While this is rather absurd, I'm surprised the reporter did not suggest the perp be plucked of all their "feathers," too.

Could a Royal Influence the U.S. Again?

Hope sprang anew in the 1930s when Princess Marina of Greece and Denmark appeared in a fashion spread modeling an ostrich feather cape from her wedding trousseau. The caption with her 1934 image reads: "A cape of magnificent shaded pink ostrich feathers and heavy georgette of the same shade was presented by the people of Oudtshoorn, Cape Province, South Africa, to H.R.H. [Her Royal Highness] Princess Marina. The cape was designed by Molyneux and is a lovely, graceful wrap." Apparently, the future Duchess of Kent was quite a fan of feathers and furs, as seen in the later image from December 1938.

Not missing a beat, Cherie Nicholas, fashion writer for Arizona's *St. Johns Herald-Observer* emphasized in her article on the trends for the new year: "The long post-war cycle is over and with it has gone the tailored career woman, trim and uncompromising with her boyish figure and her workman-like clothes. ... back comes ostrich feathers placing their glamorous seal on the return to femininity..."[829] Nicholas hoped to signal a new era being led by her royal highness Princess Marina, the new Duchess of Kent. After reviewing the unlimited possibilities of ostrich stoles such as worn by the Duchess, she wrote, "frills, feathers and furbelows mark

Left: Her Royal Highness Princess Marina, Duchess of Kent, 1934 (Shutterstock 7665068xt, Licensed Use). Right: The Duke and Duchess of Kent in Belgrave Square (London), *Queenslander Pictorial*, Dec. 21, 1938 (Fair Use).

King George VI and Queen Elizabeth on their Royal Tour, Canada, 1939. (Wikimedia Commons, Public Domain).

the lady of fashion ... an alluring creature utterly feminine in her Edwardian grandeur."[830]

The Duchess of Kent had slight to no effect on American shoppers. Nor was there an effect from Queen Elizabeth and King George VI's visit to Washington D.C. in 1939. On that trip, the queen's sported a gorgeous ostrich plume on her hat.

Another attempt for retailers to sell off boxes of bird fluff was seen in a 1944 style section of the *Herald*. Nicholas tried again to persuade her readers with another celebrity. "[I]n the romantic be-plumed portrait hat pictured, Sallie Victor [the foremost hat designer of the era] tells of the dawn of a new era of elegance interpreted through a gracious use of ostrich plumes."[831] For those wanting to appear less like the captain of a pirate ship, Nicholas suggested the more practical "daytime hat" shown on the bottom left, that is adorned with "not much more than a pouf of ostrich."[832]

The writer confidently assures readers that feather boas are making a comeback, as are evening bags made entirely of feathers. Nicholas also implied wearing ostrich feathers could make a woman beguiling, chic and smart. Alas, the following year, these tacky toppers were back in boxes and both men and women would suit up for World War II.

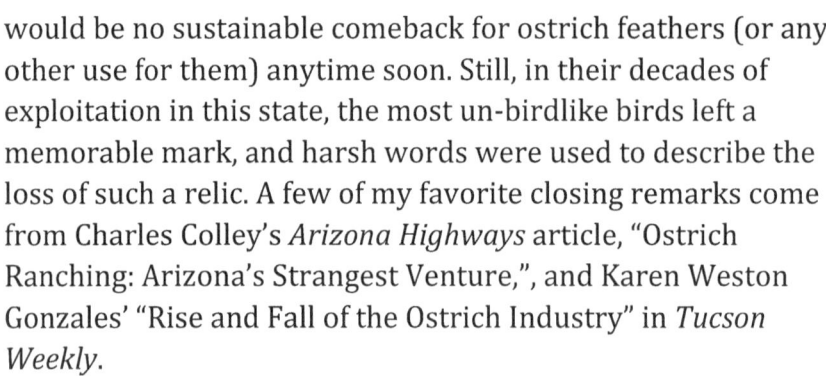

Inclusion from the *St. Johns Herald-Observer*, November 4, 1944.

It was evident that North Americans had, for the most part, moved on to other interests and there would be no sustainable comeback for ostrich feathers (or any other use for them) anytime soon. Still, in their decades of exploitation in this state, the most un-birdlike birds left a memorable mark, and harsh words were used to describe the loss of such a relic. A few of my favorite closing remarks come from Charles Colley's *Arizona Highways* article, "Ostrich Ranching: Arizona's Strangest Venture,", and Karen Weston Gonzales' "Rise and Fall of the Ostrich Industry" in *Tucson Weekly*.

Colley wrote "...the boom shattered like Humpty Dumpty's shell and not even the needs of the fan dancers of the Roaring Twenties could 'put it back together again.'"[833]

Weston Gonzales put it like this: Feather farming was a thing that "took flight briefly[,] only to hit the ground with a thud."[834]

33. The Ostrich Festival

"His joy is to run in races but rarely in a straight line..."
- Shadow Hamilton, "The Ostrich" (2015)[835]

One hundred years after the first pair of ostriches were introduced to Arizona, the City of Chandler threw its inaugural Ostrich Festival. The celebration was meant to highlight the city's founder, who once raised the notable creatures. The 1988 event was so well received that it turned into an annual soiree. The Ostrich Festival was a hit for local families who returned year after year and told all their friends. At the springtime affair, vendors sold the iconic feathers and eggs, as well as crafted items made with them. The day's admission also included musical engagements and standard fair games. Today's version has bulked up to include amusement park rides and fancy food vendors. Of course, the animals of honor always make an appearance.

> Another theme considered for the celebration was the Cotton Festival, but that idea didn't pack the same punch as a "bug-eyed, cranky animal."[r]

In its third year in operation, the festival's weekend attendance exceeded that of the World Championship Formula One motor race held at the same time. The 1990 Grand Prix in Phoenix was not held on a racetrack, but amongst the historical buildings of downtown Phoenix. That

---

[r] Michael Grady, "Weird to Honor an Ostrich? Here are Alternatives," *East Valley Tribune*, March 7, 2008.

Sunday, March 11, speedsters in their souped-up cars screeched around bank buildings. The roar of hot engines echoed a block away, to Arizona Ostrich Co.'s former showroom. The tang of burning rubber lingered just past Pan-American's first retail store. And the turning point for the final lap began by the Phoenix Ostrich Feather Manufacturing Company at 6th Ave. and Washington St. (Of course, none of those businesses were still in operation.) The Grand Prix attracted a crowd of nearly 15,000 spectators, but the following Tuesday, the headlines read: "Ostriches Outrun Formula One…". Statistics showed that Chandler drew in 75,000 festival goers on the same day.[836] The idea of ostriches outperforming or literally *outrunning* the world's fastest cars was not just a journalistic play on words. Until recently, the Ostrich Festival offered a spectacle not to be missed: ostrich races.

A Quick Note:

Ostrich racing has historically invited controversy regarding animal rights. This chapter highlights a turning point. As a historian, it is not my job to take a stance on the issue. Rather, it is my responsibility to provide a clear summary based on empirical evidence, set in context, so readers can make their own informed opinions.

The Advent of Ostrich Racing

Modern ostrich racing (ca. late 1880s) purportedly started with Edwin Cawston's family-friendly photo opportunity in Pasadena. He attached a harness to a painted Studebaker wagon on a taxidermied bird and let children pose for a picture. Another photo op allowed adults to climb aboard the bird's back. Cawston also permitted people a chance to ride live ostriches, which eventually led to a high-speed sport.[837] In time, ostrich riding became a showbiz stunt when chorus girl Florence Leslie (shown) prepared a featherback ride for the Broadway production of "The Girl Question." A 1908 interview about her riding experience quotes her saying "I should rather call it a thrilling experience!"[838]

A very early example of North American ostrich racing as a spectator sport has been found in the *San Diego Union* from 1896. That story read: "The ostrich races yesterday at Coronado track were witnessed by quite a crowd. Napoleon, the famous sprinter ... drew a buggy weighing 280 pounds and a man weighing 137 pounds, but in spite of the handicap made a half-mile in a few seconds over two minutes. He was paced by a man on a bicycle. The sight was a novel one."[839] The report provides evidence of ostriches hauling more than 50% of their own body weight, which begs some scientific exploration.

Dr. T. C. Duncan's 1888 report to the U.S. Commissioner of Agriculture touched a bit on how much weight and demand an ostrich was able to withstand. In South Africa, there had been "experiments ... with a view to test the capability of the ostrich in drawing and carrying burdens."[840] Conclusions were anecdotal. Dr. Duncan mentioned a Dr. Sparrman who directly observed mounted ostriches in use like pack camels in the Cape Colony in 1775. And earlier than that, English geographer Francis Moore wrote about an Englishman at Joar "traveling long distances upon a bridled ostrich."[841]

Girl poses for a photo at the Cawston Ostrich Farm, 1922 (Randy Young Collection/Fair Use).

Riding the Ostrich Bareback

This is a most difficult feat, yet nevertheless it is performed by one of the attendants at the Farm and is a rare sight.

———■———

You have never seen an Ostrich Farm unless you have visited "Cawston's." Visitors should not fail to see the original Farm—Cawston's.

Selected page from the Cawston Ostrich Farm fold-out brochure, ca. 1896-1935 (Public Domain).

Arizona's ostriches were ridable from day one, starting with the first two adults introduced by Clanton & Co. Evidence of this is found in the July 4, 1888 article in the *Weekly Journal-Miner* about the birds' arrival. After describing the carload of ostriches destined for the Buckeye area, the report reads: "They are very gentle and it is no difficulty for a man to ride the old birds."[842] In fact, even before those birds arrived, stories about the state's incoming troop from one month prior revealed that one of the ostriches "can carry two full-grown men on its back."[843] (By the way, with this information, some might conclude that the state's original collection of ostriches were bred from a known heavy lifter and genetically equipped for the task.)

Now, an ostrich's ability to be ridden is separate of its desire and in 1895, an example was found of either *Oom Paul* or his offspring expressing their lack of desire. At Josiah Harbert's ranch in Phoenix, a "rash individual," suspected to have been an inexperienced ranch hand, attempted to ride an ostrich with only a partially planned strategy.[844] This person first "blindfolded an ostrich and then jumped astride of him. The startled bird crashed through a high fence and pitched his rider headlong to the ground..."[845] When examining this story, I wondered if he had thought to take the blindfold off at any point. After eating a mouthful of dirt, that rider was "of the opinion that a bucking bronco is far safer..."[846]

Like with riding horses, it appears that a rider and their ostrich must be specifically trained and willing to engage in the activity for it not to harm either. T.W. Kemp, the Arizona man who was supposed to know the inner thoughts of the bird-beasts better than anyone in the world, spoke about riding them in a 1910 interview with the *El Paso Times*. He responded hesitantly. "It's easy enough to get on him, and he can stand the weight all right, but as soon as he sets off to run,

Left: Featherback rides at Casper's Farm in St. Augustine, Florida in 1948 (State Library and Archives of Florida/Fair Use). Right:
Ostrich racing at the Chandler Ostrich Festival (Michael Chow for the *Arizona Republic*, March 10, 1993/Fair Use).

you reach the ground so quickly that you never know quite how you got there."[847] Experienced rodeo rider and current ostrich breeder D.C. Cogburn has also been asked about the practice, to which he has said is absolutely doable, but not advisable because if the ostrich takes off running at 45 miles per hour, a fall would most definitely injure an inexperienced rider.[848]

Chandler's Races

From 1988 to 2017, the ostrich races at the Chandler Ostrich Festival were—hands down—the most popular event. 1993 event organizer Karry Dune described the races as a unique spectacle where jockeys could either take their chances riding bareback (some would say "featherback"), or "dressed up like old Roman legionnaires..." being pulled behind the dashing birds in custom made carts.[849] The charioteers could direct their bird through the short course with a "yee," "haw" and a broomstick.

Above: Chariot races at Casper's Farm in St. Augustine, Florida in 1948 (State Library and Archives of Florida/Fair Use). Below: Chariot racing the ostriches. Liz (Afterglow-Spins), "Ostriches!" LiveJournal, March 15, 2009. https://afterglow-spins.livejournal.com/ (Fair Use).

The races were as much a rodeo as they are fool's luck. Right out of the gate, ostriches ran in every direction, especially the wrong one. Some immediately spun around and bucked their riders off. "Remaining in the saddle is just as important as crossing the finish line," said an observer at the 1997 race, but that might only be for scoring purposes.[850] From watching recordings of the events, I've seen how ostriches that dump the extra weight and reach the end of the course could still receive a crowd's cheer of approval.

Arrival of Opposition

It wasn't long before animal rights activists targeted the century-old practice as an act of cruelty. In 1995, three individuals affiliated with the Arizona People for Animal Rights staged a demonstration at the festival. At the commencement of an ostrich race, they ran out onto the track with a chain, secured themselves to the announcer's platform and displayed a banner with an inflammatory message.[851] The protesters claimed ostriches were being exploited beyond reason. They expressed their general disgust about an event in which ostriches had to endure the horror of their fellow kind being served nearby on burger buns.

The announcer derided their disruptive behavior and the audiences urged him to resume the race. The podium pirates were promptly arrested and removed from the property. That year's Festival spokesperson, Abbie Fink, addressed the matter to the press, saying, "No birds have been injured in the history of the event."[852] The arrests did not dissuade protestors from reappearing over the next twenty years, but it did ensure more civility with future demonstrations.

Before the 2017 event, activists formally appealed to the city and local officials for a restraint on the race. United Poultry Concerns, an organization based out of Virginia, also got involved. They published a statement claiming: "The ostrich races and other animal attractions bully and ridicule captive birds and other animals to perform dangerous, demeaning, and unnatural acts."[853] UPC also sent a memorandum to supporters that listed all the email addresses for members of the Chandler Chamber of Commerce and urged followers to join the protest by filling the Chamber's inboxes with their concerns.

In addition, UPC create a Change.org petition aimed to collect signatures from around the world that might increase the pressure on Festival organizers. The petition claimed: "The ostrich races strip them of their dignity."[854] The collective signatures would be sent with an e-mail that read: "We respectfully urge you to cancel the ostrich races," with the reason being that racing "no longer reflects the consciousness of today's society towards animals."[855] Again, organizer contacts were provided to those who wanted to customize a message. 2,745 supporters signed the document.

A protestor stands outside an ostrich race event with a sign. Credit: Stephen Mounteer for Arizona Republic, March 13, 1995 (Fair Use).

The organization People for the Ethical Treatment of Animals (PETA) seconded the appeal for a restraint with an official statement in the *Arizona Republic*. They claimed that raced ostriches thought their rider was a predator pouncing on them.[856] Phoenix Zoo keeper Paige McNickle argued that the birds used for this sport "have been trained for racing," which would include desensitizing the animal to innate triggers.[857] This process would be similar to how horses are desensitized to human behaviors, décor and other distractions common to rodeos and derbies.

Some activists claimed, "ostrich skeletons are not built to be ridden by a 150-pound jockey and say the act causes panic in the animals, leading to emotional and physical distress."[858] Then president and CEO of the Chandler Chamber of Commerce Terri Kimble responded to the complaint, saying, "[ostriches] are very, very strong animals."[859] The jockeys employed for these events were physically light and small, well-trained and only rode on mature birds weighing between 350-400lbs. (By the way, the typical weight ratio carried by a racing ostrich was approximately 37%. For comparison, that's about what U.S. soldiers regularly carry in gear.)

Finally, opponents to the races argued that while ostrich ranching was a known part of state history, racing the big animals *never* was, therefore, the activity was not an appropriate inclusion at the celebration. Empirical evidence suggests the activists were right on this point. Though ostriches were ridden, Arizona breeders did not engage in racing them for sport. The Chamber of Commerce withheld the race that year, and as of 2025, the event has not been reinstituted.

Even without the races, in recent years the Ostrich Festival has brought in over 400,000 attendees per weekend. Those are staggering numbers! For context, that's four times as many people who attended global pop star Taylor Swift's largest concert to date (2024 Melbourne, "Eras Tour"). I'd argue that's yet another feather in Arizona's cap!

34. More Historical Highlights

"What remains certain & incontestable
is how much we have taken from the ostrich."
- T. Okunlola for Holding History (2021)[860]

This chapter contains an array of good, bad and ugly moments between humans and ostriches throughout ancient history. Examining the historical use of ostriches for human entertainment, which some readers may find uncomfortable, shows an evolution of both the relationship between animal and human, and of global progress towards ethical treatment. The stories presented only apply to the modern ostrich, as seen today, not to other species in the ratite family, or to any of its' evolutionary predecessors. As seen in the quote above, humans have taken much from the ostrich. If the reader is sensitive to what this implies, feel free to skip the chapter.

Where Did the Modern Ostrich Come From?

Scientists have traced the origin of the modern, un-evolved, ostrich to the Middle East. Africa quickly became their primary residence because of human trade and land migration. And, from overhunting, the deserts and savannas of Africa are now the only natural habitat for wild ostriches (though a remnant of industrial ostrich farm washouts have managed to stay alive in Australia).

With the question of origin, it also makes sense to ask: Did ostriches walk with dinosaurs? If you are thinking about the gigantic, scaly lizard-kind, then no. Those went extinct 66-

million years ago, or during the Great Flood. (There are plenty of books that argue those details. This is not one of them.) Ostriches are considered descendants of the flightless maniraptoran of the Jurassic Period such as the two-legged titan Therizinosaurus, and its bigger-brained relatives, the Oviraptor and Velociraptor. More immediately linked ancestors are believed to have appeared around 40-55 million years ago. They fluctuated in size and structure.

The modern ostrich made a distinct appearance approximately 23 million years ago, during the Miocene epoch. Their early neighbors would have been the mastodon, megalodon and great ape. Contrary to popular assumption, other ratites (cassowaries, rheas, emu and kiwi) are not "sisters" or "cousins," or in any way genetically related to the ostrich. The connection they share is more categorical, based on physical attributes, than anything else. Other than slight differences in size and skin color, the modern ostrich has never evolved into anything else and thus, is a dead-end on an evolutionary tree.

Just as soon as early humans could, we have interacted with the modern ostrich. Early industry investor and short-term Arizona ostrich raiser, Louis Chalmers, dug into this topic in 1909 and reported that from the moment humans laid eyes on the ostrich, we made full use of everything we knew the animal had to offer. "The feathers of the bird have been used as an ornament since early antiquity," he shared for readers of *The Earth*.[861] In his article, Chalmers presented some arguments for early humans sticking an ostrich feather in their hair as an ornament to increase their sex appeal.[862] If that claim seems a bit too theoretical, a more concrete example of humans incorporating ostrich products into their daily lives comes from Dina M. Ezz El-Din a professor of Egyptology.

She published the resultsof her research citing ostrich eggshell fragments being found in rock shelters of South Africa. They were carbon dated between 52,000 and 100,000 years ago. She believed the decorative ornaments made with eggshells (carved, painted, etched, etc.) are "amongst the earliest objects of any kind" that reflect the presence of humans on the continent.[863]

> "The beauty of the ostrich feather has been appreciated since recorded history began."
> -*Dub Oliver (1993)*

The indigenous Kalahari San people commonly used ostrich eggshells as flasks for carrying water, and some studies dated this practice back to people who lived 85,000 years ago.[864] In the Mesopotamian city of Kish (now in Iraq), archaeologists discovered an advancement on the concept, where ostrich eggshells were trimmed down into cups (or bowls).[865] Later examples became more complex with the addition of beeswax plugs or hand-formed pottery lids. According to Berthold Laufer of the Chicago Field Museum of Natural History, these containers are, "precious remains of the earliest civilization of which we have any knowledge."[866]

For centuries, ostriches have held spiritual significance in both Eastern and Western religions and present powerful symbolism in various artforms. Written stories of the ostrich and its beautiful egg can be found in the works of Pliny the Elder, in Arabic poetry, in the Christian Bible and the Islamic Koran. The Greek playwright Aristophanes featured ostriches in his 414-415 B.C. comedy *The Birds*. He devoted an entire song chorus to how ugly the creature was and implied that it

Morgan Seal 606, Southern Mesopotamia, ca. 1,200 to 1,000 B.C. (Pierpoint Morgan Library & Museum/Fair Use).

represented the "mother of gods" (metaphorically). Famous Renaissance Period playwright William Shakespeare perpetuated the myth of the metal-eating bird in *Henry VI* as a curse spoken by Cade against Iden: "I'll make thee eat iron like an ostrich, and swallow my sword..."[867]

Before the advent of written language, ostrich feather wearing was shown in Egyptian hieroglyphics,[868] and the birds found in pottery motifs from the indigenous Elamites of present-day Iran. The Field Museum of Natural History's Book,[s] "Ostrich Egg-shell Cups of Mesopotamia..." has a robust collection of images showing ostriches as mythical

"In nine cases out of ten... the drawing [of an ostrich] is ludicrously incorrect..."
-*Annie Martin (1890)*

characters, being hunted, tamed or fought in battles, as expressed in art forms such as engravings, mosaics, gemstone effigies and in paintings. In the 6th and 7th centuries, ostrich monoliths even stood guard over tombs in China.

---

[s] Annie Martin, *Home Life on an Ostrich Farm* (London: G. Philip, 1890), 102.

Employing Ostriches for Human Enjoyment

Ancient Assyrians were known to collect animals from around the world to be put on display in their communities as a form of public enrichment and to show off their hunting, travelling and trade accomplishments to visitors. King Ashurnasirpal II specifically included ostriches in his collection. Some historians consider this to be an early example of a zoological garden.[869] Many ostriches were sent along the old Salt Road to China to become collectibles for emperors who wanted a personal zoo on their own property. Historians recently found that ostriches were frequently gifted by rulers of this era during diplomatic meetings.[870]

Besides wearing fancy headpieces, Ancient Egyptians attached ostrich feathers to large fans that slaves waved to keep Pharaohs and other elites comfortable on hot summer days.[871] Egyptians also regularly included ostrich meat and eggs in their diet—and sometimes in their tombs.[872] In Naqada, archaeologists found a decorated ostrich egg inside a mass of graves. This eggshell had a very special job: to replace the corpse's missing head.[873] (If, after reading that, you imagined it was decorated with facial features representing the deceased, you'd be wrong—it had an image of two deer.)

Painted ostrich egg found on the island of Cyprus, ca. 700-601 B.C. (De Agostini Picture Library).

Egyptians might also be credited with employing ostriches in the first traveling circuses. Pharoah Ptolemy II Philadelphus celebrated his 2nd century ascension to the throne with ostriches in a procession far more elaborate than what Aladdin's "Genie" produced for "Prince Ali" in the Disney animated film. One description of the event claims there was an "endless array" of visual wonders and trained animals such as: "twenty-four chariots drawn by four elephants each; the royal menagerie—twelve chariots drawn by antelopes, fifteen by buffaloes, eight by pairs of ostriches, eight by zebras; also many mules, camels, etc., and twenty-four lions."[874] As a way to flaunt her status, Ptolemy's wife Arsinoe rode an ostrich in lieu of a horse.[875] This preference was mirrored by the upper class women in Ancient Rome as well. Similarly, Roman charioteers used ostriches in the harness to reflect their rank (but probably not during any actual warfare).[876]

Like Egyptians, the Romans enjoyed ostrich on their plates, but perhaps a bit too much. Besides Emperor Elagabalus' strange taste in brains, there is a legend about a man named Firmus. He supposedly made it a personal challenge to eat an entire roasted ostrich in one day. The entire book that story comes from has been declared false, in part, because this specific feat is impossible.[877]

From 753 BC to AD 476, Romans upped the ante for ostriches being used in public forms of entertainment. Ostriches were part of the Venationes games where caged animals such as lions, elephants and bears were released in an arena to be hunted and possibly killed by *bestiarii* (beast killers/hunters) before a crowd. Depending on the agility of animals employed, there was an exciting risk of accidental audience participation.

Owing to the speed of an ostrich, they were a crowd favorite.[878] In these games, the Romans were equal opportunity offenders, seeking to be satisfied by the cruel death of either participant: man, or beast.

> **Were the Bestiarii Gladiators?**
>
> No. Bestiarii fought animals (beasts), whereas gladiators competed to the death with other men. Gladiator bloodsports were not seen in the arena until 264 B.C.

Sometimes the *bestarius* was an amateur or professional hunter seeking glory or wealth. At other times, they were a criminal being sentenced to death. In the latter case, they entered the arena defenseless. If a criminal *bestarius* managed to survive one animal attack, a second animal was released to finish the job (or more, if needed).

If the Egyptians got weird, and Romans got violent, I suppose the Greeks went completely overboard with their forms of entertainment. Have you ever heard the phrase "running around like a chicken with its head cut off?" In the late 1st century, the Greek physician Galen noted that Emperor Commodus found it amusing to run ostriches through a gauntlet by spurring them into a high-speed chase around the arena, then intercepting them mid-race with the swing of a curved blade. After the ostrich's head plopped to the ground, its body attempted to finish the course. [879]

As time went on, audience tastes changed, and the focus of these circuses shifted from exploiting the wildness of an animal to exhibiting skillful training (putting the emphasis on the handler's talent). In the 1850s, a German circus entertainer named Ernst Renz brought ostriches to Prussia. At the event, acrobatic ostrich riding demonstrations were given by Turks.[880] In London, audiences at Batty's Grand National Hippodrome paid to see staged, non-lethal recreations of ostrich hunt strategies that were employed by the early Boers of South Africa.[881]

A description of the show appeared in the Berkshire newspaper. A team of three or four "hunters" on horseback would take turns pushing their horse to the max, chasing the ostrich around the performance space for an intense sprint. At just the right time, a second rider would tag the first out and pick up on the chase, without giving the ostrich a break.[882] By alternating efforts in a circular relay of sorts, the hunting team could conserve their horses' energy while wearing down the ostrich in a controlled fashion. When the ostrich finally exhausted itself and sat on the ground, the hunt portrayers took their bow.

35. Late 80's Comeback

"The ratite industry is being revived in Arizona…"
– AZ Ostrich & Emu Association (1994)[883]

The late 1980's saw a revival of ostrich ranching in Arizona and across the nation. The second major era of this industry started with another rapid boom, providing early breeders astronomical wealth, or "stupid money," as they say. For almost a decade, breeders believed that, maybe, people would finally catch on to how incredible the ostrich is as a livestock product and most importantly, as a restaurant delight. The accounts of the new ranchers read like Déjà vu. Ostrich breeders of this era followed the same unsustainable business practices as early century feather farmers. And, when faced with economic pitfalls, most ostrich-related businesses suffered the same fate.

> "The ostrich breeder market was a crazy place back then."
> *-American Ostrich Association (n.d.)*

One example might remind a reader of the late Frank Lane. Rick White, former General Manager and Vice President of the Zion View Ostrich Ranch in southern Utah, entered the industry post-boom. He shared with a represent-tative of the U.S. Department of Commerce that entrants were fascinated by "a speculative breeder's market created largely by South

---

[t] *American Ostrich Association,* "About Us," Accessed Aug. 25, 2025, https://www.americanostrichassociation.org/content.aspx?page_id=22&club_id=337926&module_id=716656.

African demand for ostrich products."[884] As White's peers across the nation were picking up second and third jobs after losing their entire life savings in the crash, he still dreamed of winning over skeptical stomachs. In his *Business America* profile piece, White fantasized about North Ameri-cans noshing on a "McOstrich" sandwich from a popular fast-food restaurant and shared his excitement over his meat sales to Japan. After only two years, White sold his business to Quill Industries, Inc. who filed for a multi-million-dollar loss that same year. The only thing White would be eating for a while were his words.

Similar to the competitive pressure created when South Africa limited trade access to ostriches in 1909, the ostrich boom of the 80s was kicked off by a global case of FOMO (Fear of Missing Out). As ostrich interests increased in the United States, the commodity was once again used as a political pawn. This time, the impetus was to end the Apartheid regime.

After WWI, South Africa had broken into a class system based on race, with white Europeans at the top and Black South Africans at the very bottom (a one-degree shift from Dutch-India and German colonial systems of exploitation and slavery). This system was radically opposed by local minorities, religious organizations and human-interest groups around the world. Outspoken Anti-Apartheid activists were regularly punished for their efforts to influence change. Well-known activists arrested for their involvement in protests were Coretta Scott King (the widow of Rev. Martin Luther King Jr.), the musician Stevie Wonder, tennis star Arthur Ashe and the future first president of South Africa, Nelson Mandela.

Growing awareness of Apartheid practices resulted in large-scale demonstrations of global disapproval such as universities in the U.S. and U.K. divesting in businesses based in South Africa. Major corporations and banks soon followed suit. There were organized boycotts of South African sports and cultural events. And in 1986, the United States passed the Comprehensive Anti-Apartheid Act that placed economic sanctions on South Africa, designed to apply pressure towards change.[885] One specific effect of this intervention was a ban on the importation of ostrich-related products. The ban was the impetus for ambitious breeders in the U.S. to expand their operations in antici- pation of meeting a higher demand.

> **What is "Apartheid"?**
> A·par·theid is the Afrikaans word for "apartness." It is similar to the English word "segregation." In context, though, these words do not have equal value.

The American Ostrich Association (AOA) reported that this gearing up was the spark that gave the industry its rebirth.[886] One *Washington Post* writer called what came next, "ostrich mania."[887] "Suddenly[,] prices for ostriches and ostrich products boomed," wrote Robert Francis for *U.S. Bird History* mag-azine.[888] Promoters declared that once again, Arizona was "poised to become a world leader in meat and leather production from these birds."[889] As interest picked up, the AOA stated[,] "Investors eagerly poured funds into such investments and prices climbed to unreal levels."[890]

Again, No One Knew How to Raise Ostriches

Many ostrich raisers of the '80s were more starstruck over promising chicks than ready to sustain a healthy troop. As a prime example, in 1987, Ed Burns of Hinton, Oklahoma went to an exotic animal auction in Missouri. At the event, he saw a little male ostrich looking sad and lonely in a cage. "He was just shivering and shaking.," Burns recalled. "Nobody

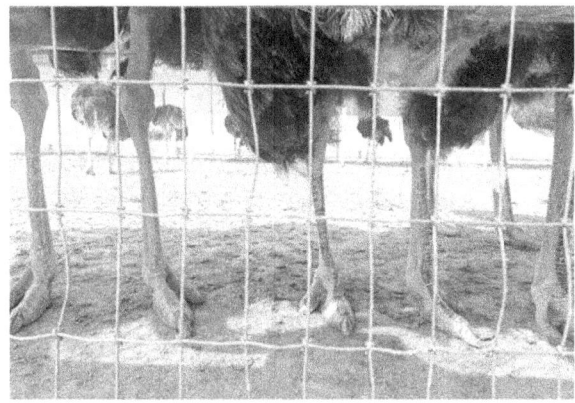

Ostrich feet and toes. Red Rock, AZ (Author collection, 2025).

thought it would last through the night. ... Well, I felt sorry for it, so I made a bid for him. ... And that's how Sharon and I got started in the ostrich business."[891] He later became the president and a board member of the AOA.

Inexperienced backyard breeders started importing birds in greater numbers and were learning on the go. Michael Lehman, current president of the AOA, has explained how even experienced livestock raisers "tried to force [ostriches] into western farming practices," which did not work.[892] "In order to farm them, you have to farm them as a wild species," he added.[893]

Dub Oliver, compiler of the 1993 title *Ostrich Ranching in America*, described the learning curve and disconnect between peers: "[W]hat worked 'here' would not work 'there'; what worked 'last month' is not working 'this month'. Ironically, while one breeder would be experiencing a very successful season, another would be experiencing considerable losses - yet the two might often be located only a few miles from each other."[894] Dr. Frank Lochner, head of the Veterinary Medicine Department at Oklahoma State University soon saw a surge in customers because "[ostrich] owners don't know how to feed or care for them."[895]

Another Species Debate

In terms of flavor, whether a red, blue, black or cross is served up for dinner will never matter because all ostrich tastes the same. Still, there was a species debate among the meat market investors. Offering a basic approval for red necks was Jim Carden, a realtor out of Weatherford, Texas, who received three Tanzanian birds from a client in 1990 in lieu of commission.[896] "They seem to be favored by some for their size," shared Penny Lynch, a breeder from Texas.[897]

Keeping with the historically preferred blue necks, Tom Broome, owner of Broome Ostrich Ranch in Panola, Texas believed they "possess many of the traits we are desiring," though admitted there were issues with the amount of inbreeding they'd experienced.[898] Barry and Nan Coy, out of Elk City, Oklahoma, insisted that only blues could hit the quality mark.[899] Another Oklahoman, Damon Carl "D.C." Cogburn, has spoken against the reds and blues, claiming that they are "okay to eat, but they are dangerous to keep and they cannot be raised sustainably."[900]

Preferring a crossbreed of red and blue necks were Mark and Penny Lynch, owners of the Circle L Ostrich Farm, who called them, "personal favorites."[901] A.D. Whitehurst Jr., farming out of Vernon, Florida, put his money on the stalwart crosses as well. He said, "I believe the future of these birds is in the meat. Therefore, a big bird (possibly a Blue/Red cross) is what I want to take to market."[902]

Standing by the South African Blacks as the best overall pick was "D.C." Cogburn, founder of the Rooster Cogburn Ostrich Ranch in Red Rock, Arizona. The South African Blacks were "a shorter bird with a fuller body, more feathers and higher quality feathers," his daughter Dana Cogburn-Barett wrote of the investment.[903] Arguing against the species, the Coys claimed, "[b]lacks are the hardest chicks to raise."[904] And

Penny Lynch claimed that the black species gets attention "not because it's necessarily any better ... but because of effective campaigns of beguiling[,] sometimes pushy (if not completely up and up) advertising tactics."[905] It appears the Cogburns were the only ranchers convinced the South African Blacks were any good. No others were imported.

> "If breeders and others have their way... the world's two largest birds will become 'the other bird meat.'"
> -United Poultry Concerns (1993)[u]

A Fatal Flaw in the Plan

A customer base for ostrich meat did not exist in the 1980s. Potential customers, had this product caught on, knew too little about ostrich meat to even consider putting it on a grocery list. Still, instead of investing money into advertising to the end user, a slew of aggressive promotions were aimed at selling birds to new breeders. This created a top-heavy business model where virtually no money could ever be made from end users because they weren't included in the plan.

Not only that, but the industry did not even have adequate participants to complete the supply chain. Supposing all the U.S. ostrich raisers' non-breeding birds matured and were ready for slaughter, there would not be enough facilities capable of processing the livestock in mass quantities and with proper considerations (there were meat, feathers, leathers, oils and bonemeal to harvest). A few "hardy souls" tried to get a customer base going by establishing a processing facility simply to get meat into circulation, the AOA shared, "but they failed under a mountain of debt."[906] Besides, the demand for sales to other breeders was more profitable that sending birds to market. Since sellers were holding out for the high-dollar breeder sale, the commercial processing market

---

[u] Dr. Karen Davis, "Special Report: Emus and Ostriches, Nowhere to Hide," United Poultry Concerns, *Poultry Press* (Fall/Winter 1993).

was stymied.[907] Without a functioning supply chain to support fulfillment, promoters were selling a pipe dream.

When asked about the industry's initial challenges, Michael Lehman, president of the AOA told podcaster Dave Miller, that there was "a lot of wishful thinking."[908] He claims the major push was geared towards a meat market of the future that would require a few years of investing in growing the population so that (hypothetical) customers could be served. Ed Burns was convinced. "There will be a slaughter market one day," said Burns.[909] "I have no crystal ball as to when – but I know it will be here."[910]

Dr. Lochner observed that "the minimum operation for profitability under ordinary circumstances should have about 2,000 birds."[911] Still, new breeders were assured of a successful return on their investment, even if they started with only one pair of chicks and patiently raised generation after generation towards that goal. Tom Mantzel, co-founder of the AOA, and an importer, stated the return on investment to be expected for the early '90s was "in excess of 75% to 100% annually."[912]

A cook carves a roasted ostrich leg for a large picnic in Lincoln Park, San Diego, ca. early 1920s (University of Southern California Libraries and California Historical Society/Public Domain).

Because of the perceived profit to be made and exponential value of a breeding bird, the demand for them rose and the market began to inflate. Susan Cook Adkins, once the Executive Director of the AOA, said that during this price hike, unethical and predatory behaviors

One of many enclosures at D.C. Cogburn's second ostrich ranch, in Southern Arizona (Author collection, 2025).

pervaded. Sadly, the AOA found that "individuals invested in ostrich[es] without ever seeing them."[913] Sometimes a new entrant would pay a deposit on chicks that would never be delivered. The sellers simply claimed the chick died and there was no replacement. Michael Lehman, current president of the AOA, has said, "It really became a scam. People were selling eggs for ridiculous prices and making assertions for how simple it was to raise ostriches and that is just not the case!"[914]

Early Organization

In the 1990s, helpful, up-to-date publications on ostrich care were still sparse and field experts few. Magazines such as *Ostrich Marketplace* and *The Ostrich News* had barely gotten off the ground. Investors struggled to make decisions when there was a lack of transparency in the industry. To alleviate some of the insecurities and address vast inconsistencies in the field, breeders organized. Almost exactly 80 years after the Arizona Ostrich Breeders' Association met in Phoenix, the American Ostrich Association formed. In March 1988, ostrich and other large bird owners met for the first time and assumed there would be a sharing of best practices and support for those who wanted to humanely, ethically and sustainably raise the best ratites in the world.[915] Among those at the inaugural session was D.C. Cogburn of Guthrie, Oklahoma (Arizona's soon-to-be ostrich king).

The U.S. Didn't See It Coming

Angered South African ostrich ranchers responded to the revival as if the U.S. was once again hijacking a national treasure. In May 1988, "Parliament passed a law making it a felony offense to export fertile ostrich or fertile ostrich eggs out of [South Africa]," effectively crippling the growth of an exciting and aggressively growing line of business.[916] Because of the restricted supply, prices of U.S.-based ostriches spiked again.

The excitement that followed created an inflation bubble that well-exceeded that of Arizona's territorial past. A U.S. breeder who had enough birds or fertile eggs to sell could ask virtually any amount. If someone wanted an ostrich, they had to fork out a fortune, get clever, or resort to crime. In the process, Cogburn observed, some breeders became extortionists overnight. Breeders starting asked for $600 per fertile egg, even though it was common knowledge that "more than half won't hatch."[917] Karen Weston Gonzales, a ranch hand at the Pacesetter Ostrich Farm in Willcox, Arizona remembered the rates being even higher. "A fertile egg was selling for $1,000," she told the *Tucson Weekly*. If a raiser wanted a guaranteed live animal, the price tag jumped exponentially, and, she continued, "six-month-old chicks were going for about $6,000." At the height of the demand, "[a]dult breeding pairs were selling for between $25,000 and $50,000."[918] Reports from the AOA and state news outlets support those extreme ranges.

Susan Franck, president and founder of the Arizona Ostrich/Emu Association out of Scottsdale, Arizona, observed that "[t]he lucrative aspects of the business ... created atmospheres of deceit, puffery, gossip and distrust."[919] Attitudes between colleagues became so soured that many farmers lost their ability to follow the tenth commandment ("Thou shall not covet"). Commandments six and eight were also potential problems (for the full list, see Exodus, chapter 20).

Because buyers felt pressure to get their hands on whatever they could get, they made desperate decisions. Some buyers looked to the black market for a bird, which was a pure gamble. "Most of the birds being shipped to the states were hatched from eggs stolen from open ostrich nests in the wild," Oliver wrote.[920] And those running such illegal egg operations often had no idea if the eggs they acquired were fertile or not. Even if they could tell, Cogburn claimed they lacked the knowledge to appropriately care for the eggs with incubators.[921] The AOA reported that these smugglers were "caught, arrested, and prosecuted by the authorities."[922]

Sometimes a broker could be found with access to birds or methods of getting them into the U.S. legally. The AOA shared that in some cases, the broker was crooked and would take payments on "non-existent birds."[923] When this was discovered and reported, scamming brokers and over-promising marketers "disappeared quickly."[924] Losses taken were often chalked up as the cost of doing business. Investors were also getting fleeced. Promoters did not openly disclose that even live chicks are no guarantee of a successful future. "[T]hey are a highly speculative investment," reported the

Deseret News, warning others that "the commercial market might not materialize."[925] Concerned AOA members began speaking up about the unethical practices and tried to educate others about potential scams. Those being outed felt livid and organizational infighting broke out.

New Possibilities & New Problems

To circumvent criminal activities in South Africa, several U.S. breeders purchased ostriches from the neighboring country of Namibia. After years of being controlled by the post-WWI League of Nations, Namibia (formerly *Deutsch-Südwestafrika)* was liberated. In 1990, they were recognized as an independent country. One of the first actions they took to boost their economy and re-establish a positive connection to the United States was to legalize ostrich exports.

Counteracting the fresh inflow of Namibian ostriches came stricter legislation for quarantines on imports. The previous year's imports of ratites received from Angola, Botswana, Portugal and Tanzania brought in arthropod ectoparasites (ticks, lice, fleas, etc.) which are known carriers of disease.[926] The USDA recommended that chicks not be allowed into the U.S. unless they could be inspected and observed for 30 days. To keep this process as inexpensive and efficient as possible for those at the quarantine station, imported chicks were required to be less than 30 pounds and shorter than three feet tall.

Imported eggs were also quarantined. I seriously doubt a tick might have gotten inside the shell with the embryo but, perhaps, they were found in packing material. The delivery had to be timed so every egg in the batch had to hatch at the quarantine station and remain with the shipment until all chicks had been observed for 30 days (which extended the quarantine period). If even one chick in a shipment carried a disease, the entire batch was either returned to its place of origin or humanely destroyed.[927]

While these standard procedures were essential for limiting the entry of sick animals, there were plenty of nuances and loopholes available to a clever ostrich breeder. Once stateside, the biggest overall risk was that extremely temperature-sensitive chicks sent to New York experienced higher fatalities due to weather conditions. When a new quarantine station opened in Miami, Florida, that risk dropped and ostrich imports increased.

With these changes, ostrich ranchers feared that the market would get flooded and prices plummet. It was a ridiculous threat to the breeders with dollar signs in their eyes. For the industry to function, however, additional imports were necessary, and pricing would have to come down to accommodate an end-user. A 1991 examination of the industry showed, "[t]he size of the total domestic flock is still far short of the 150,000 to 200,000 birds necessary to support a slaughter industry."[928] And, based on the inflated prices of yearlings from 1991 to 1994, the cost of an 8 oz. steak would start at $75. From there, the final price would tack on the cost of raising the bird, the transport fees, processing fees, packaging costs and account for the store or distributer's cut and taxes. At that point, a small serving of ostrich could be as expensive as, if not more than, wagyu beef.

Antsy responses to the Namibia and Miami stimuli were heightened by South Africa's release of political prisoner Nelson Mandela and a partial repeal of the Anti-Apartheid sanctions by U.S. President George H. W. Bush in 1991. In September 1993, Mandela requested a complete removal of sanctions (including those on ostrich products. This motion led to a panic among ostrich breeders. As readers have seen from the example in 1914, the economic impact of having a market suddenly be flooded with available products leads to mass quantity price deals which translates to a perceived drop in value of the item itself. If ostriches are again considered "a dime a dozen," then overpriced investments or the inflation "bubble" is bound to "pop," and the industry will collapse again. That effect would be devastating to industry big players who'd made big promises, unless... the ostrich raiser diversified their options and could provide more than just a trending product.

The Executive Director of the AOA, offered the following assurances to new entrants who questioned the wisdom of spending any more money: "One concern often expressed to me by newcomers," she wrote, "is 'what happens when trade sanctions against South Africa are fully removed?' The answer is that little or nothing will happen. There will be no effect..."[929]

In November 1993, President Bill Clinton signed the bill to end all remaining sanctions. As originally expected, "prices for ostriches and ostrich products plummeted."[930] As Andrew Van Dam, a data analyst writing for the *Washington Post,* put it: "The South African ostrich machine roared back to life, and the American ostrich bubble popped."[931] It was, as the AOA reported, "a perfect storm."[932] Rick "McOstrich" White shared that ostriches dropped to a fraction of their previous price.[933]

> "When the industry fell... it fell really hard."
> *-American Ostrich Association (n.d.)*

---

[v] *American Ostrich Association,* "About Us," Accessed August 25, 2025, https://www.americanostrichassociation.org/content.aspx?page_id=22&club_id=337926&module_id=716656.

Arizona's Wilcox Wasteland

Thirty-two ostrich ranches that had rapidly appeared between 1993 and 1994 in the Southeastern Arizona city of Wilcox were suddenly upside down. At this point, Weston Gonzales reported, industry members "blamed each other for not doing their part to promote their products. There was a lot of squabbling. A lot of ugly rumors circulated. Threats were made. Punches were thrown."[934]

Depending on the loans to be paid, some owners couldn't even afford to send their stock to be processed. The AOA stated "[t]here were instances where ostriches were given away for free if someone would just pick them up."[935] If that wasn't a possibility, owners took it upon themselves to butcher the birds themselves. Others gave up entirely, abandoning their properties and the ostriches on them. In 1997, one Phoenix breeder offloaded their ostriches to Maricopa County Sheriff Joe Arpaio who used the meat to feed nearly 7,000 prisoners wearing pink underwear.[936] "By the early 2000's," Gonzalez added, "most of the American ostrich industry was gone."[937]

36. Rooster Cogburn: An Arizona Legacy

*"One of the most unforgettable personalities
in the ostrich industries…"*
– Dub Oliver, Ostrich Ranching in America (1993)[938]

Rooster Cogburn's Ostrich Ranch in Red Rock, Arizona currently holds the largest private collection of South African Black ostriches in the nation (second in the world to South Africa).[939] Historically, the ranch comes in behind the Pan-American Ostrich Company as the largest collection of *any* species of ostrich in the nation (currently *the* largest). Outlasting Dr. A.J. Chandler by more than a decade, Cogburn's is the longest-continually operated ostrich ranch in the state. For all these reasons, the owners Damon Carl (D.C.) and Lucille Cogburn rank in as the current ostrich king and queen of Arizona.

The Rooster Cogburn Ostrich Ranch is nestled on 600 acres at the base of state-famous Picacho Peak, between Phoenix and Tucson. The ranch borders a two-mile stretch along the I-10 freeway and based on Arizona Department of Transportation numbers, in the three decades of ostriches living there, they've caught the attention of over 600 million drivers (over a billion if there were passengers in those cars).[940] Giant signs and waving flags invite everyone to pull over for an experience like none other. And when they do, the family offers rollicking property tours in a shamrock green monster truck, right through the pens of nearly 1,000 birds.

Cogburn's ostriches strut in the desert with Picacho Peak in the background (Author collection, 2025).

Author prepares for a monster truck tour through the ostrich enclosures (Author collection, 2025).

The roadside attraction has earned worldwide recognition and celebrity interest. Since opening for tourists, the Cogburn's ranch has been featured on Larry the Cable Guy's "Only in America," Food Network's "Chefs vs. City," PBS' popular children's program "Wild Kratts," and on CBS's Arizona Highways program (and many more). In the latter episode, CBS show host Robin Sewell allowed, "The main attraction are the big birds, but Rooster himself, is a close second."[941]

The original breeder Damon Carl "D.C." Cogburn has been popularly nicknamed "Rooster" Cogburn—a clever marketing nod to one of the lead characters from the 1969 John Wayne Western film "True Grit." When Larry the Cable Guy filmed at the ranch in 2013, he turned giddy over the reference and gave Cogburn an eyepatch to make his tour more "cool and authentic."[942]

How It Started

D.C. Cogburn's backstory is more colorful than a kaleidoscope. He is a native of Guthrie, Oklahoma—his great-grandfather having settled there in the 1890s (when it was still considered the Chickasaw Nation of Indian Territory). He was raised by a hard-knock father but rebelled against tradition when he chose a career as a competitive rodeo rider. Adjacent to that career, Cogburn also developed a clowning performance and trained animal show that involved dogs, mules, sheep, monkeys, a cat, and even a bull![943] In a trick that has never been reproduced since, Cogburn got a white bull named "Snowman" to jump through a ring of fire.[944]

Diane Simmons, writing for *Western Horseman* magazine has said, "There was a time when just about every avid rodeo fan was treated - sooner or later - to a performance by D.C. Cogburn, clown extraordinaire."[945] By 1980, at the age of 40, he'd performed in 42 states across America, and in Canada—a dream streak for many in his field. At that point, Cogburn has

said, "I could not wait to see what was over the next hill. I wanted to see a new challenge."[946]

D.C. "Rooster" Cogburn shows off the modern egg incubators they use at the ranch to hatch hundreds of eggs at a time (Author collection, 2025).

True to character, Cogburn found more ways to excite an audience with fun and memorable experiences. For a while, he and Lucille managed a roller-skating rink, which became their first multigenerational family business. Next, the Cogburns opened a family-run water park in Texas. Then D.C. helped launch an animal park in Arkansas. After a string of successful start-ups, Cogburn thought he might retire. He had achieved the white picket fence dream and could enjoy a bit of quiet with only a few cattle and some nickering horses on his pastureland. That lasted about two years.

In the summer of 1987, D.C. Cogburn ran into Leon Vandiver, the founder of the National Ostrich Breeders Association. They were both at a vet clinic at the Oklahoma State University and Vandiver had brought in some of his ostrich chicks.[947] In an instant, Cogburn was fascinated with the birds. Though he never intended to become a serious ostrich rancher like Vandiver, after talking for multiple hours about how to raise the birds, Cogburn bought his first pair of chicks, right off the man, for $1,000 each. "It was for fun," Cogburn explained.[948] Perhaps, the two cuties he took home would entertain him for a change.

Cogburn's birds [w] matured just as ostrich breeding had become a national obsession. Like so many others, he

"I am more excited about the ostrich industry than anything [else] I've ever been involved in."

-D.C. "Rooster" Cogburn (1993)

looked into monetizing their commercial products but found that he wouldn't have enough animals to provide a paycheck. He needed more ostriches, but because prices were "going through the roof," he wanted to make the most educated purchase possible. One part of that preparation took him and Lucille to Africa; the second part brought the whole family to Arizona. For two weeks, they visited Israel and Namibia and observed best practices at their ostrich farms. There, they learned about the preference given to one specific species: the "domesticated" South African Black ostrich.

The "blacks" are a hybrid species; one that has since become near impossible to acquire. They are smaller than a red or blue neck and it is generally accepted that the hens lay more eggs and grow 20% more feathers on their body (which makes their hides more decorated with quill marks, therefore, more attractive on finished products).[949] Some people claim this species is a more docile than others, though no official study has confirmed that. Though this species received an enormous amount of criticism in the 1990's, Cogburn decided to trust what he'd seen for himself, rather than the promotions being made. If this was the preferred bird of their native

---

[w] D.C. Cogburn in Oliver's *Ostrich Ranching in America* (Shreveport: Dub Oliver & Associates, 1993), 143.

Ostrich feeding zone at the Rooster Cogburn Ostrich Ranch (Author collection, 2025).

"Ostrich fishing" opportunity (Author collection, 2025).

region, why would he chance his business on any other?

Cogburn sold his red and blue ostriches off for an outrageous price and placed an order for chicks of the domesticated black species at $700 each. They were flown to New York and sat through a cold quarantine period. "Very few survived," Cogburn relayed.[950] From there, he chartered a plane to fly the surviving chicks home. Having fully revised his prior idea of a "fun" side job, Cogburn was quoted in 1993: "We fully expect to be one of the largest family-owned ostrich ranches in the world."[951]

D.C.'s daughter Dana Cogburn-Barett has explained, as their flock increase in number, "he recognized that ostriches need to be in their natural climate in order to raise large numbers efficiently."[952] That realization put the Cogburns on a

Some ostriches "dance" when tour vehicles come through their enclosure (Author collection, 2025).

search for the closest thing they could find to an ostrich's native habitat: the Salt River Valley. For a few years, the family ranch they settled on was not much to see other than some large enclosures of the wild-looking creatures watching cars fly by. Soon enough, gas station pit-stoppers and commuters were making impromptu visits to gander over the fences.

In 1999, D.C. and Lucille decided to make the best of those visits. They "put up a shade tent, [set out] a folding table, and opened to the public," their daughter shared.[953] There was no electricity for even a fan and no bathrooms for guests, but for $2, a family could interact with the birds through the fence with a cup of corn feed. Without having spent a penny on advertisement, on their first day sitting under the tent, the couple made $2,800.[954]

Since them, the business expanded to include a diverse petting zoo with (my favorite) fuzzy-headed mini donkeys, puppy-like desert tortoises, cheeky kissing goats, rainbow lorikeets and even a sting ray feeding opportunity! If guests wish to feed the ostriches, they can pass alfalfa kernels through designated spots along a fence or gleefully toss a handful overboard while off-roading through the enclosures. The most memorable option, though, is to "fish" for an ostrich from a wooden pier using handmade poles baited with juicy orange slices. Lucille Cogburn has shared that their ostriches have mastered the act of flirtation with guests to earn their treats. First thing in the morning, she has said, when the first car pulls into the parking lot, the birds get excited and run up to the petting zoo fence and feeding zones because they know it's to be show time.[955]

Though D.C. has been commended for his hard work and genius as the "master builder" behind the family legacy, three generations have contributed to the success of the animal park. [956] Even on challenging days and when contending with the Arizona heat, Cogburn's daughter Dana has said of the work, "when you see someone's face light up or tell you that this is the "best day ever," [and] watch families interact and forget their troubles for just a little while, it is all worth it. That is why we do what we do." [957] Besides putting a smile on Arizona families' and tourists' faces for more than twenty-six years (closer to thirty if we count the early trespassers), the Rooster Cogburn Ostrich Ranch supplies show birds to the Chandler Ostrich Festival and has one of the most unique shopping experiences for gift items. Of course, Cogburn's also carries those mouth-watering ruby red steaks you've read so much about.

Tragedy at the Peak

Shortly after opening the roadside attraction, tragedy struck the Cogburn's troops. Long-time residents might recall major news coverage in 2002 after a pair of hot air balloons descended into the airspace just north of the bird's pens. The glowing and hissing foreign objects sent the birds into a panic. While trying to escape the perceived threat, they started a deadly stampede.

"It was like a tornado had come through," Cogburn told the press.[958]

Dust kicked up into the air as the terrified ostriches slammed into their enclosure fencing with a clamor. Weak kneed D.C. and Lucille rushed to save as many ostriches as possible. Some of the entangled birds had to be cut free from the warped fencing wires with pliers. The losses amounted to just over 1,000 birds and it brought the whole family to tears.

"The ones that didn't die were crippled or skinned up like you wouldn't believe," Cogburn told the *Queen Creek Tribune*.[959]

University of Arizona film student Jonathan VanBallenberghe produced an eye-opening documentary about the aftermath titled *The Ostrich Testimonies* (2008, Open Lens Productions). It has since been made available online through Vimeo. Though the family diligently sought compensation in court, nothing was awarded. They appealed for four years and rallied state politicians and news outlets for another ten.

"Fifteen years of work went right down the drain," Cogburn lamented to the *Arizona Republic*.[960]

How Did the Cogburns Survive the Market Crash?

When the ostrich meat market crashed in 1994, the Cogburns survived by diversifying their options and maximizing the potential of every ostrich (and show animal) they acquired. D.C. was one of the few ranchers that was clipping and processing feathers. He had secured major contracts for feathers by big operations in Las Vegas and Brazil. He developed positive relationships with boot manufacturers for the "exotic" leather his birds provided. He also proceeded with processing birds and their eggs for the specialty meat market. Over time, Cogburn updated the ranch to improve the guest experience, and since then, he's continued to be on the lookout for new ways to make the most of his passion. In other words, his "eggs" were not all in one basket when the bottom dropped out.

Today, D.C. Cogburn is almost retired for the second time. In his late 80s, he is still considered the master caretaker for the ostriches, but he has passed down much of the park operations and management to the next generations. On monster trick tours, guests can still see him in a pair of old overalls, working a crowd with a team of talented dogs and ducks in a stage show finale.

If the audience wonders why he talks with a bit of a whistle, they can blame it on him getting a little too cozy with a long-neck. While trying to show off his bird handling skills by "kissing" one on the beak, the bird decided to go in for a more intimate tooth extraction. Rumor has it that ever since that incident, park visitors have been advised to pose for photos with the birds always behind them. That way, when

Opposite: Scene from the duck water park show. Above: Gentle goats charm guests at the "kissing booth" (Author collection, 2025).

everyone shows off a big grin, those irresistible bug-eyed birds won't be tempted to play tooth fairy. (I made that last part up, but what *is* true is that the only animal kissing allowed these days are the alfalfa pass-offs with some of the goofiest goats you could ever meet.)

On a Personal Note

While researching for this book, I've had numerous opportunities to talk with the current ostrich king of Arizona. My calls were often taken while D.C. Cogburn rumbled around his property in what he called a "sewer wagon."[961] I have also been treated to fascinating behind-the-scenes tours of the ranch. In Dub Oliver's book *Ostrich Ranching in America*, he *wrote:* "To spend 10 minutes with 'Rooster' Cogburn is an experience; to spend 2 hours with him is an adventure!"[962] I couldn't have written it any better. The rosy cheeked man in overalls might be the sweetest "shirt-off-yer-back" kind of rancher I've ever met, but when he talks, the words come out as fast as an auctioneer and he fully expects listeners to "listen up." Most of the time I did. However, if he paused to take a breath, that was my chance to ask him all the so-called "dumb" questions I could think of, like, "What's the greatest number of rocks you've ever seen in the stomach of an ostrich?" Oh, he went on for a bit about who would ever need to know that information but gave the answer anyways. "I don't know a number," he said, "but I've seen quite a pile."[963] (You're welcome, readers.)

I also asked if he had a favorite bird and, if so, what was their name. "I don't give names to the ostriches!" he claimed. "They aren't pets."[964] After a beat, he gave in and offered, "My birds names are Ostrich #1, Ostrich #2..."[965] I later learned from his grandson there was a bird named "Pretty Boy Floyd." This rooster has a reputation for giving a spunky dance performance whenever a tour vehicle came his way. "It's cute," Cogburn's grandson told me.[966] When I double backed on my question, Cogburn gruffed a bit, then admitted it was true, adding, "And that's the *only* bird that has a name!"[967] He was the first South African Black rooster they acquired and holds a special place in Cogburn's heart. Cogburn has shared: "he was such a treat to be around that we him named after another person who was also a joy to be around, my father Floyd Cogburn."[968]

Though ostriches respond positively to handler affection, there is no proof they form emotional attachments to humans (like some parrots).

37. The Future of Ostriches

"If only the state of Arizona realized what was possible…"
- D.C. "Rooster" Cogburn (2025)[969]

If you have not been enthralled by centuries of humans interacting with these disproportionately built birds, perhaps what comes next will convince you that ostriches are one of the most fascinating creatures to have ever walked the face of the earth with us. Currently, ostriches are catching the attention of the science field and are now one of the world's most exciting prospects for medical advancements. They might even provide a cure for cancer! (Or at least their eggs may.)

Mother Goose may have gotten her story wrong because ostriches are laying the golden egg in terms of new medical research, and the proof is in print. Case studies from 2010, 2018 and 2024 have already proven that antibodies created by ostriches and harvested from their eggs can effectively treat the following issues in humans: allergies caused by cedar pollen, cypress pollen, hay fever; bacterial issues such as staph infections and acne; viral infections such as the bird flu (A/HSN1), bronchitis, and coronavirus; and even problems like dermatitis and hair loss (AGA). Studies show that ostrich-made antibodies are also able to address pyoderma in canines.

Nearly anyone with a chemistry background can read the reports coming out from all over the world and follow the basic recipe towards new applications. During the Covid-19 pandemic, a doctor in Japan led a successful experiment infusing protective face masks with ostrich-made antibodies that reacted upon contact with the virus. If the person wearing the mask became exposed, the antibodies would become visible under UV light, providing an opportunity for early interventions.[970] In more recent studies being conducted, ostrich antibodies that targeted tumor markers showed encouraging results, including suppressing tumor growth.[971]

> "This is serious stuff that would solve a lot of problems!"
>
> -D.C. "Rooster" Cogburn (2025)

Gene Pfeiffer, founding president of the American Ostrich Association, has offered, "this is only the tip of the iceberg."[972]

U.S. physician Dr. Alessio Fasano, at the Massachusetts General Hospital & Harvard University, has recently isolated the protein called Zonulin, which causes autoimmune disorders, celiac disease, neurodegeneration, and tumors. He and his team are hopeful that ostriches can assist with the mass-production of Zonulin antibodies. If funding is applied toward the development of a commercially available immunization, then permanent relief is at hand for suffering patients.[973]

In Iran, a team of researchers from the Tarbiat Modares University, the Pasteur Institute of Iran, Royan Institute for Stem Cell Biology and Technology (and others) are using ostrich antibodies to inhibit the protein that causes type 1 diabetes.[974] Like the reports from Japan and the U.S., they've spelled out their workflow for a medical science journal, making this method of antibody therapy known to all.

Slow Down—What are "Antibodies?"

Antibodies are important immune cell modifiers that are naturally created during an immune system response. Antibodies (think antivenoms and antibiotics) work in

---

[x] D.C. Cogburn, phone communication to author, April 29, 2025.

opposition of an undesirable, harmful or foreign "body" within a host. Once the immune system has learned how to overcome a pathogen (either from exposure or through vaccination), corresponding proteins form into a Y-shaped chain using the undesirable pathogen as the basic model. Speaking in the most *un-science-y* way possible, these teeny-tiny molecules become our bodies' Special Ops Force, highly trained for their unique mission.

Unlike antivenoms and antibiotics, which can be made of unrelated components to disable their opposition, antibodies are built with specific protein molecules that target their signature pathogen. According to one Japanese-based research team, they found that the use of harsh disinfectants, antimicrobial agents, and antibiotics comes at a cost to the host by causing "deterioration of the resident microflora environment."[975] This side effect can be avoided with ostrich antibody therapy.

Immune cells can wear the antibody like armor, and the antibodies will continue to live within the host, awaiting an opportunity to be useful. If the signature pathogen is ever re-introduced, the antibodies will be attracted to it. Some literature describes this phenomenon as cellular memory. When encountering the pathogen a second time, the immune cell "remembers" how to overcome what it has defeated before. In this interaction, the antibodies attach to the pathogen's receptors, which will neutralize or disable its ability to attach to a healthy cell. Then, the immune cell will (typically) self-destruct, eliminating the pathogen with it.

When spontaneously exposed, this process is how we build up a resistance (or immunity) to certain diseases and conditions. Vaccinations (like the flu, chicken pox, etc.) are therapeutic exposures of weakened or inactive forms of a pathogen given under medical supervision that help prepare a body for a spontaneous exposure. Some vaccination patients experience mild symptoms while the body adjusts and overcomes the exposure. Later, if spontaneously exposed to a full-strength pathogen, the patient can expect to over-come symptoms more rapidly because the antibodies they have developed already know what to do to counter the attack.

The concept of antibody therapy asks the following questions: What if a patient did not have to fight off even the slightest version of a pathogen? What if an immuno-compromised individual did not have to risk a severe response to *any* introduction of a pathogen? And why not skip the uncomfortable and risky steps and simply receive the antibodies directly? The medical field is currently exploring the answers available with the assistance of ostriches.

Ostriches have an extraordinary immune system, able to overcome almost everything they have been exposed to in laboratory tests. Once immunized (the stage when antibodies are created), ostrich hens pass their antibodies down to the next generation, and into their infertile eggs, too. The anti-bodies can then be retrieved and administered to a human patient who needs an immune boost, without any additional demand on their system. Ostriches would essentially do the dirty work by overcoming pathogens on the patient's behalf.

How are Ostrich Antibodies Retrieved?

Hens are vaccinated with a weakened version of the target pathogen, just like a human would be. Depending on what is being introduced, the big birds may get a booster shot to ensure a successful mass production of antibodies. Two to four weeks after they have completed their vaccination schedule, antibodies are present in the hen's blood and highly concentrated in the yolk of its eggs. This being the case, the antibodies are nicknamed "immunoglobulin yolk," or just "IgY."

Yolk samples go through a purification process to remove any proteins that might cause negative reactions in humans with egg allergies (like Ovalbumin). Then, the final product can be added to a delivery method most appropriate for the condition. Existing trials have found success with delivery via syringe, lozenge, nasal spray, liquid drops, topical creams, or even being mixed in with a carrier such as an absorbent, skin-friendly oil.

In the last two decades, attempts to achieve what has been done with ostrich eggs was tried on small mammals (such as rabbits and mice). The trouble with this option has been comparatively high production costs and weaker outputs. Scientists have found that ostriches are so sensitive to vaccinations that, even though they are large animals, they need only receive the same dose as a rabbit. Because of the volume of output an ostrich egg yolk can provide, developing immunizations through them becomes a major cost-saver to the industry (and, eventually, to the end user).

One of the leading scientists behind this discovery has been Dr. Yasuhiro Tsukamoto, a veterinarian by profession and the president of the Kyoto Prefecture University in Japan. He's explored the potential of ostrich antibodies with colleagues for nearly 20 years. He founded OstriGen and Ostrich Pharma USA and has conducted his testing with a small troop of birds in Hokkaido. In trials using small mammals, he found that "[their] antibody proteins are inactivated by heat, acids, and alkalis, preventing mass production."[976]

Hypothetically, administering these antibodies to a human will prove less effective because of the presence of acids in our stomachs, alkalis in our bloodstream, saliva and bones, and because of the fevers brought on by many conditions. It is unclear how much of a mammal-produced antibody can survive the competing factors. Dr. Tsukamoto's case studies report that the IgYs from ostriches can withstand all of the above factors (including temperatures up to 120 degrees). The findings suggest IgYs are far more complementary to the human body than any other options currently available.

Considerations

The entire process is very gentle on the hen, and every procedural step can be completed within existing standards for the ethical treatment of animals. Gabi Serrato Marks, writing for the National Audubon Society has reported on the potential harm subjects experience: "The shots wouldn't make the birds sick, but would kick their immune systems into overdrive."[977] An editorial comment on the Society publication, adds that they are pleased to feature scientists turning to birds to find answers for such important issues. Though groups like PETA are diametrically opposed to animal testing, the ASPCA's official position on animal use in research is that it is acceptable if "the research is likely to produce new and substantive information that will benefit human and animal health," but only when animal-free options are unavailable.[978] Currently, animal testing procedures are regulated by the Animal Welfare Act, which is enforced by the USDA. Birds that

> "Experimenting on animals is not only cruel but also completely unnecessary & unethical."
> -People for the Ethical Treatment of Animals (2025)

---

[y] People for the Ethical Treatment of Animals, "All Your Question About Experiments on Animals," *PETA.org*, Accessed November 24, 2025, https://www.peta.org/features/animal-testing-facts-questions-answers/.

are bred for research, however, are fully excluded from those regulations (*9 CFR: 1-3*). As of 2022, *any* ratite, when intended for use as food, leather or feathers is also excluded.

Currently, the U.S. Food & Drug Administration has an evolving stance on such developments. In an April 2025 press release, they announced their intention to "phase out" animal testing in the field of antibody therapies.[979] The animal-free alternative they proposed involves artificial intelligence (AI) simulation and testing on lab-grown "human organoids" (structures created from human stem cells).[980] It is unclear when this plan will roll out and which animals will be affected. One month later, Robert F. Kennedy, Jr. claimed a reversal on the FDA's plan. Writing in defense of a troop of ostriches in Canada subject to a cull, he wrote:

> "The United States Department of Health and Human Services, including the National Institutes of Health (NIH) and the Food and Drug Administration (FDA), would like to offer our full support and assistance in conducting diagnostic testing and undertaking a long-term body of research on these ostriches," citing the "potential to study both antibody levels and cellular immunity to help further our scientific understanding."[981]

Just because these experiments have been proven effective in trials does not mean the discovery can be put into widespread use yet. Long-term studies still need to be conducted on the downstream effects, such as the half-life and vaccination booster schedules, the shelf life of commercial products, and the potential for mutations. Alternatives need to be evaluated to find safe, reliable and affordable options for

Rooster Cogburn's Ostrich Ranch in Red Rock, Arizona (Author collection, 2025).

isolating pathogen proteins. Clearances must be obtained from the FDA and market research conducted. From there, clinical trials would include humans who are willing to be part of the experience. To support these activities, though, billions of dollars must be raised, and ostrich populations must increase... again.

If the United States chooses to participate, Arizona's Salt River Valley is destined to reclaim its title as the ostrich capital of the nation. (And if so, let's not make the same mistakes this go-around.) The next step in this process would be to establish an Arizona-based research facility. There, scientists could revolutionize the medical, pharmaceutical and agricultural industries through the inclusion of ostriches in further studies. This is an exciting prospect as "ostriches have been a notable part of Arizona's history and character for over a century."[982] If research continues in this direction, ostriches may soon become one of the most important animals on earth.

Acknowledgements

A special thanks goes to named individuals who supported the production of this work and encouraged the me to keep my facts straight:

William and David Rousseau with the Rousseau Farming Company for allowing me to share part of our family history; Damon C. Cogburn, Lucille Cogburn and Danna Cogburn-Barrett with the Rooster Cogburn Ostrich Ranch for sharing their passion; Larry Cundall, longtime cattle rancher and bougie meat-eater for coyboyin' clarity; Nina U. Schaller for double-checking my comprehension of advanced science principals; Sarah Biggerstaff with the Chandler Museum for archival assistance; and to Carol Lynds and Jim Burge relatives the Pickrells and Tostons, for encouraging the full retelling of their family history.

D.C. Cogburn with author (Author collection, 2025).

Molony

(Blank Page)

Endnotes

Chapter 1

[1] "Ostrich Farm Sold," *Arizona Republican*, May 16, 1901, 8.

[2] Sylvia Bender-Lamb, "An Economic Analysis of the Ostrich Industry in Arizona's Salt River Valley," April 18, 1978, 1. (Found in the Arizona Historical Society Small Manuscript Collection - MSM 48.)

[3] 1907 Advertisement in the *Phoenix Gazette*, as cited in Kristen Kraklio's "Feather fad created Arizona's ostrich industry," *Arizona Republic,* March 21, 2015.

[4] Dub Oliver, *Ostrich Ranching in America* (Shreveport: Dub Oliver & Associates, 1993), 7.

[5] Thomas C. Duncan (M.D., Ph.D.), "Ostrich Farming in America," in *Report of the Commissioner of Agriculture for the Year 1888* (Washington: Government Printing Office, 1889), 685.

[6] Karen Kraklio, "Feathers in Our Cap," *Arizona Highways* 90, no. 10 (October 2014), 8.

[7] Rep. Carl T. Hayden, "The Ostrich Industry," *Congressional Record of the 62nd Congress, U.S. House of Representatives* 49 (February 7, 1913), 60.

[8] John A. Lesku, Leith C. Meyer, Andrea Fuller, Shane K. Maloney, Giacomo Dell'Omo, Alexi L. Vyssotski, and Niels C. Rattenborg, "Ostriches Sleep Like Platypuses," *Plos One* 6, no. 8 (2011), 1-7, https://doi.org/10.1371/journal.pone.0023203.

[9] "The Arizona Ostrich," *Arizona Graphic* 1, no. 11 (1899), 4.

[10] "How to Farm an Ostrich," *Marion Commonwealth*, December 14, 1882, 1. (Reprinted or extracted from the *New York Sun*.)

[11] "Way of the Ostrich," *Evening Capital*, February 27, 1900, 4.

[12] "Ostrich," *San Diego Zoo*, 2025, https://animals.sandiegozoo.org/animals/ostrich.

Chapter 2

[13] Cawston Ostrich Farm, *Souvenir Book*, 1909. (Held at the Smithsonian Institute.)

[14] "Ostrich Farming in the United States," *Journal of the Royal Society of Arts* 60, no. 3095 (1912), 476-477.

[15] Blanche K. Murray, "Ostriches in Arizona," *Arizona Highways,* 15, no. 11 (1939), 22.

[16] "Ostrich Feathers," *Millinery Trade Review* 14, no. 3 (1889), 19.

[17] "Milliners Meet," *Buffalo Courier Express,* August 9, 1901, 3.

[18] *Buffalo Courier Express,* August 9, 1901.

[19] *Buffalo Courier Express,* August 9, 1901.

[20] Roscoe G. Wilson, "Ostrich Farms Contributed to Fashion World," *Arizona Days and Ways,* March 2, 1958, 27.

[21] Watson Pickrell, "Ostriches," in *Yearbook of the United States Department of Agriculture, 1905* (Washington: Government Printing Office, 1906), 403.

[22] Pickrell, "Ostriches," 403.

[23] Wilson, "Ostrich Farms...," 26.

[24] Pickrell, "Ostriches," 403.

[25] James A. Geissinger, "On an Arizona Ostrich Farm," *The Presbyterian Banner* (January 28, 1909), 8.

[26] Murray, "Ostriches in Arizona," 23.

[27] Murray, 23.

[28] Annie Martin, *Home Life on an Ostrich Farm* (London: G. Philip, 1890), 110.

Chapter 3

[29] "Trade Conditions," *Millinery Trade Review* 29, no. 7 (July 1904), 44.

[30] Louis Henry Chalmers, "The Ostrich in the Salt River Valley," *The Earth: Salt River Valley of Arizona, Special* 6, no. 8 (August 1909), 21.

[31] Duncan, "Ostrich Farming in America," 666.

[32] Sarah A. Stein, *Plumes: Ostrich Feathers, Jews, and a Lost World of Global Commerce* (New Haven: Yale University, 2008), 6.

[33] Stein, *Plumes*, 6.

[34] The second lasted from 1889 to 1902.

[35] Watson Pickrell, "Ostrich," in *Cyclopedia of Farm Animals*, ed. L. H. Bailey (New York: MacMillan, 1922), 511.

[36] Pickrell, "Ostrich," in *Cyclopedia*, 511.

[37] James S. Stewart, "What Are the Kinds of Ostrich and Which One is Best?," in Oliver's *Ostrich Ranching in America*, 17-18.

[38] C. W. Wright, "Alfalfa & Millinery," *Agricultural Southwest* 8, no. 22 (Aug. 16, 1912), 1.

[39] Damon C. Cogburn, phone communication to author, August 28, 2025.

[40] "The Ostrich," *Scientific American* 65, no. 23 (December 5, 1891), 359.

Chapter 4

[41] Henry Miles, ed. "Strange Farms, Unusual Means of Making Money," *Montreal Pharmaceutical Journal* 27, no. 12 (December 1916), 235.

[42] Berthold Laufer, "Ostrich Egg-shell Cups of Mesopotamia and the Ostrich in Ancient and Modern Times" (Chicago: Field Museum of Natural History, 1926), 43.

[43] "The Ostrich in America," *Arizona Republican*, February 27, 1905, 3.

[44] E. H. Rydall, "Ostrich Farming in California," *American Farmer* 5, no. 4 (April 1, 1899), 286.

[45] Duncan, "Ostrich Farming in America," 666.

[46] Damon C. Cogburn, phone communication to author, May 21, 2025.

[47] Rydall, "Ostrich Farming in California," 286.

[48] Rydall, 286.

[49] They were all about eight years old.

[50] *Arizona Republican*, February 27, 1905.

[51] Miles, "Strange Farms…," 235.

[52] Tom Pulley, "Orange County was Once the Ostrich Capital of America," *County Courier* 39, no. 5 (Santa Ana: Orange County Historical Society, May 2009), 1.

[53] "African Colonist," *New Bern Weekly Journal*, November 16, 1882, 2.

[54] *New Bern Weekly Journal*, November 16, 1882.

[55] *New Bern Weekly Journal*, November 16, 1882.

[56] *New Bern Weekly Journal*, November 16, 1882.

[57] *Marion Commonwealth*, December 14, 1882.

[58] Martin, *Home Life on an Ostrich Farm*, 110-111.

[59] "Mr. Protheroe's Herd of Ostriches," *Morning Press*, December 8, 1882, 4. (Reprinted or extracted from the *New York Sun*.)

[60] "Shipping Ostriches to California," *Democratic Leader*, January 3, 1883, 4.

[61] Laufer, "Ostrich Egg-shell Cups…," 47.

[62] "British and Foreign Items," *The Mercury*, January 27, 1883.

[63] William G. Le Duc, "Domestic Ostrich Farming," *The Courier*, December 13, 1883, 3.

[64] Pulley, "Orange County was Once…," 1.

[65] Pulley, 1.

[66] Charles Frederick Holder, "An Ostrich Ranch," *Chautauquan* VII, no. 3 (Dec. 1886), 153.

[67] "Ostrich Farming in California," *Los Angeles Herald*, January 7, 1883, 3.

[68] *Los Angeles Herald*, January 7, 1883.

[69] Rydall, "Ostrich Farming in California," 286.

[70] Laufer, "Ostrich Egg-shell Cups…," 47.

[71] *Arizona Republican*, February 27, 1905.

Chapter 5

[72] *Arizona Graphic,* "The Arizona Ostrich," 4.

[73] Lowell Parker, "Fashion Foibles Led to Flourishing Industry," *Arizona Republic,* January 20, 1974, 6.

[74] Johannes Leo Africanus, *Cosmographia et Geographia de Africa* (1526), ts. Clare Richie to *A Geographical Historie of Africa* (London, 1600): 347-348.

[75] "A New Industry," *Arizona Weekly Star,* June 7, 1888, 3.

[76] *San Diego Zoo,* 2025.

[77] Martin, *Home Life on an Ostrich Farm,* 112.

[78] Martin, 112.

[79] "An Ostrich Ranch in Arizona," *Poultry Monthly* 17, no. 5 (May 1895), 156.

[80] *Arizona Graphic,* "The Arizona Ostrich," 4.

[81] Duncan, "Ostrich Farming in America," 696.

[82] Duncan, 696.

[83] *Poultry Monthly,* "An Ostrich Ranch in Arizona," 156.

[84] Laufer, "Ostrich Egg-shell Cups…," 48-49.

[85] Laufer, 48-49.

[86] Damon C. Cogburn, phone communication to author, April 29, 2025.

Chapter 6

[87] Pickrell, "Ostrich," in *Cyclopedia,* 511.

[88] Pickrell, "Ostrich," in *Cyclopedia,* 511.

[89] "Ostriches for California," *Phoenix Weekly Herald,* December 13, 1883, 2. (They established the American Ostrich Company in Fallbrook, San Diego Co.)

[90] William Dutcher, "The Ostrich," *Bird-Lore* 7, no. 2 (April 1, 1905), 154.

[91] Ed J. Johnson to a South African Associate, January 1884, as quoted in Jeannette DeWyze's "San Diego's Ostrich Speculators," *San Diego Reader,* May 12, 1994, https://www.sandiegoreader.com/news/1994/may/12/cover-san-diego-ostrich-speculators/.

[92] Pulley, "Orange County was Once…," 3.

[93] Pulley, 3.

[94] Duncan, "Ostrich Farming in America," 666.

[95] *Scientific American,* "The Ostrich," 359.

[96] Duncan, "Ostrich Farming in America," 666.

[97] Holder, "An Ostrich Ranch," 152.

[98] "Ostrich Feathers," *Arizona Sentinel,* September 18, 1866, 1.

[99] Duncan, "Ostrich Farming in America," 666.

[100] "Seasick Ostriches," *Daily Tombstone,* April 13, 1886, 3.

[101] Andrea Ringer, "The Captive Lives of Ostriches as Belligerent Animal Workers and Bad Mothers," in *Modern American History* 8, no. 2 (Boston: Cambridge University Press, July 2025), 115.

[102] Some records say 34, others say 36.

[103] *Daily Tombstone,* April 13, 1886.

[104] *Daily Tombstone,* April 13, 1886.

[105] "Ostriches," *Tucson Citizen,* April 16, 1886, 4.

[106] *Arizona Republican,* February 27, 1905.

Chapter 7

[107] "Ostrich Farming," advertisement of the American Ostrich Company in *Westerner* 7, no. 3 (Seattle: Westerner Co., August 1907), 17. (On file at the University of Washington Library – Pacific Northwest Collection.)

[108] Dutcher, "The Ostrich," 154-155.

[109] Parker, "Fashion Foibles," 6.

[110] "Cawston Ostrich Farm," *Picryl* Public Domain Media, https://picryl.com/collections/cawston-ostrich-farm-7ee4ea.
[111] Pulley, "Orange County was Once…," 5.
[112] Before closing, the California Ostrich Co. moved from Anaheim to Fullerton.
[113] Pulley, "Orange County was Once…," 4.
[114] Robin Doughty, "Ostrich Farming American Style," *Agricultural History* 47, no. 2 (April 1973), 142.
[115] *Arizona Republican*, February 27, 1905.
[116] Pulley, "Orange County was Once…," 5.

Chapter 8
[117] "An Ostrich Farm for Arizona," *Arizona Sentinel*, June 9, 1888, 2.
[118] "Arizona Ostriches," *The Oasis* 1, no. 20 (September 21, 1893), 1.
[119] *Arizona Daily Star*, July 13, 1888.
[120] "Arizona Ostriches," *Weekly Journal-Miner*, July 4, 1888, 1.
[121] *Arizona Weekly Star*, June 7, 1888.
[122] *Arizona Sentinel*, June 9, 1888.
[123] Editorial, *Arizona Weekly Enterprise*, June 30, 1888, 3.
[124] Charles C. Colley, "Ostrich Ranching: Arizona's Strangest Venture," *Arizona Highways* 55, no. 5 (May 1979), 41.
[125] Murray, "Ostriches in Arizona," 22.
[126] Colley, "Ostrich Ranching: Arizona's Strangest Venture," 41.
[127] "Ostriches Sold," *Arizona Daily Star*, July 13, 1888, 4.
[128] *Arizona Weekly Star*, June 7, 1888.
[129] Editorial, *Arizona Sentinel*, October 22, 1887, 3.

Chapter 9
[130] 1899-1900 Phoenix City Directory.
[131] Wilson, "Ostrich Farms…," 26.
[132] Colley, "Ostrich Ranching: Arizona's Strangest Venture," 41.
[133] "Ostrich Farm Sold," *Coconino Sun*, May 25, 1901, 2.
[134] *Arizona Daily Star*, July 13, 1888.
[135] *The Oasis,* "Arizona Ostriches," 1.
[136] "Ostrich Farming," *Clifton Clarion*, June 19, 1889.
[137] Colley, "Ostrich Ranching: Arizona's Strangest Venture," 42.
[138] Murray, "Ostriches in Arizona," 22.
[139] Colley, "Ostrich Ranching: Arizona's Strangest Venture," 42.
[140] Murray, "Ostriches in Arizona," 23.
[141] *The Oasis,* "Arizona Ostriches," 1.
[142] *Poultry Monthly,* "An Ostrich Ranch in Arizona," 156.
[143] "Omnivorous Birds," *Arizona Republican*, September 4, 1894, 1.
[144] Murray, "Ostriches in Arizona," 22.
[145] Chalmers, "The Ostrich in the Salt River Valley," 21.
[146] *Arizona Graphic,* "The Arizona Ostrich," 4.
[147] *Arizona Graphic,* 4.
[148] Dutcher, "The Ostrich," 155.

Chapter 10
[149] 1899-1900 Phoenix City Directory.
[150] *Arizona Graphic,* "The Arizona Ostrich," 4.
[151] Job 39:14, Holy Bible (Amplified Version).
[152] Dutcher, "The Ostrich," 156.
[153] Pickrell, "Ostriches," 400.

[154] *The Oasis,* "Arizona Ostriches," 1.

[155] As cited in Laufer's "Ostrich Egg-shell Cups…," 14. Original item available through the LOC https://www.loc.gov/item/2021667228/

[156] Colley, "Ostrich Ranching: Arizona's Strangest Venture," 42.

[157] "Ostrich-Hunting," *Pinal Drill,* October 7, 1882, 2.

[158] *The Oasis,* "Arizona Ostriches," 1.

[159] Pickrell, "Ostriches," 401.

[160] *The Oasis,* "Arizona Ostriches," 1.

[161] Job 39:16, Holy Bible (The Message).

[162] Ringer, "The Captive Lives of Ostriches…,"117.

[163] Pickrell, "Ostrich," in *Cyclopedia,* 512.

[164] Geissinger, "On an Arizona Ostrich Farm," 9.

[165] *Arizona Republican,* December 23, 1914.

Chapter 11

[166] 1915-1916 Arizona State Business Directory.

[167] Pickrell, "Ostriches," 399.

[168] Thomas W. Kemp, "Opinion of an Expert: The Ostriches in the Salt River Valley," *Arizona Republican,* October 30, 1910, 9.

[169] "Ostriches," *Arizona Republican,* April 1, 1901, 11.

[170] 1899-1900 Phoenix City Directory.

[171] Wilson, "Ostrich Farms…," 26.

[172] *Coconino Sun,* "Ostrich Farm Sold," May 25, 1901.

[173] *Arizona Republican,* February 27, 1905.

[174] Pulley, "Orange County was Once…," 4.

[175] "Funeral of A. Y. Pearson," *Arizona Republican,* January 28, 1903, 4.

[176] Dutcher, "The Ostrich," 155.

[177] Pickrell, "Ostriches," 400.

[178] "The Ostrich Center," *Arizona Silver Belt,* March 29, 1900, 3.

[179] Pulley, "Orange County was Once…," 4.

[180] Pickrell, "Ostriches," 400.

[181] *Arizona Silver Belt,* "The Ostrich Center," March 29, 1900. Note: James E. Bark was a prominent cattleman in Arizona Territory. He was once the president of the Arizona Cattle Growers Association. He partnered with Frank Criswell.

[182] Pickrell, "Ostriches," 400.

[183] *Arizona Silver Belt,* "The Ostrich Center," March 29, 1900.

[184] Pulley, "Orange County was Once…," 4.

[185] *Arizona Silver Belt,* "The Ostrich Center," March 29, 1900.

[186] *Coconino Sun,* "Ostrich Farm Sold," May 25, 1901.

[187] "About the Corridors," *Los Angeles Evening Express,* May 18, 1901, 12.

[188] *Los Angeles Evening Express,* May 18, 1901.

[189] *Arizona Republican,* "Ostrich Farm Sold," May 16, 1901.

[190] *Coconino Sun,* "Ostrich Farm Sold," May 25, 1901.

[191] *Arizona Republican,* January 28, 1903.

Chapter 12

[192] Bender-Lamb, "An Economic Analysis…," 1.

[193] Dutcher, "The Ostrich," 155.

[194] "Ostrich Autopsy," *Buffalo Courier,* June 16, 1901, 22.

[195] "Ostrich in Hospital," *Buffalo Courier Express,* June 11, 1901, 7.

[196] *Buffalo Courier,* "Ostrich Autopsy," June 16, 1901.

[197] *Buffalo Courier Express,* "Ostrich in Hospital," June 11, 1901.

[198] *Buffalo Courier Express,* June 11, 1901.

[199] *Buffalo Courier Express,* June 11, 1901.

[200] "Ostrich Returned," *Buffalo Review*, July 4, 1901, 6.

[201] Martin, *Home Life on an Ostrich Farm*, 153-154.

[202] Martin, 153-154.

[203] Dutcher, "The Ostrich," 155.

[204] Pickrell, "Ostriches," 400.

Chapter 13

[205] Sisley Barnes, "Preening Plumes," *Westways* 67, no. 5 (May 1975), 54.

[206] Al. D. Beasley, ed., *Phoenix, Arizona, Maricopa County: 20th Century Phoenix, Illustrated* (Phoenix: n.p., 1907), 106.

[207] Pickrell, "Ostriches," 403.

[208] Pickrell, 403.

[209] Pickrell, 403.

[210] Dutcher, "The Ostrich," 156.

[211] Murray, "Ostriches in Arizona," 27.

[212] Doughty, "Ostrich Farming American Style," 142.

[213] Duncan, "Ostrich Farming in America," 697.

[214] Colley, "Ostrich Ranching: Arizona's Strangest Venture," 45.

[215] Pickrell, "Ostriches," 403.

[216] "An Ostrich Item," *Arizona Republican*, December 30, 1910, 11.

[217] *Arizona Republican*, December 30, 1910.

[218] *Arizona Republican*, December 30, 1910.

[219] *Arizona Republican*, December 30, 1910.

[220] Holder, "An Ostrich Ranch," 154.

[221] Stein, *Plumes*, 13.

Chapter 14

[222] Bender-Lamb, "An Economic Analysis…," 1.

[223] *Millinery Trade Review*, "Trade Conditions," 44.

[224] *Millinery Trade Review*, 44.

[225] Murray, "Ostriches in Arizona," 27.

[226] *Arizona Republican*, February 27, 1905.

[227] Murray, "Ostriches in Arizona," 27.

[228] "Doings in Phoenix and the Salt River Valley," *Arizona Silver Belt*, November 3, 1904, 2.

[229] *Arizona Republican*, February 27, 1905.

[230] "Ostriches," *Arizona Republican,* April 1, 1908, 11.

[231] *Arizona Republican,* April 1, 1908, 13.

[232] "Ostrich Plucking," *Arizona Republican*, September 25, 1906, 4.

[233] Wilson, "Ostrich Farms…," 27.

[234] *Arizona Silver Belt*, "The Ostrich Center," March 29, 1900.

[235] *Arizona Republican*, February 27, 1905.

[236] Milo's last name was spelled McNeil until around 1920 when he started spelling it McNeal. He appears the only person in his family to have made that change.

[237] *Arizona Republican*, February 27, 1905.

[238] "The Ostrich in Arizona," *Arizona Republican*, May 31, 1905, 8.

Chapter 15

[239] "Ostriches In California," *Daily Morning Times,* December 16, 1882, 2.

[240] Examples: 1. Mark Boardman, "Facing Down a Lynch Mob," *True West* (blog), March 18, 2022, https://truewestmagazine.com/facing-down-a-lynch-mob/ ; 2. Gary L. Roberts, "Wyatt Earp: The Search for Order on the Last Frontier," in *A Wyatt Earp Anthology*

(Denton: Univ. of North Texas Press, 2019), 19; 3. Casey Tefertiller, *Wyatt Earp: The Life Behind the Legend* (New York: John Wiley & Sons, 1997), 149.

[241] Examples: 1. Chuck Hornung, citing The *Daily Nugget* of March 27, 1882 in *Wyatt Earp's Cow-boy Campaign,* (North Carolina: McFarland & Co., 2016), 128; 2. "Tombstone, Arizona: Archive of Earp Associate, E. B. Gage," *Heritage Auctions,* https://historical.ha.com/itm/miscellaneous/ephemera/tombstone-arizona-archive-of-earp-associate-e-b-gage/a/6035-47308.s; 3. Peter Brand as cited in James Gressinger's "Wyatt Earp's Vendetta Posse: Who Were These Guys?," *Southern Arizona Guide,* n.d., https://southernarizonaguide.com/wyatt-earps-vendetta-posse-who-were-these-guys/. 3. Casey Tefertiller, *Wyatt Earp: The Life Behind the Legend* (New York: John Wiley & Sons, 1997), 238; 4. John D. Rose, "Wyatt Earp's Tombstone Home Site Discovered," *Wyatt Earp Explorers,* 2018, https://www.wyattearpexplorers.com/wyatts-house.html.

[242] E.B. Gage's property in Tombstone was named the Loma de Plata and the property in Prescott became known as the Gage/Murphy Mansion.

[243] Beasley, *20th Century Phoenix, Illustrated,* 106. Note: This amount is over $20.5 million in 2025.

[244] Murray, "Ostriches in Arizona," 27.

[245] *Arizona Republican,* April 1, 1908, 11.

[246] Advertisement, *Arizona Republic,* October 25, 1907, 2.

[247] Murray, "Ostriches in Arizona," 27.

[248] Murray, 27.

[249] "Have Big Plans for Bird Farm," *Imperial Valley Press,* April 22, 1915, 5.

[250] Liza Daly, "The Ostrich for the Defence (1912)," *Liza Daly* (blog), March 4, 2022, https://lizadaly.com/pages/utopian-novels/ostrich-for-the-defence.html.

[251] Miles, "Strange Farms…," 235.

[252] "Articles of Incorporation of International Ostrich Farm and Feather Company," *Border Vidette,* October 30, 1909, 2.

[253] Daly, "The Ostrich for the Defence (1912)."

[254] Daly, "The Ostrich."

[255] "Belgian Capital: Locally Invested," *Arizona Republican,* April 19, 1910, 8.

[256] "Ostriches Are Not Valuable," *Arizona Republican,* December 6, 1917, 10.

[257] *Arizona Republican,* December 23, 1914.

[258] *Arizona Republican,* April 10, 1910.

[259] Heard Farm, "Our History - The Story of the Heard Farm," *HeardFarm.com* (website), December 2, 2021, https://heardfarm.com/blog/our-history-the-story-of-heard-farm/. Note: The Bartlett-Heard Land and Cattle Company featured cattle, citrus and cotton.

[260] J. H. McClintock (Col), "An American Community of the Salt River Valley in the Making," *Arizona Republican,* November 6, 1911, 56.

[261] "Important is Ostrich Sale," *Arizona Republican,* November 11, 1910, 1.

[262] "Mesa Goes Deeper into Ostrich Business," *Arizona Daily Star,* April 7, 1911, 4.

[263] *Arizona Daily Star,* April 7, 1911.

[264] *Arizona Daily Star,* April 7, 1911.

[265] *Arizona Daily Star,* April 7, 1911.

[266] "Another Ostrich Farm," *Arizona Republican,* November 4, 1911, 10.

[267] 1. "New Ostrich Farm," *Los Angeles Times,* April 19, 1907, 14; 2. Paul R. Spitzzeri, "Feathering the Nest: A Quartet of Photos of the Los Angeles Ostrich Farm, Lincoln Heights, August 1924," *Homestead Museum,* August 11, 2003, https://homesteadmuseum.blog/2023/08/11/feathering-the-nest-a-quartet-of-photos-of-the-los-angeles-ostrich-farm-lincoln-heights-august-1924/. Note: The other men were L.H. Hughes, J.E. Sturges.

[268] "Ostrich Feather Manufacturing Co.," *Arizona Republican,* May 10, 1909, 7.

[269] "Rural Route 2," *Arizona Republican,* July 3, 1909, 9.

Chapter 16

270 Michael Lehman in "Zagat Documentary: Interview with Michael Lehman," *Central Oregon Ostrich*, n.d., https://centraloregonostrich.com/.

271 Pickrell, "Ostriches," 399.

272 "An Organization of Ostrich Breeders," *Arizona Republican*, April 26, 1908, 8.

273 Murray, "Ostriches in Arizona," 23.

274 Lester Ward "Budge" Ruffner, *All Hell Needs is Water* (Tucson: Univ. of Arizona Press, 1972), 67.

275 Colley, "Ostrich Ranching: Arizona's Strangest Venture," 42.

276 Ruffner, *All Hell Needs*, 67.

277 Bender-Lamb, "An Economic Analysis…,"1.

278 Pickrell, "Ostriches," 399.

279 Chalmers, "The Ostrich in the Salt River Valley," 21.

280 Martin, *Home Life on an Ostrich Farm*, 134.

281 *Arizona Republican,* April 1, 1908, 11.

282 Pickrell, "Ostriches," 399.

283 Doughty, "Ostrich Farming American Style," 140.

284 Murray, "Ostriches in Arizona," 27.

285 Susan Franck, "History of Ostrich Ranching in Arizona," in Oliver's *Ostrich Ranching in America*, 9.

286 Murray, "Ostriches in Arizona," 27.

287 Paige McNickle, as quoted in Jerod MacDonald-Evoy's "A brief history of the Chandler Ostrich Festival," *Arizona Republic*, March 10, 2017, https://www.azcentral.com/story/news/local/chandler/2017/03/10/history-and-protests-over-chandler-ostrich-festival/98502344/.

288 1. 4 birds per 1 acre: Kraklio, "Feathers in Our Cap," 8; 2. 100 or more birds per 1.25 acres: Tony Jones, "Birds of a different feather could bring lucrative new industry to Arizona," *The Arrow*, October 9, 1992, 20.

289 Leon Vandiver, "Exotic Livestock: A Small-Scale Agriculture Alternative," *University of California Sustainable Agriculture Research and Education Program* (brochure), (January 1989), https://ucanr.edu/node/130928/printable/print.

290 Vincent Gabrielle, "The Strange Tale of the Great 1911 Trans-Saharan Ostrich Heist," *Atlas Obscura*, April 22, 2019, https://www.atlasobscura.com/articles/great-ostrich-heist.

291 "Those Who Would Know of Ostrich," *Arizona Republican*, November 4, 1910, 9.

292 Wright, "Alfalfa and Millinery," 1.

293 Pickrell, "Ostriches," 399-406.

294 Ibid Pickrell, 403.

295 Watson Pickrell, "Ostrich Farming by Watson Pickrell," *Arizona Republican*, October 13, 1906, 5.

296 "Watson Pickrell Died in Omaha, Neb.," *Arizona Republican*, September 7, 1907, 5.

297 "Arizona Leads World in Ostrich Culture," *Daily Arizona Silver Belt*, April 3, 1908, 6.

298 *Daily Arizona Silver Belt*, April 3, 1908.

299 *Arizona Republican*, November 4, 1910.

300 "Ostrich Investigator from South Africa," *Arizona Republican*, March 8, 1910, 3.

301 *Arizona Republican*, March 8, 1910.

302 *Arizona Republican*, March 8, 1910.

303 Kemp, "Opinion of an Expert," *Arizona Republican*, October 30, 1910.

304 Kemp, October 30, 1910.

305 Kemp, October 30, 1910.

306 Kemp, October 30, 1910.

Chapter 17

307 Colley, "Ostrich Ranching: Arizona's Strangest Venture," 42.

308 Patrick Pester, "The World's Fastest Animals," *LiveScience.com*, September 10, 2021, https://www.livescience.com/59822-fastest-animals.html.

309 Murray, "Ostriches in Arizona," 28.

310 Nina U. Schaller, Bernd Herkner, Rikk Villa, and Peter Aerts, "The intertarsal joint of the ostrich (Struthio camelus): Anatomical examination and function of passive structures in locomotion," *Journal of Anatomy* 214, no. 6 (May 22, 2009), 830, https://onlinelibrary.wiley.com/doi/10.1111/j.1469-7580.2009.01083.x.

311 Nina Schaller, "Birds on the run: what makes ostriches so fast?" *Science In School* 6, no. 21 (November 22, 2011), https://www.scienceinschool.org/article/2011/ostrich/.

312 Geissinger, "On an Arizona Ostrich Farm," 9.

313 Fay E. Clark, Jasmine Burdass, Annalise Kavanagh, and Annabel King, "Palaeognath birds innovate to solve a novel foraging problem," *Scientific Reports* 15, 4512 (2025), https://doi.org/10.1038/s41598-025-88217-8.

314 Clark, et al., 2025.

315 Clark, et al., 2025.

316 Kaya Burgess, "Emus climb the intelligence pecking order but ostriches are birdbrains," *The Times,* February 20, 2025, https://www.thetimes.com/uk/science/article/emus-climb-the-intelligence-pecking-order-but-ostriches-are-birdbrains-xbxxgxzhb

317 "Animal Justice Urges CFIA to Rethink Ostrich Cull, Allow Independent Testing," Animal Justice League, September 23, 2025, https://animaljustice.ca/media-releases/animal-justice-urges-cfia-to-rethink-ostrich-cull-allow-independent-testing.

318 "Ostrich Farm at the Fair: Sixty Birds from California Show Off their Fine Plumes," *Our Horticultural Visitor* 10, no. 7 (July 1904), 3.

319 *Our Horticultural Visitor*, 3.

320 1. Riley Black, "Walnut: the True Measure of a Dinosaur's Brain," *National Geographic,* January 28, 2013, https://www.nationalgeographic.com/science/article/walnut-the-true-measure-of-a-dinosaurs-brain; 2. Charles Q. Choi, "Biggest Dinosaurs Had Brains the Size of Tennis Balls," *Live Science*, January 23, 2013, https://www.livescience.com/26539-giant-sauropods-small-brains.html.

321 Andrew Coletti, "Ancient Eaters: Elagabalus, the Roman Doctor Frank-N-Furter (203-222 CE)," *PassTheFlamingo* (blog), April 26, 2017, https://passtheflamingo.com/2017/04/26/ancient-eaters-elagabalus-the-roman-doctor-frank-n-furter-203-222-ce/.

322 Coletti, April 26, 2017.

323 Job 39: 13-18 (The Message).

324 Martin, *Home Life on an Ostrich Farm*, 106.

325 Wright, "Alfalfa and Millinery," 4.

326 McNickle, as quoted in *Arizona Republic*, March 10, 2017.

327 Cogburn, to author, April 29, 2025.

328 Amanda NLN, as quoted in Peter Hendra's "Farm north of Kingston a social media sensation," *The Whig Standard*, April 28, 2022, https://www.thewhig.com /news/local-news/farm-north-of-kingston-a-social-media-sensation#:~:text= Amanda%20said%20she%20enjoys%20the,really%20been%20such%20a% 20delight.%E2%80%9D

329 *Useless Farm*, "Meet Useless Farm: Karen the Emu," Accessed October 10, 2025, https://uselessfarm.com/pages/meet-the-farm

330 Hendra, *The Whig Standard*, April 28, 2022.

331 Karen Weston Gonzales in Sam Negri's "No Dummies These Big Ostriches," *Arizona Highways* 81, no. 1 (January 2005), 31.

332 Joe Hendrick in Sheri Johnson's "Chandler Ostrich Fest Pits 9 Eager Birds in Variety of Events," *Arizona Republic*, March 12, 1989, 22.

333 Negri, "No Dummies…," 31.

334 Walt Mason, "Rippling Rhymes: The Ostrich," *Arizona Republican*, September 8, 1915, 4.

335 Mary Graham Bonner, "Daddy's Evening Fairy Tale: Poor Mrs. Ostrich," *Arizona State Miner*, July 17, 1926.

336 *Poultry Monthly*, "An Ostrich Ranch in Arizona," 156.

337 *Poultry Monthly*, 156.

338 Editorial, *Arizona Daily Star*, February 7, 1883, 2.

339 *The Oasis*, "Arizona Ostriches," 1.

Chapter 18

340 *Arizona Daily Star*, April 7, 1911.

341 MacDonald-Evoy, *Arizona Republic*, March 10, 2017.

342 Blanche K. Murray, "Dr. A.J. Chandler, Empire Builder," *Arizona Highways*, 15, no. 4 (1939), 8.

343 Murray, 9.

344 Editorial, *Arizona Weekly Enterprise*, August 4, 1888.

345 "The Quarantine," *Tombstone Epitaph*, December 29, 1888, 1.

346 "Ostrich Trust Secures More Valuable Birds in Arizona," *Copper Era and Morenci Leader*, August 2, 1906, 1.

347 *Morenci Leader*, August 2, 1906.

348 "Ostrich Shipment," *Arizona Republican*, December 11, 1906, 8.

349 *Arizona Republican*, December 11, 1906.

350 *Arizona Republican*, December 11, 1906.

351 "Luncheon of Ostrich Eggs," *Arizona Republican*, December 25, 1911, 2.

352 *Los Angeles Times*, April 19, 1907.

353 Editorial, *Arizona Republican*, March 15, 1911, 15.

354 "Grand Opening Today," (Ad.), *Los Angeles Times*, April 21, 1907, 20.

355 *Los Angeles Times*, April 19, 1907.

356 "Shipment of Feathers," *Arizona Republican*, May 28, 1910, 10.

357 *The Oasis*, June 4, 1910, 5. (Editorial reprint from the *Phoenix Gazette*.)

358 "Improved Lands," (Mesa Improvement Co. Ad.) in *Arizona Republican*, November 5, 1911, 11.

359 *Arizona Republican*, March 15, 1911.

360 *Arizona Republican*, March 15, 1911.

361 "Ostriches in El Paso," *El Paso Times*, June 24, 1965, 12.

362 "El Paso's Very Latest Industry: Ostrich Farm," *El Paso Times*, September 30, 1911, 2.

363 "Ostrich Farm for Valley is Assured," *El Paso Herald*, September 11, 1911, 4.

364 Peter W. Eveler, "The Southwest Ostrich Farm of Old El Paso," *Password* 12, no. 3 (Fall, 1967), 90-91.

365 "Ship Ostriches from Arizona to Chicago," *Tucson Citizen*, November 17, 1911, 2.

366 "Mesa: Will Instruct People of the East," *Arizona Republican*, November 14, 1911, 12.

Chapter 19

367 "Yuma is Best Field in the World for Ostrich Industry," *Arizona Sentinel*, Oct 30, 1913, 1.

368 *Arizona Sentinel*, October 30, 1913.

369 "Two Ostrich Farms in the Yuma Valley," *Arizona Daily Star*, August 22, 1912, 2.

370 *Arizona Daily Star*, August 22, 1912

371 "Awful Experience with Gila Monster," *Arizona Republican*, October 21, 1909, 2.

372 Jean Beach King, *Arizona Charlie: A Legendary Cowboy, Klondike Stampeder and Wild West Showman* (Phoenix: Heritage Publishers, 1989), 21.

373 Tom Horn, *Life of Tom Horn, Government Scout and Interpreter* (Denver: Louthan Book Company, 1904), 106-107.

374 Horn, 106-107.

375 Horn, 106-107.

376 "The San Carlos Indians Attack the Meadows Family," *Tulare County Times*, July 28, 1882, 3. Note: This contains the transcribed letter from Charlie Meadows to Rhoda Kansas McGinnis in California.

377 King, *Arizona Charlie*, 22. Note: Maggie Meadows's recollection of the event was preserved in a letter to Charlie about it dated January 23, 1932. This letter is found in the Century House Museum in Yuma, Arizona.

378 Horn, *Life of Tom Horn*, 109.

379 "The Wild West Show," *Armidale Express and New England General Advertiser*, January 30, 1891, 3.

380 King, *Arizona Charlie*, 70.

381 Editorial, *The Oasis*, December 4, 1909, 10. (Reprint from *Yuma Enterprise.*)

382 Editorial, *Border Vidette*, March 12, 1910, 1. (Reprint from *Yuma Enterprise.*)

383 Editorial, *Yuma Examiner*, May 26, 1910, 1.

384 "Yuma's First Ostrich," *Yuma Examiner*, April 8, 1910, 4.

385 Editorial, *The Oasis*, January 21, 1911, 2. (Reprint from *Yuma Sun.*)

386 "Fine Ostrich Plumes," *Arizona Sentinel and Yuma Wekly Examiner*, December 21, 1911, 8.

387 King, *Arizona Charlie*, 240.

388 "Young Ostriches Burn," *Arizona Sentinel and Yuma Weekly Examiner*, January 30, 1913, 4.

389 Editorial, *Winslow Daily Mail*, July 12, 1913, 1.

390 Editorial, *Tombstone Epitaph*, October 12, 1913, 2.

391 *Tombstone Epitaph*, October 12, 1913.

392 "Dr. Williams of the State University, Visits Yuma…", *Arizona Sentinel and Yuma Weekly Examiner*, November 19, 1914, 1.

393 "Ostrich Raising in Yuma County," *Tombstone Epitaph*, March 15, 1914, 2.

394 Edwin L. Hansberger Sr., Delia Fuquay Hansberger, and James LeRoy Hansberger, *Dates, Pecans & Ostriches: Some Memories of Life in the Yuma Valley* (Yuma: Yuma County Historical Society, 1970), 41.

395 Hansberger Sr., Hansberger & Hansberger, *Dates, Pecans & Ostriches*, 41.

396 *Epitaph*, March 15, 1914.

397 Hansberger Sr., Hansberger & Hansberger, *Dates, Pecans & Ostriches*, 41.

Chapter 20

398 Geissinger, "On an Arizona Ostrich Farm," 9.

399 Wilson, "Ostrich Farms…," 27.

400 Geissinger, "On an Arizona Ostrich Farm," 8.

401 Wilson, "Ostrich Farms…," 27.

402 Chalmers, "The Ostrich in the Salt River Valley," 21.

403 Wilson, "Ostrich Farms…," 27.

404 Murray, "Ostriches in Arizona," 27.

405 Colley, "Ostrich Ranching: Arizona's Strangest Venture," 42.

406 Kemp, "Opinion of an Expert," *Arizona Republican*, October 30, 1910.

407 1. Lisa Hegarty, "Pan-American Ostrich Company," *Litchfield Heritage Center Newsletter* (Spring, 2024), 3; 2. *Journal of the Royal Society of Arts*, "Ostrich Farming in the United States," 191.

408 Kemp, "Opinion of an Expert," *Arizona Republican*, October 30, 1910.

409 Wilson, "Ostrich Farms…," 27.

410 Murray, "Ostriches in Arizona," 23.

411 Pickrell, "Ostriches," 403.

412 "$150 Ostriches Sell for $5 Now," *Quad-City Times*, February 24, 1915, 11.

413 Felix J. Koch, "The Ostrich Feather Industry in the West Vs. Africa," *Overland Monthly* 58, no. 6 (December 1911), 470.

[414] Koch, 470.

[415] Kemp, "Opinion of an Expert," *Arizona Republican*, October 30, 1910.

[416] Chandler Museum, "George T. Peabody, Chandler Chamber of Commerce Founder," *Chandlerpedia*, June 14, 2022, https://chandlerpedia.atlassian.net/wiki /spaces/CHANDLERPE/pages/1304789050/Week+18+George+T.+Peabody+Chandler+C hamber+of+Commerce+Founder.

[417] "Chandler Visitor," *Arizona Republican*, September 22, 1912, 18.

[418] "Chandler Company Elects New Officers," *Arizona Republican*, December 12, 1914, 6.

[419] "New Kind of Chamber," *Arizona Republican*, March 5, 1915, 7.

[420] Chandler Museum, "George T. Peabody."

[421] "Mesa – 18 Miles from Phoenix - The Chandler Ranch," *Arizona Republican*, November 11, 1906, 31.

[422] "Fertile Chandler Ranch…," (Ad.), *Arizona Republican* July 2, 1911, 12.

[423] "'Come and See for Yourselves,' says Wizard of Chandler Town," *Arizona Republican*, November 17, 1912, 21.

[424] "San Marcos Hotel at Chandler Opened," *Arizona Republican*, November 5, 1913, 3.

[425] *Arizona Republican*, November 11, 1906.

[426] *Arizona Republican*, November 5, 1913, 3. Note: The doors opened on November 3, 1913.

[427] Chandler Museum, "George T. Peabody."

[428] "Intensive Farming," *Arizona Republican*, March 28, 1914, 10.

Chapter 21

[429] Editorial, *Arizona Republican*, May 19, 1914, 5.

[430] "Fine Moving Picture of Scenes in the Valley," *Arizona Republic*, October 8, 1910, 7.

[431] *Arizona Republic*, October 8, 1910.

[432] Flora A. Bell, "From Arizona," *Slater News-Rustler*, April 4, 1913, 2.

[433] "Seeking for Information," *Arizona Republican*, September 8, 1913, 12.

[434] *Arizona Republican,* September 8, 1913.

[435] Commonwealth of Australia, "Ostrich Farming," *Parliamentary Debates, Session 1913, vol. LXXI* (1914), case 5.7, 2146.

[436] Commonwealth, 2147.

[437] Commonwealth, 2147.

[438] Commonwealth, 2148.

[439] 1914 Phoenix and Maricopa County Directory.

[440] "Sixty Ostriches to Feed Guests of Fred Harvey Houses," *Arizona Republican*, November 27, 1914, 2.

[441] "For Sale – Live Stock," *Arizona Republic*, December 1, 1914, 8.

[442] "Local Men Buy 150 Ostriches," *Chandler Arizonan*, November 27, 1914, 1.

[443] In December 1911, both Margaret Ann "Maggie" Toston and Thomas Toston entered land contracts with Dr. A.J. Chandler via Mesa Improvement Company. They obtained a mortgage for 160 acres in January of 1912. In 1913, they received the deeds to the land, about one mile north of Chandler townsite. In July 1914, their mortgages were satisfied. By October 1914, all of Thomas' prior holdings were sold and the only property in the family was the NE ¼ of the NE ¼ of Section 28 (T1S R5E). In addition to these original properties, in 1912 Maggie purchased 40 acres on the N ½ of the NE ¼ of the SW ¼ of Section 28. She sold that portion to Dwight L. Lecky in March 1913.

[444] Dorothy Combs, "Margaret Ann 'Maggie' Todd Toston" [Memorial ID 110859207, *FindAGrave*. Accessed July 21, 2025, https://www.findagrave.com/memorial/110859207/margaret_ann-toston.

[445] Combs, "Margaret Ann 'Maggie' Todd Toston."

[446] "Went to Her Western Lover," St. *Louis Globe-Democrat*, January 25, 1895, 3.

[447] "Local Layout," *Livingston Enterprise*, March 3, 1900, 5.

[448] "Three Are Hurt in Chandler in One Day," *Tucson Citizen*, June 14, 1913, 5.

Chapter 22

449 Hayden, "The Ostrich Industry" (Speech), 58.

450 United States Senate, "Carl Hayden Retires, January 3, 1969," *Senate.gov*, Accessed October 29, 2025. https://www.senate.gov/artandhistory/history/minute/Carl_Hayden_retires.htm.

451 United States Senate, "Carl Hayden Retires."

452 Hayden, "The Ostrich Industry" (Speech), 58.

453 Hayden, 60.

454 In 1911 and 1912, the Union of South Africa's Department of Agriculture published "Experiments with Ostriches," the results of tests as observed by Prof. J. E. Duerden of Rhodes University College, Gramstown.

455 Hayden, "The Ostrich Industry" (Speech), 58.

456 Hayden, 58-59.

457 Hayden, 59.

458 Hayden, 58-59.

459 Hayden, 60.

460 Hayden, 60.

461 Bell, *Slater News-Rustler*, April 4, 1913.

462 Hayden, "The Ostrich Industry" (Speech), 60.

463 Murray, "Ostriches in Arizona," 28.

464 "Industry is in its Infancy," *Arizona Republican*, Dec 22, 1913, 11.

465 Hayden, "The Ostrich Industry" (Speech), 59.

466 Hayden, 59.

467 "Appropriations for the Department of Agriculture for the fiscal year ending June 30, 1915," Public-No. 122-63rd Congress (H.R. 13679), 6.

468 1. "Hunting Site for Experimental Farm," *Arizona Republican*, August 6, 1913, 3; 2. United States Department of the Interior, National Register of Historic Places, *Registration Form for University of Arizona Campus Agricultural Center at 4101 N. Cambell Ave.*, November 20, 2023, sec. 8, 5.

469 U.S. Department of Agriculture, "Agricultural Experiment Stations of the United States, Their Locations and Directors," in *Yearbook of the United States Department of Agriculture, 1914* (Washington: Government Printing Office, 1915), 507.

470 "Tucson to Have Experimental Ostrich Farm," *Tucson Citizen*, September 12, 1914, 6.

471 "Ostriches Shared Range," *Arizona Land & People* 36, no. 1 (Tucson: University of Arizona, March 1985): 16.

472 Editorial, *Snowflake Herald*, September 19, 1914, 2.

473 1. Statistic from *Arizona Republic*, December 1, 1914; 2. Donation from *Tucson Citizen*, September 12, 1914.

474 *Arizona Republican*, November 27, 1914.

475 Doughty, "Ostrich Farming American Style," 142.

476 H. C. Cross, "Miscellaneous Information on the Ostrich Industry," in *United States Department of Agriculture, Bureau of Animal Husbandry, Animal Husbandry Division*, December 15, 1915.

477 H. C. Cross, "Miscellaneous Information," December 1916.

478 "Nat Luce Goes Back into Government Work," *California Poultry Journal* V, no. 10 (August 1920): 287.

479 "Government Poultry Work," *California Poultry Journal* V, no. 9 (July 1920): 267.

480 Doughty, "Ostrich Farming American Style," 142.

481 Doughty, 142.

482 "Ostriches Shared Range," 16.

483 "Pima Values Enhance by Ajo Smelter," *Arizona Daily Star*, July 15, 1917, 8.

484 Editorial, *Copper Era and Morenci Leader*, February 9, 1917, 7.

485 "Ostrich is Piece de Resistance at Banquet," *Tucson Citizen*, January 20, 1918, 14.

486 H. C. Cross, "Miscellaneous Information," November 15, 1916.

487 H. C. Cross, "Miscellaneous Information," March 11, 1918.

488 "Appropriations for the Department of Agriculture," 6.

489 H. C. Cross, "Miscellaneous Information," February 15, 1918.

490 H. C. Cross, "Chronological Record of the Ostrich Breeding Work from November 7, 1917," *United States Department of Agriculture, Bureau of Animal Husbandry, Animal Husbandry Division* [National Archives Record #1549640, November 17, 1917 – July 19, 1919], February 7, 1919. Note: Cross was the Senior Poultryman until July 21, 1920.

491 H. C. Cross, "Miscellaneous Information," December 19, 1915.

492 Arthur Douglass, *Ostrich Farming in South Africa* (London: Cassell, Petter, Galpin & Co., 1881), 141.

493 Nat E. Luce, "Record of the Work Being Conducted at the U.S. Poultry Experiment Station," *United States Department of Agriculture, Bureau of Animal Husbandry, Animal Husbandry Division,* [National Archives Record #1549640, July 21,1920 – December 30, 1921], April 20, 1920.

494 Letter From H. C. Cross to Harry M. Lamon August 10, 1918, in H. C. Cross, "Miscellaneous Information."

495 Letter dated December 19, 1919 was sent to Francisco Martines and Martha Gerald in Tollison.

496 H. C. Cross, "Chronological Record," May 8, 1919. Note: This was from the day of the auction.

497 Cross, May 8, 1919.

498 H. C. Cross, "Chronological Record," May 15-16, 1919.

499 "Poultry Work in the Southwest," *California Poultry Journal* VI, no. 7 (May 1921), 190.

500 H. C. Cross, "Record of the Ostrich Breeding Work at the U.S. Poultry Experiment Station, Season 1919-1920," *United States Department of Agriculture, Bureau of Animal Husbandry, Animal Husbandry Division* [National Archives Record #1549640, July 20, 1919 - July 20, 1920], July 21, 1920.

501 Nat E. Luce, "History of the U.S. Poultry Experiment Station," (Manuscript), February 8, 1921, in *United States Department of Agriculture, Bureau of Animal Husbandry, Animal Husbandry Division,* [National Archives Record #1549640, December 15, 1915-October 4, 1917], 1.

502 Gardner Griffith, "Chicken Day at Glendale, Arizona May 20, 1921," *California Poultry Journal* VI, no. 8 (June 1921): 2-3.

503 Luce, "History of the U.S. Poultry Experiment Station," 1.

504 "Nat E. Luce is Dead," *San Bernardino County Sun*, July 13, 1924, 18.

505 Nat E. Luce, "Record of the Work," April 20, 1920.

506 H. C. Cross, "Field Day at the U.S. Poultry Experiment Station," (Meeting notes), Nov. 18, 1920, in Luce, "Record of the Work," July 21,1920 – December 30, 1921.

507 Glendale District Chamber of Commerce, "Petition to the United States Department of Agriculture, December 30, 1920," *United States Department of Agriculture, Bureau of Animal Husbandry, Animal Husbandry Division* [National Archives Record #154961642]. (Emphasis added.)

508 Luce, "Record of the Work," Nov. 22, 1920.

509 H. C. Cross, "Miscellaneous Information," December 30, 1920.

510 Glendale District Chamber of Commerce, "Petition."

511 "Legislative Briefs," *Tucson Citizen*, February 10, 1921, 1.

512 Editorial, *Bisbee Daily Review*, March 23, 1921, 4.

513 Gardner Griffith, "Chicken Day at Glendale, Arizona May 20, 1921," *California Poultry Journal* VI, no. 8 (June 1921): 1.

514 Nat E. Luce, "Record of the Work Being Conducted at the U.S. Poultry Experiment Station," *United States Department of Agriculture, Bureau of Animal Husbandry, Animal*

Husbandry Division, [National Archives Record #1549641, January 1, 1922 – November 16, 1924.], January 16, 1922.

[515] Nat E. Luce, "Record of the Work Being Conducted at the U.S. Poultry Experiment Station," *United States Department of Agriculture, Bureau of Animal Husbandry, Animal Husbandry Division*, [National Archives Record #1549640, July 21, 1920 – December 30, 1921], May 18, 1921.

[516] "Glendale is Center of Poultry Raising Industry in Valley," *Arizona Republican*, November 11, 1921, 19.

[517] *Arizona Republican*, November 11, 1921.

[518] Luce, "History of the U.S. Poultry Experiment Station," 9.

[519] M. E. Bemis, "Poultry Notes from Arizona," *California Poultry Journal* V, no. 11 (September 1920), 303.

[520] Luce, "History of the U.S. Poultry Experiment Station," 9.

[521] "Arizona Chicken Day is the Great Event," *Arizona Republican*, May 20, 1921, 9.

[522] Luce, "Record of the Work," October 10, 1921.

[523] Luce, August 3, 1921.

[524] Luce, "Record of the Work," May 27, 1922.

[525] "Out Again," *Arizona Republican*, Feb. 10, 1924, 7.

[526] Griffith, "Chicken Day," 1.

Chapter 23

[527] Geissinger, "On an Arizona Ostrich Farm," 8.

[528] Ruffner, *All Hell Needs*, 67.

[529] *Poultry Monthly*, "An Ostrich Ranch in Arizona," 156.

[530] *Arizona Graphic,* "The Arizona Ostrich," 4.

[531] *Poultry Monthly*, "An Ostrich Ranch in Arizona," 156.

[532] *Poultry Monthly*, 156.

[533] *Arizona Graphic,* "The Arizona Ostrich," 4.

[534] "Ostrich-Hunting," *Pinal Drill*, October 7, 1882, 2.

[535] *Pinal Drill*, October 7, 1882.

[536] *Pinal Drill*, October 7, 1882.

[537] *Pinal Drill*, October 7, 1882.

[538] Chalmers, "The Ostrich in the Salt River Valley," 22.

[539] *Pinal Drill*, October 7, 1882.

[540] *Pinal Drill*, October 7, 1882.

[541] *Pinal Drill*, October 7, 1882.

[542] Murray, "Ostriches in Arizona," 23.

[543] Murray, 23.

[544] *The Arizona Republican*, December 11, 1906.

[545] Pickrell, "Ostriches," 405.

[546] *Poultry Monthly,* "An Ostrich Ranch in Arizona," 156.

[547] *El Paso Times*, September 30, 1911.

[548] *Marion Commonwealth*, December 14, 1882, 1.

[549] "Mesa Rancher is Killed," *Mesa Tribune*, July 30, 1935, 1.

[550] "Edmund Ellsworth Company (1856)," *The Church of Jesus Christ of Latter-Day Saints* (Church History Biographies, 2025), https://history.churchofjesuschrist.org/chd/organization/pioneer-company/edmund-ellsworth-company.

[551] Pete Ellsworth, interview by Joyce McBride, *Show Low Historical Society Museum*, January 13, 2008, https://azmemory.azlibrary.gov/nodes/view/164800.

[552] "Birthday Party," *Arizona Republican*, June 25, 1907, 8.

[553] "Hunting for Trouble," *Arizona Republican*, January 5, 1912, 8.

[554] "Reception to Local Players," *Arizona Republican*, June 24, 1907, 8.

[555] *Arizona Republican*, June 24, 1907.

[556] *Arizona Republican*, January 5, 1912.

[557] *Arizona Republican*, January 5, 1912.

[558] *Arizona Republican*, January 5, 1912.

[559] Hegarty, "Pan-American," 3.

[560] Pickrell, "Ostriches," 405.

[561] Duncan, "Ostrich Farming in America," 700.

[562] Karen Weston Gonzales, "Rise and Fall of the Ostrich Industry," *Tucson Weekly*, May 9, 2002, https://www.tucsonweekly.com/tucson/rise-and-fall-of-the-ostrich-industry/Content?oid=1070205.

[563] "A Freak Ostrich," *Arizona Republican*, June 30, 1909, 13.

Chapter 24

[564] "Herding 200 Ostriches On Road A Task," *Chandler Arizonan*, November 13, 1914, 1.

[565] "Girls Get Big Coin," *Daily Arizona Silver Belt*, May 26, 1910, 5.

[566] *Daily Arizona Silver Belt*, May 26, 1910.

[567] *Daily Arizona Silver Belt*, May 26, 1910.

[568] "E. B. Gage Passes Away at 'Frisco," *Tombstone Epitaph*, March 16, 1913, 4.

[569] "A Chance to Get in on the Ground Floor," *Arizona Republican*, November 145, 1914, 7.

[570] Murray, "Ostriches in Arizona," 28.

[571] "OSTRICHES," *Arizona Republican*, November 22, 1914, 22.

[572] "Chandler to have Big Ostrich Farm," *Chandler Arizonan*, November 12, 1.

[573] *Chandler Arizonan*, November 12.

[574] "Chandler Luncheon," *Arizona Republican*, December 11, 1914, 3.

[575] "On Ostrich Farm," *Arizona Daily Star*, September 10, 1911, 9.

[576] Alan Thurber, "Tragic Ostrich Stampede Recalled," *Arizona Republic*, June 17, 1984, B1.

[577] Helen H. Sergeant, *House by the Buckeye Road* (San Antonio: Naylor Co., 1960), 75-76.

[578] *Chandler Arizonan*, November 13, 1914.

[579] "Special: Ostriches in a Stampede; Woman Meets her Death," *Waukegan News-Sun*, November 13, 1914, 1.

[580] *Chandler Arizonan*, November 13, 1914.

[581] "The Week at the San Marcos," *Arizona Republican*, November 22, 1914, 24.

[582] Martin, *Home Life on an Ostrich Farm*, 142.

[583] Martin, 142.

[584] Martin, 142.

[585] Martin, 24.

[586] Hegarty, "Pan-American," 3.

[587] *Chandler Arizonan*, November 13, 1914.

[588] *Chandler Arizonan*, November 13, 1914.

[589] Sergeant, *House by the Buckeye Road*, 75.

[590] "Ostrich Industry in Arizona Hurt by Dame Fashion," *Bisbee Daily Review*, November 22, 1914, 7.

Chapter 25

[591] Mary E. Wilkins Freeman, "The Ostrich," *Harper's New Monthly* CXI, no. 663 (August 1905).

[592] Lovell T. Rousseau Obit, *Arizona Republic*, September 14, 2000, 26.

[593] Thurber, "Tragic Ostrich Stampede."

[594] Martin, *Home Life on an Ostrich Farm*, 106-107.

[595] *Arizona Republican*, November 20, 1914.

[596] Thurber, "Tragic Ostrich Stampede."

[597] "Ostriches Stampede," *Kentucky Advocate*, November 18, 1914, 4.

[598] Sergeant, *House by the Buckeye Road*, 75-76.

[599] "Ostrich Round Up in Salt River Bottom," *Arizona Republican*, November 20, 1914, 9.

[600] Hegarty, "Pan-American," 3.

[601] Murray, "Ostriches in Arizona," 28.

[602] Chandler Museum, "The 1914 Ostrich Drive and Rough Neck," *Chandlerpedia*, June 14, 2022, https://chandlerpedia.atlassian.net/wiki/spaces/CHANDLERPE /pages/1305673775/Week+39+The+1914+Ostrich+Drive+and+Rough+Neck.

[603] "Stampede of 300 Ostriches Causes Death," *Arizona Republican*, November 13, 1914, 4.

[604] Thurber, "Tragic Ostrich Stampede."

[605] Thurber, "Tragic Ostrich Stampede."

[606] "Ostriches Stampede; Kill Woman and Horse, In Arizona," *Stockton Evening and Sunday Record*, November 13, 1914, 1.

[607] "Ostriches Scare, Woman is Killed," *Billings Daily Tribune*, November 14, 1914, 8.

[608] *Waukegan News-Sun*, November 13, 1914.

[609] "From Around the Planet," *Semi-Weekly Leader*, November 21, 1914, 2.

[610] *Arizona Republican*, November 13, 1914.

[611] *Stockton Evening and Sunday Record*, November 13, 1914.

[612] "In Memoriam of Mrs. L. D. Rousseau," *Kentucky Interior Journal*, December 8, 1914, 2.

Chapter 26

[613] "Ostrich Hunting: An Arizona Sport," *Arizona Republican*, Nov. 15, 1914, 9.

[614] *Stockton Evening and Sunday Record*, November 13, 1914.

[615] *Stockton Evening and Sunday Record*, November 13, 1914.

[616] *Arizona Republican*, November 20, 1914.

[617] *Stockton Evening and Sunday Record*, November 13, 1914.

[618] *Arizona Republican*, November 20, 1914.

[619] "Roosevelt Dam is Making New Record," *Bisbee Daily Review*, November 19, 1914, 8.

[620] Murray, "Ostriches in Arizona," 28.

[621] *Chandler Arizonan*, November 13, 1914.

[622] *Chandler Arizonan*, November 13, 1914.

[623] American Rivers, "Gila River: The Origin of Wilderness," *AmericanRivers.org*. Accessed July 15, 2025, https://www.americanrivers.org/river/gila-river/#:~: text=The%20Backstory,due%20to%20large%20irrigation%20diversions.

[624] "More Ostriches for Chandler," *Arizona Republican*, November 27, 1914, 7.

[625] Roscoe G. Willson, "Arizona Days with Roscoe G. Willson," Arizona Republic, August 22, 1954, 80.

[626] Willson, "Arizona Days," 80.

[627] Willson, "Arizona Days," 80.

[628] Colley, "Ostrich Ranching: Arizona's Strangest Venture," 40.

[629] *Arizona Republican*, November 20, 1914.

[630] Sergeant, *House by the Buckeye Road*, 76.

Chapter 27

[631] "It's a Gay Life, Chasing Ostriches," *Chandler Arizonan*, December 4, 1914, 3.

[632] *Arizona Republican*, November 15, 1914.

[633] *Stockton Evening and Sunday Record*, November 13, 1914.

[634] *Arizona Republican*, November 20, 1914.

[635] *Arizona Republican*, November 27, 1914.

[636] "Statement of the Ownership, Management, Circulation, Etc.," *Chandler Arizonan* July 13, 1913, 2.

[637] *Arizona Republican*, November 27, 1914.

[638] *Arizona Republican*, November 27, 1914.

[639] *Arizona Republican*, November 15, 1914.

[640] *Arizona Republican*, November 15, 1914.

[641] *Arizona Republican*, November 15, 1914.

[642] *Arizona Republican*, November 15, 1914.

[643] *Arizona Republican*, November 22, 1914.

[644] "Phoenix Boys Capture Another Stray Ostrich," *Arizona Republican*, November 24, 1914, 10.

[645] Martin, *Home Life on an Ostrich Farm*, 145.

[646] *Arizona Republican*, November 15, 1914.

[647] Sergeant, *House by the Buckeye Road*, 76.

[648] "Wandering Ostrich," *Arizona Daily Star*, November 27, 1914, 4.

[649] *Arizona Republican*, November 27, 1914.

[650] *Arizona Republican*, November 15, 1914.

[651] "Arizona's Greek Camel Driver," *Phoenix Weekly Herald*, August 30, 1883, 4. (Reprinted from *Tombstone Epitaph*.)

[652] "Arizona Camels Sold," *Mohave County Miner*, January 27, 1884, 1.

[653] "The Phantom that Terrified all Arizona for a Time," *Mohave County Miner*, February 25, 1893, 3.

[654] *Arizona Republican*, November 20, 1914.

[655] "Isn't it Horrible? Ostrich: A Suicide," *Bisbee Daily Review*, March 24, 1915, 6.

[656] Michael Grady, "Chandler Bash Celebrates City's History with Hotheaded, Long-Necked Ostriches," *East Valley Tribune*, March 10, 2006, https://www.eastvalleytribune.com/get_out/chandler-bash-celebrates-city-s-history-with-hotheaded-long-necked-ostriches/article_7182101b-98a1-5d2f-b7e6-f1d816448d35.html.

Chapter 28

[657] "Ostrich Feathers," *Arizona Sentinel*, Sep 18, 1886, 1.

[658] Rebecca Bales, "7 Deadliest Birds on Earth and What Makes Them So Dangerous," *A-Z Animals,* last updated 2025, accessed July 16, 2025, https://a-z-animals.com/animals/birds/bird-facts/deadliest-birds/.

[659] John P. Rafferty, "6 of the World's Most Dangerous Birds," *Encyclopedia Britannica,* last updated June 13, 2025, https://www.britannica.com/list/6-of-the-worlds-most-dangerous-birds.

[660] Talon Homer, "The World's Most Dangerous Bird and 9 Runners-ups," *How Stuff Works*, Nov 12, 2024, https://animals.howstuffworks.com/birds/most-dangerous-bird.htm.

[661] Martin, *Home Life on an Ostrich Farm*, 113.

[662] Pickrell, "Ostrich," in *Cyclopedia*, 513.

[663] *Bisbee Daily Review*, March 24, 1915.

[664] *Bisbee Daily Review*, March 24, 1915.

[665] *Bisbee Daily Review*, March 24, 1915.

[666] 1. "Roughneck, Most Vicious Ostrich, is Killed; Neck Caught in a Wire Fence," *El Paso Herald*, March 22, 1915, 9; 2. *Bisbee Daily Review*, March 24, 1915.

[667] *El Paso Herald*, March 22, 1915.

[668] *El Paso Herald*, March 22, 1915.

[669] "*Bisbee Daily Review*, March 24, 1915.

[670] *El Paso Herald*, March 22, 1915.

[671] "Bad Ostrich Attacks Men," *Arizona Republican*, December 12, 1914, 6.

[672] *Arizona Republican*, December 12, 1914.

[673] *Arizona Republican*, December 12, 1914.

[674] *Arizona Republican*, December 12, 1914.

[675] Murray, "Ostriches in Arizona," 28.

[676] Murray, 28.

[677] Murray, 28.

[678] Murray, 28.

[679] Sergeant, *House by the Buckeye Road*, 75-76.

680 Martin, *Home Life on an Ostrich Farm*, 114. Emphasis added.
681 Martin, 114.
682 "An Ostrich a Bad Patient," *Buffalo News*, November 10, 1901, 17.
683 *Buffalo News*, November 10, 1901.
684 "Arizona Coyotes Make Meal on Ostriches," *Albuquerque Journal*, September 6, 1907, 3.
685 "Ostriches Victims of Lightning Bolt," *Arizona Republican*, August 22, 1911, 4.
686*Arizona Republican*, August 22, 1911.
687 Gonzales in Negri, "No Dummies…," 30-31.
688 Murray, "Ostriches in Arizona," 27.
689 *Waukegan News-Sun*, November 13, 1914.
690 Rydall, "Ostrich Farming in California," 286.
691 *Anaheim Gazette* (Fall 1883), as quoted by Tom Pulley in *County Courier*, 2009, 3.
692 Le Duc, "Domestic Ostrich Farming," 3.
693 Murray, "Ostriches in Arizona," 28.
694 Editorial, *Arizona Sentinel*, April 24, 1886, 3.
695 *Tucson Citizen*, April 16, 1886.
696 Editorial, *Arizona Sentinel*, May 1, 1886, 3.
697 *Arizona Department of Health Services*, "A History of the Arizona State Public Health Laboratory," n.d., https://www.azdhs.gov/documents/preparedness/state-laboratory/centennial/AZ-State-Lab_The-Early-Years.pdf.
698 "Meserves' Ostrich Still Roams the Mesa," *Tucson Citizen*, December 1, 1914, 8.
699 "Compelling Stranger Injured Furniture," *Arizona Republican*, December 3, 1914, 7.
700 "Ostrich Wagon Tips Over," *Arizona Republican*, December 4, 1914, 5.
701 *Arizona Republican*, December 4, 1914.
702 *Chandler Arizonan*, December 4, 1914.
703 *Chandler Arizonan*, December 4, 1914.
704 "Waging War on Emus," *Kalgoorie Miner*, November 5, 1932, 4.
705 "New Strategy in a War on the Emu," *Sunday Herald*, July 5, 1953, 13.
706 Joshua NLN, "The Great Emu War of 1932: When Australia Fought an Army of Feathers," *Vocal Media - History* (February 2025), https://vocal.media/history/ the-great-emu-war-of-1932-when-australia-fought-an-army-of-feathers.

Chapter 29
707 "The Spectator," *Outlook* 84, no. 6 (Oct 1906), 311-312.
708 "Scott Tells About the Ostriches in Magazine," *Arizona Republican*, January 30, 1914, 8.
709 *Arizona Republican*, January 30, 1914.
710 "The Lion Theater…" *Arizona Republican*, July 5, 1914, 16.
711 Doughty, "Ostrich Farming American Style," 141.
712 Geissinger, "On an Arizona Ostrich Farm," 8.
713 Geissinger, 8.
714 Geissinger, 8.
715 Parker, "Fashion Foibles," 6.
716 "The Home of the Ostrich" (Ad.), *Arizona Republican*, October 8, 1906, 8.
717 "High School Class Trip to the Valley," *Yuma Examiner*, May 20, 1910, 4.
718 "Needs an Ostrich in his Business," *Arizona Republican*, October 2, 1910, 10.
719 *Arizona Republican*, October 2, 1910.
720 *Arizona Republican*, October 2, 1910.
721 "The Spectator," 311-312.
722 *Arizona Republican*, October 2, 1910.
723 *Arizona Republican*, October 2, 1910.
724 Duncan, "Ostrich Farming in America," 700.
725 *Arizona Republican*, October 2, 1910.
726 *Arizona Republican*, October 2, 1910.

[727] "Recalling a Search for a Feathered Fortune," *Fort Worth Star-Telegram*, June 1, 1997, 23.

[728] *Fort Worth Star-Telegram*, June 1, 1997.

[729] *Fort Worth Star-Telegram*, June 1, 1997.

[730] *Fort Worth Star-Telegram*, June 1, 1997.

[731] Willetta Riggs, quoted in Michael Grady's "Chandler Bash," March 10, 2006.

[732] "A Grand Success: The Plucking and Quilling at the Ostrich Farm Yesterday," *Arizona Republican*, April 2, 1905, 11.

[733] "Plucking the Ostriches," *Border Vidette*, January 1, 1910, 1.

[734] *Border Vidette*, January 1, 1910.

[735] "Crowds View Little Ostriches," *Arizona Republican*, March 19, 1914, 6.

[736] "Hatching Ostriches in City Store Window," *Arizona Republican*, March 18, 1914, 16.

[737] *Arizona Republican*, March 19, 1914.

[738] Wilson, "Ostrich Farms...," 27.

[739] "Ostrich Feather Thief was Easily Convicted," *Arizona Republican*, June 2, 1910, 14.

[740] "Doings of the Legislature," *Coconino Sun*, March 19, 1909, 1.

[741] "Would Poison Ostrich for Board of Trade," *Arizona Republican*, October 6, 1910, 4.

[742] Pulley, "Orange County was Once...," 3.

[743] Pulley, 3.

[744] "The Spectator," 311-312.

[745] "The Spectator," 311-312.

[746] "The Spectator," 312.

[747] Holder, "An Ostrich Ranch," 153.

[748] "The Spectator," 312.

[749] Doughty, "Ostrich Farming American Style," 136.

[750] "Rural Route No. 3," *Arizona Republican*, January 30, 1909, 7.

[751] *Arizona Republican*, December 11, 1914.

[752] *Arizona Republican*, December 11, 1914.

[753] *Border Vidette*, January 1, 1910.

[754] "Yuma is a Coming Cattle Raising Center," *Arizona Sentinel and Yuma Weekly Examiner*, November 19, 1914, 1.

[755] "Ostriches – 3000 – Ostriches," *Imperial Valley Press*, October 27, 1912, 3.

[756] "Record Shipment of Ostriches from Here," *Arizona Republican*, December 10, 1914, 2.

[757] "Chico is Discussing Large Ostrich Farm," *Daily People's Cause*, December 9, 1914, 4.

[758] "Frank Lane is Now Ostrich King," *Arizona Republican*, December 27, 1914, 2.

[759] *Arizona Republican*, December 27, 1914.

[760] *Imperial Valley Press*, April 22, 1915.

Chapter 30

[761] Oliver, *Ostrich Ranching in America*, 35.

[762] Pickrell, "Ostriches," 406.

[763] "Ostriches for Thanksgiving Dinner," *Arizona Republican*, November 17, 1914, 7.

[764] "Thanksgiving Indeed!," *Chicago Tribune*, November 17, 1914, 5.

[765] "Baby Ostriches for C. Q. Hotel Dinner," *Bisbee Daily Review*, November 25, 1914, 8.

[766] "C.A.A. Eats Ostrich Today," *Chicago Tribune*, November 25, 1914, 1.

[767] *Arizona Republican*, November 27, 1914.

[768] "President Wilson Issues Thanksgiving Proclamation," *Parker Post*, November 7, 1914, 2.

[769] "Elks Serve Ostrich in Place of Turkey," *Arizona Sentinel and Yuma Weekly Examiner*, November 26, 1914, 1.

[770] Editorial, *Arizona Republican*, December 3, 1914, 4.

[771] "The Spectator," 311-312.

[772] *Arizona Republican*, December 23, 1914.

[773] *Arizona Republican*, December 23, 1914.

774 Leviticus 11:13-16, Holy Bible (English Standard Version). Scripture reference: "And these you shall detest among the birds; they shall not be eaten; they are detestable: the eagle, the bearded vulture, the black vulture, the kite, the falcon of any kind, every raven of any kind, the ostrich, the nighthawk, the sea gull, the hawk of any kind..."
775 Cogburn, to author, April 29, 2025.
776 Rydall, "Ostrich Farming in California," 290.
777 Martin, *Home Life on an Ostrich Farm*, 149.
778 Oliver, *Ostrich Ranching in America*, 271.
779 Martin, *Home Life on an Ostrich Farm*, 150.
780 "Twenty-Five Years Ago," *Arizona Daily Star*, January 20, 1943, 4.
781 Martin, *Home Life on an Ostrich Farm*, 126.
782 *Arizona Republican*, December 25, 1911.

Chapter 31
783 Kenneth Arline, "Where the Ostrich Once Roamed," *Phoenix Gazette*, June 19, 1976, 2.
784 "Appertainin' to the Ostrich," *Millinery Trade Review* 29, no. 5 (May 1904), 41.
785 Dutcher, "The Ostrich," 156.
786 Dutcher, 156.
787 Koch, "The Ostrich Feather Industry," 470.
788 Doughty, "Ostrich Farming American Style," 134.
789 There are different versions of this story, but one of the more reliable retellings is available at https://www.historicuk.com/HistoryUK/HistoryofBritain/White-Feather-Movement/.
790 "The Importation of Plumage Prohibition Bill," *The Spectator*, February 28, 1914, 19.
791 "The Need for the Plumage Bill," *The Spectator* March 7, 1914, 10-11.
792 "Of Interest to Ostrich Men," *Arizona Republican*, July 8, 1914, 3. (Reprint of "The Anti-Plumage Bill" from the *Journal of Agriculture of South Africa*.)
793 *Arizona Republican*, July 8, 1914.
794 *Quad-City Times*, February 24, 1915.
795 Murray, "Ostriches in Arizona," 28.
796 *Arizona Republican*, November 14, 1914.
797 *Arizona Republican*, November 14, 1914.
798 *Bisbee Daily Review*, November 22, 1914.
799 *Tucson Citizen*, December 1, 1914.
800 *Quad-City Times*, February 24, 1915.
801 Colley in "Ostrich Ranching...," *Arizona Highways* (1979) reports the Sacaton agency having four ostriches, while Ruffner in *All Hell Needs is Water*, reports there being twelve.
802 *Quad-City Times*, February 24, 1915.
803 Sergeant, *House by the Buckeye Road*, 75.
804 Sergeant, *House by the Buckeye Road*, 75-76.
805 Oliver, *Ostrich Ranching in America*, 43.
806 "Ostriches Sold," *Arizona Republican*, November 16, 1916, 8.
807 Wilson, "Ostrich Farms...," 27.
808 Wilson, 27.
809 "Ostriches Will Be Fed to Hogs," *Arizona Republican*, November 29, 1916, 4.
810 H. C. Cross, "Chronological Record," March 10, 1919.
811 Doughty, "Ostrich Farming American Style," 143.
812 *Quad-City Times*, February 24, 1915.
813 *Quad-City Times*, February 24, 1915..
814 "Save Your Ostrich," *Buffalo Courier Express*, May 18, 1917, 9.
815 Parker, "Fashion Foibles," 6.
816 Chandler Museum, "The 1914 Ostrich Drive."

[817] Murray, "Ostriches in Arizona," 28.

[818] Willetta Riggs, quoted in Michael Grady's "Chandler Bash," March 10, 2006.

[819] Doughty, "Ostrich Farming American Style," 145.

[820] Cogburn, to author, April 29, 2025.

Chapter 32

[821] Anne Rittenhouse, "Dress," *Buffalo Courier*, April 25, 1919, 9.

[822] Rittenhouse, *Buffalo Courier*, April 25, 1919.

[823] Rittenhouse, *Buffalo Courier*, April 25, 1919.

[824] "New Use for Ostrich Tips," *Buckeye Valley News*, March 3, 1920, 3.

[825] Colley, "Ostrich Ranching: Arizona's Strangest Venture," 45.

[826] "Ostriches Again Valuable," *Arizona Republican*, September 8, 1920, 4.

[827] "Meanest Thief Plucks Plumes of Ostriches Near Chandler…" *Arizona Republican*, January 16, 1924, 2.

[828] *Arizona Republican*, January 16, 1924.

[829] Cherie Nicholas, "Style Pendulum Swing to Handsome Ostrich Finery," *St. Johns Herald-Observer*, December 24, 1938, 5.

[830] Nicholas, "Style Pendulum," December 24, 1938.

[831] Cherie Nicholas, "Lavish Ostrich, Fine Feathers Bespeak New Elegance," *St. Johns Herald-Observer*, November 4, 1944, 5.

[832] Nicholas, "Lavish Ostrich," November 4, 1944.

[833] Colley, "Ostrich Ranching: Arizona's Strangest Venture," 41.

[834] Weston Gonzales, "Rise and Fall."

Chapter 33

[835] Shadow Hamilton, "The Ostrich," *Poetry Soup*, last modified 2015, accessed July 21, 2025, https://www.poetrysoup.com/poem/the_ostrich_635339.

[836] "Ostriches Outrun Formula One Cars," *Arizona Republic*, March 13, 1990, 22.

[837] Doughty, "Ostrich Farming American Style," 135.

[838] "Trained Ostrich Used as a Mount," *Los Angeles Herald*, August 6, 1908, 5.

[839] "Ostrich Driving," *San Diego Union*, May 25, 1896, 5.

[840] Francis Moore, *Travels into the Inland Parts of Africa (1738)*, as cited in Duncan's, "Ostrich Farming in America," 700.

[841] Moore, 700.

[842] "Arizona Ostriches," *Weekly Journal-Miner*, July 4, 1888, 1.

[843] "A New Industry," *Arizona Republican*, June 7, 1888, 3.

[844] *Poultry Monthly*, "An Ostrich Ranch in Arizona," 157.

[845] *Poultry Monthly*, 156-157.

[846] *Poultry Monthly*, 157.

[847] *El Paso Times*, September 30, 1911.

[848] Damon C. Cogburn, phone communication to author, May 11, 2025.

[849] Bob Petrie, "Worth the Effort," *Arizona Republic*, March 10, 1993, 172.

[850] Scott Craven, "Chandler's Ostrich Festival is a Novel Attraction," *Arizona Republic*, March 7, 1997, 176.

[851] "3 Arrested in Protest at Ostrich Festival," *Arizona Republic*, March 13, 1995, 12.

[852] *Arizona Republic*, March 13, 1995.

[853] United Poultry Concerns, "Urge Chamber of Commerce to Eliminate Ostrich Races at Chandler Ostrich Festival," *Poultry Press* (Spring 2017), https://www.upc-online.org/pp/spring2017/eliminate_chandler_ostrich_races.html.

[854] *United Poultry Concerns*. "Stop Ostrich Races." Change.org. January 26, 2017. https://www.change.org/p/chandler-chamber-of-commerce-stop-ostrich-races.

[855] *United Poultry Concerns*, "Stop Ostrich Races."

[856] Jerod MacDonald-Evoy, "Ostriches, Long Part of Chandler History," *Arizona Republic*, March 11, 2017, A15.

[857] McNickle, as quoted in *Arizona Republic*, March 10, 2017.

[858] MacDonald-Evoy, "Long Part of Chandler," March 11, 2017, A15.

[859] Terri Kimble in MacDonald-Evoy's "Long Part of Chandler," March 11, 2017, A15.

Chapter 34

[860] Theophilus Okunlola, "The Ostrich has Given Its All," *HoldingHistory.com*, last modified January 11, 2021, accessed August 24, 2025, https://www.holdinghistory.org/post/the-ostrich-has-given-its-all.

[861] Chalmers, "The Ostrich in the Salt River Valley," 21.

[862] Chalmers, 21.

[863] Dina M. Ezz El-Din, "Ostrich Eggs of Predynastic Egypt," *Journal of the General Union of Arab Archaeologists*11, no. 1, 40, https://jguaa.journals.ekb.eg/article_2754_9a36080136c91901261c665144ee1d0d.pdf.

[864] Alice C. Linsley, "The Ostrich in Biblical Symbolism," *Biblical Anthropology*, October 2, 2010, https://biblicalanthropology.blogspot.com/2010/10/ostrich-in-biblical-symbolism.html. Note: Author is citing Texier, P.J., Porraz, G., Parkington, J., Rigaud, J.P., Poggenpoel, C., Miller, C., Tribolo, C., Cartwright, C., Coudenneau, A., Klein, R., Steele, T., Verna, C. "A Howiesons Poort tradition of engraving ostrich eggshell containers dated to 60,000 years ago at Diepkloof Rock Shelter, South Africa," in *Proceedings of the National Academy of Sciences of the United States of America* 107, no. 14 (April 6, 2010), 6180-5, DOI: 10.1073/pnas.0913047107.

[865] Laufer, "Ostrich Egg-shell Cups…," 6.

[866] Laufer, 3.

[867] William Shakespeare, *Henry VI* (1594), Part 2, Act 4, Scene 10.

[868] Laufer, "Ostrich Egg-shell Cups…," 19.

[869] Rozmiarek, M. and Wtodarczyk, A. "Ostrich Hunting as a Form of Sporting Pursuit in the Nineteenth Century British Press," *Sport and Tourism Central European Journal* (*Sport i Turystka. Srodkowoeuropejskie Czasopismo Naukowe*) 7, No. 1 (2024), 16.

[870] Rozmiarek and Wtodarczyk, "Ostrich Hunting, 16.

[871] Laufer, "Ostrich Egg-shell Cups…," 19.

[872] Flinders Petrie and James E. Quibell, *Naqada and Ballas, 1895* (London: Quaritch Publishing, 1896), 28. Regarding Body #1480.

[873] Petrie and Quibell, *Naqada and Ballas*, 28. Regarding Body #1480.

[874] William Stearns Davis, *Readings in Ancient History: Illustrative Extracts from the Sources, 2 Vols.* (Boston: Allyn and Bacon, 1912-1913), Vol. I: Greece and the East, 329-332.

[875] Rozmiarek and Wtodarczyk, "Ostrich Hunting, 16.

[876] Rozmiarek and Wtodarczyk, "Ostrich Hunting, 16. Note: Citing from Jaroslaw O. Horbanczuk, *Strusie [Ostriches]* (Warszawa [Warsaw, Poland]: Zaktad Wydawniczo-Reprodukcyjny Auto-Graf [Autograf Publishing and Reproduciton Plant], 2001), 10.

[877] The *Historia Augusta* has had numerous sections proven false and even fraudulent. The ostrich eating tale is found in the section titled "Quadrigae Tyrannorum (Four tyrants: The Lives of Firmus, Saturninus, Proculus and Bonosus)."

[878] "Bon Appetit Wednesday! Ancient Roman Ostrich Ragoût," *Antiquity Now*, February 4, 2015, https://antiquitynow.org/2015/02/04/bon-appetit-wednesday-ancient-roman-ostrich-ragout/#:~:text=As%20food%2C%20ostriches%20seem%20to,recipe%20we're%20featuring%20today.

[879] Rozmiarek and Wtodarczyk, "Ostrich Hunting, 16. Note: Citing "Sufferings of Guillotined Persons," *Leicester Chronicle*, October 5, 1833, 1. The news story reads: "Gallian [Greek physician Galen] records, that the Emperor Commodus was so skillful in the decapitation

of ostriches, that these birds did not at first pause in their speed, after the loss of their heads."

880 Rozmiarek and Wtodarczyk, "Ostrich Hunting, 17.

881 "Batty's Hippodrome," *Morning Advertiser*, July 10, 1851, 6.

882 *Reading Mercury*, June 11, 1853, 4, as cited in Rozmiarek, M. and Wtodarczyk, A. "Ostrich Hunting,", 20.

Chapter 35

883 Linda J. Lynch (President of the AZ Ostrich & Emu Assoc.) and Phil Patton (Treasurer), in Secretary of State Richard Mahoney's "Voters Read All About It!," *State of Arizona 1994 Ballot Propositions on the General Election*, November 8, 1994, 12.

884 Rick White in Curtice K. Cultice's "Where's the Beef?," *Business America* 117, No. 4 (May 1996), 27.

885 Stephen Kaufman, "Pressure to End Apartheid Began at Grass Roots in U.S.," *U.S. Mission to International Organizations in Geneva*, Sept. 17, 2013, https://geneva.usmission.gov/2013/12/17/pressure-to-end-apartheid-began-at-grass-roots-in-u-s/.

886 *American Ostrich Association*, "About Us," Accessed August 25, 2025, https://www.americanostrichassociation.org/content.aspx?page_id=22&club_id=337926&module_id=716656.

887 Andrew Van Dam, "The Great Llama (and Ostrich and Emu Collapse)," *Washington Post*, March 8, 2024, https://www.washingtonpost.com/business/2024/03/07/llama-emu-ostrich-herds-down/.

888 Robert Francis, "The Ostrich: America's Once and Future Bird," *U.S. Bird History*, August 29, 2023, https://usbirdhistory.com/american-ostriches/.

889 Susan D. Franck (Ex. Dir. of United Ratite Producers of AZ & Pres./Founder of the Arizona Ostrich), in Mahoney's "Voters Read All About It!," November 8, 1994, 12.

890 *American Ostrich Association*, "About Us."

891 Oliver, *Ostrich Ranching in America*, 116.

892 Michael Lehman, "As exotic farms are on decline nationwide, Oregon ranchers are hopeful for the future," April 15, 2024. *Think Out Loud* podcast with Dave Miller, Oregon Public Broadcasting (OPB), MP3 audio, 14:08, https://www.opb.org/article/2024/04/05/oregon-ranchers-hopeful-future/.

893 Lehman, *Think Out Loud*, April 15, 2024.

894 Oliver, *Ostrich Ranching in America*, 80.

895 *University of California Sustainable Agriculture Research and Education Program*, "Exotic Livestock: A Small-Scale Agriculture Alternative" (brochure), (January 1989), https://ucanr.edu/node/130928/printable/print.

896 Jim Carden in Oliver's *Ostrich Ranching in America*, 150.

897 Penny Lynch in Oliver's *Ostrich Ranching in America*, 139.

898 Tom Broome in Oliver's *Ostrich Ranching in America*, 126.

899 Barry Coy, in Oliver's *Ostrich Ranching in America*, 212.

900 Cogburn, to author, April 29, 2025.

901 Lynch in Oliver's *Ostrich Ranching in America*, 140.

902 A.D. Whitehurst, Jr. in Oliver's *Ostrich Ranching in America*, 186.

903 Dana Cogburn-Barrett, "Rooster Cogburn Ostrich Ranch Story" (manuscript), *Rooster Cogburn Ostrich Ranch*, July 18, 2025.

904 Coy, in Oliver's *Ostrich Ranching in America*, 212.

905 Lynch in Oliver's *Ostrich Ranching in America*, 140.

906 *American Ostrich Association*, "About Us."

907 *American Ostrich Association*, "About Us."

908 Lehman, *Think Out Loud*, April 15, 2024.

909 Ed Burns in Oliver's *Ostrich Ranching in America*, 118.

910 Burns, 118.

911 *University of California,* "Exotic Livestock."

912 Tom Mantzel in Oliver's *Ostrich Ranching in America*, 39.

913 *American Ostrich Association,* "About Us."

914 Lehman, "Zagat Documentary."

915 *American Ostrich Association,* "Welcome," Accessed August 25, 2025, https://www.americanostrichassociation.org/.

916 Oliver, *Ostrich Ranching in America*, 44.

917 Cogburn, to author, April 29, 2025.

918 Weston Gonzales, "Rise and Fall."

919 Franck in Oliver's *Ostrich Ranching in America*, 132.

920 Dub Oliver, *Ostrich Ranching in America*, 45.

921 Cogburn, to author, April 29, 2025.

922 *American Ostrich Association,* "About Us."

923 *American Ostrich Association,* "About Us."

924 *American Ostrich Association,* "About Us."

925 David DeWitte, "Ostrich Ranchers Told to Get Their Heads Out of the Sand," *Deseret News*, July 17, 1994, https://www.deseret.com/1994/7/17/19120102/ostrich-ranchers-told-to-get-their-heads-out-of-the-sand/.

926 James W. Mertina and Jack L. Schiater, "Exotic Ectoparasites of Ostriches Recently Imported into the United States," *Journal of Wildlife Diseases* 27, no. 1 (1991), 180.

927 Susan Cook Adkins, "Importation - Hottest Ostrich Issue Ever," in Oliver's *Ostrich Ranching in America*, 75-76.

928 Mertina and Schiater, "Exotic Ectoparasites of Ostriches," 180.

929 Cook Adkins, in Oliver's *Ostrich Ranching in America*, 79.

930 Francis, "America's Once and Future Bird."

931 Andrew Van Dam, "The Great Llama," March 8, 2024.

932 *American Ostrich Association,* "About Us."

933 White in Cultice's "Where's the Beef?," 26.

934 Weston Gonzales, "Rise and Fall."

935 *American Ostrich Association,* "About Us."

936 Associated Press, "County Jail Inmates in Arizona Will Soon Get the Gift of Ostrich Meat," *Los Angeles Times*, July 23, 1997, https://www.latimes.com/archives/la-xpm-1997-jul-23-mn-15502-story.html.

937 *American Ostrich Association,* "About Us."

Chapter 36

938 Oliver, *Ostrich Ranching in America*, 92.

939 Cogburn, to author, April 29, 2025.

940 ADOT, *Average Annual Daily Traffic Report 2018,* https://azdot.gov/sites/default/files/2019/05/2018-AADT-INTERSTATES.pdf.

941 Robin Sewell in "Mount Lemmon: A Scenic Drive to Arizona's Secret Town," *Arizona Highways TV (CBS 5),* posted to YouTube on Sep. 23, 2024, https://www.youtube.com/watch?v=yIbDR_iJduk.

942 Larry the Cable Guy (Daniel L. Whitney) in "Only in America With Larry the Cable Guy," *History Channel*, Season 3, Episode 1: Larry Herds Dinosaurs, Aired May 8, 2013.

943 Diane Ciarloni Simmons, "Whatever Happened to D.C. Cogburn?," *Western Horseman* 56, no. 5 (May 1991), 122.

944 Cogburn-Barrett, "Rooster Cogburn*,"* July 18, 2025.

945 Simmons, "Whatever Happened to D.C. Cogburn?," 122.

946 D.C. Cogburn, phone communication to author, April 29, 2025.

947 Dub Oliver, *Ostrich Ranching in America*, 143.

948 Cogburn, to author, April 29, 2025.

[949] Cogburn, to author, August 28, 2025.

[950] Cogburn, to author, April 29, 2025.

[951] D.C. Cogburn, in Oliver's *Ostrich Ranching in America*, 144.

[952] Cogburn-Barrett, "Rooster Cogburn," July 18, 2025.

[953] Cogburn-Barrett, "Rooster Cogburn," July 18, 2025.

[954] Cogburn, to author, April 29, 2025.

[955] Negri, "No Dummies...," 31.

[956] Cogburn-Barrett, "Rooster Cogburn," July 18, 2025.

[957] Cogburn-Barrett, "Rooster Cogburn," July 18, 2025.

[958] Henry Molski, "Dream to Revolutionize Ostrich Industry Crumbles," *Arizona Republic*, August 9, 2014, https://www.azcentral.com/story/life/az-narratives/2014/08/10/ostrich-industry-dream-dies/13855611/.

[959] Ken Sain, "Bird supplier for Ostrich Fest has weathered hard times," *Queen Creek Tribune*, March 12, 2023, https://www.themesatribune.com/get_out/bird-supplier-for-ostrich-fest-has-weathered-hard-times/article_f6c7d3c0-c1ec-11ed-8e59-8fdf597da209.html.

[960] Molski, "Dream to Revolutionize," August 9, 2014.

[961] Cogburn, to author, April 29, 2025.

[962] Oliver, *Ostrich Ranching in America*, 141.

[963] Cogburn, to author, April 29, 2025.

[964] Cogburn, April 29, 2025.

[965] Cogburn, April 29, 2025..

[966] Tanner Barrett, personal communication to author, May 11, 2025.

[967] D.C. Cogburn, personal communication to author, May 16, 2025.

[968] D.C. Cogburn, personal communication to author, September 22, 2025.

Chapter 37

[969] Cogburn, to author, April 29, 2025.

[970] *Reuters*, "Japan researchers use ostrich cells to make glowing COVID-19 detection masks," December 10, 2021, https://www.reuters.com/business/healhcare-pharmaceuticals/japan-researchers-use-ostrich-cells-make-glowing-covid-19-detection-masks-2021-12-10/.

[971] Dr. Yasuhiro Tsukamoto email communication to D.C. Cogburn, May 18, 2025.

[972] Gene F. Pfeiffer, in Oliver's *Ostrich Ranching in America*,165. Note: Pfeiffer was the first President of the AOA.

[973] Dr. Alessio Fasano, "Zonulin, Regulation of Tight Junctions and Autoimmune Diseases," *Annual New York Academy of Sciences* no.1, article 1258 (July 2012), 25-33, DOI: 10.1111/j.1749–6632.2012.06538.x.

[974] Hamid Dabiri, Majid Sadeghizadeh, Vahab Ziael, Zahra Moghadasi, Ali Maham, Ensiyeh Hajizadeh-Saffier, and Mahdi Habibi=Anbouhi, "Development of an ostrich-derived single-chain variable fragment against PTPRN extracellular domain," *Nature Portfolio* no.14, article 3689 (February 2024), DOI: 10.1038/s41598–024–53386–5.

[975] Dr. Yasuhiro Tsukamoto, Osamu Maeda, Genshi Shigekwa, Stuart Greenberg, Barry Hendler, "Ostrich Antibody and Its Application to Skin Diseases, a Review and Case Report," Health 10, no. 10 (2018), 1357-1370, DOI: 10.4236/health.2018.1010105.

[976] Dr. Yasuhiro Tsukamoto, Barry Hendler, Stu Greenberg, "Application of Ostrich Antibodies to the Restoration of Hair Growth, a Preliminary and Case Report," *Journal of Cosmetics, Dermatological Sciences and Applications* 8, no. 4 (October 2018), 179-184, DOI: 10.4236/jcdsa.2018.84019.

[977] Gabi Serrato Marks, "How the Biggest Birds on Earth Could Help Fend Off Epidemics," *Audubon.org*, March 21, 2019. https://www.audubon.org/magazine/how-big gest-birds-earth-could-help-fend-epidemics?int_query=ostrich&int_src=site _search.

978 *American Society for the Prevention of Cruelty to Animals,* "Animals in Research: General Considerations." ASPCA.org. Accessed November 24, 2025. https://www.aspca.org/about-us/aspca-policy-and-position-statements/animals-research-general-considerations.

979 United States Food & Drug Administration, "FDA Announces Plan to Phase Out Animal Testing Requirement for Monoclonal Antibodies and Other Drugs" (Press Release), *FDA.gov* (April 10, 2025), https://www.fda.gov/news-events/press-announcements/fda-announces-plan-phase-out-animal-testing-requirement-monoclonal-antibodies-and-other-drugs.

980 United States Food & Drug Administration, "FDA Announces Plan to Phase Out Animal Testing Requirement for Monoclonal Antibodies and Other Drugs" (Press Release), *FDA.gov* (April 10, 2025), https://www.fda.gov/news-events/press-announcements/fda-announces-plan-phase-out-animal-testing-requirement-monoclonal-antibodies-and-other-drugs.

981 Kennedy Jr., Robert F. (Sec.), "Re: H5N1 Infected Ostriches at Universal Ostrich Farm in Edgewood, B.C." (Letter) to Paul MacKinnon, President of the Canadian Food Inspection Agency, May 23, 2025.

982 Janelle Molony, "Arizona Ostrich rancher makes flock available for research," *Queen Creek Tribune*, June 8, 2025, pages 14-16.

Bibliography

Archives

"Appropriations for the Department of Agriculture for the fiscal year ending June 30, 1915," Public-No. 122-63rd Congress (H.R. 13679), 6.

Cross, H. C. "Chronological Record of the Ostrich Breeding Work from November 7, 1917." *United States Department of Agriculture, Bureau of Animal Husbandry, Animal Husbandry Division* [National Archives Record #1549640, November 17, 1917 – July 19, 1919].

Cross, H. C. "Field Day at the U.S. Poultry Experiment Station," (Meeting notes), Nov. 18, 1920, in Nat E. Luce, "Record of the Work Being Conducted at the U.S. Poultry Experiment Station," *United States Department of Agriculture, Bureau of Animal Husbandry, Animal Husbandry Division* [National Archives Record #1549640, July 21,1920-December 30, 1921].

Cross, H. C. "Miscellaneous Information on the Ostrich Industry," in *United States Department of Agriculture, Bureau of Animal Husbandry, Animal Husbandry Division* [National Archives Record #1549640, December 15, 1915 – October 4, 1917].

Cross, H. C. "Record of the Ostrich Breeding Work at the U.S. Poultry Experiment Station, Season 1919-1920," *United States Department of Agriculture, Bureau of Animal Husbandry, Animal Husbandry Division* [National Archives Record #1549640, July 20, 1919 – July 20, 1920].

Glendale District Chamber of Commerce, "Petition to the United States Department of Agriculture, December 30, 1920," *United States Department of Agriculture, Bureau of Animal Husbandry, Animal Husbandry Division* [National Archives Record #154961642].

Luce, Nat E. "History of the U.S. Poultry Experiment Station," (Manuscript), February 8, 1921, in *United States Department of Agriculture, Bureau of Animal Husbandry, Animal Husbandry Division* [National Archives Record #1549640, December 15, 1915-October 4, 1917], 1-11.

Luce, Nat E. "Record of the Work Being Conducted at the U.S. Poultry Experiment Station," *United States Department of Agriculture, Bureau of Animal Husbandry, Animal Husbandry Division* [National Archives Record #1549640, July 21,1920-December 30, 1921].

Luce, Nat E. "Record of the Work Being Conducted at the U.S. Poultry Experiment Station," *United States Department of Agriculture, Bureau of Animal Husbandry, Animal Husbandry Division,* [National Archives Record #1549641, January 1, 1922 – November 16, 1924.].

Ostrich depiction in Wonders of Creation [Turkish manuscript W.659/ CPS_W.659.137b_Fp_DD] (Walters Art Museum, Henry Walters Collection).

Sylvia Bender-Lamb, "An Economic Analysis of the Ostrich Industry in Arizona's Salt River Valley," April 18, 1978 (Arizona Historical Society, Small Manuscript Collection - MSM 48).

Books & Articles

Adkins, Susan Cook. "Importation - Hottest Ostrich Issue Ever." Quoted in in Dub Oliver, *Ostrich Ranching in America* (Shreveport: Dub Oliver & Associates, 1993), 75-76.

Africanus, Johannes Leo. *Cosmographia et Geographia de Africa* (1526). Transcribed by Clare Richie to *A Geographical Historie of Africa.* London, 1600. (Available through Early English Books Online.)

American Ostrich Association. "About Us." Accessed August 25, 2025. https://www.americanostrichassociation.org/content.aspx?page_id=22&club_i d=337926&module_id=716656.

American Ostrich Association. "Welcome." Accessed August 25, 2025. https://www.americanostrichassociation.org/.

American Society for the Prevention of Cruelty to Animals, "Animals in Research: General Considerations." ASPCA.org. Accessed November 24, 2025. https://www.aspca.org/about-us/aspca-policy-and-position-statements/animals-research-general-considerations.

American Rivers. "Gila River: The Origin of Wilderness." Accessed July 15, 2025. https://www.americanrivers.org/river/gilariver/#:~:text=The%20Backstory,du e%20to%20large%20irrigation%20diversions.

Animal Justice League. "Animal Justice Urges CFIA to Rethink Ostrich Cull, Allow Independent Testing." September 23, 2025. https://animaljustice.ca/ media-releases/animal-justice-urges-cfia-to-rethink-ostrich-cull-allow-independent-testing.

Antiquity Now. "Bon Appetit Wednesday! Ancient Roman Ostrich Ragoût." February 4, 2015, https://antiquitynow.org/2015/02/04/bon-appetit-wednesday-ancient-roman-ostrich-ragout/#:~:text=As%20food%2C%20 ostriches%20seem%20to,recipe%20we're%20featuring%20today.

Arline, Kenneth. "Where the Ostrich Once Roamed." *Phoenix Gazette*, June 19, 1976, 2.

Arizona Department of Health Services. "A History of the Arizona State Public Health Laboratory." n.d., accessed August 28, 2025. https://www.azdhs.gov/ documents/preparedness/state-laboratory/centennial/AZ-State-Lab_The-Early-Years.pdf.

Arizona Department of Transportation (ADOT). "Average Annual Daily Traffic Report 2018." https://azdot.gov/sites/default/files/2019/05/2018-AADT-INTERSTATES.pdf.

Associated Press. "County Jail Inmates in Arizona Will Soon Get the Gift of Ostrich Meat." *Los Angeles Times*, July 23, 1997. https://www.latimes.com/ archives/la-xpm-1997-jul-23-mn-15502-story.html.

Bales, Rebecca. "7 Deadliest Birds on Earth and What Makes Them So Dangerous." *A-Z Animals,* last updated 2025, accessed July 16, 2025. https://a-z-animals.com/animals/birds/bird-facts/deadliest-birds/.

Barnes, Sisley. "Preening Plumes," *Westways* 67, no. 5 (May 1975): 54-55.

Beasley, Al D. (ed.). *Phoenix, Arizona, Maricopa County: 20th Century Phoenix, Illustrated.* Phoenix: n.p., 1907.

Bell, Flora A. "From Arizona." *Slater News-Rustler*, April 4, 1913, 2.

Bemis, M. E. "Poultry Notes from Arizona." *California Poultry Journal* V, no. 11 (September 1920): 303.

Bemis, M. E. "Poultry Work in the Southwest." *California Poultry Journal* VI, no. 7 (May 1921): 189-190.

Bennett, Arnold. "The White Feather: A Sketch of English Recruiting." *Collier's Weekly*, 1914.

Bibliography

Black, Riley. "Walnut: the True Measure of a Dinosaur's Brain." *National Geographic*. January 28, 2013, https://www.nationalgeographic.com/science/article/walnut-the-true-measure-of-a-dinosaurs-brain.

Boardman, Mark. "Facing Down a Lynch Mob." *True West* (blog). March 18, 2022. https://truewestmagazine.com/facing-down-a-lynch-mob/.

Bonner, Mary Graham. "Daddy's Evening Fairy Tale: Poor Mrs. Ostrich." *Arizona State Miner*, July 17, 1926.

Brand, Peter. "Wyatt Earp's Vendetta Posse." Quoted in James Gressinger, "Wyatt Earp's Vendetta Posse: Who Were These Guys?" *Southern Arizona Guide*, n.d., accessed September 15, 2025. https://southernarizonaguide.com/wyatt-earps-vendetta-posse-who-were-these-guys/.

Broome, Tom. Quoted in in Dub Oliver, *Ostrich Ranching in America* (Shreveport: Dub Oliver & Associates, 1993): 126.

Burgess, Kaya. "Emus climb the intelligence pecking order but ostriches are birdbrains." *The Times,* February 20, 2025, https://www.thetimes.com/uk/science/article/emus-climb-the-intelligence-pecking-order-but-ostriches-are-birdbrains-xbxxgxzhb.

Burns, Ed. Quoted in in Dub Oliver, *Ostrich Ranching in America* (Shreveport: Dub Oliver & Associates, 1993): 118.

California Poultry Journal. "Government Poultry Work." *California Poultry Journal* V, no. 9 (July 1920): 267.

California Poultry Journal. "Nat Luce Goes Back into Government Work." *California Poultry Journal* V, no. 10 (August 1920): 287.

Carden, Jim. Quoted in in Dub Oliver, *Ostrich Ranching in America* (Shreveport: Dub Oliver & Associates, 1993): 150.

Cawston Ostrich Farm, Souvenir Book, 1909. (Held at the Smithsonian Institute.)

Chalmers, Louis Henry. "The Ostrich in the Salt River Valley." *The Earth: Salt River Valley of Arizona, Special* 6, no. 8 (August 1909): 21-23.

Chandler Museum. "George T. Peabody, Chandler Chamber of Commerce Founder." *Chandlerpedia*, June 14, 2022, https://chandlerpedia.atlassian.net/wiki/spaces/CHANDLERPE/pages/1304789050/Week+18+George+T.+Peabody+Chandler+Chamber+of+Commerce+Founder.

Chandler Museum. "The 1914 Ostrich Drive and Rough Neck." *Chandlerpedia*, June 14, 2022, https://chandlerpedia.atlassian.net/wiki/spaces/CHANDLERPE/pages/1305673775/Week+39+The+1914+Ostrich+Drive+and+Rough+Neck.

Church of Jesus Christ of Latter-Day Saints. "Edmund Ellsworth Company (1856)." Church History Biographies, 2025. https://history.churchofjesuschrist.org/chd/organization/pioneer-company/edmund-ellsworth-company.

Clark, F.E.; Burdass, J.; Kavanagh, A.; & King, A. "Palaeognath birds innovate to solve a novel foraging problem." *Scientific Reports* 15, 4512 (2025). https://doi.org/10.1038/s41598-025-88217-8.

Coletti, Andrew. "Ancient Eaters: Elagabalus, the Roman Doctor Frank-N-Furter (203-222 CE)." *PassTheFlamingo* (blog), April 26, 2017. https://passtheflamingo.com/2017/04/26/ancient-eaters-elagabalus-the-roman-doctor-frank-n-furter-203-222-ce/.

Colley, Charles C. "Ostrich Ranching: Arizona's Strangest Venture." *Arizona Highways* 55, no. 5 (May 1979): 40-45.

Cogburn-Barrett, Dana. "Rooster Cogburn Ostrich Ranch Story" (manuscript). *Rooster Cogburn Ostrich Ranch,* July 18, 2025.

Combs, Dorothy. "Margaret Ann 'Maggie' Todd Toston." *FindAGrave.com* [Memorial ID 110859207], Accessed July 21, 2025, https://www.findagrave.com/memorial/110859207/margaret_ann-toston.

Commonwealth of Australia. "Ostrich Farming," *Parliamentary Debates, Session 1913, vol. LXXI* (1914), case 5.7 (2146-2155).

Coy, Barry. Quoted in Dub Oliver, *Ostrich Ranching in America* (Shreveport: Dub Oliver & Associates, 1993): 212.

Craven, Scott. "Chandler's Ostrich Festival is a Novel Attraction," *Arizona Republic*, March 7, 1997, 176.

Dabiri, H.; Sadeghizadeh, M.; Ziael, V.; Moghadasi, z.; Maham, A.; Hajizadeh-Saffier, E.; & Habibi-Anbouhi, M. "Development of an ostrich-derived single-chain variable fragment against PTPRN extracellular domain." *Nature Portfolio* no.14, article 3689 (February 2024). DOI: 10.1038/s41598–024–53386–5.

Daly, Liza. "The Ostrich for the Defence (1912)." *Liza Daly* (blog), March 4, 2022. https://lizadaly.com/pages/utopian-novels/ostrich-for-the-defence.html.

Davis, Dr. Karen. "Special Report: Emus and Ostriches, Nowhere to Hide." United Poultry Concerns, *Poultry Press* (Fall/Winter 1993). https://www.upc-online.org/pp/fall93/nowhere_to_hide.html.

Davis, William Stearns. *Readings in Ancient History: Illustrative Extracts from the Sources, Vol. I: Greece and the East.* Boston: Allyn and Bacon, 1912-1913.

DeWitte, David. "Ostrich Ranchers Told to Get Their Heads Out of the Sand." *Deseret News*, July 17, 1994, https://www.deseret.com/1994/7/17/19120102/ostrich-ranchers-told-to-get-their-heads-out-of-the-sand/.

DeWyze, Jeannette. "San Diego's Ostrich Speculators." *San Diego Reader*, May 12, 1994. https://www.sandiegoreader.com/news/1994/may/12/cover-san-diego-ostrich-speculators/.

Doughty, Robin. "Ostrich Farming American Style." *Agricultural History* 47, no. 2, (April 1973): 133-145.

Douglass, Arthur. *Ostrich Farming in South Africa* (London: Cassell, Petter, Galpin & Co., 1881).

Duncan, T. C. "Ostrich Farming in America." In *Report of the Commissioner of Agriculture for the Year 1888*. Washington: Government Printing Office, 1889: (666-685).

Dutcher, William. "The Ostrich." *Bird-Lore* 7, no. 2 (April 1, 1905): 153-156.

Ellsworth, Pete. Interview by Joyce McBride. *Show Low Historical Society Museum*, January 13, 2008. https://azmemory.azlibrary.gov/nodes/view/164800.

Eveler, Peter W. "The Southwest Ostrich Farm of Old El Paso." *Password* 12, no. 3 (Fall, 1967): 90-91.

Ezz El-Din, Dina M. "Ostrich Eggs of Predynastic Egypt." *Journal of the General Union of Arab Archaeologists* 11, no. 1: 40-56. https://jguaa.journals.ekb.eg/article_2754_9a36080136c91901261c665144ee1d0d.pdf.

Fasano, Dr. Alessio. "Zonulin, Regulation of Tight Junctions and Autoimmune Diseases." *Annual New York Academy of Sciences* no.1, article 1258, (July 2012): 25-33. DOI: 10.1111/j.1749–6632.2012.06538.x.

Franck, Susan. "History of Ostrich Ranching in Arizona." In Dub Oliver, *Ostrich Ranching in America* (Shreveport: Dub Oliver & Associates, 1993), 6-11.

Franck, Susan. Quoted in Dub Oliver, *Ostrich Ranching in America* (Shreveport: Dub Oliver & Associates, 1993), 132.

Franck, Susan D. Quoted in Secretary of State Richard Mahoney, "Voters Read All About It!" *State of Arizona 1994 Ballot Propositions on the General Election*, November 8, 1994, 12.

Francis, Robert. "The Ostrich: America's Once and Future Bird." *U.S. Bird History*, August 29, 2023. https://usbirdhistory.com/american-ostriches/.

Bibliography

Gabrielle, Vincent. "The Strange Tale of the Great 1911 Trans-Saharan Ostrich Heist." *Atlas Obscura*, April 22, 2019. https://www.atlasobscura.com/articles/great-ostrich-heist.

Geissinger, James A. "On an Arizona Ostrich Farm." *The Presbyterian Banner* (January 28, 1909), 8.

Grady, Michael. "Chandler Bash Celebrates City's History with Hotheaded, Long-Necked Ostriches." *East Valley Tribune*, March 10, 2006. https://www.east valleytribune.com/get_out/chandler-bash-celebrates-city-s-history-with-hotheaded-long-necked-ostriches/article_7182101b-98a1-5d2f-b7e6-f1d816448d35.html.

Griffith, Gardner. "Chicken Day at Glendale, Arizona May 20, 1921." *California Poultry Journal* VI, no. 8 (June 1921): 1-3.

Hamilton, Shadow. "The Ostrich." *Poetry Soup*, last modified 2015, accessed July 21, 2025. https://www.poetrysoup.com/poem/the_ostrich_635339.

Hayden, Carl T. (Rep.). "The Ostrich Industry" (Speech), February 7, 1913, *Congressional Record of the 62nd Congress, House of Representatives* 49, (December 2, 1912 to March 4, 1913): 57-60.

Heard Farm. "Our History - The Story of the Heard Farm." December 2, 2021. https://heardfarm.com/blog/our-history-the-story-of-heard-farm/.

Hegarty, Lisa. "Pan-American Ostrich Company." *Litchfield Heritage Center Newsletter* (Spring, 2024): 3.

Hendra, Peter. "Farm north of Kingston a social media sensation." *The Whig Standard*, April 28, 2022, https://www.thewhig.com/news/local-news/farm-north-of-kingston-a-social-mediasensation#:~:text=Amanda%20said%20she%20enjoys%20the,really%20been%20such%20a%20delight.%E2%80%9D.

Hendrick, Joe. Quoted in Sheri Johnson, "Chandler Ostrich Fest Pits 9 Eager Birds in Variety of Events." *Arizona Republic*, March 12, 1989, 22.

Heritage Auctions. "Tombstone, Arizona: Archive of Earp Associate, E. B. Gage." Accessed September 19, 2025. https://historical.ha.com/itm/miscellaneous/ephemera/tombstone-arizona-archive-of-earp-associate-e-b-gage/a/6035-47308.s.

Holder, Charles Frederick. "An Ostrich Ranch." *Chautauquan* VII, no. 3 (December 1886): 153.

Homer, Talon. "The World's Most Dangerous Bird and 9 Runners-ups." *How Stuff Works*, Nov 12, 2024. https://animals.howstuffworks.com/birds/most-dangerous-bird.htm.

Horn, Tom. *Life of Tom Horn, Government Scout and Interpreter*. Denver: Louthan Book Company, 1904.

Hornung, Chuck. Citing The *Daily Nugget* of March 27, 1882 in *Wyatt Earp's Cow-boy Campaign*, (North Carolina: McFarland & Co., 2016).

Jones, Tony. "Birds of a different feather could bring lucrative new industry to Arizona." *The Arrow*, October 9, 1992, 20.

Journal of the Royal Society of Arts. "Ostrich Farming in the United States." *Journal of the Royal Society of Arts* 60, no. 3095 (1912): 476-477.

Kaufman, Stephen. "Pressure to End Apartheid Began at Grass Roots in U.S." *U.S. Mission to International Organizations in Geneva*, Sept. 17, 2013. https://geneva.usmission.gov/2013/12/17/pressure-to-end-apartheid-began-at-grass-roots-in-u-s/.

Kemp, Thomas W. "Opinion of an Expert: The Ostriches in the Salt River Valley." *Arizona Republican*, October 30, 1910, 9.

Kennedy Jr., Robert F. (Sec.). "Re: H5N1 Infected Ostriches at Universal Ostrich Farm in Edgewood, B.C." (Letter) to Paul MacKinnon, President of the Canadian Food Inspection Agency, May 23, 2025.

Kraklio, Karen. "Feathers in Our Cap," *Arizona Highways* 90, no. 10 (October 2014): 8.

Kimble, Terri. Quoted in MacDonald-Evoy, "Ostriches, Long Part of Chandler History." *Arizona Republic*, March 11, 2017, A3 & A15.

King, Jean Beach. *Arizona Charlie: A Legendary Cowboy, Klondike Stampeder and Wild West Showman*. Phoenix: Heritage Publishers, 1989.

Koch, Felix J. "The Ostrich Feather Industry in the West Vs. Africa." *Overland Monthly* 58, no. 6 (December 1911): 470-474.

Laufer, Berthold. "Ostrich Egg-shell Cups of Mesopotamia and the Ostrich in Ancient and Modern Times." Chicago: Field Museum of Natural History, 1926.

Lesku, J.A.; Meyer, L.C.; Fuller, A., Maloney, S.K.; Dell'Omo, G.; Vyssotski, A.L.; & Rattenborg, N.C. "Ostriches Sleep Like Platypuses." *Plos One* 6, no. 8 (2011): 1-7. https://doi.org/10.1371/journal.pone.0023203.

Linsley, Alice C. "The Ostrich in Biblical Symbolism." *Biblical Anthropology*, October 2, 2010. https://biblicalanthropology.blogspot.com/2010/10/ostrich-in-biblical-symbolism.html.

Luck, Sara. *Under the Desert Sky* (New York: Pocket Books, 2016).

Lynch, Linda J. & Patton, Phil. Quoted in Secretary of State Richard Mahoney's "Voters Read All About It!" *State of Arizona 1994 Ballot Propositions on the General Election*, November 8, 1994, 12.

Lynch, Penny. Quoted in Dub Oliver, *Ostrich Ranching in America* (Shreveport: Dub Oliver & Associates, 1993), 139.

MacDonald-Evoy, Jerod. "A brief history of the Chandler Ostrich Festival." *Arizona Republic*, March 10, 2017, (A13 & A15) https://www.azcentral.com/story/news/local/chandler/2017/03/10/history-and-protests-over-chandler-ostrich-festival/98502344/.

Mantzel, Tom. Quoted in Dub Oliver, *Ostrich Ranching in America* (Shreveport: Dub Oliver & Associates, 1993), 36-39.

Martin, Anne. *Home Life on an Ostrich Farm*. London: G. Philip, 1890.

Mason, Walt. "Rippling Rhymes: The Ostrich." *Arizona Republican*, September 8, 1915, 4.

McNickle, Paige. Quoted in Jerod MacDonald-Evoy, "A brief history of the Chandler Ostrich Festival." *Arizona Republic*, March 10, 2017. https://www.azcentral.com/story/news/local/chandler/2017/03/10/history-and-protests-over-chandler-ostrich-festival/98502344/.

Mertina, James W. & Schiater, Jack L. "Exotic Ectoparasites of Ostriches Recently Imported into the United States." *Journal of Wildlife Diseases* 27, no. 1 (1991): 180-182.

Miles, Henry (Ed.) "Strange Farms, Unusual Means of Making Money." *Montreal Pharmaceutical Journal* 27, no. 12 (December 1916): 235.

Millinery Trade Review. "Appertainin' to the Ostrich." *Millinery Trade Review* 29, no. 5 (May 1904): 41-42.

Millinery Trade Review. "Ostrich Feathers." *Millinery Trade Review* 14, no. 3 (1889), 19.

Millinery Trade Review. "Trade Conditions." *Millinery Trade Review* 29, no. 7 (July 1904): 44.

Molony, Janelle. "Arizona Ostrich rancher makes flock available for research." *Queen Creek Tribune*, June 8, 2025, 14-16.

Molski, Henry. "Dream to Revolutionize Ostrich Industry Crumbles." *Arizona Republic*, August 9, 2014. https://www.azcentral.com/story/life/az-narratives/2014/08/10/ostrich-industry-dream-dies/13855611/.

Murray, Blanche K., "Ostriches in Arizona." *Arizona Highways*, 15, no. 11 (1939): 22-28.

Murray, Blanche K. "Dr. A.J. Chandler, Empire Builder." *Arizona Highways*, 15, no. 4, (1939): 8-26.

Negri, Sam. "No Dummies These Big Ostriches." *Arizona Highways* 81, no. 1 (January 2005): (30-31).

Nicholas, Cherie. "Style Pendulum Swing to Handsome Ostrich Finery." *St. Johns Herald-Observer*, December 24, 1938, 5.

Nicholas, Cherie. "Lavish Ostrich, Fine Feathers Bespeak New Elegance." *St. Johns Herald-Observer*, November 4, 1944, 5.

Okunlola, Theophilus. "The Ostrich has Given Its All." *HoldingHistory.com*, last modified January 11, 2021, accessed August 24, 2025, https://www.holdinghistory.org/post/the-ostrich-has-given-its-all.

Oliver, Dub. *Ostrich Ranching in America*. Shreveport: Dub Oliver & Associates, 1993.

"Ostriches Shared Range," *Arizona Land & People* 36, no. 1 (Tucson: University of Arizona, March 1985): 16.

Our Horticultural Visitor. "Ostrich Farm at the Fair: Sixty Birds from California Show Off their Fine Plumes." *Our Horticultural Visitor* 10, no. 7 (July 1904): 3.

Outlook. "The Spectator." *Outlook* 84, no. 6 (Oct 1906): 311-312.

Parker, Lowell. "Fashion Foibles Led to Flourishing Industry." *Arizona Republic*, January 20, 1974, 6.

People for the Ethical Treatment of Animals. "All Your Question About Experiments on Animals." PETA.org, Accessed November 24, 2025. https://www.peta.org/features/animal-testing-facts-questions-answers/.

Petrie, Bob. "Worth the Effort." *Arizona Republic*, March 10, 1993, 161 & 172.

Pester, Patrick. "The World's Fastest Animals." *LiveScience.com*, September 10, 2021. https://www.livescience.com/59822-fastest-animals.html.

Petrie, Flinders & Quibell, James E. *Naqada and Ballas, 1895*. London: Quaritch Publishing, 1896. (Regarding Body #1480.) Available at https://archive.org/details/cu31924028740826.

Pickrell, Watson. "Ostrich." In *Cyclopedia of Farm Animals*, edited by L. H. Bailey, 511. New York: MacMillan, 1922.

Pickrell, Watson. "Ostrich Farming by Watson Pickrell." *Arizona Republican*, October 13, 1906, 5.

Pickrell, Watson. "Ostriches." In *Yearbook of the United States Department of Agriculture, 1905*, 399-406. Washington: Government Printing Office, 1906.

Pliny. *The Historie of the World Commonly Called, The Naturall Historie of C. Plinius Secundus*, transcribed by Philemon Holland, amplified by Claire Richie. London: Adam Islip, 1601.

Pfeiffer, Gene F. Quoted in Dub Oliver, *Ostrich Ranching in America* (Shreveport: Dub Oliver & Associates, 1993):165. Note: Pfeiffer was the first President of the AOA.

Poultry Monthly. "An Ostrich Ranch in Arizona," *Poultry Monthly* 17, no. 5 (May 1895): 156.

Pulley, Tom. "Orange County was Once the Ostrich Capital of America." *County Courier* 39, no. 5. Santa Ana: Orange County Historical Society (May 2009): 1.

Rafferty, John P. "6 of the World's Most Dangerous Birds." *Encyclopedia Britannica,* last updated June 13, 2025. https://www.britannica.com/list/6-of-the-worlds-most-dangerous-birds.

Riggs, Willetta. Quoted in Michael Grady, "Chandler Bash Celebrates City's History…" *East Valley Tribune*, March 10, 2006.

Ringer, Andrea. "The Captive Lives of Ostriches as Belligerent Animal Workers and Bad Mothers." In *Modern American History* 8, no. 2 (Boston: Cambridge University Press, July 2025). 115-119. DOI 10.1017/mah.2024.52.

Roberts, Gary L. "Wyatt Earp: The Search for Order on the Last Frontier," in *A Wyatt Earp Anthology* (Denton: Univ. of North Texas Press, 2019), 2-25.

Rose, John D. "Wyatt Earp's Tombstone Home Site Discovered." *Wyatt Earp Explorers*, 2018. https://www.wyattearpexplorers.com/wyatts-house.html.

Reuters. "Japan researchers use ostrich cells to make glowing COVID-19 detection Masks." December 10, 2021. https://www.reuters.com/business/healhcare-pharmaceuticals/japan-researchers-use-ostrich-cells-make-glowing-covid-19-detection-masks-2021-12-10/.

Rozmiarek, M. and Wtodarczyk, A. "Ostrich Hunting as a Form of Sporting Pursuit in the Nineteenth Century British Press." *Sport and Tourism Central European Journal* (*Sport i Turystka. Srodkowoeuropejskie Czasopismo Naukowe*) 7, No. 1 (2024): (11-26).

Ruffner, Lester Ward "Budge." *All Hell Needs is Water*. Tucson: Univ. of Arizona Press, 1972.

Rydall, E. H. "Ostrich Farming in California." *American Farmer* 5, no. 4 (April 1, 1899): 286.

Sain, Ken. "Bird supplier for Ostrich Fest has weathered hard times." *Queen Creek Tribune*, March 12, 2023. https://www.themesatribune.com/get_out/bird-supplier-for-ostrich-fest-has-weathered-hard-times/article_f6c7d3c0-c1ec-11ed-8e59-8fdf597da209.html.

San Diego Zoo. "Ostrich." *San Diego Zoo*, 2025. https://animals.sandiegozoo.org/animals/ostrich.

Schaller, N.U.; Herkner, B.; Villa, R.; & Aerts, P. "The intertarsal joint of the ostrich (Struthio camelus): Anatomical examination and function of passive structures in locomotion." *Journal of Anatomy* 214, no. 6 (May 22, 2009): 830-847. https://onlinelibrary.wiley.com/doi/10.1111/j.1469-7580.2009.01083.x.

Schaller, Nina. "Birds on the run: what makes ostriches so fast?" *Science In School* 6, no. 21 (November 22, 2011). https://www.scienceinschool.org/article/2011/ostrich/.

Scientific American. "The Ostrich." *Scientific American* 65, no. 23 (December 5, 1891): 359.

Sergeant, Helen H. *House by the Buckeye Road*. San Antonio: Naylor Co., 1960.

Serrato Marks, Gabi. "How the Biggest Birds on Earth Could Help Fend Off Epidemics." *Audubon.org* (March 21, 2019). https://www.audubon.org/magazine/how-biggest-birds-earth-could-help-fend-epidemics?int_query=ostrich&int_src=site_search.

Shakespeare, William. *Henry VI* (1594), Part 2, Act 4, Scene 10.

Simmons, Diane Ciarloni. "Whatever Happened to D.C. Cogburn?" *Western Horseman* 56, no. 5 (May 1991): 122-126.

Spitzzeri, Paul R. "Feathering the Nest: A Quartet of Photos of the Los Angeles Ostrich Farm, Lincoln Heights, August 1924." *Homestead Museum*, August 11, 2003. https://homesteadmuseum.blog/2023/08/11/feathering-the-nest-a-quartet-of-photos-of-the-los-angeles-ostrich-farm-lincoln-heights-august-1924/.

Stein, Sarah A. *Plumes: Ostrich Feathers, Jews, and a Lost World of Global Commerce*. New Haven: Yale University, 2008.

Stewart, James S. "What Are the Kinds of Ostrich and Which One is Best?" In Dub Oliver, *Ostrich Ranching in America,* 17-21 (Shreveport: Dub Oliver & Associates, 1993).

"The Great Emu War of 1932: When Australia Fought an Army of Feathers." *Vocal Media - History* (February 2025). https://vocal.media/history/the-great-emu-war-of-1932-when-australia-fought-an-army-of-feathers.

Tefertiller, Casey. *Wyatt Earp: The Life Behind the Legend* (New York: John Wiley & Sons, 1997).

Bibliography

Thurber, Alan. "Tragic Ostrich Stampede Recalled." *Arizona Republic*, June 17, 1984, B1-11.

Tsukamoto, Dr. Y.; Hendler, B.; Greenberg, S. "Application of Ostrich Antibodies to the Restoration of Hair Growth, a Preliminary and Case Report." *Journal of Cosmetics, Dermatological Sciences and Applications* 8, no. 4 (October 2018), 179-184. DOI: 10.4236/jcdsa.2018.84019.

Tsukamoto, Dr. Y.; Maeda, O.; Shigekwa, G.; Greenberg, S.; Hendler, B. "Ostrich Antibody and Its Application to Skin Diseases, a Review and Case Report." *Health* 10, no. 10 (2018), 1357-1370. DOI: 10.4236/health.2018.1010105.

Weston Gonzales, Karen. "Rise and Fall of the Ostrich Industry." *Tucson Weekly*, May 9, 2002. https://www.tucsonweekly.com/tucson/rise-and-fall-of-the-ostrich-industry/Content?oid=1070205.

Weston Gonzales, Karen. Quoted in Sam Negri, "No Dummies These Big Ostriches." *Arizona Highways* 81, no. 1 (January 2005): 30-31.

White, Rick. Quoted in Curtice K. Cultice, "Where's the Beef?" *Business America* 117, No. 4 (May 1996): 27.

Whitehurst Jr., A.D. In Dub Oliver, *Ostrich Ranching in America* (Shreveport: Dub Oliver & Associates, 1993), 186.

Wilkins Freeman, Mary E. "The Ostrich." *Harper's New Monthly* CXI, no. 663 (August 1905).

Willson, Roscoe G. "Arizona Days with Roscoe G. Willson." *Arizona Republic*, August 22, 1954, 80.

Wilson, Roscoe G. "Ostrich Farms Contributed to Fashion World." *Arizona Days and Ways,* March 2, 1958, 26-27.

Wright, C. W. "Alfalfa and Millinery." *Agricultural Southwest* 8, no. 22 (August 16, 1912): 1-12.

United Poultry Concerns. "Stop Ostrich Races." Change.org. January 26, 2017. https://www.change.org/p/chandler-chamber-of-commerce-stop-ostrich-races.

United Poultry Concerns. "Urge Chamber of Commerce to Eliminate Ostrich Races at Chandler Ostrich Festival." *Poultry Press* (Spring 2017). https://www.upc-online.org/pp/spring2017/eliminate_chandler_ostrich_races.html.

United States Department of Agriculture, "Agricultural Experiment Stations of the United States, Their Locations and Directors," in *Yearbook of the United States Department of Agriculture, 1914* (Washington: Government Printing Office, 1915), 507.

United States Department of the Interior. *Registration Form for University of Arizona Campus Agricultural Center at 4101 N. Cambell Ave.* National Register of Historic Places, November 20, 2023, sec. 8, 5.

United States Food & Drug Administration, "FDA Announces Plan to Phase Out Animal Testing Requirement for Monoclonal Antibodies and Other Drugs" (Press Release), FDA.gov (April 10, 2025), https://www.fda.gov/news-events/press-announcements/fda-announces-plan-phase-out-animal-testing-requirement-monoclonal-antibodies-and-other-drugs.

United States Senate, "Carl Hayden Retires, January 3, 1969," *Senate.gov*, Accessed October 29, 2025. https://www.senate.gov/artandhistory/history/minute/Carl_Hayden_retires.htm.

University of California. "Exotic Livestock: A Small-Scale Agriculture Alternative" (brochure). *Sustainable Agriculture Research and Education Program,* (January 1989). https://ucanr.edu/node/130928/printable/print.

Useless Farm. "Meet Useless Farm: Karen the Emu." Accessed October 10, 2025. https://uselessfarm.com/pages/meet-the-farm.

Van Dam, Andrew. "The Great Llama (and Ostrich and Emu Collapse)."
  Washington Post, March 8, 2024. https://www.washingtonpost.com/business/
  2024/03/07/llama-emu-ostrich-herds-down/.
Vandiver, Leon. "Exotic Livestock: A Small-Scale Agriculture Alternative."
  *University of California Sustainable Agriculture Research and Education
  Program* (brochure), (January 1989). https://ucanr.edu/node/130928/
  printable/print.

Directories

1899-1900 Phoenix City Directory
1909-1910 Arizona State Business Directory
1911-1912 Arizona State Business Directory
1912 Phoenix City and Salt River Valley Directory
1914 Phoenix and Maricopa County Directory
1915-1916 Arizona State Business Directory
1917 Phoenix, Arizona City Directory
1918 Phoenix Metropolitan Area City Directory

Film & Audio

Larry the Cable Guy (Daniel L. Whitney). "Only in America With Larry the
  Cable Guy." *History Channel*, Season 3, Episode 1, May 8, 2013.
Lehman, Michael. "Zagat Documentary: Interview with Michael Lehman,"
  Central Oregon Ostrich, n.d. https://centraloregonostrich.com/.
Miller, Dave. "As exotic farms are on decline nationwide, Oregon ranchers are
  hopeful for the future." April 15, 2024. *Think Out Loud.* Oregon Public
  Broadcasting (OPB). Podcast, MP3 audio, 14:08. https://www.opb.org/
  article/2024/04/05/oregon-ranchers-hopeful-future/.
Rib Ticklers. "Ostrich Sounds – Noises." YouTube, Oct. 6, 2021. https://youtu.be/
  cZ00FltTmwc?si=1fuLikpWRCLYklul
Sewell, Robin. "Mount Lemmon: A Scenic Drive to Arizona's Secret Town."
  Arizona Highways TV. YouTube, Sep. 23, 2024.
  https://www.youtube.com/watch?v=yIbDR_iJduk.
VanBallenberghe, Jonathan, dir. *The Ostrich Testimonies.* 2008: Tucson, AZ:
  Open Lens Productions. DVD and Vimeo. https://vimeo.com/111413
  1426?share=copy#t=1126.098.

Images

Alamy (stock photos)
Ancestry.com
American Numismatic Society
A. O. Boeres Co. Postcard Collection
Arizona Historical Society Library
Arizona Magazine
Arizona Museum of Natural History
Arizona State Library, Arizona State Archives
Arizona State Library, History and Archives Division (Public Records)
Beagles' Postcard Collection
Biographical Sketches of the Class of 1858, Dartmouth College by Samuel Lankton Gerould (Telegraph Publishing Co., 1905).
Buffalo and Erie County Historical Society
California Digital Library, Randy Young Collection
California Historical Society, C. C. Pierce Photo Collection
Cawston Ostrich Farm fold-out brochure, ca. 1896-1935

Bibliography

Chandler Museum Collection
Charles D. Arnold, Official Views of Pan-American Exposition
Claremont Colleges Library, David Boule Collection
De Agostini Picture Library
Dwight B. Heard Investment Company
FindAGrave.com
Gollwitzer Schmuckfedern
Google Maps
Harper's Weekly
Hannon Library, Dept. of Archives and Special Collections
Library of Congress
LiveJournal Blog
Los Angeles Public Library, Nicholas Beyelia Collection
Los Angeles Public Library Digital Collection
Kongelige Bibliotek manuscript collection
Metropolitan Museum of Art
Museum of Veterinary Anatomy
Millinery Trade Review
National Cowboy and Western Heritage Museum, Willard H. Porter Rodeo Collection
New York Public Library Digital Collection, Lewis W. Hine Collection
Omaha Public Library & Univ. of Nebraska, Trans-Mississippi International Exposition Collection

Phoenix Gazette
Phoenix Public Library, Susan Arreola Postcard Collection
Picryl Public Domain Media
Pierpoint Morgan Library & Museum
Poultry Monthly
Public Brodcasting Service, PBS.org
Westerner
Wikimedia Commons
Salt River Project
Salt River Project, Walter Lubken's Photographs of the Salt River Valley
San Diego State University, John and Jane Adams Postcard Collection
Shutterstock (stock photos)
Smithsonian Institute
South Pasadena Public Library
State Library and Archives of Florida
Sudan Times
Queenslander Pictorial (December 21, 1938)
Tempe History Museum
Tichnor Bros. Inc. Postcard Collection
University of Southern California Libraries and California Historical Society
University of Queensland, Henry William Mobsby Papers
Valley Metro
Walters Art Museum Collection, Henry Walters Collection
Yuma County Highway Department

Newspapers

Albuquerque Journal (New Mexico)
Arizona Daily Star (Arizona)
Arizona Graphic (Arizona)
Arizona Republican/Arizona Republic (Arizona)
Arizona Sentinel (Arizona)
Arizona Sentinel and Yuma Weekly Examiner (Arizona)
Arizona Silver Belt/ Daily Arizona Silver Belt (Arizona)
Arizona Weekly Enterprise (Arizona)
Arizona Weekly Star (Arizona)
Armidale Express and New England General Advertiser (New South Wales, AUS)
Bisbee Daily Review (Arizona)
Border Vidette (Arizona)
Billings Daily Tribune (Montana)

Buffalo Courier (New York)
Buffalo Courier Express (New York)
Buffalo News (New York)
Buffalo Review (Arizona)
Chandler Arizonan (Arizona)
Chicago Tribune (Illinois)
Clifton Clarion (Arizona)
Coconino Sun (Arizona)
Copper Era and Morenci Leader (Arizona)
Daily Morning Times (Sydney, AUS)
Daily People's Cause (California)
Daily Tombstone (Arizona)
Democratic Leader (Wyoming)
Deseret News (Utah)
East Valley Tribune (Arizona)
El Paso Herald (Texas)
El Paso Times (Texas)

Evening Capital (Maryland)
Fort Worth Star-Telegram (Texas)
Imperial Valley Press (California)
Kalgoorie Miner (Western Australia, AUS)
Kentucky Advocate (Kentucky)
Livingston Enterprise (Tennessee)
Los Angeles Evening Express (California)
Los Angeles Herald (California)
Los Angeles Times (California)
Marion Commonwealth (South Australia, AUS)
Mesa Tribune (Arizona)
Mohave County Miner (Arizona)
Morning Advertiser (London, U.K.)
Morning Press (California)
New Bern Weekly Journal (North Carolina)
New York Sun (New York)
New York Times (New York)
Parker Post (Arizona)
Phoenix Gazette (Arizona)
Phoenix Weekly Herald (Arizona)
Pinal Drill (Arizona)
Quad-City Times (Iowa)
Queen Creek Tribune (Arizona)
Reading Mercury (Reading, U.K.)

San Bernardino County Sun (California)
San Diego Reader (California)
San Diego Union (California)
Semi-Weekly Leader (Mississippi)
Slater News-Rustler (Missouri)
Snowflake Herald (Arizona)
St. Johns Herald-Observer (Arizona)
St. Louis Globe-Democrat (Missouri)
Stockton Evening and Sunday Record (California)
Sunday Herald (New South Wales, AUS)
The Courier (Queensland, AUS)
The Mercury (Tasmania, AUS)
The Oasis (Arizona)
The Times (London, U.K.)
Times Leader (Pennsylvania)
Tombstone Epitaph (Arizona)
Tucson Citizen (Arizona)
Tulare County Times (California)
Washington Post (Washington)
Waukegan News-Sun (Illinois)
Weekly Journal-Miner (Arizona)
Winslow Daily Mail (Arizona)
Yuma Weekly Examiner (Arizona)
Yuma Sun (Arizona)

Index

Index

Index

Index

Appendix Items

A. Ostrich Owners in Early State History

Established between 1888-1900
Arizona Ostrich Co. (Phoenix-Central)
Josiah Harbert (Phoenix-West)
M. E. Clanton & Co. (Arlington/Buckeye)
Pearson Ostrich Company (Cashion/Avondale)

Established between 1901-1905
Arizona Ostrich Company, reopened (Phoenix-Central)
Big-Five Company (Phoenix-West)
McNeil-Wylie Ostrich Farm (Phoenix-Central)
National Ostrich Company (Phoenix-West)
Pearson Ostrich Show Farm (Phoenix-West)
Phoenix-American Ostrich Company (Cashion/Avondale)*
Tempe Ostrich Company (Tempe-South)
W. S. Pickrell & Co. (brokerage) (Phoenix)

Established between 1906-1909
Arizona Ostrich Farm (Phoenix-Central)
Biechteler Bros. Ostrich Farm (Yuma)
Desert Ostrich Co. (Glendale-West)
International Ostrich Farm and Feather Co. (Nogales)**
J. H. Meadows Ostrich Farm (Yuma)
Louis Janssens' Ostrich Farm (Phoenix-South)
Mesa Ostrich Farm (Mesa)
Pan-American Ostrich Company (Cashion/Avondale)*
William Hartranft (Glendale-West)
Salt River Valley Ostrich Farm (Phoenix-West)***
Spangler Co. (Mesa)
T.W. Kemp & Co. (Tempe)

*See original Pearson Ostrich Company, est. 1903.
**Never realized.
***Renamed Wickey Ostrich Farm.

Established between 1910-1913
Belgo-American Ostrich Company (Phoenix-South)
Ernest Ellsworth (Mesa)
G. Thieleman (Phoenix-South)
H. C. Meyers (Chandler)
Hansberger & Sons (Gadsden, Yuma Co.)
Meyers Ostrich Farm (Glendale-West)
Louis Ellsworth (Mesa)
Maricopa Ostrich Farm
Salt River Valley Ostrich Co. (Glendale-West)
William J. Clemens (Mesa-South)
Mr. Cummings
Mr. Ivey
Mr. Lenarm

Established approximately 1914
A. G. Barnes
Chandler Ostrich Farm (Chandler)
Dr. Charles Meserve (Tucson)
Charles Peterson (Chandler)
Dwight L. Lecky (Chandler)
F. Brown
Frank D. Lane (Cashion/Avondale)
George Alkire (Phoenix-West)
H. C. Cleveland (Phoenix)
Hiram Claridge (Thatcher)
J. M. Sanders
John W. Heffner (Chandler)
Lovell & Clobby
Morrison Brothers Ostrich Farm (Chandler)
Mr. Blount (Wenden, Yuma Co.)
O. M. McCulloch
Peabody Ranch (Chandler)
Samuel H. Mitchell (Phoenix-Central)
S. E. Sparks
Toston Ranch (Chandler)
United States Ostrich Experimental Station at UofA (Tucson)
Wayne H. Heffner (Chandler)
Dr./Rev. Wilbur Fisk (Tempe)

Appendix

Established 1915 or later
Clemmens Ostrich Farm (Phoenix)
Frances A. Shaw Jr. (Phoenix-Central)
I. S. Bewley (Glendale)
Pearson Ostrich Farm (Phoenix-South)*
Mesa City Ostrich Company (Mesa)
Perkins Ostrich Farm (Phoenix-Central)
Sacaton Indian Agency (Sacaton)
United States Ostrich Experimental Station (Glendale-West)**
University Ostrich Farm at UofA (Tucson)
W. A. Lane (Glendale)

*Owned by Judge L.L. Pearson, est. 1922.
**Originally in Tucson (est. 1914).

B. Official Positions on Humane Animal Farming

Audubon Society

"The Audubon Societies are not opposed to the use of feather ornaments which can be obtained without cruelty or the sacrifice of the lives of birds. …Ostrich feathers are legitimate as well as beautiful decorations and are approved by the Audubon Societies. Their use does not entail the sacrifice of life, nor does it cause the slightest suffering to the Ostrich…"

William Dutcher, President of the National Association of Audubon Societies, for Bird -Lore *Magazine (April 1905)*

American Society for the Prevention of Cruelty to Animals

"The welfare of an animal includes its physical and mental state … Any animal kept by man, must at least, be protected from unnecessary suffering."

"Five Freedoms:
1. Freedom from Hunger and Thirst by ready access to fresh water and diet to maintain health and vigor.
2. Freedom from Discomfort by providing an appropriate environment including shelter and a comfortable resting area.
3. Freedom from Pain, Injury or Disease by prevention or rapid diagnosis and treatment.
4. Freedom to Express Normal Behavior by providing sufficient space, proper facilities and company of the animal's own kind.
5. Freedom from Fear and Distress by ensuring conditions and treatment which avoid mental suffering."

ASPCA.org (2025)
Guiding Principles

Appendix

Animal Welfare Council

"The Animal Welfare Council members support the use of animals in recreation, entertainment, industry and sports. We are dedicated to advancing the responsible and humane use of animals in these activities."

"Animal welfare proponents seek to improve the treatment and well-being of animals. Animal welfare proponents believe that humans can interact with animals in entertainment, industry, sport and recreation, and industry, but that the interaction should include provisions for the proper care and management for all animals involved."

AnimalWelfareCouncil.org (2025)
Homepage & Welfare vs. Rights

People for the Ethical Treatment of Animals (PETA)

"PETA and our millions of supporters around the world know that animals aren't ours to use for food—they're unique, feeling individuals with their own wants and needs."

"The only truly humane foods are vegan ones."

PETA.org (2025)
Cows, Chickens, Fish, and Other Animals Used for Food

United Poultry Concerns

"The mania to degrade ostriches and emus into just one more commodity item must be stopped. Those who see the ostrich and the emu only as slabs of bloody meat, 'less cholesterol,' luggage, trinkets, cash cows, and cowboy boots, defile the living beauty of these birds."

UPC-online.org/Ostriches (2025)
"Nowhere to Hide"

C. Watch "1932: The Great Emu War"

1932: The Great Emu War (Short Film)
Directed by Kyle Harrington
(Flightless Films, 2020), 30 min. 37 sec.

Smartphone users can scan the QR code below to open the film link:

Web Address to View:
https://www.youtube.com/watch?v=dkmflJne_yU

Official:
@KyleDavidH (on Twitter/X)
@PlywoodAndPixels (on Instagram)

Legal Disclaimer:
Flightless Films is not affiliated with the author, nor did they pay for a mention in the book. Any questions or comments about their content should be directed to the Flightless Films production team at FlightlessFilmsContact@gmail.com

Appendix

D. Watch "The Ostrich Testimonies"

The Ostrich Testimonies
Directed by Jonathan VanBallenberghe
(Tucson: Open Lens Productions, 2008), 1 hour, 9 min.

Smartphone users can scan the QR code below to open the film link:

Web Address to View:
https://vimeo.com/1114131426?share=copy#t=1126.098

TinyUrl (takes you to the same video):
https://tinyurl.com/OTFilm2008

Official: www.OpenLensProductions.com
Online: Vimeo.com/Showcase.OpenLensProductions

Legal Disclaimer:
The film Director has made documentary access freely available to the public as of August 28, 2025. If there are issues with the link or code (because let's face it, technology changes rapidly), please reach out to the
Director at openlensproductions@gmail.com and/or to the author at www.JanelleMolony.com/contact

E. Tips for Cooking Ostrich

- Ostrich meat needs to be marinated, seasoned and cooked as a red meat. It has a light, clean flavor and can be enjoyed with only the slightest spices or oils.

- Even when fully cooked, it may still be red. Because of its molecular composition, ostrich does not brown like other red meats. Please use a meat thermometer and watch the internal temperature carefully to avoid overcooking.
125° = RARE
150° = MEDIUM
150°> Just don't.

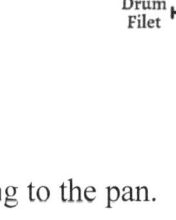

- Prepare on a FLAT skillet to avoid loss of moisture.

- Prepare to marinate and/or baste with your preferred oil, butter or tallow to preserve moisture and prevent sticking to the pan.

- For the best experience, cook and eat ostrich on the same day. If you have too large a cut, sliced it into smaller steaks and freeze for individual cooking later.

A simple and light marinade I've enjoyed: sesame oil, soy sauce, lemon juice, chopped or sliced ginger and chopped garlic (to taste). Marinate for 30 minutes. Use butter and reserved liquid to baste during cooking. Don't overdo anything. Let ostrich be the star of the mealtime show.
– Janelle Molony

About the Author

Janelle Molony is a family historian and nonfiction writer on Women, Wars & the West. She is popularly known as the "Hottie Historian" and has been featured on numerous television programs, radio shows and podcast episodes. Her work has been featured in the *Annals of Wyoming, Michigan Historical Review, Minnesota Genealogist, History Nebraska, the Wild West History Association Journal, Tombstone Epitaph*, and other notable publications.

Molony has earned literary acclaim and honors from the American Writing Awards, Writer's Digest, Readers' Favorite, BookFest, National Indie Excellence, the National Federation of Press Women, the Nonfiction Authors Association, and Women Writing the West (among others). In addition to writing, Molony was the program host of the YouTube interview series, "Women of Wyoming: Then & Now." She endeavors to continue freelancing as long as her sweet husband is willing to put up with it.

Official:
www.JanelleMolony.com
YouTube.com/@JanelleMolony
Socials: @AuthorJanelleMolony

Janelle Molony's Family Lineage

John "Jack" Alexander Rousseau (1782-1870)
Sarah "Sallie" Elizabeth Buster (1795-1861)

First born son:
James Alexander Rousseau (1813-1882)
Sarah Jane Daglish (1815-1872)

1. Mary Ann Rousseau (1843-1882)
2. Sarah Elizabeth Rousseau (1849-1931)
   (md.) Walter Percival Cave (1843-1898)

   a. William Lee Cave (1869-1919)
   b. Florence Evelyn Cave (1871-1947)
   c. Sarah "Jenny" Cave (1874-1935)
      (md.) Joseph Arther Molony (1871-1940)

      i. Joseph Arthur Molony Jr. (1909-1970)
      ii. Walter Beverly Molony (1898-1974)
          (md.) Marguerite Elenor Robertson (1904-1948)

          1. Beverly Richard Molony (1926-2015)
          2. Ronald Molony (1933-2011)
          3. Reginald Delbert Molony (1936-2019)

             a. Ryan Molony
                (md.) **Janelle Molony**

   d. James John Cave (1876-1905)
   e. Walter Percival Cave (1881-1905)
   f. Daisy Mae Cave (1884-1948)
   g. Lester Percival Cave (1887-1918)

3. John James Rousseau (1852-1914)
4. Albert Miller Rousseau (1856-1920)

About

The Arizona Rousseau's Family Lineage

John "Jack" Alexander Rousseau (1782-1870)
Sarah "Sallie" Elizabeth Buster (1795-1861)

Fifth born son:
John Wesley Rousseau (1824-1901)
Martha Curtis Stewart (1831-1907)

1. Lovell Dogan Rousseau (1843-1882)
   (md.) **Desdemona "Desde" Jones** (1856-1914)
   a. Clyde Joseph Rousseau (1882-1945)
      (md.) Frances A. Bowman (1892-1980)
   b. William V. Rousseau (1884-1944)
      (md.) Mary Margaret Rankin (1892-1974)
      i. Lovell Thomas Rousseau (1914-2000)
      ii. Desda Marie Rousseau (1918-2001)
      iii. William "Billy" Rousseau (1920-2009)
           (md.) Isabel Ivy Pendergast (1930-2014)
           1. **William "Will" Rousseau** (1958-)
           2. Clyde Rousseau (1960-)
           3. **David Rousseau** (1961-)
   c. *Seven other children that followed.*
2. *Five other children that followed.*

Don't miss out on these other great reads
from the historian you love!

From Where I Sat

(fiction, forthcoming) Social Media @RousseauProject

Escaping the Civil War is extra hard when one's family is tied up in political schemes. To avoid the next round of drafts, a grand plan brings four families from Pella, Iowa together for the greatest adventure of their lives on the Overland-California trail. Between the endless starry nights and daytime gunfights with menacing Indians, Mrs. Sarah Rousseau logs the wagon train's progress in her pocket diary. As a wheelchair-bound woman, she's not able to help when supplies run low and desperate choices must be made before they reach the snow-covered Sierra Nevadas standing between them and their California dreams. All she can do is write down what happens next. Follow all four families as they travel across the Plains, for better or for worse.

"The balance of the journey, will be welcomed by trail fans."

Robert Clark, Overland-California Trails Association, Editor of *Overland Journal* (2020)

More

Emigrant Tales of the Platte River Raids

(non-fiction, 2023)
Learn: JanelleMolony.com/EmigrantTales
Buy: TinyUrl.com/PlatteRiverRaidss
Audio: TinyUrl.com/PRRAudio

While the Civil War raged in the east, the Platte River Raids would begin an entirely new battle for the American West. In July of 1864, Northern Plains Indians in Idaho Territory (Wyoming) appeared to be on a warpath to cease all emigrant travel on the Bozeman, Oregon, and Overland Trails by any means.

On a signal, hundreds of warriors launched a series of attacks and robberies on unsuspecting emigrants through the winding "Black Hills." Shots rang out and arrows whizzed as miners, doctors, farmers, families, and war widows rallied their covered wagons together. Some fought to defend their stock and protect their families. Others helped bury the bodies of those who did not survive.

Read the eyewitness testimonies of over 60 survivors, vetted by living descendants, mapped out, annotated, and presented in one accord for the first time in literary history.

"It's like having a front row seat for the action!"

Julia Brunia Thompsen, Descendant of the Jongewaard-Rysdam wagon train from Pella, IA (2023)

POEMS FROM THE ASYLUM (non-fiction, 2021)

Learn: JanelleMolony.com/PoemsFromTheAsylum
Buy: TinyUrl.com/AsylumPoems
Audio: TinyUrl.com/PFTAAudio
Socials @SevenYearsInsane

Biography and complete anthology of poems written in 1932 by Martha Nasch, patient-inmate #20864 at the St. Peter State Hospital for the Insane.

After noticing something strange from a secret medical procedure in 1927, St. Paul, Minnesota, Martha Nasch's doctor claimed she just had a "case of nerves." With a signature from her adulterous husband, Martha was committed against her will to the asylum. She spent nearly seven years in the Minnesota hospital during the Great Depression and tried to escape twice. Martha's poems from behind bars include shocking eyewitness accounts of patient treatment and a long-suffering adoration for her only child.

Inside, she sought an explanation for her mysterious condition that led her to a spiritual answer for the mystifying "curse." Would her findings make her a metaphysical guru of the Breatharian lifestyle, or would she become the laughingstock of her Depression-era family?

"Martha's story restores dignity and self-respect ... to so many women diagnosed with a mental illness."

Mary Ann Lancette Palumbo, St. Paul Historian, MN (2022)

More

WHAT DID YOU ENJOY ABOUT THIS BOOK?

You are encouraged to share your thoughts with the reading community in the following ways:

1. Leave a short review on Amazon

https://tinyurl.com/AMZAuthorMolony

2. Leave a short review on GoodReads

https://tinyurl.com/GRAuthorMolony

3. Post a photo and review on your social media channels.

4. Submit a review to your favorite historical organization, writing association, or other interest group that might also get a kick out of the story (though, hopefully not an *ostrich* kick).

Thank you in advance!

M Press Publishing
Phoenix, Arizona